SECOND EDITION

CURRENT CONTROVERSIES
ON
FAMILY VIOLENCE

SECOND EDITION

CURRENT CONTROVERSIES
ON
FAMILY VIOLENCE

Editors

Donileen R. Loseke
University of South Florida

Richard J. Gelles
University of Pennsylvania

Mary M. Cavanaugh
University of Pennsylvania

SAGE Publications
Thousand Oaks ▪ London ▪ New Delhi

For information:

Sage Publications, Inc.
2455 Teller Road
Thousand Oaks, California 91320
E-mail: order@sagepub.com

Sage Publications Ltd.
1 Oliver's Yard
55 City Road
London EC1Y 1SP
United Kingdom

Sage Publications India Pvt. Ltd.
B-42, Panchsheel Enclave
Post Box 4109
New Delhi 110 017 India

Printed in the United States of America

Library of Congress Cataloging-in-Publication Data

Current controversies on family violence / Donileen R. Loseke, Richard J. Gelles, and Mary M. Cavanaugh, editors.—2nd ed.
        p. cm.
Includes bibliographical references and index.
ISBN 0-7619-2105-2 (cloth)
ISBN 0-7619-2106-0 (pbk.)
    1. Family violence—United States 2. Victims of family violence—United States. 3. Family violence—United States—Prevention. I. Loseke, Donileen R., 1947-II. Gelles, Richard J. III. Cavanaugh, Mary M.
HQ809.3.U5C87 2005
362.82′92—dc22

                                                2004007765

This book is printed on acid-free paper.

04   05   06   07   10   9   8   7   6   5   4   3   2   1

Acquisitions Editor:	Arthur T. Pomponio
Editorial Assistant:	Veronica Novak
Production Editor:	Denise Santoyo
Copy Editor:	Pam Suwinsky
Typesetter:	C&M Digitals (P) Ltd.
Indexer:	Kathy Paparchontis
Cover Designer:	Edgar Abarca

Contents

Introduction

Understanding Controversies on Family Violence

Donileen R. Loseke

Richard J. Gelles

Mary M. Cavanaugh

For more than 30 years, the introductions to books and articles about child abuse, violence against women, domestic violence, or intimate violence invariably began by pointing out the public and professional inattention to private and intimate violence. In the 1970s, such introductions were "calls to arms" about the unacknowledged significance of the problem of family violence. In the 1980s and 1990s, these introductions were designed to keep family violence on the public and professional agenda.

Now, in the early years of the twenty-first century, such introductions seem trite and overdone. After all, each year the president of the United States declares April to be "Child Abuse Prevention Month," and October to be "Domestic Violence Awareness Month." Public opinion surveys, content analysis of mass media, and reviews of annual state and federal legislative activity clearly demonstrate that the public, professionals, and policymakers alike are concerned about family violence. Awareness no longer is a major problem.

❖   FAMILY VIOLENCE AND SOCIAL CHANGE

One reason why family violence in the past was considered a private trouble was that this violence often was defined as simply a "normal" part of family life. Members of the general public tended to have an image of family violence as parents "spanking" their children, or husbands and wives "slapping" one another in the heat of arguments. Logically, there was no reason to worry about such violence because it likely would not lead to negative consequences. Encouraging the general public to condemn violence therefore required changing the idea that violence inside homes was "normal" and inconsequential.

One mechanism for changing these attitudes was to *name* the problem. Thus, advocates and researchers did not refer to violent acts as "discipline" or "marital discord," but instead called the violence "abuse." The term of *abuse* is an evaluation that the behavior is not tolerable, that there are limits to what is acceptable, that outsiders can—and perhaps should—intervene. By definition, "abuse" should not be a "normal" part of family life.

In order to transform family violence from a private trouble to a social issue, other changes were needed surrounding ideas about family, marriage, parenting, and gender. For example, defining violence as a matter of public concern required challenging deeply held beliefs that what goes on inside the privacy of one's home is not the concern of others: Condemning child abuse challenges traditional beliefs that parents should have the right to discipline their children as they see fit, while condemning wife abuse challenges traditional notions that men have the right to control their wives as they see fit.

In brief, the transformation of family violence from behaviors that were invisible, ignored, denied, or minimized into something that is a topic of public concern required many changes in how people think about family, gender, parenting, and violence. In some ways, the magnitude of this change in such a short period of time is remarkable. As late as the 1970s, for example, there were complaints that police often failed to respond to calls for help when violence involved family members, or that police used a "stitch rule" to determine whether or not to arrest a violent husband: An arrest would be made only when a woman's injuries required a certain number of stitches. Also, until quite recently, laws surrounding rape explicitly excluded women who were raped by their husbands. According to law, women gave their husbands consent to sex—all sex—when they married.

The transformation of public and political concern, however, was hardly seamless. Attempts to generate concern for the formerly defined "private troubles" of family violence did not immediately galvanize an unaware public and apathetic public policy system. Advocates often clashed with politicians about whether or not family violence existed at all and, if it did, whether it was a significant enough problem to warrant special agencies, programs, and policies. Also predictably, social change has been uneven. True, there are shelters for battered women, but there are too few. True, there are multiple interventions for abused children, but these too often are characterized more by their failures than by their successes. So, too, there has been uneven social change in attitudes: While many people believe that shelters for battered women are life-saving resources, others believe they should be closed because they are "homes for runaway wives" that promote family dissolution. Likewise, child abuse intervention is applauded as life saving by some, while others argue that it interferes with parental rights to discipline their children. And, while Americans tend to deplore extreme abuse that yields devastating consequences, other forms of violence—such as pushes, shoves, slaps, and spanks—are not condemned; they are still considered a normal and legitimate part of family life.

One recent example of such a bifurcation of attitudes about family violence is the Federal Adoption and Safe Families Act of 1997. The main provisions of the act prescribed steps that states must take to protect the safety and well-being of abused and neglected children. Yet, the act specifically states that nothing in it should be interpreted as a prohibition against parents using "reasonable corporal punishment" on their children. But what is "reasonable" corporal punishment? The legislation did not specifically define what is—and what is not—"reasonable." *Reasonable* lies only in the eyes of the beholder.

Social change has been uneven, and, critically, family violence in its many forms remains surrounded by controversies. For example, naming the violence as abuse was necessary to highlight its moral intolerability. Yet this naming was not without unintended consequences, because the more pejorative the term, the less likely offenders will admit what they did and the more reluctant victims are to come forward and seek help because it is embarrassing. There also are continuing controversies among members of the general public, who approach the topic with very different kinds of understandings and values. What is evaluated as a simple "exercise in parental authority" by one person is evaluated as "child abuse" by another; what is "sibling rivalry" to one person is "sibling abuse" to another.

❖ SOCIAL CHANGE AND FAMILY VIOLENCE EXPERTS

Social change also is found in the scholarly work surrounding this topic. Although family violence scholars in the past invariably began by noting the lack of knowledge about it, there now is so much knowledge that some professional and academic organizations have established Web sites dedicated solely to interpreting, organizing, and synthesizing new research. Theory and scientific research on family violence are regularly contained in general journals of biology, psychology, sociology, women's studies, history, political science, and cultural studies. There are several academic journals (such as *Child Abuse and Neglect, Journal of Elder Abuse and Neglect, Journal of Violence Against Women, Journal of Family Violence, Violence and Victims,* the *Journal of Interpersonal Violence*) devoted entirely to this topic. This is a remarkable social change.

But it is not change without controversy. While apathetic politicians were a convenient and common enemy for early advocates, controversies soon arose between and among advocates, researchers, and practitioners. Researchers, social service providers, and social advocates whose work revolves around family violence disagree about how best to approach this personal and social problem. Indeed, family violence researchers, practitioners, and advocates do not even agree on how to define the topic itself. This book, for example, has *family* in its title, but some people argue that this label is inappropriate because public and academic attention should focus on violence among *intimates,* whether or not those intimates are family members. Still others argue that the focus of attention should be on typical *victims* of violence—women, children, elderly people—who can experience violence by family members, other intimates, social service providers, employers, and complete strangers.

Disagreements about naming the problem are only the tip of the iceberg of controversies among those whose work revolves around family violence. There were, obviously, sufficient controversies and passion in the field of family violence to allow us to publish the first edition of this book in 1993. A comparison of the first and second editions demonstrates that some controversies continue to stir passion, others have faded into the background as either less relevant or somewhat settled by evidence or agreement, and new controversies have emerged.

❖ THE ORGANIZATION OF THIS VOLUME

This edition is about some of the most important and hotly debated issues surrounding family violence in its myriad forms. "Controversies in Conceptualization" is Section I, because when violence is defined as a particular type of problem, the stage is set for policy and practice interventions. What type of problem is family violence? Is it a problem of individual psychopathology (Dutton & Bodnarchuk)? Is violence caused by gender inequality (Yllö)? Is it a problem created by a variety of social structures, social forces, and social processes (Loseke)?

Section II centers on "Controversies in Definition and Measurement." Once violence is conceptualized as a particular type of problem, a set of research questions follows: How, specifically, should violence be defined? How should it be measured? What people should be the focus of research attention? The three controversies in this section each demonstrate how different answers to these questions lead to remarkably different research results. First, is women's violence toward men a serious social problem? If violence is measured in terms of behaviors, then women's violence against men is as serious as men's violence against women (Straus). Yet if violence is defined and measured in terms of its gendered contexts, consequences, and meanings, it makes little sense to talk about similarities in sheer number of violent acts done by women and by men (Loseke & Kurz). Second, depending on how "date rape" is defined and measured, it either is a problem affecting a large minority of women (Cook & Koss), or a problem affecting a much smaller number of women (Gilbert). Third, what is "spanking" of small children? Is it an effective and sometimes necessary parental technique of control and socialization (Rosemond)? Or is it an always ineffective and never necessary form of violence (Straus)?

Section III, "Controversies in Cause," turns to two specific controversies about the causes of violence. Both involve comparing a view that seems only common sense with an opposing perspective. First, do alcohol or other drugs cause violence? In the public imagination they do, and in this section that understanding is supported by research (Flanzer). The opposing view is that alcohol and other drugs are associated with violence but are not its cause (Gelles & Cavanaugh). Second, what is the relationship between abused elderly people and their abusive offspring? While it seems logical that the perception of stress created by the burden of caring for elderly people might lead caretakers to become abusive (Steinmetz), perhaps it is the deviant and abusive adult children who are dependent on the elderly parents they abuse (Pillemer).

Section IV turns to "Controversies of Social Intervention." What should the public *do* about violence? While what should be done depends on how the problem and its causes are conceptualized, defined, and measured, social interventions cannot wait until controversies are resolved. Not surprisingly, social interventions themselves can become surrounded by controversy. This section considers four such controversies. First, is the battered woman syndrome a sensible and important legal defense for abused women who kill their abusive partners (Osthoff & Maguigan), or is it a false hope that actually hinders women in court (Downs & Fisher)? Second, should young children be educated in how to prevent their own abuse (Plummer), or are child sexual abuse education programs ineffective at best, harmful at worst (Reppucci, Haugaard, & Antonishak)? Third, should there be guidelines allowing workers at child abuse hotlines to filter out some calls so that they have more time to respond to the most serious cases (Besharov), or should policy encourage bringing in even more such reports (Finkelhor)? And last, are programs attempting to "save families" better for children than taking children out of their homes and placing them into foster care, with its well-known problems and failures (Wexler), or do policies to "preserve families" put abused and neglected children at risk for even more harm (Gelles)?

By highlighting controversies, the chapters in this volume explode the myth that a group of experts, such as those in family violence, hold a united vision of "the truth." But just as idealized images of home and loved ones often stand in stark contrast to lived realities, public images of experts as holders of singular and agreed-upon objective truths most often stand in contrast to the realities. Indeed, *all* professional groups are much like families, where there is a "front stage" of presentation to outsiders and a "back stage" of interactions among group members. Like families in a traditional sense, members of professional groups, such as experts on family violence, often sweep disagreements under the carpet and project a public face of agreement and accord. Disagreements among professionals of *all* types tend to occur primarily behind closed doors—in the pages of journals read only by other professionals or in conferences attended only by like-minded others. Similar to family members in a traditional sense, members of professional groups are reluctant to publicly air their "dirty laundry."

The chapters in this volume are written by individuals who are members of the professional family of experts on family violence. This group is composed of people who have taken on the various tasks of researching, writing about, and intervening in this violence. Members of this group are a family in a sense that we share common goals—in one way or another, all want to change some aspect of how the public evaluates and responds to family violence. This also is a family in the sense that all are engaged in a joint enterprise, in which the efforts of each person often can influence the work of others. As with families in a traditional sense, we do not all agree. Such controversy should be expected.

❖ SOURCES OF CONTROVERSY

There are multiple sources of controversy among family violence experts. First and most simply, public and scholarly attention to this violence has a relatively short history. Only four decades have passed since child abuse first received particular attention; it has been only during the past three decades that wife abuse and elder abuse have been specific topics of concern, and most social service interventions have an even shorter history. Making sense of any social problem is difficult; something as complex as family violence cannot be understood, much less resolved, in the short span of a few decades. Regrettably, it is only in fiction—including that presented through the mass media—that human troubles are easily understood and quickly fixed.

The complexity of family violence and the many questions it raises also have drawn the attention of people who approach their work from different perspectives and with different goals. Authors of chapters in this volume use frameworks as diverse as psychology, sociology, political science, law, women's studies, social welfare, and Christianity. Various authors identify themselves as academic or public policy researchers, therapists, lawyers, victim advocates, or educators. An important source of controversy is that the experts do not share a theoretical perspective, a common vocabulary of discourse, or a specific agenda for their work.

The short history of family violence as a social problem, coupled with the multiple perspectives of family violence experts, at least partially accounts for the presence of controversies. Four additional characteristics of this topic lead to disagreements that can be heated, long lasting, and resistant to resolution.

First, while family violence in its many forms is an *academic* puzzle to be *studied*, this violence is first and foremost a *practical* problem to be *resolved*. Debates among experts do not, and should not, disguise the fact that the topic at hand is immediate and critical: It is about real people who experience sometimes life-threatening violence, and it is about people who commit this violence. Debates about immediate and practical concerns are more heated than are controversies over obscure issues having little relevance to the real world. The topic is immediate, practical, and urgent. So, too, are the debates and disagreements.

Second, family violence is a *political* issue. Family violence experts can be powerful because they can influence what is done to stop violence, to help victims, to rehabilitate and/or punish offenders. When one side of a controversy "wins," even if only momentarily, social policies can be designed, public attitudes can be shaped, behaviors can change. *All* controversies in this volume have implications for practical action: What types of changes are needed? Will interventions focus on changing individuals or on changing social forces or social institutions? Where will social service providers look in the lives of their individual clients for causes and hence resolutions of violence? Controversies and disagreements increase in intensity as the practical and political stakes become higher.

Third, controversies can become heated and resist resolution when the issues at hand cannot be resolved solely by reason and logic. Although only sometimes explicit, views of *morality* underlie all definitions and measurements of family violence. Each definition and argument involves making moral evaluations: What behaviors are evaluated as acceptable or at least tolerable? What behaviors are evaluated as wrong? What values should be preserved? Controversies with clear moral dimensions can become emotionally charged, because morality is as much about feeling as about thinking.

This *emotional* dimension of the topic is a fourth reason that controversies surrounding family violence can be so heated. The public image of professionals as people who are somehow immune to human feeling does not describe professionals in general, and it certainly does not describe family violence professionals in particular. In the course of their work, many of the authors of these chapters have repeatedly seen the horrific details of cases of physical, sexual, and emotional abuse; many have witnessed firsthand the sometimes disastrous unintended consequences of well-intentioned social policies. Researchers and practitioners working in this area often feel sadness, rage, anger, and frustration. Such emotions can influence arguments and can lead to disagreements that are emotionally charged.

The relative newness and complexity of the topic, experts' divergent perspectives and agendas, the high practical and political consequences of what experts say, the moral dimension of the work, and the inextricable combination of rationality and passion associated with these concerns have combined to yield controversy. To be clear, controversy is good, because this is how knowledge is advanced: Controversy leads to debate, debate encourages reflection, reflection leads to research, and research leads to refining and elaborating ideas. At the same time, for controversies to be beneficial, they must be swept out from the musty pages of academic journals and from the dark rooms of professional conferences into the bright light of public scrutiny.

Although we do not naively believe that the controversies presented in this volume can be neatly resolved, we do believe that closing off debate is counterproductive when so little is known about such important issues. There is reason, then, for this particular volume. Taken as a whole, the chapters presented here do not answer questions. Rather, they encourage debate and reflection about complex theoretical, moral, practical, and political questions.

❖ EVALUATING CONTROVERSIES

Clearly, the organization of this volume differs from that of most mass media treatments of family violence—or any other social problem. In this world of 30-second sound bites and television talk shows, the expert of the moment often seems to convey "simple truths." Such mass media images are calming because they allow audiences to believe there are simple solutions to complex problems. But that is the world of the mass media. When taken as a whole, the chapters in this volume reflect real life. Family violence is a complex theoretical, moral, practical, and political problem. Therefore, the discussions in these chapters are complex, and they contain no simple truths. Certainly, it would be the route to ignorance if readers simply dismiss all viewpoints in these chapters because the "experts do not agree." Rather, chapters in this volume require readers to weigh the evidence and make their own judgments about the validity and importance of the views in these chapters.

Evaluating discussions of any type, but especially those surrounding such a morally charged topic as family violence, is very difficult work for at least two reasons. First, arguments are cognitively evaluated by comparing them to existing knowledge and personal experience. People have a tendency simply to accept views that confirm what already is known; there is a tendency simply to reject views that challenge taken-for-granted assumptions about how the world works. In these instances, people tend to be not critical enough of statements confirming existing understandings, and too critical of those challenging existing knowledge. Second, feeling influences cognitive evaluations. There is a tendency to reject too quickly arguments that lead to negative feelings such as anger or hopelessness or frustration, and a tendency to accept too quickly arguments that lead to positive feelings such as hopefulness. In these instances, arguments are evaluated on criteria of feeling rather than thinking.

Although evaluation always is difficult, and especially difficult for topics such as family violence, there are evaluation criteria that nonetheless can be used to examine views such as those contained in this volume. Surely, readers should ask questions associated with the critical reasoning of science: Is the argument logical? What is the quality of evidence? Does the evidence support the argument? Even for a topic as volatile as family violence, logical and objective standards apply.

At the same time, generally accepted scientific criteria are not enough to evaluate the views contained in these chapters. For example, scientific criteria are a yardstick measuring an *academic* standard of knowledge that prizes impartiality and generalizability of evidence. However, family violence is not just an academic puzzle to be studied; it is a practical problem to be resolved. At times, evidence might not conform to academic standards, yet it nonetheless is adequate to address particular practical questions. In addition, while family violence is associated with strong feelings and moral evaluations, scientific criteria are concerned only with logic and objectivity. Much that might reasonably pertain to understanding violence escapes empirical conceptualization and measurement.

In brief, although it is important to examine these opposing viewpoints in terms of their logic and empirical support, readers should remember that academic research is only one way of knowing about the social world. It likewise is important to remember that, because the arguments made by some of the authors in this volume are new, scientific evidence supporting or refuting them is not yet available; that authors write from many different perspectives and have different agendas; that what does and does not constitute adequate evidence can vary; and that the evidence for arguments made by some of the authors never could be found in statistics. The messiness of the subject matter therefore leads to complexities in evaluation.

We are grateful to all of the contributors to this volume who have demonstrated that the best spokespersons for the various sides of controversies can and will engage in debate. Although these chapters do not offer a simple truth about myriad questions of family violence, the high quality of the presentations here repeatedly demonstrate how equally intelligent and dedicated people can come to quite different conclusions.

SECTION I

Controversies in Conceptualization

This book is about controversies, and many disagreements about specific issues have the common beginning of failure to agree on conceptual frameworks. Conceptual frameworks answer the question: What type of problem are we dealing with? Is violence a problem of individual people? Is it rather created by characteristics of the social order? If so, which characteristics of the social order are most important? Conceptualizing violence as a particular type of problem explicitly answers questions about the problem's cause, and this, in turn, implicitly answers questions about what should be done to eliminate violence.

Here we offer the three most common general frameworks for conceptualizing family violence. Donald Dutton and Mark Bodnarchuk introduce a *psychological* perspective, Kersti Yllö argues for a *feminist* framework, and Donileen Loseke introduces a *sociological* view.

For two reasons, it is logical to begin this section with the psychological perspective. First, early conceptualizations of family violence were highly influenced by psychology, as researchers focused on examining the personality characteristics of abusive parents, abused children, and abusive and abused spouses. Second, the psychological perspective is the commonsense perspective of many—if not most—Americans, who tend to think of troublesome behaviors of all sorts as consequences of individual psychopathology. While all forms of family violence—child abuse, elder abuse, spouse abuse—have been conceptualized as psychological problems, Dutton and Bodnarchuk in their chapter focus on exploring personality disorders of men who are violent toward their wives. Within this framework, violence is conceptualized as a problem of *individual men.*

In the second chapter, Yllö promotes a feminist perspective on violence. Like Dutton and Bodnarchuk, Yllö also focuses on the particular problem of men's violence toward women, yet she criticizes the psychological framework for its narrow focus on examining personality characteristics of offenders. Her feminist conceptualization of violence against women by men emphasizes the importance of the complex consequences of gender inequality, as well as how gender, race, and social class must be simultaneously understood as the cause of violence. This feminist framework conceptualizes violence by men as a *tactic of coercive control.*

The sociological perspective is presented by Loseke, who maintains that this framework emphasizes understanding the complexity of violence. While sociology does not deny the consequences of individual psychopathology, it minimizes these consequences and rather emphasizes how violence is an outcome of myriad characteristics of the social order, such as a lack of community, economic inequality, and particularly the characteristics of family as a social institution. This sociological perspective conceptualizes violence of all types as a consequence of *social structures, social forces,* and *social processes.*

The theoretical perspectives of psychology, feminism, and sociology are like lenses of a camera: Each framework "takes a picture" of violence that brings some aspects of human existence into sharp focus. Psychological perspectives yield sharp images of *individual* characteristics and behaviors. In comparison, the feminist lens takes pictures of women victims and men offenders as they live within the *gendered* contexts of the social order. Finally, the sociological lens yields a picture of *social life.*

As photographers know, decisions to use a particular camera lens require deciding what should be in the picture and what will not be captured at all, or what will be in a blurry background. Psychology zooms in to take a very detailed picture of individual characteristics, but in so doing does not bring into focus what we all know about human behavior: Environments matter. Feminism zooms out to place gender in sharp focus, but a feminist lens is incapable of taking pictures of other than violence in which men are offenders and women are victims. Finally, sociology offers the widest view of both people and their environments, but because a great deal is included in the picture, nothing really is in sharp focus.

In some respects, readers who evaluate these controversies are similar to judges of a photography competition. Is there a "best" picture—a best conceptual framework—for family violence? There is much to be said for considering that different conceptualizations likely will be the "best" at *different times*. Some violence on some occasions by some people is most certainly the consequence of psychopathology; some individual instances of violence most clearly are a tactic of male control of women; some violence is obviously associated with social structures, social processes, or social forces. It is possible, then, to argue that each framework is particularly good for understanding some specific instances of violence while irrelevant or even misleading when used to understand others.

Evaluating the *general* usefulness of these frameworks is difficult. First, conceptual frameworks implicitly lead to advocating particular routes to problem resolution. This will be a recurring theme in this volume: Where is the best place to invest our attention and resources in order to eliminate violence? Controversies in conceptualization lead to controversies in intervention. Do we invest our time and money to investigate individual psychopathology and try to change individual people? Do we invest in understanding the multiple consequences of the gendered nature of social life and attempt to change those? Do we focus on understanding and ameliorating inequality, on changing the characteristics of community or family? Because each framework is implicated in causing at least some violence, in a perfect world we would pursue all these possibilities. But our world is not perfect. In practice, embracing one conceptualization often leads to ignoring or minimizing others. Evaluating the usefulness of conceptual frameworks should include assessing their potential value in resolving the problem of violence.

At the same time, how we evaluate the potential usefulness of frameworks to eliminate violence is difficult, because our logical and cognitive evaluations are influenced by our feelings and beliefs. Many American readers of chapters in this section will find it fairly easy to embrace the psychological perspective, because it points to a seemingly easy route to problem resolution: individual therapy. In comparison, both the sociological and feminist frameworks challenge typical cultural beliefs. A sociological route to eliminating violence requires nothing less than changing the structure of the American social order. Likewise, problem resolution from a feminist framework requires a complete transformation of the structures and practices of gender. Evaluating frameworks therefore requires examining how our vaguely articulated but deeply held feelings and beliefs about how the world "should work" influence our cognitive appraisals. What might seem to be the easiest route to change might—or might not—be the most effective.

Evaluating the appropriateness and usefulness of these three frameworks also is difficult because of the characteristics of the research supporting each of them. These chapters offer a glimpse into what will be another recurring theme in this book: Real or perceived problems in research underlie and fuel controversies. This is a specific topic for Loseke, who, in her chapter, advises caution in evaluating *all* research on family violence. According to her, this research is characterized by a lack of clear definitions of key concepts, by dubious statistical analyses, and by faulty generalizations of research findings. In addition, another recurring theme in this volume is that authors sometimes accuse one another of intentionally ignoring, misrepresenting, or misinterpreting research. In this section, Dutton and Bodnarchuk make the grave accusation that the "essence of feminist theory has been to preserve its own ideology at the cost of ignoring or dismissing empirical data that do not serve its ideological ends." To them, this is due to feminists' exclusive focus on wife abuse. Yllö explicitly responds to this criticism. While she complains that feminists themselves "deepen the chasm by dismissing non-feminist insights too quickly," she argues that the feminist exclusive focus on the abuse of women by men "has made an enormous contribution to our understanding of wife abuse."

Is violence caused by the characteristics of individual people? By gender? By a larger range of social processes, social forces, social institutions? These are controversies in conceptualization.

individual differences in male violence (among other things, such as female violence or gay violence) are ignored or disregarded.

In surveys of wife assault incidence (for example, Straus & Gelles, 1992), the majority of males, according to their wives, are not abusive; a smaller group is abusive once; and a still smaller group is repeatedly abusive. This latter group probably constitutes 8–12 percent of the male population, large enough to constitute a significant social problem, but too small to be explained by gender analysis or evolutionary theories (Dutton, 1995). An explanation attributing spousal assault to "maleness" would lead to a prediction of a normal distribution of male violence, not the highly skewed distribution found in national surveys. It certainly would not predict that 88 percent of males would be described by their female partners as *not* physically abusive. Feminism cannot consider individual differences in males, since it is committed to a generic view of males or "maleness" per se as the cause of wife assault. As Bograd (1988) wrote in *Feminist Perspectives on Wife Assault*, all feminist researchers, clinicians, and activists address a primary question: "Why do men beat their wives?" (p. 13), and further, "Instead of examining why this particular man beats his particular wife, feminists seek to understand why men in general use physical force" (p. 13).

Despite the feminist claim that their sociological view can be combined with more fine-grained psychological analyses, it rarely is. In fact, there has been a resistance to examining psychological factors connected to spouse assault because such examination is incompatible with "gender analysis," the paradigm of feminism. Feminist theory has also resisted the study of female violence, husband battering, lesbian battering, and gay violence, since these forms of intimate violence are also incompatible with gender analysis, despite a considerable empirical basis documenting these forms of abuse (Dutton, 1994). Studies such as the survey by Lie, Schilit, Bush, Montague, and Reyes (1991), showing lesbian verbal, sexual, and physical abuse rates to be higher than heterosexual rates, are simply dismissed, as are studies showing female intimate violence to be equal or higher in incidence than male intimate violence (Magdol et al., 1997; Archer, 2000). The essence of feminist theory has been to preserve its own ideology at the cost of ignoring or dismissing empirical data that do not serve its ideological ends. The notion that special characteristics of a small group of males may generate intimate violence is incompatible with gender power ideology. Similarly, any work showing that male violence stems from a psychological feeling of powerlessness is ignored (Dutton, 1994).

Personality disorders are defined as self-reproducing dysfunctional patterns of interaction (Millon, 1997). In some cases, they are general to all social relationships; in others, they manifest primarily in intimate relationships. Dutton (1998) described an "abusive personality" characterized by shame-based rage, a tendency to project blame, attachment anxiety manifested as rage, and sustained rageful outbursts, primarily in intimate relationships. This "abusive personality" was constructed around a fragile core called "borderline personality."

A variety of researchers have found an extremely high incidence of personality disorders in assaultive populations. Studies have found incidence rates of personality disorders to be 80–90 percent in both court-referred and self-referred wife assaulters (Saunders, 1992; Hamberger & Hastings, 1986, 1988, 1989; Dutton & Starzomski, 1994), compared to estimates in the general population, which tend to range from 15 percent to 20 percent (Kernberg, 1977). As the violence becomes more severe and chronic, the likelihood of psychopathology in these men approaches 100 percent (Hart, Dutton, & Newlove, 1993; Dutton & Hart, 1992a, 1992b). Across several studies, implemented by independent researchers, the prevalence of personality disorder in wife assaulters has been found to be extremely high. These men are not mere products of male sex role conditioning or "male privilege"; they possess characteristics that differentiate them from the majority of men who are not repeat abusers.

❖ EARLY RESEARCH ON PERSONALITY DISORDERS

By the 1980s the Millon Clinical Multiaxial Inventory (MCMI: 1987) joined the Minnesota Multiphasic Personality Inventory (MMPI) as a broad assessment instrument able to detect personality disorder. The MCMI was intended to configure closely to *DSM-IV* definitions of PD. Having a self-report instrument allowed lengthy structured interviews to be avoided and generated more attention to PD. The initial studies investigating incidence of PD among abusive males were conducted by Hamberger and Hastings (1986). These researchers identified eight subgroups comprised of various combinations of three factors that could account for 88 percent of the entire wife assault subject sample.

Dutton (1988) argued that repeat offenders were personality disordered and that three specific forms of PD were most prevalent among wife assaulters: Antisocial, Borderline, and "Overcontrolled."

Hamberger and Hastings (1986) refined their eight clusters to three groups corresponding to their initial factors: "Schizoid/Borderline," "Narcissistic/Antisocial," and "Passive/Dependent/Compulsive." Each subgroup scored high on one factor and low on the other two factors. This "three factor solution," or three subtypes of batterers, has been found repeatedly (albeit under different labels) in various studies. In a study of psychophysiological functioning of batterers, Gottman et al. (1995) established differential patterns of psychophysiological reactivity in what they termed "Antisocial" (Type 1) batterers and "Impulsive" (Type 2) batterers.

Hamberger and Hastings began to report the existence of an expanded non–PD group emerging from their data in 1988. Whether or not this was a response to political pressure to de-pathologize their work is not known. Lohr, Hamberger, and Bonge (1988) cluster analyzed the eight PD scales on the MCMI-II in a sample of 196 men. This time, a cluster was found that showed no elevations on any PD scale (39 percent of the sample, compared to 12 percent in the 1986 paper). A second cluster (35 percent) was termed Negativistic/Avoidant (Overcontrolled), while a third (26 percent) was labeled Aggressive (Antisocial/Narcissistic-Paranoid).

A later study by Hamberger, Lohr, Bonge, and Tolin (1996) used a sample of 833 court-referred men, but unfortunately, this study relied on self-reports of relationship violence, which typically is underreported by batterers (Dutton & Hemphill, 1992). Using a two-stage clustering technique, they again obtained three large clusters and three smaller clusters. Cluster 1, or the Dependent-Passive Aggressive (Overcontrolled), comprised 18 percent of the sample. Their average MCMI scale elevations exceeded baseline (> 75: clinically present) on the Dependent, Passive Aggressive-Negativistic and Avoidant subscales. Cluster 2, or the Instrumental, accounted for 26 percent of the sample; this group showed elevations of Antisocial or Narcissistic subscales. Cluster 3, or the no PD group, comprised 40 percent of the sample, an increase from the original 12 percent. The Borderline or Emotionally Volatile cluster seemed to have disappeared.

Two problems exist with this approach. The first is that the MCMI was not meant to be factor or cluster analyzed; it was intended for individual assessment. The second is that the authors do not report Desirability scores for their sample. Men entering treatment groups who perceive a strong judgmental aspect to treatment and who are assessed early in treatment may attempt to underreport all pathology, including trauma symptoms and violence experienced in the family of origin (Dutton & Starzomski, 1993; Dutton & Hemphill, 1992). Another example is clearly exemplified in a recent paper by Gondolf (1999), which attempts to show that personality disorders are overdiagnosed in batterers. Gondolf published data showing that a large percentage of a batterer sample had no personality disorders, but his sample also scored extremely high on the Desirability scale used to assess pathology. Fifty-five percent of his sample was above the 75th percentile criterion on the Desirability scale of the MCMI-III, and although he does not report means or standard deviations for the Disclosure and Debasement scales, they appear low from the percentile data. Gondolf drew his sample from "psychoeducational" treatment groups (the majority following the Duluth Model: Pence & Paymar, 1986). The setting and treatment of this model creates a shaming atmosphere for clients, one that instantly puts them on the defensive (Dutton, 1998). Gondolf's low scores could simply have occurred because men were underreporting on any item that read as signifying psychological problems. This social desirability pattern could lead to underreporting of "undesirable" traits (psychopathology). While the MCMI does correct for desirability, there are not, as yet, studies to indicate that the correction factors are sufficient. Hence, assessments of PD based solely on self-report may underrepresent the actual incidence of PD. Assessors need to closely examine scale scores on the MCMI-III, especially the Desirability subscale.

Hart, Dutton, and Newlove (1993) investigated the incidence of personality disorders in court and self-referred wife assaulters using the MCMI-II (Millon, 1987) and a structured interview called the Personality Disorder Examination (PDE: Loranger, 1988). The PDE results were more modest than the MCMI, with a prevalence rate around 50 percent. The MCMI-II results indicated that 80–90 percent of the sample (court and self-referred, $n = 85$) met the criteria for some personality disorder. The most frequent PD was what came to be called "Negativistic" (Passive-Aggressive + Aggressive-Sadistic). Almost 60 percent of the sample achieved base rate scores equal to 85 or higher, signifying that this particular PD was central and prominent in the psychological makeup of these men. In contrast to Gondolf's (1999) sample, the mean Desirability score for court-referred men was 53.4, for self-referred 50.7. Hart et al. (1993) argued that the court-ordered men approximated a random selection of spouse assaulters (compared to self-referred), as the criminal justice system operated somewhat capriciously.

Saunders (1992) performed a cluster analysis of 182 men being assessed for wife assault treatment and reported on 13 potential differentiating variables. He also found a trimodel set of patterns described as Family Only (overcontrolled), Emotionally Volatile (impulsive), and Generally Violent (instrumental). His Instrumental group (26 percent of the sample) reported severe abuse victimization as children but low levels of depression and anger. They were violent both within and outside the marriage. The Emotionally Volatile group (17 percent of the sample) was the most psychologically abusive and had the highest anger and depression scores. Overcontrolled (Dependent PD) comprised 52 percent of the sample.

Murphy, Meyer, and O'Leary (1993) compared batterers with nonviolent men in discordant relationships and well-adjusted men, using the MCMI-II. Each sample contained 24 men. Batterers had significantly higher elevations on Borderline, Narcissistic, Aggressive-Sadistic, and Passive-Aggressive PD than non-batterers. More important, Desirability scores did not differ among groups, although Debasement was higher among batterers, possibly reflecting a pervasive remorse about their violence. Severe physical abuse in the family of origin was related to presence of psychopathology. One conclusion that emerges from the previous review is that, when social desirability scores are equivalent, batterers exhibit significantly more psychopathology than controls. When they differ, groups emerge that show significantly higher social desirability scores while appearing to have no PD elevations. Personality pathology, it seems, is something that respondents attempt to conceal when they are assessed for wife battering (Dutton & Hemphill, 1992).

Holtzworth-Munroe and Stuart (1994) published a review of previous studies clustering men involved in domestic violence, reiterating the tripartite typology of batterers and again describing instrumental and impulsive batterers. The impulsive batterers (whom they labeled Dysphoric/Borderline), primarily confine violence to their family, carry out moderate to severe violence, and engage in sexual and psychological abuse. These batterers are emotionally volatile (and were so labeled by Saunders, 1992), psychologically distressed, have Borderline and Schizoid personality disorders, elevated levels of depression, and substance abuse problems. Holtzworth-Munroe and Stuart (1994) estimate that *impulsive batterers make up 25 percent of treatment samples.* The instrumental cluster (called Generally Violent/Antisocial) batterers, engage in more violence outside the home than the other abusive men, carry out moderate to severe violence, and engage in psychological and sexual abuse. They may have an antisocial personality disorder or psychopathy and may abuse alcohol and/or drugs. Their use of violence is frequently instrumental. Holtzworth-Munroe and Stuart (1994) suggest that *the instrumental group also makes up 25 percent of all batterers*. A third group (which they called "Family Only") appears to be *overcontrolled, and makes up 52 percent of the sample* (when men are recruited from the community as well as batterer treatment groups). It is important to note that the authors were not insisting on respondents achieving criteria on a test such as the MCMI to make these determinations.

Holtzworth-Munroe, Meehan, Herron, and Rehman (2000) conducted an empirical confirmation of their earlier work, comparing 102 maritally violent men. This time data formed four clusters, the difference being that the Antisocial (Instrumental) cluster was subdivided into two groups, depending on level of antisocial behavior. Consistent with Dutton's (1994, 1995, 1998) findings, Borderline/Dysphoric exhibited the highest level of fear of abandonment and had the highest scores on Fearful Attachment and Spouse-Specific Dependency. Their wives reported them to be the most jealous of all groups. They also had significantly higher scores on the BPO (Oldham et al., 1985) scale (M = 74, S.D. = 14.3) compared to a mean score of 48 for nonviolent males. Their BPO score was also higher than for any other batterer group. Dutton (1994) found a BPO score of 72 for batterers and 74 for independently diagnosed borderlines. As in the Dutton work, Holtzworth-Munroe et al. (2000) also had the highest reports of parental rejection.

Gottman et al. (1995) recruited a "severely violent sample" of couples in which male-perpetrated battering was occurring. The psychophysiological responding of these men was monitored *in vivo* while arguing with their partners in a laboratory conflict. Two distinct patterns of psychophysiological responding were obtained. Type 1 batterers demonstrated unexpected heart rate decreases during intimate conflict. They were also more likely to be generally violent and to have scale elevations on the MCMI-II for Antisocial and Aggressive-Sadistic behavior.

Type 2 batterers showed psychophysiological increases during intimate conflict. Tweed and Dutton (1998) examined these two groups, which they called "Instrumental" (Type 1) and "Impulsive" (Type 2), on a variety of psychological measures. The Instrumental group showed an Antisocial-Narcissistic-Aggressive-Sadistic profile on the MCMI and reported more severe physical violence. The Impulsive group showed elevations on Borderline, Avoidant, and Passive-Aggressive, higher scores on the Oldham et al. (1985) BPO measure of borderline personality organization (more about this following), higher chronic anger, and a fearful attachment style on the Relationship Style Questionnaire (RSQ: Bartholomew & Horowitz, 1991).

Specific Disorders 1: Borderline Personality Organization

In a series of studies on what he called the "abusive personality," Dutton (1995, 1998) described a number of associated psychological features of abusiveness that clustered around Oldham et al.'s (1985) measure of BPO. The BPO scale assessed a disorder of the self-characterized by feelings of inner emptiness, a terror of being alone, temporary deficits in reality testing, and tendencies to use projection and splitting as defenses against anxiety. The associated features, all of which correlated significantly with BPO, include a fearful attachment style (Dutton, Saunders, Starzomski, & Bartholomew, 1994), high scores on chronic anger (Dutton & Starzomski, 1994) and trauma symptoms (Dutton, 1995), a tendency to construe intimate conflicts as due to the personality of the intimate other, and a negative attitude toward women (Starzomski, 1995). With its basis in BPO and with its clinical signs of impulsiveness and hyper-emotionality in intimate relationships, the abusive personality described in this work seems more closely aligned with Impulsive or Type 2 batterers. Tweed and Dutton (1998) confirmed this in a comparison of "instrumental" and "impulsive" batterers; impulsive men had BPO scores of 75 (identical to Oldham et al.'s (1985) reported mean for borderlines), while instrumental and control batterers had significantly lower BPO scores. More recently, Edwards, Scott, Yarvis, Paizis, and Panizzon (2003) found that measures of Borderline and Antisocial Personality Disorder were significantly correlated with physical aggression (spouse assault) in a forensic sample (43 men convicted of wife assault, 40 convicted of nonviolent crimes). Their high-violence groups had higher scores on all pathology scales of the Personality Assessment Instrument (PAI: Morey, 1991). The authors relate personality disorder to spousal violence via the mediating variable of impulse control.

Some studies have also found BPD to be predictive of intimate violence in female perpetrators. Zanarini et al. (2003) found that BPD symptomatology increased with sexual relations and included intimate abusiveness for both male and female subjects. Fortunata and Kohn (2003) found that lesbian batterers were also more likely to report both borderline and antisocial personality traits on the MCMI-III.

BPO self-report scores of batterers, controls, and various community groups (college students, psychiatric outpatients, gay couples) all correlated significantly with intimate partners' reports of emotional abusiveness and, in the case of batterers, with physical abusiveness. Dutton (1995, 1998) found evidence in retrospective reports of abusive men for a triad of developmental factors contributing to BPO: witnessing abuse in the family of origin, being shamed by a parent, and insecure attachment. It was hypothesized that the modal family constellation for producing abusive men was an abusive and shaming father and a mother incapable of providing consistent attachment (probably due to dealing with the abusive father). The transmission of abuse by this personality type occurs through a conjunction of two primary personality features: the inability to modulate arousal, generating extreme volatility and anger, and the tendency to externalize blame onto the intimate other, providing a target for the unmodulated rage. This latter feature appears to develop through a failure in "object relations" (Dutton, 1998; Celani, 1994) or through an attachment disorder (Dutton et al., 1994; Dutton, 1998). Treatment systems that would be compatible with cognitive-behavioral treatment for batterers (Dutton, 1998) would include systems by Linehan (1993) and Arntz (1994).

Specific Disorders 2: Psychopathic Batterers

Psychopathy is characterized as a personality disorder that involves a variety of distinct interpersonal and affective characteristics and socially deviant behaviors (Hare, 1993, 1996). Hare's *Psychopathy Checklist-Revised* (*PCL-R:* Hare, 1991), the primary assessment tool for this disorder, generates two factors for psychopathy. Factor 1 is composed of interpersonal and emotional features, including shallow affect, grandiosity, lack of empathy, glibness, and manipulativeness. Factor 2 characterizes the behavioral pattern that presents for most psychopaths as one of irresponsibility, impulsivity, violence or aggression, and promiscuity. As Hare (1993, 1995) notes, psychopaths may be serious violent offenders, men who assault their partners, or even stock promoters. As Langhinrichsen-Rohling, Huss, and Ramsey (2000) point out, even though a particular batterer may not meet the actuarial cutoff on the *PCL-R*, and thus may not be classified as a psychopath per se, the presence of a significant number of the more severe interpersonal and affective characteristics could still be important for discriminating this class of batterer. Finally, the generalized and instrumental violence identified in the generally violent batterer (Dutton, 1998; Holtzworth-Munroe & Stuart, 1994) is also quite characteristic of offenders with psychopathic personalities.

Langhinrichsen-Rohling et al. (2000) argue that psychopaths who score high on Factor 1 of the *PCL* commit more instrumental violence with less provocation and arousal and tend to have a more distant relationship with the victim. Hence, the quintessential psychopath seems defined more by Factor 1 scores (lack of empathy, manipulativeness, shallow affect, pathological lying, glibness) than by the social deviance scores generated by Factor 2. Thus, similar to the batterer typologies, the most common type of violence across all batterers is reactive or impulsive. Those who are capable of committing planned acts of violence for control or gain, however, are more likely to be psychopathic.

Notwithstanding the other similarities, it is this pattern of generalized and instrumental violence identified in the generally violent batterer that most clearly demonstrates the likelihood that these men are psychopathic. Moreover, it is this difference that separates the generally violent batterer from other men who perpetrate domestic violence so strikingly. The existing theories regarding the causal mechanisms underlying abuse probably do little to explain the etiology of this particular subtype. Edwards et al. (2003) found that "Antisocial Personality Disorder" (ASPD), which is similar to but not synonymous with psychopathy, was a significant predictor of wife assault in their sample. A key moderating variable between ASPD and violence seems to be a lack of empathy and a sense of entitlement.

❖ THE BACKLASH AGAINST "PATHOLOGIZING WIFE ASSAULT"

The main resistance to accepting personality disorders as important explanatory criteria for wife assault comes from sociological feminism. The feminist perspective on wife assault complains that wife assault was being pathologized, which deflects attention from social causes and from the radical social restructuring needed to end patriarchy (Yllö & Bograd, 1988). Yet the data reported earlier in the chapter clearly show that personality disorders are central to intimate abusiveness in North American samples. Gender studies handle this empirical disconfirmation by simply ignoring it, a tendency that is at odds with academic values of free inquiry and the construction of empirically testable and falsifiable hypotheses. The analysis offered by feminism is a paradigm that would be unacceptable if applied to any other social problem. Imagine researchers suggesting that they wanted to study "why blacks in general were violent" or "why women in general became rock groupies." These proposals would, with good reason, be vilified. Yet feminists continue to ask why men in general beat their wives. Data about female abusiveness, lesbian battering, and female-perpetrated child abuse all exist (Dutton, 1994; Archer, 2000), yet continue to be willfully ignored by dogmatic feminist analysis.

Studies on the impact of personality disorders indicate they are related to intimate aggression across a wide variety of groups: male batterers, college students, clinic outpatients, gay male couples, lesbian couples, and heterosexual females. In cultures where intimate violence is disapproved but where intimacy remains problematic, personality problems remain a robust predictor of intimate violence.

❖ REFERENCES

Archer, J. (2000). Sex differences in aggression between heterosexual partners: A meta-analytic review. *Psychological Bulletin, 126*(5), 651–680.

Arntz, A. (1994). Treatment of borderline personality disorder: A challenge for cognitive-behavioral therapy. *Behavioral Research & Therapy, 32*(4), 419–430.

Bartholomew, K., & Horowitz, L. M. (1991). Attachment styles among young adults: A test of a four-category model. *Journal of Personality and Social Psychology, 61*, 226–244.

Bograd, M. (1988). Feminist perspectives on wife abuse: An introduction. In M. Bograd & K. Ylló (Eds.), *Feminist perspectives on wife abuse*. Beverly Hills: Sage.

Celani, D. (1994). *The illusion of love*. New York: Columbia University Press.

Dutton, D. G. (1988). *Domestic assault of women: Psychological and criminal justice perspectives*. Boston: Allyn & Bacon.

Dutton, D. G. (1994). Patriarchy and wife assault: The ecological fallacy. *Violence and Victims, 9*(2), 125–140.

Dutton, D. G. (1995). *The domestic assault of women*. Vancouver, BC: University of British Columbia Press.

Dutton, D. G. (1998). *The abusive personality: Violence and control in intimate relationships*. New York: Guilford.

Dutton, D. G., & Hart, S. D. (1992a). Risk factors for family violence in a federally incarcerated population. *International Journal of Law and Psychiatry, 15*, 101–112.

Dutton, D. G., & Hart, S. D. (1992b). Evidence of long-term, specific effects of childhood abuse and neglect on criminal behavior in men. *International Journal of Offender Therapy and Comparative Criminology, 36,* 129–137.

Dutton, D. G., & Hemphill, K. J. (1992). Patterns of socially desirable responding among perpetrators and victims of wife assault. *Violence and Victims, 7,* 29–39.

Dutton, D. G., Saunders, K., Starzomski, A. J., & Bartholomew, K. (1994). Intimacy-anger and insecure attachment as precursors of abuse in intimate relationships. *Journal of Applied Social Psychology, 24,* 1367–1386.

Dutton, D. G., & Starzomski, A. J. (1993). Borderline personality in perpetrators of psychological and physical abuse. *Violence and Victims, 8,* 327–337.

Dutton, D. G., & Starzomski, A. J. (1994). Psychological differences between court-referred and self-referred wife assaulters. *Criminal Justice and Behavior: An International Journal, 21,* 203–222.

Edwards, D. W., Scott, C. L., Yarvis, R. M., Paizis, C. L., & Panizzon, M. S. (2003) Impulsiveness, impulsive aggression, personality disorder and spousal violence. *Violence and Victims, 18*(1), 3–14.

Fortunata, B., & Kohn, C. S. (2003). Demographic, psychosocial and personality characteristics of lesbian batterers. *Violence and Victims, 18*(5), 557–568.

Gondolf, E. W. (1999). MCMI-III results for batterer program participants in four cities: Less "pathological" than expected. *Journal of Family Violence, 14,* 1–17.

Gottman, J. M., Jacobson, N. S., Rushe, R. H., Short, J. W., Babcock, J., La Taillade, J. J., & Waltz, J. (1995). The relationship between heart rate activity, emotionally aggressive behavior and general violence in batterers. *Journal of Family Psychology, 9,* 1–41.

Hamberger, L. K., & Hastings, J. E. (1986). Personality correlates of men who abuse their partners: A cross-validational study. *Journal of Family Violence, 1,* 323–341.

Hamberger, L. K., & Hastings, J. E. (1988). Personality characteristics of spouse abusers: A controlled comparison. *Violence and Victims, 3,* 5–30.

Hamberger, L. K., & Hastings, J. E. (1989). Counseling male spouse abusers: Characteristics of treatment completers and dropouts. *Violence and Victims, 4,* 275–286.

Hamberger, L. K., Lohr, J. M., Bonge, D., & Tolin, D. F. (1996). A large empirical typology of male spouse abusers and its relationship to dimensions of abuse. *Violence and Victims, 11,* 277–292.

Hare, R. D. (1991). *The Hare psychopathy checklist-Revised.* Toronto: Multi-Health Systems.

Hare, R. D. (1993). *Without conscience: The disturbing world of the psychopaths among us.* New York: Pocket Books.

Hare, R. D. (1995). Psychopathy: Theory, research and implications for society. An introduction. *Issues in Criminological and Legal Psychology, 24,* 4–5.

Hare, R. D. (1996). Psychopathy: A clinical construct whose time has come. *Criminal Justice and Behavior, 23,* 25–54.

Hart, S. D., Dutton, D. G., & Newlove, T. (1993). The prevalence of personality disorder among wife assaulters. *Journal of Personality Disorders, 7,* 329–341.

Holtzworth-Munroe, A., Meehan, J., Herron, K., & Rehman, U. (2000). Testing the Holtzworth-Munroe and Stuart typology. *Journal of Consulting and Clinical Psychology, 68,* 1000–1019.

Holtzworth-Munroe, A., & Stuart, G. L. (1994). Typologies of male batterers: Three subtypes and the differences among them. *Psychological Bulletin, 116,* 476–497.

Kernberg, O. (1977). The structural diagnosis of borderline personality organization. In P. Hartocollis (Ed.), *Borderline personality disorders: The concept, the syndrome, the patient.* New York: International Universities Press.

Langhinrichsen-Rohling, J., Huss, M. T., & Ramsey, S. (2000). The clinical utility of batterer typologies. *Journal of Family Violence, 15,* 37–54.

Lie, G., Schilit, R., Bush, J., Montague, M., & Reyes, L. (1991). Lesbians in currently aggressive relationships: How frequently do they report aggressive past relationships? *Violence and Victims, 6,* 121–135.

Linehan, M. (1993). *Cognitive-behavioral treatment of borderline personality disorder.* New York: Guilford.

Lohr, J. M., Hamberger, L. K., & Bonge, D. (1988). The nature of irrational beliefs in different personality clusters of spouse abusers. *Journal of Rational Emotive and Cognitive Behavior Therapy, 6,* 273–285.

Loranger, A. W. (1988). *Personality Disorder Examination (PDE) manual.* Yonkers, NY: DV Communications.

Magdol, L., Moffitt, T. E., Caspi, A, Newman, D. L., Fagan, J., & Silva, P. A. (1997). Gender differences in partner violence in a birth cohort of 21 year olds: Bridging the gap between clinical and epidemiological approaches. *Journal of Consulting and Clinical Psychology, 65,* 68–78.

Millon, T. (1987). On the genesis and prevalence of the borderline personality disorder: A social learning thesis. *Journal of Personality Disorders, 1,* 354–372.

Millon, T. (1997). *The Millon inventories: Clinical personality assessment.* New York: Guilford.

Morey, L. C. (1991). *The Personality Assessment Inventory: Professional manual.* Odessa, FL: Psychological Assessment Resources.

Murphy, C. M., Meyer, S. L., & O'Leary, K. D. (1993). Family origin violence and MCMI-II psychopathology among partner assaultive men. *Violence and Victims, 8,* 165–176.

Oldham, J., Clarkin, J., Appelbaum, A., Carr, A., Kernberg, P., Lotterman, A., & Haas, G. (1985). A self-report instrument for borderline personality organization. In T. H. McGlashan (Ed.), *The Borderline: Current empirical research. The progress in psychiatry series* (pp. 1–18). Washington, DC: American Psychiatric Press.

Pence, E., & Paymar, M. (1986). *Power and control: Tactics of men who batter.* Duluth: Minnesota Program Development.

Saunders, D. G. (1992). A typology of men who batter: Three types derived from cluster analysis. *American Orthopsychiatry, 62,* 264–275.

Starzomski, A. (1995) *Attachment and attribution in abusive males.* Unpublished M.A. thesis. Department of Psychology, University of British Columbia.

Straus, M. A., & Gelles, R. J. (1992). *Physical violence in American families.* New Brunswick, NJ: Transaction.

Tweed, R., & Dutton, D. G. (1998). A comparison of impulsive and instrumental subgroups of batterers. *Violence and Victims, 13,* 217–230.

Yllö, K., & Bograd, M. (1988). *Feminist perspectives on wife assault.* Newbury Park, CA: Sage.

Zanarini, M. C., Parachini, E. A., Frankenburg, F. R., Holman, J. B., Hennen, J., Reich, D. B., & Silk, K. R. (2003). Sexual relationship difficulties among borderline patients and axis II comparison subjects. *Journal of Nervous and Mental Disorders 191*(7), 479–482.

2

Through a Feminist Lens

*Gender, Diversity, and Violence:
Extending the Feminist Framework*

Kersti A. Yllö

V iolence within the family is as complex as it is disturbing. Compressed into one assault are our deepest human emotions, our sense of self, our power, and our hopes and fears about love and intimacy, as well as the social construction of marriage and its place within the larger society. Despite the issue's complexity, the most fundamental feminist insight into all of this is quite simple: Domestic violence cannot be adequately understood unless gender and power are taken into account.

Looking at domestic violence through a feminist lens is not a simple matter, however. Developing a theoretical, empirical, political, and personal understanding of violence requires us to analyze its

---

AUTHOR'S NOTE: Thanks are given to Michelle Harris for her comments and suggestions.

complex gendered nature. This involves the psychologies of perpetrator and victim and their interactions, gendered expectations about family relationships and dynamics, and the patriarchal ideology and structure of society within which individuals and relationships are embedded. Increasingly, feminists of color are pointing to the important impact of race/ethnicity and class in shaping all of these dimensions. Although there is a range of feminist perspectives, there is a broad consensus that family violence is profoundly shaped by gender and power.

Feminist understanding of domestic violence has its roots in social action. Feminist academic work, theoretical analyses, and methodological debates flow out of feminist practice. The feminist perspective, with its origins in social movements, is strong on practical programs and critiques of prevailing perspectives. But it is not yet a fully developed, distinctive framework for the explanation of domestic violence, and in this limitation we are in good company, for no single view is complete. Although a feminist lens may not be sufficient for seeing the full picture of domestic violence, I believe that it is a necessary lens without which any other analytic perspective is flawed. Gender and power are key elements of domestic violence, whether one takes a sociological or a psychological perspective.

After briefly reviewing the gender and power analysis so central to the feminist perspective, I turn to one of the pressing issues feminists are now addressing: a fuller, more nuanced incorporation of race/ethnicity and class into our analysis. The feminist focus on women as a victimized class has obscured the diversity among women (as well as among the men who perpetrate the violence). I point to new directions in feminist theory that, I believe, hold the potential to move us to a more inclusive and more powerful analysis.

❖ DOMESTIC VIOLENCE, GENDER, AND CONTROL

As social constructionists point out, the phenomena we study (including physical violence) are not simply "out there" to be discovered through direct observation. Rather, definitions of problems are socially created through ongoing controversy as well as collaboration. Observation is always theory laden, and this is especially true when the phenomenon under scrutiny is as politically and emotionally fraught as violence (see Yllö, 1988).

The focus we choose for our work (including our theoretical formulations, our empirical research, our policy recommendations, and our social activism) is crucially important. As the title of this volume, *Current Controversies on Family Violence*, suggests, the editors regard the family as the overarching rubric for defining the problem. It then falls to feminists, who tend to focus on *domestic violence* (a term that has become synonymous with battering), to explain why our analysis is largely limited to woman abuse. In the *Handbook of Marriage and the Family*, for example, Suzanne Steinmetz (1987) dismisses feminist theory as "constricted" and of "limited utility as a theory of family violence" (p. 749).

An important question that has been largely overlooked during the 30-year explosion of the family violence field is whether "family violence" is a unitary phenomenon that requires an overarching theory. I argue that feminist analysis has made an enormous contribution to our understanding of wife abuse, yet it has produced relatively less insight into child abuse or elder abuse. However, I do not regard this as evidence that feminist theory is constricted, since it has also made significant contributions to our understanding of stranger rape, acquaintance rape, sexual harassment in the workplace, and murder. Further, this analysis of violence against women (whether in the family or outside it) rests within even broader feminist analysis of all aspects of women's lives in patriarchal society. A feminist analysis of violence connects it to the pervasive sexism in our norms, values, and institutions.

When a man rapes his wife because he feels that it is her "wifely duty" to submit, this is not just a conflict of individual interests, as a sociological analysis might contend. This conflict is deeply gendered, and the husband's perceived entitlement has strong institutional support. When a man with a personality disorder batters his wife when she burns his dinner or tries to get a job, our understanding of the violence is incomplete if we deny the gendered aspects of his controlling behavior. To say simply that domestic violence is about gender and power may seem like nothing more than a sound bite. But it is far more than that— it is a concise expression of a complex body of feminist theory and research. A full discussion of this work would fill volumes; in this chapter I can only outline the coercive control view of domestic violence.

In her review essay on feminism and family research, Myra Marx Ferree (1990) states that "feminists agree that male dominance within families is part of a wider system of male power, is neither natural nor inevitable, and occurs at women's cost" (p. 866). Feminist work in family violence explores and articulates the ways in which violence against women in the home is a critical component of the system of male power. Violence grows out of inequality within marriage (and other intimate relations that are modeled on marriage) and reinforces male dominance and female subordination within the home and outside it. In other words, violence against women (whether in the form of sexual harassment at work, rape by a date, or a beating at home) is a part of male control (Hanmer & Maynard, 1987; Dobash & Dobash, 1998). It is not gender neutral any more than the economic division of labor or the institution of marriage is gender neutral.

The conceptualization of violence as coercive control was not deduced from an abstract theoretical model. Rather, it grew inductively out of the day-to-day work of battered women and activists who struggled to make sense of the victimization they saw. As the shelter movement grew and survivors and activists joined together to discuss their experiences, a clearer vision of what domestic violence is and how to challenge it emerged.

A control model of domestic violence, known as the "Power and Control Wheel," developed by the Domestic Abuse Intervention Project in Duluth, Minnesota, is shown in Figure 2.1. This model has been used across the country in batterers' groups, support groups, and training sessions, as well as in empirical studies (see Shepard & Pence, 1999). It provides a valuable, concise framework for seeing the interconnections between violence and other forms of coercive control or *control tactics.* The wheel connects physical and sexual violence to the hub of power and control with a number of "spokes": minimization and denial, intimidation, isolation, emotional abuse, economic abuse, use of children, threats, and assertion of male privilege.

When one looks at these control tactics in a bit more detail, through research based on extensive interviews with battered women and batterers (Jones & Schechter, 1992; Ptacek, 1988), the close-up picture of domestic violence that develops is one of domination. The following is an interview excerpt from my study of women who were physically abused during their pregnancies.

S., a 31-year-old white woman, describes the control and violence in her marriage that eventually resulted in a miscarriage:

> I didn't even realize he was gaining control and I was too dumb to know any better. . . . He was gaining control bit by bit until he was checking my pantyhose when I'd come home from the supermarket to see if they were inside out. . . . He'd time me. He'd check the

Figure 2.1 Power and Control Wheel

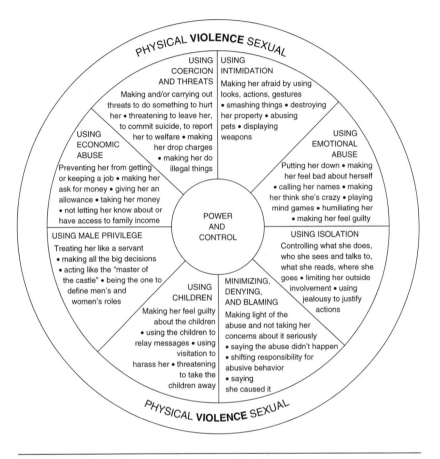

SOURCE: Reprinted with permission from Minnesota Program Development, Inc., Domestic Abuse Intervention Project, 206 W. 4th Street, Duluth, MN 55806.

mileage on the car. . . . I was living like a prisoner. . . . One day I was at Zayers with him . . . and I was looking at a sweater. He insisted I was looking at a guy. I didn't even know there was a guy in the area, because it got to the point that I, I had to walk like I had horse-blinders on. . . . You don't look anybody in the eye. You don't look up because you are afraid.

At one point, S. was insulted by a friend of her husband's, and she was furious. She recalls:

I told him, who the hell was he? And I threw a glass of root beer in his face. My husband gave me a back hand, so I just went upstairs to the bedroom and got into a nightgown. And he kept telling me to come downstairs and I said "No—just leave me alone." . . . He come up and went right through the door. Knocked the whole top panel off the door and got into the room. Ripped the nightgown right off my back, just bounced me off every wall in that bedroom. Then he threw me down the stairs and . . . outside in the snow and just kept kicking me and saying it was too soon for me to be pregnant. . . . His friend was almost rooting him on.

The coercive control model of domestic violence is an important theoretical alternative to psychological explanations focused only on personality disorders and the sociology of interpersonal conflict. It identifies violence as a tactic of entitlement and power that is deeply gendered, rather than as a symptom of a disorder or as a conflict tactic that is individual and gender neutral. It has deepened our understanding of family violence in substantial and significant ways. However, it is not the final analysis. Although it provides a potent description of violence and its context, it should be seen as the beginning, not the completion of our work.

❖ COMMONALITY AND DIVERSITY

One area where feminist theory has fallen short concerns the racial/ethnic and class diversity among women. Drawing on radical feminist analysis, we have conceptualized women as a class, oppressed in a dichotomous sex/gender system. During the last decade, important work by feminists of color have challenged this view as simplistic and limiting (Crenshaw, 1994; Richie, 1996). This conceptualization is constricted by what Adrienne Rich (1979) called "white solipsism"—a type of tunnel vision in which white experience is assumed to describe human experience.

We are currently undergoing a period of rich intellectual and political debate about the interconnections among gender, race, and class and their implications for understanding violence. I suggest that feminist theory stands out among the different family violence frameworks in addressing these issues. Race is far more than a variable affecting rates of violence or a factor to be controlled. Like gender, race/ethnicity infuses all aspects of family life and its social context. I next touch upon promising theoretical work, mostly by women of color, that needs more attention and integration into our analyses and practices.

An important concept for analyzing diversity and violence is the idea of intersectionality, developed by legal scholar Kimberlé Crenshaw (1993, 1994). She makes the point that:

> although violence is a common issue among women, such violence usually occurs within a specific context—that often varies considerably depending on the race, class, and other social characteristics of the woman. . . . These characteristics can be better understood and addressed through a framework that links them to broader structures of subordination which intersect sometimes in fairly predictable ways. (1993, p. 15)

Further, she suggests that we consider both structural and political intersectionality. Structurally, the intersection of race, class, and gender creates particular circumstances for different battered women. Deciding how to respond to abuse is very different for a Latina who is trying to establish legal residence through her husband than it is for an employed white woman who is a U.S. citizen. Politically, intersectionality has implications for activism and intervention. Crenshaw urges us to supersede identity politics and the notion of unitary groups in conflict (blacks versus whites, males versus females, gays versus straights, and so on) and to recognize each of these groups as multidimensional within themselves and, at their best, effective coalitions. So, women can be a coalition of gay, straight, Latina, middle class, poor, African American, white, and so on with structural and political commonalties and differences. A feminist theory that emphasizes only the commonality of gender erases the texture of women's lives and is less useful than it might be. Feminist scholars and activists who are mindful of these intersections can develop theory, research, and interventions to move us forward.

In *The Color of Privilege: Three Blasphemies on Race and Feminism* (1996), Aida Hurtado offers a useful and challenging framework for considering intersectionality, although she does not address domestic violence directly. She develops a theory of gender subordination as relational, explaining why subordination is experienced differently by white women and women of color. It is often tempting to see these as differences in attitude—as simple reflections of culture (for example, different values regarding family)—or social location (the greater likelihood that women of color live in poverty). Hurtado argues that the theoretically important factor is women's *relationship* to white male power. She points out that women of color have been exploited for their labor and sexuality, yet they have been rejected as legitimate reproducers of white men's offspring. White women, in contrast, have been seduced into compliance because they are needed to biologically reproduce the next generation of the power structure (p. vii). White women, especially of the upper and middle classes, live *within* circles of power and are intimately connected to those who subordinate them.

Hurtado's theory is particularly useful in an analysis of violence in the home, because she helps us see how feminist theory to date has been myopic. The political consciousness that has informed the women's movement grew out of an examination of the public/private distinction and the realization by white, educated women that gender oppression occurred in the intimacy of their own homes. The radical slogan, "The personal is political," according to Hurtado, "identifies and rejects the public-private distinction as a tool by which women are excluded from public participation while the daily tyrannies of men are protected from public scrutiny" (p. 18). From this viewpoint, battering is a prime example of this intimate oppression, and much of feminist activism has attempted to bring it to public attention, to sanction it through the criminal justice system, and to offer women refuge from their homes.

This work has undoubtedly been important and has saved lives. It has, however, assumed that the private/public split applies similarly to all women. Hurtado contends that "the political consciousness of women of Color stems from an awareness that the public is personally political" (p. 18). People of color have not had the luxury of a private realm. Through welfare programs, public housing, sterilization programs, police presence, and disproportionate arrest and incarceration rates, public systems of social control invade their private realm. Poor women of color are acutely aware of their distance from the white male power structure that may evict or deport them or imprison their sons. Their activism, then, more often focuses on these public issues rather than the subordination or abuse they may experience from their intimate partners who are, otherwise, relatively powerless. Their experiences with the racism of the criminal justice system and other service providers make them reluctant to use the same avenues of redress that white battered women turn to.

In contrast, women who are physically integrated into the centers of power have a very different experience of gender subordination. Thus white feminists have been more concerned with expectations of docility, gender socialization, housework, body image, and intimate violence. These observations have been made before; however, the implication usually has been that some essential difference exists between the submissive, white women victimized within their homes and the strong, black women heading families. A relational theory of gender subordination offers a clear structural explanation for the differences: They reflect women's connection to or distance from white male power.

As Hurtado points out, the women's movement is the only political movement in history to develop its own clinical approach—feminist therapy (p. 18). There is a real question about the extent to which therapy, which deals with oppression at the individual and interpersonal level, can address the needs of all women. So far, feminist therapy has focused heavily on issues of intimacy with white men and has been utilized largely by those women who are struggling with the seduction of men in power. Yet, feminist therapy, like feminist theory, is addressing the challenges posed by feminists of color who question its assumptions (Bograd, 1999). This is not to argue that feminist therapy has not made important contributions, but rather that we should not assume that approaches of value for some women will be of value for all women. Further, a truly radical feminist therapy will help to transcend the divisions between those women privileged by their association with white male power and those distanced and oppressed by it.

The discussion in this chapter has been largely about gender subordination and rather little about family violence. Nevertheless, I hope that the implications for our work, both scholarly and applied, are becoming clear. The feminist approach to violence will become more analytically powerful and more practically useful if we add to its depth and complexity by addressing the intersection of race/ethnicity, class, and gender. It is not enough to include these factors as variables in models that ignore the structural conditions of oppression. Nor is it enough to invoke "race/class/gender" as a political mantra in superficial analyses. There is an enormous amount of intellectual, political, and practical work to be done to reach more synthetic understandings and solutions.

❖ RESEARCH AND INTERVENTION AT THE INTERSECTION

The feminist analysis of intimate violence to date has emphasized women's commonality. The point feminists have made over and over again has been that *all* women are vulnerable to such violence, which cuts across racial, ethnic, and class lines. This position has proven to be very effective politically precisely because of the relational character of gender subordination that Hurtado identifies. Whether we're training judges, police, or medical doctors, or lobbying for stronger criminal justice sanctions or the Violence against Women Act, we have made the point that the victims can be *"your* sisters, daughters, and friends." We have seen that Social Security is sacred, while welfare is vilified. Therefore, we have emphasized the connections to the white men in power and downplayed violence in poor communities of color because we knew that funding would not be forthcoming if victims were seen as "other." Political favor flows more easily to "worthy" (read white, middle-class) victims. Using this strategy, feminists have successfully changed laws, policies, and procedures and gained funding for services that have helped large numbers of women.

However, Crenshaw (1994, p. 105) points out that there is a thin line between debunking the stereotypical beliefs that only poor and minority women are battered and pushing them aside to focus on victims for whom mainstream politicians and media are more likely to express concern.

Unfortunately, one of the unintended consequences of this approach is that the differences among women have been "white-washed" and that those who are most victimized have been pushed aside. The reality that poor women (who are disproportionately women of color) experience more extensive and severe violence coupled with fewer options tends to become lost.

Angela Browne and her colleagues (Browne & Bassuk, 1997) have done important work on the relationship between poverty and intimate violence. Their well-designed study of housed and homeless poor women revealed horrific rates of physical and sexual abuse. The researchers found that an astounding 83 percent of very low-income mothers had been victims of severe physical violence and/or sexual abuse during their lifetimes. Homelessness and substance abuse were closely connected problems. The enormity of these women's troubles can be more fully understood through such examinations of class, poverty, and the welfare system; a gender analysis alone is inadequate.

The gender-race-class intersection was an unexpected finding in a study by Eileen Abel (1999) that compared female "victims" with women who had been adjudicated as "batterers." The study was based on a sample of women drawn from three domestic violence victim service programs ($N = 51$) and three batterer intervention programs ($N = 67$) in the state of Florida. There were few statistical differences between the "victims" and "batterers" in exposure to violence *by their partners*, except that the women identified as batterers were *more* likely to have been threatened and forced to have sex than their victim counterparts. The women who had been labeled as batterers were also more likely to have previously sought medical treatment (62 percent versus 38 percent), whereas victims were more likely to have previously used domestic violence victim services (67 percent versus 33 percent). Abel discovered another important difference between the two groups: Women of color were overrepresented in the batterers group (42 percent nonwhite) compared to the victims group (26 percent). The mean income of women in the batterers group was $26,000; in the victims group it was more than $46,000. So, despite higher levels of victimization and injury, poorer and minority women are more likely to be mandated into batterer treatment through the criminal justice system, while victim services are more likely to offer support to white, financially more stable women. While the Abel study offered no details of the women's use of violence or the process by which they came to be in the two groups, her research does raise questions about the impact of class and race on battered women's experiences with state intervention and social services.

The race-gender intersection also proved critical in a study of 1,870 partner violence reports to police by Bourg and Stock (in Marin & Russo, 1999). They found that, overall, men were more likely to be identified as batterers; however women who were so identified were more likely to be charged with a serious crime. In particular, "black women were more likely to be arrested on felony charges (84%) than white men were (19%) *for similar behavior*" (p. 23, emphasis mine). Given the overall high arrest rates in communities of color, it is not surprising that black women are arrested and charged disproportionately.

These studies provide support for the proposition that individuals' distance from the white male power structure shapes their chances of abuse as well as the response of social services and the criminal justice system. However, these studies offer just a glimpse of how race intersects with gender in the institutional response to violence, since race was not their main focus. One study that does take this intersection as its central concern is Beth Richie's *Compelled to Crime: The Gender Entrapment of Battered Black Women* (1995). Her research on battered women jailed on Rikers Island, New York, reveals just how complex the race/class/gender intersection is. The battered African American women she interviewed were entrapped in a series of paradoxes. For example, Richie found that the battered women in her sample were more likely to come from stable families in which their parents had high expectations of them. These women struggled to maintain relationships despite ongoing abuse because they were so committed to traditional gender norms and family values. Unfortunately for these women, these efforts led to illegal activities in response to violence and coercion by their male partners (p. 4). Women from more disadvantaged and unstable families were more likely to walk away from violent partners because they had few expectations of an enduring family.

Compounding what Richie refers to as the battered women's "gender entrapment" in their abusive relationships are their experiences with social services and the criminal justice system. Compared to the white battered women in the study, the African American women were less likely to turn to social services for help. Further, none wanted their partners arrested or jailed, whereas the white women had often turned to the police for help. Here, Hurtado's (1996) emphasis on distance from the white male power structure is illuminating. The institutions that feminists have worked hard to make responsive to battered women have certainly changed, but those changes seem to better serve white women rather than all women.

Richie's (1996) study serves as a warning to those who ignore race or who might too easily assume that the effects of race, class, and gender are simply additive. Although Richie focused on the most extreme cases, her nuanced analysis of the intersection of race, class, and gender serves as a model of feminist research that can guide us in further work on the full spectrum of family violence.

❖ LOOKING FORWARD

Feminists have made enormous contributions to our understanding of and interventions in intimate violence. Gender and coercive control remain critical conceptual tools in this work. The challenge before us is to deepen and extend our analysis. The centrality of gender is the subject of as much controversy as ever. From researchers using the Conflict Tactics Scales comes the assertion that women are as violent as men in the home (Straus, this volume). Antifeminist activists use these data to champion an artificial "equality" of abuse that erases the terror and injury of battering and undermines programs designed to intervene with violent men and support battered women. In response, feminists must work hard to elucidate women's shared subjection. We must not relent in asserting women's commonality of experience with coercive control. The Power and Control Wheel (which has been translated into dozens of languages and dialects) speaks to battered women of every color in disparate communities around the globe.

Yet, as surely as we must assert women's commonality in response to the antifeminist backlash, we must recognize, understand, and draw on the power of the diversity among us. A feminist analysis that assumes gender oppression is a unitary phenomenon will fall far short of its transformative potential. The social location of a black battered woman or an abused illegal immigrant is profoundly different from that of a beaten middle-class white woman—despite the subjection of all three to the coercive control of their partners. These differences are not essential to racial or ethnic groups. Rather, they reflect cultural differences, structural inequalities, and our differing relationships to white male power.

Doing feminist work in this field is, in many ways, more challenging than ever. It is certainly true that we have been heard and have more funding and more influence than in the early years of the movement. We have succeeded in making what was once a private trouble into a public issue. Feminist research and activism have influenced institutional realms from the police and courts to medical, mental health, and social services. After more than 25 years of work, we are at a point where the once glaring indifference to violence against women has been confronted and, in many places, transformed. There have been dramatic changes in law, policy, protocols, and practice. In a recent address titled "The Color of Violence against Women," Angela Davis (2000) pays tribute to the anti-violence movement that has criminalized the once-private act of battering. Yet she challenges us by arguing that "given the racist and patriarchal patterns of the state, it is difficult to envision the state as the holder of solutions to the problem of violence against women of color." A critical task now is to develop more of what some have called "culturally sensitive" or "culturally competent" analysis and interventions. We must remember that this cultural sensitivity must be linked to challenges of structural inequalities and power relations. The work before us is, in many ways, more complex and difficult than what we have accomplished thus far.

The final point I make is not about feminism or violence per se, but about the nature of the debate and controversy around these issues.

I am disturbed by the deep cleavages that have resulted from attacks, counterattacks, and highbrow name calling. Feminist scholars and activists with strong convictions are labeled ideologues, "feminist fundamentalists" (Erickson, 1992), and "dogmatic" (Dutton, this volume). At the same time, feminists deepen the chasm by dismissing nonfeminist insights too quickly and hastily deciding who "gets it" and who doesn't. In the early years of family violence research and the battered women's movement, these divisions were largely focused on gender politics. More recently, challenges from scholars and activists of color (some feminists, some not) are pushing us forward toward more inclusive and transformative work. Our contentious history should give us pause. White feminists taking up the challenge to address race must recognize the potential dangers of this work. As Jim Ptacek (1999) notes, "In a fiercely divided society, public discussions of class, race, and violence entail risks. Wittingly or unwittingly, those who name these interconnections arouse powerful racist images, even when their goals are to displace them" (p. 19).

One way that white feminists can further the work on the race/ class/gender intersection is to interrogate our own racial privilege (Lewis, 1997). "Culturally sensitive" theories and interventions focused on people of color should not be seen as alternatives to the prevailing work, which is somehow assumed to be culturally neutral. Race is not a black issue any more than gender is a women's issue.

I believe that our future work cannot evade these difficult matters. Openness and respectful listening to different viewpoints will be essential. Careful consideration of potential unintended consequences of our work will be more important than ever. Recognition of the power of the coalitions (rather than the divisions) among us will be crucial. It will not be easy to answer Angela Davis's (2000) question, "How do we develop analyses and organizing strategies against violence against women that acknowledge the race of gender and the gender of race?" It will be difficult. But in addressing this question, I believe, lies the radical potential of feminism.

❖ REFERENCES

Abel, E. (1999). *Comparing the social service utilization, exposure to violence, and trauma symptomology of domestic violence "victims" and female "batterers."* Paper presented at the 7th International Family Violence Research Conference, University of New Hampshire.

Bograd, M. (1999). Strengthening domestic violence theories: Intersections of race, class, sexual orientation, and gender. *Journal of Marital and Family Therapy, 25,* 275–289.

Browne, A., & Bassuk, S. (1997). Intimate violence in the lives of homeless and poor housed women. *American Journal of Orthopsychiatry, 67*(2), 261–278.

Crenshaw, K. (1993). Race, gender, and violence against women. In M. Minow (Ed.), *Family matters: Readings on family lives and the law* (pp. 230–232). New York: New Press.

Crenshaw, K. (1994). Mapping the margins: Intersectionality, identity politics, and violence against women of color. In M. Fineman & R. Mykitiuk (Eds.), *The public nature of private violence* (pp. 93–118). New York: Routledge.

Davis, A. (2000). *The color of violence against women.* Keynote address of the Color of Violence Conference at the University of California at Santa Cruz. Retrieved April 29, 2004, from www.arc.org/C__Lines/CL Archive/story3_3_02.html

Dobash, R. E., & Dobash, R. P. (1998). *Rethinking violence against women.* Thousand Oaks, CA: Sage.

Erickson, B. (1992). Feminist fundamentalism: Reactions to Avis, Kaufman, and Bograd. *Journal of Marital and Family Therapy, 18,* 263–267.

Ferree, M. M. (1990). Beyond separate spheres: Feminism and family research. *Journal of Marriage and the Family, 52,* 866–884.

Hanmer, J., & Maynard, M. (1987). *Women, violence, and social control.* Atlantic Highlands, NJ: Humanities.

Hurtado, A. (1996). *The color of privilege: Three blasphemies on race and feminism.* Ann Arbor: University of Michigan Press.

Jones, A., & Schechter, S. (1992). *When love goes wrong.* New York: Harper Collins.

Lewis, A. (1997). *Theorizing whiteness: Interrogating racial privilege.* Working Paper #568, Center for Research on Social Organization, University of Michigan.

Marin, A., & Russo, N. (1999). Feminist-perspectives on male violence against women. In M. Harway & J. O'Neil (Eds.), *What causes men's violence against women?* (pp. 18–35). Thousand Oaks, CA: Sage.

Ptacek, J. (1988). "Why do men batter their wives?" In K. Yllö & M. Bograd (Eds.), *Feminist perspectives on wife abuse* (pp. 133–157). Newbury Park, CA: Sage.

Ptacek, J. (1999). *Battered women in the courtroom.* Boston: Northeastern University Press.

Rich, A. (1979). *On lies, secrets, and silence: Selected prose, 1966–1978.* New York: Norton.

Richie, B. E. (1995). *Compelled to crime: The gender entrapment of battered black women.* New York: Routledge.

Richie, B. E. (1996). Battered black women: A challenge for the black community. *Black Scholar, 16*(2), 40–44.

Shepard, M., & Pence, E. (Eds.). (1999). *Coordinating community response: Lessons from Duluth and beyond.* Thousand Oaks, CA: Sage.

Steinmetz, S. K. (1987). Family violence: Past, present, and future. In M. B. Sussman & S. K. Steinmetz (Eds.), *Handbook of marriage and the family* (pp. 725–765). New York: Plenum.

Yllö, K. (1988). Political and methodological debates in wife abuse research. In K. Yllö & M. Bograd (Eds.), *Feminist perspectives on wife abuse* (pp. 28–50). Newbury Park, CA: Sage.

3

Through a Sociological Lens

The Complexities of Family Violence

Donileen R. Loseke

"Family violence" is an umbrella term that encompasses a vast variety of behaviors and people, including violence by parents toward children, violence by children toward parents, violence by men toward women, violence by women toward men, violence by adults toward elderly people, and violence between siblings. In this chapter I explore how sociological perspectives can help in understanding the phenomena of family violence as well as help in understanding the sources of the many controversies surrounding it.

❖ THINKING SOCIOLOGICALLY ABOUT FAMILY VIOLENCE

While terms such as "family violence," "wife abuse," or "child abuse" most often are used without definition, a sociological perspective called *social constructionism* emphasizes examining the power and meanings of words (Loseke, 2003).

What is family?

The title of this book, *Current Controversies on Family Violence*, directs attention to violence happening in a particular *place*—in families. This makes sense for the simple reason that FBI statistics (Federal Bureau of Investigation, 1999) indicate that there is an astonishing amount of violence in American families. It also makes sense to focus on violence in families because, regardless of recurring complaints that actual families often fail their members, family remains an important cultural ideal: Most adults marry and desire children; the right to legal marriage is an important part of gay and lesbian political agendas. In theory and in practice, family is critical to Americans.

While concentrating on violence in families makes sense, it raises a seemingly simplistic question: What *is* a "family"? For example, although there is more violence among people who cohabit than among those who are formally married (Anderson, 1997), are unmarried couples a family? And, if cohabiting heterosexual couples are family, then perhaps cohabiting lesbian and gay couples also should be included, because these relationships contain violence (Renzetti, 1992). What about couples who are merely dating—or who dated in the past? Here, too, there is much violence (Greenfield et al., 1998), but should these types of relationships be classified as family? In the same way, child sexual abuse is perpetrated by men who are "dating" children's mothers (Patton, 1991, p. 228). Are such men family? In brief, "family" in this current historical era is a rubber-band term. At times, it seems to expand to include people in many types of relationships.

The definition of *family* is critical for examining and understanding violence, because different types of relationships are associated with different characteristics, problems, and possibilities. There are experiential and practical differences between couples who are merely dating and those who are cohabiting, between cohabiting and married couples, and between heterosexual and homosexual couples. Children abused by their biological or legal fathers are in different circumstances than those abused by their mothers' informal partners. Muddled thinking results when differences are ignored; it matters how *family* is defined.

What is violence?

Examining and understanding family violence also requires careful attention to defining *violence*. What, specifically, do family violence researchers examine? What, specifically, do members of the public worry about?

There are good reasons why the concern should be with *all* violence: The presence of violence violates cultural images of families as places of peace and solidarity. Yet statistics from national studies consistently paint a picture of American homes as riddled with violence. Pushes, shoves, slaps, and spanks are routine features of family life, and this violence seemingly is done by *everyone* to *anyone:* Siblings are violent toward one another, children hit parents, parents hit children, men hit women, women hit men (see, for example, Straus, Gelles, & Steinmetz, 1980).

While this statistical portrait challenges cultural images, many— perhaps most—Americans are not terribly concerned with this high prevalence of violence. Instead, there is a common understanding in the United States that not *all* violence is a problem that must be resolved. Violence in self-defense and for other "good reasons," such as child discipline, often is evaluated as "legitimate"; violence between siblings, as well as some types of violence, such as pushes, slaps, and shoves, often are evaluated as "normal" parts of family life.

Members of the public, academic researchers, and social policy- makers generally are not particularly concerned with "legitimate" or "normal" violence. Instead, concern is with abuse—violence evaluated as *not* normal, and as *not* legitimate. In popular understandings, *abuse* is violence that produces "victims," people evaluated as suffering greatly and unjustly through no fault of their own (Loseke, 2003). Concern with *abusive* violence yields a picture of American homes as characterized primarily by the presence of child abuse, wife abuse, and elder abuse.

This focus on abusive violence raises two important questions. First, as Richard Gelles and Murray Straus noted some years ago (1979), "abuse" is a *moral evaluation*. Given this, what is—and is not— included as abuse depends on the moral judgments of people using the term. Individual researchers and members of the public have wildly different ideas about what is—and is not—abusive.

A second question is raised by a focus on abusive violence with children, women, and elderly people as the typical victims: Why limit attention to violence experienced in *families?* After all, children are victims of violence in day care centers, elderly people are victims of violence in nursing homes, women are stalked and raped by strangers. Some observers therefore claim that rather than limiting attention to violence in *families*, it makes more sense to examine the myriad forms of violence experienced by particular *people*: children, women, or the elderly.

A sociological perspective encourages asking questions about the topic: What particular people are being included in definitions of family? What particular behaviors are being included in definitions of violence? Should the focus be on violence happening in families or on violence happening to particular types of people? Answers to these questions influence what is found, how it can be understood, and how it might be resolved.

❖ THINKING SOCIOLOGICALLY
   ABOUT RESEARCH AND STATISTICS

Observers note how divergent definitions of both family and violence have led to conflicting findings, to difficulty in comparing studies (Geffner, Rosenbaum, & Hughes, 1988; Tolliver, Valle, Dopke, Serra, & Milner, 1998), and to problems in developing theories (Azar, 1991). That is only the tip of the iceberg of dilemmas, because research on family violence of all types is plagued by myriad problems (see Belsky, 1993, for one review). Rather than detailing typical problems faced by researchers, I focus on some important questions that should be asked in order to evaluate research.

One critical question is about the *samples* used to gather the data: Who was talked to and/or what records were examined? With the notable exceptions of the Family Violence National Studies (see Straus, this volume) and national crime victimization surveys (Greenfield et al., 1998), the great majority of research on this topic uses *non-random* samples. These commonly involve examining organizational records or talking with clients or service providers in places such as child welfare services, Child Protective Services, counseling centers, or shelters for battered women. Two typical biases result from such commonly used samples.

First, these samples result in bias surrounding estimates of relationships between violence and economic class. This is a well-known empirical association: As income goes down, the amount of violence (both in and out of families) goes up (Greenfield et al., 1998). While national probability samples find this association, data drawn from social service agencies *magnify* it. In the case of child abuse, this is because protective service workers are likely to simply assume child abuse is occurring when parents are poor (Howitt, 1992; Lane, Rubin, Monteith, & Christian, 2003; O'Toole, Turbett, & Napka, 1983). In technical terms, providers tend to *overdiagnose* abuse in poor families. It follows that children from poor families will be *overrepresented* in research relying on information from child protection agencies. In the case of wife abuse, women often rely on shelters because they do not have the money to pay for a hotel (Loseke, 1992). Poor women therefore are *overrepresented* in research using shelters as sites for data collection. Hence, while national random sample studies *do* show associations between all forms of violence and income, these associations are magnified when data are collected from social service agencies.

There is a second bias resulting from research samples that rely on social service agencies. By definition, women in shelters have experiences severe enough to lead them to leave their homes; by definition, parents being monitored by protective service agencies are people whose behaviors are evaluated as extreme enough to warrant intervention. Yet data from such samples all too often are generalized. Data on the characteristics and experiences of women shelter residents are generalized to *all* battered women; data on the characteristics and experiences of parents monitored by child protective agencies are generalized to *all* abusive parents.

Thinking sociologically about research also requires being thoughtful in interpreting statistics, especially those presented in the mass media.

The mass media are well known for their tendencies to offer glib, "sound bite" answers to perplexing and complicated questions, as well as for their tendencies to magnify and distort information in ways that increase audience interest (Loseke, 2003). It is not that uncommon, for example, to hear statements such as "Abused children grow up to be abusive adults," or for so-called relationship experts on talk shows to tell a troubled woman, "Your husband hit you because his parents hit him." Such statements contain two types of statistical errors.

First, associations between violence and particular characteristics of people often are enormously inflated. Data testing the "intergenerational transmission of abuse" theory, for example, do *not* support the deterministic statement that "abused children grow up to be abusive adults." While there is a moderate association between experiencing child abuse and becoming a child abuser (Black, Heyman, & Slep, 2001), that association is nowhere near perfect (Kaufman & Zigler, 1993). Likewise, there is only a weak-to-moderate association between experiencing child abuse and becoming an abusive spouse (Stith et al., 2000).

Second, statistical associations measure characteristics or behaviors of *categories* of people (such as poor people/not poor people, or abused as a child/not abused as a child). Categorical associations *cannot* be used to make predictions about individual people in these categories. It is an error in logic to predict that any given *individual* will be violent because she or he is poor or because she or he was abused as a child.

Thinking sociologically about research and statistical findings requires asking how key terms were defined, how samples lead to biases, how data can be inappropriately generalized, and how categorical association cannot be used to predict individual characteristics and behaviors.

❖ THINKING SOCIOLOGICALLY ABOUT THE RISK FACTORS OF VIOLENCE

While it is difficult to talk about the "causes" of violence (or of anything else) because the determinants of human behavior are incredibly complex, it is possible to talk about *risk factors:* the characteristics of people, experiences, and environments that put individuals at a greater (or lesser) risk for using violence. These risk factors occur on several levels.

The Biological Level

Because humans are physical creatures, it follows that there can be *biological* risk factors for violence. At this time, little is known about biological risk factors because this research is in its infancy. While very few people believe that biological factors ultimately will account for more than a small amount of family violence, some violence does appear to be associated with intellectual deficits, organic problems, head injuries, and hormones (see Barnett, Miller-Perrin, & Perrin, 1997, for a review). Critically, biological risk factors are potentially helpful only for understanding the behavior of people who are violent in *all* spheres of their lives. Biology *cannot* be referenced when people use violence against family members but not against strangers, employers, or friends.

The Psychological Level

Humans are characterized by complex and symbolic thinking, remembering, emotions, needs, and desires. It follows that there can be *psychological* risk factors for violence. Psychological risk factors of violence that routinely are relayed through the mass media often are trite and mundane and rely on circular reasoning. For example, arguments that violence is caused by "stress" or "low self-esteem" say little, because, *except at the most extreme,* such terms resist empirical measurement. Yet even when psychological diagnosis is done rigorously by highly trained professionals, references to individual-level psychopathology are necessary only to understand the *most extreme* violent behavior (O'Leary, 1993). Psychological theories are of no help in understanding why "spankings," "pushes," "shoves," and "slaps" are a routine feature of family life; they become necessary when violence is obviously and most certainly abusive.

While recognizing biological and psychological risk factors, sociological perspectives strongly argue that these rarely are sufficient, and often are not even necessary, to understand violence. The search for the risk factors of violence cannot end at the level of individual biology or psychology.

The Interactional Level

Because family violence involves people who know one another, violence might be associated with characteristics of *interaction.* Some observers, for example, use categories such as "common couple violence" (Carlson, 1997; Johnson, 1995) or "mutual combat" (Straus, this volume) to conceptualize violence between adults that results from the complexities of family life when disagreements can lead to arguments and arguments can lead to violence.

While marriage counselors offering couples therapy focus on changing patterns of interaction associated with violence, much caution is in order, because "common couples violence" is only one form of violence between adults. The other form is "wife abuse" (Loseke & Kurz, and Yllö, this volume). This is one-way violence, where women are victims and men are offenders using violence to control women. While wife abuse involves an interactional dynamic because men interactionally intimidate women (Lloyd, 1999), it is a grave error to speculate that battered women are implicated in this interactional dynamic.

The interactional level therefore can account for only some violence. Too much emphasis on this interactional level can divert attention from understanding the complexity of violence (Bograd, 1984); it can serve to unjustly blame victims.

The Social Structural Level

While recognizing that in some ways each family is unique, sociological perspectives focus on examining characteristics shared by many, if not most, families. A full understanding of something as complex as family violence requires looking closely at how social environments can be a risk factor for violence.

Not surprisingly, because family violence can be conceptualized as including many types of behaviors (from "spanking" to "murder") involving victims and offenders in any and all family categories, there is not one sociological theory that can adequately account for all violence. Feminism (Yllö, this volume), for example, is a form of sociological theory that explores the consequences of the gendered social environment. Theories informed by feminism are excellent in examining the social conditions and forces allowing and even encouraging the victimization of women by men. Yet, as Yllö comments, feminist-inspired theories are not particularly useful in understanding other forms of violence, such as child abuse, sibling abuse, or elder abuse. In addition, because feminist theories begin with the a priori labeling of women as victims and men as offenders, they also are unable to conceptualize women's violence toward men except as violence done in self-defense.

While sociological theories of family violence are woefully undeveloped, two general theories of crime and violence have obvious relevance to the topic of family violence.

Control Theory. Rather than asking why some people *are* violent, control theory asks why most people are *not* violent. The theoretical answer is that people are controlled by bonds to other people and to social institutions and by the fear of punishment. Some research has demonstrated this relationship for family violence: Men who have strong attachments to and who fear negative sanctions from significant others are less likely to be wife abusers than are men who do not have such attachments (Lackey & Williams, 1995). Likewise, the threat of arrest for wife abuse is a deterrent (control) primarily for men who have valued attachments to home, work, and community (Sherman, 1992).

Resource Theory. This perspective helps to understand relationships between income and violence. Resource theory maintains that force (violence) is a resource that can be used to resolve conflicts, and that in our modern world it is most often a resource of "last resort," used when all else fails (Goode, 1971). This theory could be used to note that economically advantaged parents wishing to punish or control their children can take away their children's computers, televisions, or private phones. In many instances, this would be sufficient to bring a child's behavior into line with parental expectations, so there would be no need for physical force. Because economically disadvantaged parents cannot take away possessions their children do not have, they might turn to the use of physical force more quickly. In the same way, men with high income and social standing have a variety of resources by which to control their wives; men without such resources might more quickly turn to physical force (Anderson, 1997).

Control and resource theories are general perspectives that help understand risk factors for many types of crime, including family violence. In addition, sociology often characterizes family as a social institution, and this leads to other types of risk factors for violence.

Family as a Social Institution. Each social institution (such as family, economy, religion, or education) has three characteristics. First, social institutions include more-or-less agreed-upon *ideas*. Although there has been significant social change, the institution of family includes ideas such as families should be private, parents should care for their children, family members should be emotionally close and share activities, and so on. Second, social institutions include *practices*—the ways people typically act toward one another. Again, although there has been considerable social change, typical practices in American families include a division of labor between spouses, economic dependence of children on their parents, parental socialization of their children, and so on. Finally, social institutions include *arrangements*—objective characteristics of the social world that are outside individual control. In the case of family, these include laws surrounding marriage, divorce, and child protective services, as well as the characteristics of child and elder care, and the organization of employment.

In multiple and complex ways, these—and many other—institutional characteristics of family can be conceptualized as risk factors for violence. For example, in ideas and in practice, family is associated with privacy, and increasing levels of privacy lead to social isolation, which is associated with higher rates of family violence of all types (Belsky, 1993; Williams, 1992). Likewise, the gendered core of typical divisions of labor, as well as stereotypical ideas about gender, are associated with wife abuse (Brown & Hendricks, 1998); strong beliefs that parents have the right to discipline and control their children are associated with child abuse (Belsky, 1993). Furthermore, the idealized image that family members should know the intimate details of one another's lives leads families to be emotional hotbeds: Family members often know better than any one else what can be said or done that will most deeply hurt another.

Examining the characteristics of family as a social institution leads to a perplexing realization that the very characteristics drawing people to value family relationships create a fertile ground for violence. Ideas about how families should be organized, typical ways family members behave toward one another, and the characteristics of the social structures supporting these ideas and expectations allow—if not downright encourage—violence.

❖ THE IMPORTANCE OF THINKING SOCIOLOGICALLY

My goal in this chapter was to demonstrate how thinking sociologically about family violence means thinking in complex ways. This is the power of sociological perspectives: To think about and question research before accepting findings, to understand differences between statistical associations and predictions about individual behavior, to understand that humans are complex creatures and that what goes on inside us is influenced by what goes on outside us. Sociology is a way of thinking about the world.

Yet clearly, sociological perspectives are not as popular as psychological perspectives, especially those routinely paraded through the mass media. The compelling nature of psychological perspectives makes sense because they seem to pose simple solutions to severe and complex problems: If violence is about individual psychopathology, then violent people merely need to be "repaired" and the problems will be resolved. The allure of psychological perspectives also is that these theories pertain primarily to people who use extreme violence, and these are the people who are the object of public fascination.

Finally, psychological theories are undoubtedly more popular than sociological theories because they do not challenge us to think about relationships between social organization and violence. Sociological perspectives encourage us to explore how family violence—in its many forms—can be a consequence of a lack of community or of poverty. These perspectives encourage us to explore how the ideas, practices, and arrangements of the institution of family can create a fertile ground for violence. Yes, indeed, sociological perspectives raise difficult questions. Yet violence cannot be understood or stopped if such questions are swept under the carpet simply because they are troublesome.

❖ REFERENCES

Anderson, K. L. (1997). Gender, status, and domestic violence: An integration of feminist and family violence approaches. *Journal of Marriage and the Family, 59*, 655–669.

Azar, S. T. (1991). Models of child abuse: A metatheoretical analysis. *Criminal Justice and Behavior, 18*, 30–46.

Barnett, O. W., Miller-Perrin, C. L., & Perrin, R. D. (1997). *Family violence across the lifespan: An introduction.* Thousand Oaks, CA: Sage.

Belsky, J. (1993). Etiology of child maltreatment: A developmental-ecological analysis. *Psychological Bulletin, 113*, 413–434.

Black, D. A., Heyman, R. E., & Slep, A. M. S. (2001). Risk factors for child physical abuse. *Aggression and Violent Behavior, 6*, 121–188.

Bograd, M. (1984). Family systems approaches to wife battering: A feminist critique. *American Journal of Orthopsychiatry, 54*, 558–568.

Brown, M. P., & Hendricks, J. E. (1998). Wife abuse. In N. A. Jackson & G. C. Oates (Eds.), *Violence in intimate relationships: Examining sociological and psychological issues* (pp. 119–136). Boston: Butterworth-Heinemann.

Carlson, B. E. (1997). A stress and coping approach to intervention with abused women. *Family Relations, 46*, 291–298.

Federal Bureau of Investigation. (1999). The structure of family violence: An analysis of selected incidents. Retrieved September 12, 2003: http://www.fbi.gov/ucr/nibrs/famvi021.pdf

Geffner, R., Rosenbaum, A., & Hughes, H. (1988). Research issues concerning family violence. In V. B. Van Hasselt, R. Morison, A. S. Bellack, & M. Hersen (Eds.), *Handbook of family violence* (pp. 457–481). New York: Plenum.

Gelles, R. J., & Straus, M. A. (1979). Determinants of violence in the family: Toward a theoretical integration. In W. R. Burr, R. Hill, F. I. Nye, & I. L. Reiss (Eds.), *Contemporary theories about the family, Vol. 1* (pp. 549–580). New York: Free Press.

Goode, W. J. (1971). Force and violence in the family. *Journal of Marriage and the Family, 33,* 624–636.

Greenfield, L. A., Rand, M. R., Craven, D., Klaus, P. A., Perkins, C. A., Ringel, C., Warchol, G., & Maston, C. (1998). *Violence by intimates: Analysis of data on crime by current or former spouses, boyfriends, and girlfriends.* Washington, DC: U.S. Department of Justice, Bureau of Justice Statistics (NCJ-167237).

Howitt, D. (1992). *Child abuse errors: When good intentions go wrong.* New Brunswick, NJ: Rutgers University Press.

Johnson, M. P. (1995). Patriarchal terrorism and common couple violence: Two forms of violence against women. *Journal of Marriage and the Family, 57,* 283–294.

Kaufman, J., & Zigler, E. (1993). The intergenerational transmission of abuse is overstated. In R. J. Gelles & D. R. Loseke (Eds.), *Current controversies on family violence* (1st ed.; pp. 209–221). Newbury Park, CA: Sage.

Lackey, C., & Williams, K. R. (1995). Social bonding and the cessation of partner violence across generations. *Journal of Marriage and the Family, 57,* 295–305.

Lane, W. G., Rubin, D., Monteith, R., & Christian, C. W. (2003). Racial differences in the evaluation of pediatric fractures for physical abuse. *Journal of the American Medical Association, 288,* 1603–1609.

Lloyd, S. A. (1999). The interpersonal and communication dynamics of wife battering. In X. B. Arriaga & S. Oskamp (Eds.), *Violence in intimate relationships* (pp. 91–111). Thousand Oaks, CA: Sage.

Loseke, D. R. (1992). *The battered woman and shelters: The social construction of wife abuse.* New York: State University of New York Press.

Loseke, D. R. (2003). *Thinking about social problems: An introduction to constructionist perspectives,* 2nd ed. New York: Aldine DeGruyter.

O'Leary, D. K. (1993). Through a psychological lens: Personality traits, personality disorders, and levels of violence. In R. J. Gelles & D. R. Loseke (Eds.), *Current controversies on family violence* (1st ed., pp. 7–30). Newbury Park, CA: Sage.

O'Toole, R., Turbett, P., & Napka, C. (1983). Theories, professional knowledge, and the diagnosis of child abuse. In D. Finkelhor, R. J. Gelles, G. Hotaling, & M. A. Straus (Eds.), *The dark side of families* (pp. 349–362). Beverly Hills, CA: Sage.

Patton, M. Q. (1991). Patterns, themes, and lessons. In M. Q. Patton (Ed.), *Family sexual abuse: Frontline research and evaluation* (pp. 223–242). Newbury Park, CA: Sage.

Renzetti, C. M. (1992). *Violent betrayal: Partner abuse in lesbian relationships.* Newbury Park, CA: Sage.

Sherman, L. W. (1992). *Policing domestic violence: Experiments and dilemmas.* New York: Free Press.

Straus, M. A., Gelles, R. J., & Steinmetz, S. K. (1980). *Behind closed doors: Violence in the American family.* Garden City, NY: Doubleday.

Stith, S. M., Rosen, K. H., Middleton, K. A., Busch, A. L., Lundeberg, K., & Carlton, R. P. (2000). The intergenerational transmission of spouse abuse: A meta-analysis. *Journal of Marriage and the Family, 62,* 640–654.

Tolliver, R., Valle, L. A., Dopke, C. A., Serra, L. D., & Milner, J. S. (1998). Child physical abuse. In N. A. Jackson & G. C. Oates (Eds.), *Violence in intimate relationships: Examining sociological and psychological issues* (pp. 1–24). Boston: Butterworth-Heinemann.

Williams, K. R. (1992). Social sources of marital violence and deterrence: Testing an integrated theory of assaults between partners. *Journal of Marriage and the Family, 54,* 620–629.

SECTION II

Controversies in Definition and Measurement

O nce violence has been defined as a particular type of problem, the next question is how to explicitly define and measure it so that research can be done to examine its causes and consequences. At the heart of each controversy in this section are different images of what, specifically, should be defined and measured as a social problem that should be resolved.

The first controversy is as old as the study of family violence itself: How troublesome is women's violence toward men? Murray Straus believes that women's violence is a major social problem that should be publicly condemned and eliminated. In contrast, Donileen Loseke and Demi Kurz argue that women's violence toward men is not the same as men's violence toward women, and that public attention and social resources should not be diverted from the problem of wife abuse. The second controversy in this section involves date rape: What is "date rape," and how much of it is there? Sarah Cook and Mary Koss offer a definition of rape that is expanded from traditional folk understandings of rape as a forcible crime committed by a stranger against a woman who vehemently says "No." Using such a definition in research, they find that the incidence of such rape is incredibly high—as many as 1 in 4 women experience this during their college years. In contrast, Neil Gilbert contends that a more traditional definition of rape is best, and this narrower definition, not surprisingly, greatly reduces estimates of the incidence rate of rape. The third controversy is about spanking: Is spanking a necessary and effective form of punishment or control of small children? John Rosemond argues that parents should have the right to use corporal punishment because it is effective and because it sometimes is necessary. In the opposing view, Murray Straus believes that parents should never, ever use physical punishment, regardless of the situation.

In various ways, the three controversies in this section demonstrate how definitions and measurements matter. First, in the controversy surrounding violence by women, Straus defines violence as specific *behaviors*, such as a push, slap, kick, choke, and so on. Research using this behavioral definition of violence consistently finds that women initiate and carry out physical assaults on their partners as often as do men. Loseke and Kurz, in comparison, believe that a behavioral definition of violence misses the major point: Violence is *gendered* in its *contexts*, its *meanings*, and its *consequences*. Once the sheer counts of women's and men's violent behaviors are placed within these contexts, men's violence and women's violence are very dissimilar.

In the same way, the controversy surrounding date rape is about definitions and measurements. In their chapter, Cook and Koss contend that rape includes "nonforcible assaults if intercourse is obtained with someone unable to consent" for any reason, including intoxication. Furthermore, they believe that the public image of "rape" as a forcible act committed by a stranger leads to women often failing to define themselves as victims when they are raped without physical assault by a date or acquaintance. With this definition, research includes as rape victims women who could not offer true consent to intercourse because they were intoxicated; it includes women whose experiences met the legal definition of rape although the women, themselves, do not believe they were raped. In comparison, Neil Gilbert maintains that "there is a notable discrepancy between Koss's definition of rape and the way most of the women she labels as victims interpreted their experiences." Arguing against including either intoxicated women or women who do not define themselves as rape victims, Gilbert's estimates of the prevalence of date rape are much smaller than those of Koss and Cook.

Finally, how is spanking defined? Rosemond offers a specific definition of spanking: Spanking is punishment done with love. According to him, when love is lacking, spanking is violence, not discipline. Within his definition, the same behavior of spanking could be evaluated either as discipline—and therefore morally acceptable—or violence—and therefore morally unacceptable. Conversely, Straus defines spanking behaviorally. It does not matter whether or not it was done by a caring parent; it does not matter why it was done. Spanking is a behavior and, according to Straus, it is the behavior—not the motive—that leads to a variety of negative consequences.

Which of these definitions and measurements are correct? There are no scientific criteria for answering this question, because each definition—of violence, of date rape, of spanking—reflects judgments of *morality*. Are acts of violence wrong regardless of their contexts, consequences, meanings, or intentions? Should *all* violence be condemned? Is violence about behaviors or is it about consequences? Are there "good reasons" for violence? What does it mean to be a "victim"? These are matters of moral decision making.

Although dealing with different questions, the authors of these three controversies fall into two categories. In one group are those who believe that the public should *expand* its common definition of the forms of violence that should be morally condemned. For example, Straus argues that public concern about the problems of men's violence against women should expand to include concern about women's violence against men. He argues this is necessary because it is "intrinsically wrong" to assault a partner, because women's violence "produces a substantial percentage of all injuries and fatalities from partner violence," and that even when women's assaults do not result in injury, they "put women in danger of much more severe retaliation by men." Cook and Koss likewise defend their definition of rape, which is expanded from more traditional understandings of this crime. According to them, their expanded definition is not new—it is contained in current law that defines rape as including *nonforcible* assaults, and that includes intercourse with a woman legally unable to consent due to intoxication. Furthermore, they argue that women's *failure to label themselves* as victims "does not mean the incident never happened." Finally, in arguing against spanking, Straus offers considerable evidence demonstrating that, despite common myths, spanking is no more effective—and probably less effective—in both the short run and the long term than other noncorporal forms of punishment and control, and that, again despite common myths, spanking has negative consequences. In brief, on one side of each of these controversies are people who believe the public should expand the types of violence that are defined as morally intolerable.

In a second group are authors who do *not* promote expanding definitions of what should be morally condemned and accorded the status of a social problem. While none of these authors argues that violence is "good," or that violence is preferable to no violence, each of their arguments focuses on the social and political implications of attempting to expand definitions of morally intolerable violence. Loseke and Kurz, for example, assert that focusing on women's use of violence "quickly leads to polemics where women's violence is used to justify men's violence, where women are evaluated as not deserving sympathy or support." They believe Straus's assertion that we should train women that "no violence is allowed" has troublesome implications, because so much of women's violence is in self-defense. In arguing against an expanded definition of rape, Gilbert maintains that such expansion "trivializes the trauma and pain suffered by the all too many women who are truly victims," and shows an "immense disregard for the way college women interpreted their own experiences." Finally, Rosemond asserts that while he does "not feel passionately about spankings either one way or the other," he does "feel passionately about government deciding how parents can and cannot discipline" their children. Given his concern that governments increasingly are dictating how parents can discipline their children, Rosemond believes that Straus's simple "advice" to never spank can be used as a tool for governments to *prohibit* spanking by making it a criminal offense. In brief, Loseke and Kurz do *not* condone women's violence, Gilbert does *not* applaud a range of less-than-mutual sexual encounters, Rosemond does *not* support routine spanking. Each of these authors, however, believes that attempts to expand the public's definitions of morally intolerable violence have unacceptable personal, social, and political costs.

In two ways, the controversies in this section offer further examples of problems in evaluating the strength of arguments. Straus, for example, supports his argument that women are as violent as men by offering readers statistical evidence from literally 100 scientific studies. Yet Loseke and Kurz summarily dismiss this evidence by maintaining that studies showing that "women are violent, too" measure only behaviors, and behaviors are meaningless unless placed into their contexts. Likewise, Cook and Koss offer readers multiple citations to studies supporting their assertions that date rape is a significant social problem affecting a very high percentage of women. Gilbert dismisses this evidence by alleging that cited studies are the consequences of "advocacy research," which, according to him, obtain inflated findings by measuring the problem very broadly, by measuring the most affected group and then generalizing to "all women," and by changing definitions and revising data when the research is criticized.

These chapters also show how different forms of evidence can be used to support arguments. In both his chapters, Straus relies exclusively on statistics from scientific studies. Cook and Koss do the same in supporting their argument about date rape. In comparison, Gilbert uses far fewer statistics than do Cook and Koss, and relies more heavily on logical reasoning as well as readers' commonsense understandings of rape. In turn, Loseke and Kurz rely even less on statistical presentations, and more heavily on the results of interview studies. Finally, Rosemond's argument does not proceed by referencing either statistics or the research of others. Rather, his is a logical argument, strengthened by its appeals to everyday practical knowledge. Indeed, one of his major points is that *both* the "anti-spanking ideologues" and the "pro-spanking ideologues" ignore common sense.

How, then, should readers evaluate these arguments? That depends: How should violence be defined and measured? What types of violence should be morally condemned? What are the costs and what are the benefits of expanding—or contracting—images of the violence to be condemned? Experts do not agree.

4

Women's Violence Toward Men Is a Serious Social Problem

Murray A. Straus

The first purpose of this chapter is to review research showing that women initiate and carry out physical assaults on their partners as often as do men. A second purpose is to show that, despite the much

AUTHOR'S NOTE: This chapter is a revision and updating of a paper presented at the 1989 meeting of the American Society of Criminology. It is a pleasure to acknowledge the comments and criticism of the members of the 1989–90 Family Research Laboratory Seminar, and also Angela Browne, Glenda Kaufman Kantor, Coramae Mann, Daniel Saunders, Kirk R. Williams, and Kersti A. Yllö. However, this does not imply their agreement with this chapter. Part of the data are from the National Family Violence Resurvey, funded by National Institute of Mental Health grant R01MH40027 (Richard J. Gelles and Murray A. Straus, co-investigators) by a grant for "Family Violence Research Training" from the National Institute of Mental Health (grant T32 MH15161).

lower probability of physical injury resulting from attacks by women, women produce a substantial percentage of all injuries and fatalities from partner violence.

"Minor" assaults perpetrated by women are also a major problem, even when they do not result in injury, because they put women in danger of much more severe retaliation by men. They also help perpetuate the implicit cultural norms that make the marriage license a hitting license (Straus & Hotaling, 1980). It will be argued that in order to end "wife beating," it is essential for women also to end what many regard as a "harmless" pattern of slapping, kicking, or throwing something at a male partner who persists in some outrageous behavior and "won't listen to reason."

The chapter focuses on physical assaults, even though they are not necessarily the most damaging type of abuse. One can hurt a partner deeply—even drive them to suicide—without ever lifting a finger. Verbal aggression may be even more damaging than physical attacks (Vissing, Straus, Gelles, & Harrop, 1991). This chapter focuses exclusively on physical assaults because, with rare exception, the controversy has been focused on this type of violence by women. Detailed methodological and sociology of science analyses of the controversy can be found in Felson (2002) and Straus (1999).

❖ DEFINING AND MEASURING ASSAULT

The National Crime Panel Report defined *assault* as "an unlawful physical attack by one person upon another" (U.S. Department of Justice, 1976). It is important to note that neither this definition, nor the definition used for reporting assaults to the FBI (Federal Bureau of Investigation, 1995), requires injury or bodily contact. Nevertheless, injury will be considered in this chapter for two reasons. First, the presence of injury makes a difference in what the police, prosecutors, and juries do. Second, numerous studies show that a substantial proportion of serious injuries and homicides of partners are perpetrated by women.

❖ GENDER DIFFERENCES
    IN PARTNER ASSAULT AND HOMICIDE

Violence by women against male partners has been a difficult and controversial issue caused by differences in research methodologies and in moral agendas (Straus, 1999). One of the major discrepancies in research is between what can be called "family conflict" studies, such as the National Family Violence Surveys, and "crime studies," such as the National Crime Victimization Survey. Family conflict studies ask respondents about problems and conflicts in their *family*, while crime studies focus on examining police reports or asking respondents if they have been victims of *crime*.

Without exception, family conflict studies find approximately equal rates of assaults by women and men (Archer, 2000; Fiebert, 1997). In comparison, and also without exception, crime studies find much higher rates of assaults by men. Family conflict and crime studies also yield extremely different answers to questions about the overall prevalence of assaults on partners: Crime studies find a fraction of the rates found by family conflict studies. Both the low overall rate of assault and the high percentage of assaults by men found in crime studies probably occur because crime studies deal with only the small part of all domestic assaults that study respondents experience as a "crime." Assaults perceived as crimes rather than as "family fights" occur relatively rarely and involve perpetration by men much more often than by women (Straus, 1999).

Family Conflict Studies

National Family Violence Surveys. These studies have obtained data from nationally representative samples of 2,143 married and cohabiting couples in 1975 and 6,002 couples in 1985. In both surveys, the rate of female-to-male assault was slightly higher than the rate of male-to-female assault (Straus & Gelles, 1986, 1990). Because the seeming equality in assault rates may occur because of a tendency by men to underreport their own assaults (Dutton, 1988; Stets & Straus, 1990), the assault rates were recomputed for this chapter on the basis of information provided by the 2,994 women in the 1985 National Family Violence Survey. The resulting overall rate for assaults by women was 124 per 1,000 couples, as compared to 122 per 1,000 for assaults by men *as reported by their female partners.* This difference is not great enough to be statistically reliable.

Separate rates were also computed for minor and severe assaults. The rate of minor assaults by women was 78 per 1,000 couples, compared with a rate for men of 72 per 1,000. The severe assault rate was 46 per 1,000 couples for assaults by women and 50 per 1,000 for assaults by men. Neither difference is statistically significant. Since these rates are based exclusively on information provided by women respondents, the near-equality in assault rates cannot be attributed to a gender bias in reporting.

Other Family Violence Surveys. There have been more than 100 family violence surveys, which have used a variety of measures and reported similar results. This includes research by respected scholars such as Scanzoni (1978) and O'Leary, Malone, and Tyree (1994); and large-scale studies such as the Los Angeles Epidemiology Catchment Area study (Sorenson & Telles, 1991), the National Survey of Households and Families (Brush, 1990), the Dunedin, New Zealand, birth cohort study (Moffitt, Caspi, Rutter, & Silva, 2001), and a statewide survey conducted for the Kentucky Commission on Women.

The Kentucky study raises a troublesome question of scientific ethics, because it is one of several in which the data on assaults by women were intentionally suppressed. The existence of that data became known only because Hornung, McCullough, and Sugimoto (1981) obtained the computer tape and found that, among the violent couples, 38 percent were attacks by women on men who, as reported by the women themselves, had not attacked them. More often, the strategy to maintain the myth that partner assault is exclusively a male crime has been to omit questions that ask about violence by women, as for example in the Canadian National Survey of Violence against Women.

Samples of "Battered Women." Studies of residents in shelters for battered women are sometimes cited to show that it is only male partners who are violent. However, these studies display the pattern of deception and cover-up noted in the previous paragraph. They rarely obtain or report information on assaults by women; and when they do, they ask only about women's use of violence in self-defense. One of the few exceptions is Walker (1984), who found that 1 out of 4 women in battering relationships responded affirmatively when asked if she had "used physical force to get something you wanted" (p. 174). Giles-Sims (1983) also found that in the year prior to coming to a shelter, 50 percent of the women reported assaulting their partner, and in the six months after leaving the shelter, 41.7 percent reported an assault against a partner. Giles-Sims's case study data suggest that is not likely these assaults were in self-defense.

Dating Couples. Sugarman and Hotaling (1989) summarized the results of 21 studies of violence in dating relationships. They found an average assault rate of 329 per 1,000 for men and 393 per 1,000 for women; that is, a higher proportion of females than males self-reported perpetrating an assault on a dating partner. Other studies (Pirog-Good & Stets, 1989; Stets & Straus, 1990) further confirm the equal or higher rate of assault by women in dating relationships. The most extensive of these is the International Dating Violence Study. Preliminary results based on research on more than 8,000 couples at 33 universities in 16 countries show that the pattern of equal or higher rates of violence by women is a worldwide phenomenon (Straus & Members of the International Dating Violence Research Consortium, 2004).

Crime Studies

National Crime Victimization Survey. Conducted for the Department of Justice by the Bureau of the Census, the National Crime Victimization Survey (NCVS) is an annual study of approximately 60,000 house-holds. In comparison to family violence surveys, the NCVS finds a very low prevalence rate of assault: fewer than 10 per 1,000 couples. The NCVS rate for assaults by female partners was 11 per 1,000, and for male partners 77 per 1,000. Thus, according to the NCVS, the rate of domestic assaults by men is seven times greater than the rate of assault by female partners.

The extremely low rate of assaults by both men and women found by the NCVS may occur because the NCVS is presented to respondents as a study of *crime.* The problem is that it takes relatively rare circumstances, such as an injury or an attack by a former partner, to perceive an attack as a "crime" (Langan & Innes, 1986). This is probably why the NCVS produces such totally implausible statistics such as a 75 percent injury rate (compared with an injury rate of less than 3 percent in the family violence surveys), and more assaults by former partners than by current partners.

Police Calls. Data on calls to the police about domestic assaults are biased in ways that are similar to the bias of the National Crime Survey. Like the NCVS, at least 93 percent of the cases are missed (Kaufman Kantor & Straus, 1990), probably because there was no injury or fear of serious injury great enough to warrant calling the police. Since the cases for which police are called tend to involve injury, or chronic severe assault, and because that tends to be a male pattern, assaults by women rarely are recorded in police records. Another reason assaults by women are rare in police statistics is that many men are reluctant to involve the police (Felson, 2002) and admit that they cannot "handle their wife." These artifacts produce a rate of assaults by men that is hugely greater than the rate of assault by women.

National Violence Against Women Survey (NVAW). Sponsored by the National Institute of Justice and the Centers for Disease Control, the NVAW surveyed 8,000 women and 8,000 men representing 16,000 households (Tjaden & Thoennes, 2000). The initially released results reported that men physically assaulted their female partners at three times the rate at which women engaged in such behavior. This was interpreted as evidence showing that domestic violence is a male crime. There were, however, several problems with this widely disseminated conclusion. First, although the rate of perpetration by men was three times greater, an unbiased interpretation would have also noted that women committed a third of domestic assaults—one-third of offenders cannot be ignored. Second, buried in publications released a year later was a table giving the past-year prevalence rates, as contrasted with the lifetime prevalence rates released earlier. Past-year prevalence rates are the most usual way of reporting crime statistics, and they are considered to be more accurate because they do not depend on recall of events long past. When past-year prevalence rates are used, women committed 39 percent of the partner assaults. Third, the NVAW survey was presented to respondents as a study of crime and personal safety, and therefore respondents were implicitly encouraged to restrict their reports to "real crimes," thus excluding most instances of assault by a partner, and especially "harmless" assaults by women. Thus, a study that, in my opinion, was carried out to refute the idea of gender symmetry in partner violence instead gave strong support to the conclusion that women physically attack partners at about the same rate as do men.

Partner Homicide Rates. Homicides are widely believed to be the most completely recorded crime and therefore to be relatively free from the reporting biases just described. Homicide rates published by the FBI show that only 14 percent of homicide offenders are women (Federal Bureau of Investigation, 1988). However, the percentage of women offenders varies tremendously according to the relationship between offender and victim.

Female-perpetrated homicides of *strangers* occur at a rate that is less than a twentieth the male rate. The female share goes up somewhat for murders of *acquaintances*. As for murders of *family members*, women commit them at a rate that is almost half the rate of men in the period 1976–79 and more than a third of the male rate during the period 1980–84. However, "family" includes all relatives, whereas the main focus of this chapter is couples. There are two gender-specific estimates of the rates for partner homicides (Browne & Williams, 1989; Straus, 1986). These two studies found that women murder male partners at rates that are 56 percent and 62 percent as great as the rate of partner homicides by men. This is far from equality, but it indicates that, in partner relationships, even when the assaults are so extreme as to result in death, a substantial proportion are committed by women, whereas as noted previously, for murders of strangers, the female rate is only a twentieth of the male rate.

❖ SHOULD INJURY BE PART OF
    THE DEFINITION OF PARTNER VIOLENCE?

As pointed out elsewhere (Straus, 1980), female assault rates based on the Conflict Tactics Scales (CTS) used in the Family Violence Surveys can be misleading if the study does not also examine the purpose of the violence and the injuries resulting from assaults. The 1985 National Family Violence Survey included questions on who initiated violence and questions on injuries. The revised CTS (Straus, Hamby, Boney-McCoy, & Sugarman, 1996) includes supplemental questions on injury.

Injury-Adjusted Rates. Stets and Straus (1990) and Brush (1990) provide data that can be used to adjust the assault rates to take into account whether or not the assault resulted in an injury. Stets and Straus found a rate of 3 percent for injury-producing assaults by men and 0.4 percent for injury-producing assaults by women. Somewhat lower injury rates were found by Brush for another large national sample: 1.2 percent for injury-producing assaults by men and 0.2 percent for injury-producing assaults by women. An "injury-adjusted" rate was computed using the higher of the two injury estimates. The resulting rate of "injury-producing assaults" by men is 3.7 per 1,000, and the rate of injury-producing assaults by women is much lower: 0.6 per 1,000. Thus, the injury-adjusted rate for assaults by men is six times greater than the rate of domestic assaults by women.

Although the injury-adjusted rates highlight the greater injury inflicted by male offenders, there are several disadvantages to rates based on injury (Straus, 1990, pp. 79–83). One of the disadvantages, for example, is that the criterion of injury contradicts the domestic assault legislation and new police policies, which are major achievements in the efforts to end violence against women. These statutes and policies premise restraining orders and encourage arrest on the basis of attacks. The woman does not have to suffer an observable injury for action to be taken.

Another disadvantage of using injury as a criterion for domestic assault is that injury-based rates omit the 97 percent of assaults by men that do not result in injury but that are nonetheless a serious social problem. Without an adjustment for injury, National Family Violence Survey produces an estimate of more than 6 million women assaulted by a male partner each year, of which 1.8 million are "severe" assaults (Straus & Gelles, 1990). If the injury-adjusted rate is used, the estimate is reduced to 188,000 assaulted women per year. The figure of 1.8 million seriously assaulted women each year has been used in many legislative hearings and countless feminist publications to indicate the prevalence of the problem. If that estimate was replaced by 188,000, it would understate the extent of the problem and could handicap efforts to educate the public and secure funding for shelters and other services. Fortunately, that is not necessary. Both estimates can be used, since each highlights a different aspect of the problem.

❖ SELF-DEFENSE AND ASSAULTS BY WOMEN

For many years I explained the high rate of attacks on partners by female partners as largely a *response* to or a defense against assault by their partner. However, new evidence raises questions about that interpretation.

Homicide

For lethal assaults by women, some studies suggest that a substantial proportion are self-defense, retaliation, or acts of desperation following years of brutal victimization (Browne, 1987; Browne & Williams, 1989; Jurik & Gregware, 1989). However, Jurik and Gregware's (1989) investigation of 24 cases in which women killed male partners found that the victim initiated use of physical force in 40 percent of the cases, and that only 21 percent were in response to "prior abuse" or "threat of abuse/death." They also found that 60 percent of the women had a previous criminal record. Likewise, Mann's (1990) study of the circumstances surrounding partner homicides by women shows that many women who murder their partners are impulsive, violent, and have criminal records.

National Family Violence Survey

Female-Only Violence. Of the 495 couples in the 1985 National Family Violence Survey for whom one or more assaults were reported by a woman respondent, the man was the only violent partner in 25.9 percent of the cases; the female partner was the only one to be violent in 25.5 percent of the cases; and both were violent in 48.6 percent of the cases. Thus, a minimum estimate of violence by women that is *not* self-defense because she is the only one to have used violence in the past 12 months is 25 percent. Brush (1990) reports similar results for the couples in the National Survey of Families and Households and the National Comorbidity Study.

Perhaps the real gender difference occurs in assaults that are severe enough to carry a high risk of causing an injury, such as punching, kicking, and attacks with weapons. This hypothesis was investigated using the 211 women who reported one or more instances of a "severe" assault. The resulting percentages were similar: Both used violence in 35.2 percent, male only in 35.2 percent, and female only in 29.6 percent.

Regardless of whether the analysis is based on all assaults or is focused on dangerous assaults, about as many women as men attacked a partner who had *not* hit them during the one-year referent period. This is inconsistent with the "self-defense" explanation for the high rate of domestic assault by women. However, it is possible that, among the couples where both assaulted, all the women were acting in self-defense. Even if that unlikely assumption were correct, it would still remain that 25–30 percent of violent relationships are violent solely because of attacks by the female partner.

Initiation of Attacks. The 1985 National Family Violence Survey asked respondents, "Let's talk about the last time you and your partner got into a physical fight and . . . (the most severe act previously mentioned) . . . happened. In that particular instance, who started the physical conflict, you or your partner?" According to the 446 women involved in a violent relationship, their partners struck the first blow in 42.3 percent of the cases, they hit first in 53.1 percent of the cases, and they could not remember or could not disentangle who hit first in the remaining 3.1 percent of the cases. Similar results were obtained by other studies (Archer, 2000).

Is the High Rate of Assault
by Women Explainable as Self-Defense?

It is remarkable that when research does not preclude the possibility of women being the instigators of violence by omitting data on female perpetrators, every study finds that women initiate violence in a large proportion of cases. Let us assume that many of the assaults initiated by women are in response to fear derived from a long prior history of victimization. Even if that is the case, it is a response that tends to elicit further assaults by male partners (Bowker, 1983; Feld & Straus, 1989; Gelles & Straus, 1988, chap. 7; Straus, 1974) and therefore helps to perpetuate or increase partner violence.

❖ GENDER AND CHRONICITY OF ASSAULT

Although the prevalence rate of assaults by women is about the same as that for men, men may engage in more *repeated* attacks. This hypothesis was investigated by computing the mean number of assaults among couples for which at least one assault was reported by a female respondent. According to these 495 women, their partners averaged 7.2 assaults during the year, and they themselves averaged six assaults. Although the frequency of assault by men is greater than the frequency of assault by women, the difference is not large enough to be statistically dependable. If the analysis is restricted to the 165 cases of severe assault, the men averaged 6.1 and the women 4.3 assaults, which is a 42 percent greater frequency of severe assault by men and is just short of being statistically significant. If one disregards the tests of statistical significance, these comparisons support the hypothesized greater chronicity of violence by men. At the same time, the fact that the average number of assaults by men is higher should not obscure the fact that the violent *women* carried out an average of six minor and five severe assaults per year, indicating a repetitive pattern by women as well as men.

❖ CONTEXT, MEANING, AND MOTIVES

The symmetry between males and females in the number and severity of assaults, important as it is, ignores the context, meaning, and consequences of these assaults. Feminist scholars believe that there are important differences between men and women in the motivation for assaults on a partner. However, less injury seems to be the only difference that has been well documented by empirical research. A few studies suggest, but do not demonstrate, differences in context, meaning, or motives. For example, a meta-analysis of research on gender differences in aggression by Eagly and Steffen (1986) found no overall difference in aggression by men and women, but less aggression by women if the act would produce harm to the target. From this, one can infer that women are more reluctant to inflict injury. Greenblat (1983) interpreted her data as showing that men typically hit or threaten to hit in order to force some specific behavior on pain of injury, whereas women typically slap a partner or pound on his chest as an expression of outrage or in frustration from his having turned a deaf ear toward repeated attempts to discuss some critical issue. Despite the surface difference, both are uses of physical violence for coercion. One of the very few empirical studies to investigate the motives for partner violence by women found that the predominant explanation offered by the women in the study was to coerce the partners into doing something (Fiebert & Gonzalez, 1997). A careful review of the research by Felson (2002) led to the conclusion that there was no clear evidence indicating differences in the context, meaning, and motives for assaults by male and female partners. Moreover, even if there were differences in context, meanings, and motives, that would not indicate the absence of assault by women. Nor would it refute the hypothesis that assaults by women help legitimize male violence. Only empirical research can resolve that issue.

❖ FEMALE OFFENDERS CAUSE
SUBSTANTIAL INJURY AND DEATH

It is important to realize that, although the rate of injury inflicted by women is lower, it is a large enough proportion of the injuries and deaths to be a severe social and public health problem by itself. Studies have found that 12–40 percent of injuries and homicides are inflicted by women. The NVAW survey found that women's violence led to

40 percent of all the past year's injuries, created 27 percent of the injuries requiring medical attention, and accounted for 38 percent of the victims who lost time from work and 31 percent of the victims who feared bodily injury (Tjaden & Thoennes, 2000). Other research has found that women's violence resulted in 12 percent of assault-related injuries requiring medical attention (Stets & Straus, 1990), 50 percent of injuries needing medical attention among a sample of high school students (Molidor & Tolman, 1998), 40 percent of injuries suffered by college student dating partners (Makepeace, 1989), and a third of all homicides of domestic partners (Rennison, 2000).

The fact that men inflict a larger percentage of the severe injuries and deaths does not diminish that the proportion perpetrated by women is a serious health, crime, and family problem.

❖ VIOLENCE BY WOMEN INCREASES THE PROBABILITY OF VIOLENCE AGAINST WOMEN

There seems to be an implicit cultural norm permitting or encouraging minor assaults by women in certain circumstances. Stark and McEvoy (1970) found about equal support for a wife hitting a husband as for a husband hitting a wife; Greenblat (1983) found that both men and women are *more* accepting of women hitting husbands than of husbands hitting wives, and she suggests this is because female aggressors are far less likely to do physical harm. These norms tolerating low-level violence by women are transmitted and learned in many ways. For example, even casual observation of the mass media suggests that just about every day, there are scenes depicting a man who makes an insulting or outrageous statement and an indignant woman who responds by "slapping the cad." This presents an implicit model of assault as a morally correct behavior to millions of women.

Although the previous section of this chapter demonstrated that women are responsible for an important proportion of serious injuries and deaths of partners, I assume that most of the assaults by women fall into the "slap the cad" genre and are not intended to, and only rarely cause, physical injury. The danger to women is shown by studies finding that minor violence by women increases the probability of severe assaults by men (Bowker, 1983; Feld & Straus, 1989; Gelles & Straus, 1988, pp. 146–156). Sometimes this is immediate and severe retaliation. But regardless of whether that occurs, a more indirect and probably more important effect may occur because such morally correct slapping acts out and reinforces the traditional tolerance of assault in marriage. The moral justification of assault implicit when a woman slaps or throws something at a partner for something outrageous reinforces the moral justification for slapping *her* when she is doing something outrageous, being obstinate, nasty, or "not listening to reason" as he sees it. To the extent that this is correct, one of the many steps needed for primary prevention of assaults on women is for women to forsake even "harmless" physical attacks on male partners and children. Women must insist on nonviolence by their sisters, just as they rightfully insist on it for men.

It is painful to recognize the high rate of domestic assaults by women. Moreover, the statistics are likely to be used by misogynists and apologists for male violence. My view of recognizing violence by women is parallel to Hart's (1986, p. 10) view on the importance of recognizing battering within lesbian relationships. It is painful, but to do otherwise obstructs a potentially important means of reducing assaults by men—raising the consciousness of women about the implicit norms that are reinforced by a ritualized slap for outrageous behavior on the part of their partners.

It follows from this discussion that efforts to prevent assaults by men must also include attention to assaults by women. Although this may seem like "victim blaming," there is an important difference: Recognizing that violence by women is one of the many causes of violence against women does not justify violence by men. It is the responsibility of men as well as women to refrain from physical attacks (including retaliation), at home as elsewhere, no matter what the provocation.

❖ GENDER DIFFERENCES
    IN TRENDS IN PARTNER VIOLENCE

The acceptability of hitting a partner and the actual rate of partner violence in the United States has been decreasing in the past 25 years. This decrease has been primarily in violence by male partners (Straus, 1995; Straus & Gelles, 1986; Straus & Kaufman Kantor, 1997). Yet despite the decrease, partner violence by both men and women remains the most frequent form of interpersonal violence in American society.

The fact that violence and approval of violence by male partners has decreased, whereas violence and approval of violence by female partners has not, may reflect the fact that almost all programs to end partner violence were created by and continue to be a major effort of the women's movement. Consequently, they are based on the assumption that partner violence is perpetrated almost exclusively by men. The voluminous research summarized in this chapter shows that this assumption is false. Most partner violence is mutual. Therefore, as indicated previously, rather than ignoring assaults by female partners, primary prevention of violence *against* women requires strong efforts to end assaults *by* women. However, the needed change must be made with extreme care. First, it must be done in ways that simultaneously refute the idea that violence by women justifies or excuses violence by their partners. Second, although women may assault partners at approximately the same rate as men, assaults by men usually inflict greater physical, financial, and emotional injury. This means that male violence against women is typically the more serious crime. Thus, major focus on violence by women does not necessarily mean equal focus. Finally, in many societies women lack full economic, social, political, and human rights. In such cultural contexts, equality for women needs to be given priority as an even more fundamental aspect of primary prevention. Otherwise, focusing on partner violence by women can further exacerbate the oppression of women.

❖ CONCLUSIONS

Ending assaults *by* women needs to be added to efforts to prevent assaults *on* women for a number of reasons. Perhaps the most fundamental reason is the intrinsic moral wrong of assaulting a partner. A second reason is the fact that women inflict a third of the injuries and deaths from partner violence. Third, women who hit their partners "model" violence for children, and this is associated with an increase in psychological problems of children. The harm to children from assaults by women is at least as strong as from assaults by men (Holden, Geffner, & Jouriles, 1998; Jaffe, Wolfe, & Wilson, 1990; Straus, 1991). Fourth is the danger of escalation when women engage in "harmless" minor violence. Feld and Straus (1989) found that if the female partner also engaged in an assault, it increased the probability that assaults will persist or escalate in severity over the one-year period of their study; whereas if only one partner engaged in physical attacks, the probability of cessation increased. Finally, when women assault their partners, it validates the traditional cultural norms tolerating a certain level of violence between partners and therefore helps perpetuate a system in which they are the predominant victims.

It should be emphasized that the preventive effect of reducing violence by women, including "harmless" minor violence, has not been demonstrated by the evidence in this chapter. It is a plausible inference and a hypotheses for further research. However, it is important not to wait for the results of such research before implementing steps to end partner violence by women because, as pointed out, it would be equivalent to ignoring the legal and moral wrong of such behavior, and ignoring the physical and psychological injuries to their partners and children. The steps can include posters and public service announcements, police arrest policies, treatment programs for female offenders, and school-based prevention programs addressed to girls as well as to boys (Foshee, 2004). These steps must be made with extreme care for a number of reasons, not the least of which is to avoid implying that violence by women justifies or excuses violence by their partners. Moreover, although women may assault their partners at approximately the same rate as men, the first priority in services for victims and in prevention and control must continue to be directed toward assaults by men because these tend to result in greater physical, financial, and emotional injury.

❖ RESPONSE TO LOSEKE AND KURZ

The objections that Loseke and Kurz (this volume) raise to my chapter reflect three major differences between us: theoretical differences, methodological differences, and differences in our moral agendas.

Theoretical Differences

The theoretical difference is epitomized in a single word in the titles to our chapters. My chapter refers to violence by women as "a" social problem, whereas their chapter asserts that violence against women is "the" social problem. I do not believe that either violence by men or by women is "the" problem. Society faces multiple and interrelated problems with violence, and the correction of one usually depends on dealing with the configuration of problems in which it is embedded. Thus, violence against women is *a* serious social problem, but it is also only one aspect of the problem of violence in American, and many other, societies. From the theoretical perspectives that social problems are interrelated, and that violence is a multiply determined interactive event, an adequate solution to the problem of violence against women requires addressing the behavior of both participants in that interactive sequence, as well as addressing many other phenomena that increase the risk of violence.

The *single-problem* focus epitomized in Loseke and Kurz's title is part of a larger theoretical difference: a *single-cause* theoretical approach. A single-cause approach has long been rejected by social scientists. One exception, however, is the subgroup of feminist social scientists who assume that a patriarchal social system and male dominance and privilege explains almost all cases of violence against women.

It is appropriate and necessary for feminist scholars to focus their research on this one of the many causes of violence against women. Society is indebted to the feminists for bringing gender-based oppression and violence to the fore. At the same time, denying the importance of other causes of violence against women, such as stress, alcoholism, violent socialization, criminal propensities, and violence by women, is something that would be ridiculed and rejected if it came from social scientists of any other theoretical persuasion. The following section suggests why we accept this scientific error from feminists but not from others.

The Moral Agenda

One of the reasons social scientists and the public at large are willing to accept a single-cause approach advocated by feminists is the recognition of and indignation by most social scientists over past and continuing oppression and discrimination against women. As a result, there is a tendency to accept almost anything that will change this aspect of society. Liberal social scientists tend deliberately to close their eyes to excesses and incorrect statements by feminists because they do not want to undermine feminist efforts to bring about a more equitable society. Thus, avowedly feminist scholars have suppressed data on violence by women. Social scientists I know who do not claim to be feminists have also published only the part of their data that shows violence by men.

History is full of atrocities carried out in the service of a moral agenda. These make suppression and denial of evidence on female violence trivial by comparison. But to those like myself, for whom ending *all* violence, from spanking by parents to nations engaging in war, it is as essential to confront violence by women against male partners as it is to confront the high rate of violence by men.

Both Loseke and Kurz and I are against all violence, and both they and I are against all forms of gender inequality. The difference between us is in priorities for research and action. I infer that they rank ending oppression of women as number 1. Ending all violence is also very important, but not number 1. On the other hand, I rank ending all violence as number 1 and ending oppression of women as also very important, but not number 1. They are willing to accept certain costs to achieve equality for women, and I am willing to accept certain costs to achieve a nonviolent society. For example, although domestic violence victims who need the services of a shelter are overwhelmingly women, I am willing to accept the cost of radical male advocacy groups misusing the results of my research to oppose shelters for domestic violence victims that do not provide the same services for male victims. I am willing to accept the rare instances in which they have been successful as a bearable cost, because there is no way of avoiding it without suppressing the evidence on female violence.

Violence by both men and women against a partner are criminal acts and morally repulsive, except in the rare cases of self-defense. The moral priorities of Loseke and Kurz represent a legitimate difference in assessing the long-run costs and benefits for women of recognizing that women assault their partners at about the same rate as men. I think my moral priorities promise a greater long-run benefit to women because, for the reasons given in my chapter, ending violence *by* women will help end violence *against* women. In addition to the other reasons in my chapter explaining why ending violence by women will help end violence against women, I should have pointed out that it will end the training in violence of the next generation of both men and women that is provided when children grow up watching their mothers hit their fathers. As my chapter shows, this occurs just as often as fathers hitting mothers, and mothers are the first to hit as often as fathers.

Methodological Differences

One key methodological difference is that I believe that feminist research, like all other research, cannot be limited to in-depth qualitative studies. Qualitative studies are essential, but so are large-scale surveys. Each has its own limitations, and each has the power to shed light on a different aspect of violence between partners. Moreover, there is also something not quite appropriate when Loseke and Kurz reject the results of large-scale surveys showing symmetry in physical assault, but accept the results of large-scale surveys showing a predominance of male perpetrators in respect to sexual coercion.

As for the purported deficiencies in the CTS mentioned by Loseke and Kurz, none is correct. The space I have been given for this rejoinder does not permit me to respond to each of these purported deficiencies, so I respond to just the first of them. Readers can find the others on my Web site, http://pubpages.unh.edu/~mas2, by clicking on "Detailed Response to Loseke and Kurz."

Loseke and Kurz argue that "research based on representative samples [using the CTS] will *underestimate* the amount of extreme violence experienced by women because severely abused women will not participate in the survey" (italics in original). That is certainly true, but it is even more likely that male victims of female violence avoid participation in such surveys. Assaulting or being assaulted by a partner is shameful. It took a major and still continuing effort by feminists to get women to report such assaults to police. The same shame and reluctance to participate in surveys occurs for male victims. However, for men, there is the additional shame and reluctance stemming from the type of masculinity that expects a "real man" to be able to handle such situations, and that lead police to scoff at or laugh at men who do file a complaint (Mills, 2003).

Other Inaccuracies in the Loseke-Kurz Article

There are a large number of other incorrect statements in the Loseke-Kurz chapter. As in the case of the erroneous deficiencies of the CTS, the space available to me permits including only the first two of them. The others are on my Web site.

Loseke and Kurz claim that I "trivialize . . . the complex meaning of violence and its impact on the lives of women." Their demonstration of this, however, is a statement out of context, which reverses its meaning. They say I characterize "women's typical violence as motivated by their desire to 'slap the cad.'" On the contrary, the "slap the cad" phrase was not to show that this is typical. It was in a section of my chapter designed to show that even such trivial violence increases the risk of being attacked by a male partner. This is the opposite of failing to recognize the impact of violence on the lives of women.

Moreover, the sentence preceding pointed out that "the previous section . . . demonstrated that women are responsible for an important proportion of serious injuries and deaths of partners." This is not trivial violence.

Loseke and Kurz say that I do "not incorporate gender at the level of measurement." This is the opposite of what the record of my research shows. For example, the Conflict Tactics Scales (CTS) was designed to investigate gender differences in partner violence. In order to show that there is more violence by male than female partners, the CTS asks about assaults by both partners. My intention to show greater male violence was thwarted by the results. Other examples abound. I carried out the first empirical study of partner violence to *measure* (not just talk about) feminist concepts such as inequality in power and resources and social norms tolerating partner violence (for example, Straus, 1976).

In conclusion, I have always believed and acted on the belief that a feminist approach is both valid and necessary. By a "feminist approach," I mean taking into account phenomena that represent gendered inequality and oppression. That is why I have taken that approach in much of the research just cited. Feminist advocacy is needed and is critical to free society of its sexist structure. But it has gone beyond stimulating and motivating research to self-censorship and attempts to suppress the results of other researchers whose findings do not conform to the feminist assumption that only men assault partners. It undermined feminist credibility not just among researchers, but also among the general public. That is tragic.

It is necessary to recognize without delay and to alert women to the fact that violence against partners by women is prevalent and is one of the many causes of violence against women, just as violence by men is prevalent and is one of the many causes of violence by women. There is a difference between explanation and blame. The fact that violence by women is part of the interactive sequence of events that constitutes most partner violence does not excuse men any more than it excuses women. It important to recognize this fact, primarily for the protection of women but also to protect the reputation of feminist scholarship. It is important for the protection of women because each cause that is identified provides an opportunity to develop programs to eliminate or reduce that cause, and therefore to reduce partner violence. Each cause that is identified and acted on adds to the effectiveness of the effort to prevent violence against women.

❖ REFERENCES

Archer, J. (2000). Sex differences in aggression between heterosexual partners: A meta-analytic review. *Psychological Bulletin, 126*(5), 651–680.

Bowker, L. H. (1983). *Beating wife beating.* Lexington, MA: Lexington Books.

Browne, A. (1987). *When battered women kill.* New York: Free Press.

Browne, A., & Williams, K. R. (1989). Exploring the effect of resource availability and the likelihood of female-perpetrated homicides. *Law and Society Review, 23*(1), 75–94.

Brush, L. D. (1990). Violent acts and injurious outcomes in married couples: Methodological issues in the National Survey of Families and Households. *Gender and Society, 4*(1), 56–67.

Dutton, D. G. (1988). Profiling of wife assaulters: Preliminary evidence for a trimodal analysis. *Violence and Victims, 3*(1), 5–29.

Eagly, A. H., & Steffen, V. J. (1986). Gender and aggressive behavior: A meta-analytic review of the social psychological literature. *Psychological Bulletin, 100*(3), 309–330.

Federal Bureau of Investigation. (1988). *Crime in the United States: Uniform crime reports.* Washington, DC: U.S. Government Printing Office.

Federal Bureau of Investigation. (1995). *Crime in the United States, 1993: Uniform crime reports:* Washington, DC: U.S. Department of Justice.

Feld, S. L., & Straus, M. A. (1989). Escalation and desistance of wife assault in marriage. *Criminology, 27*(1), 141–161.

Felson, R. B. (2002). *Violence and gender reexamined.* Washington, DC: American Psychological Press.

Fiebert, M. S. (1997). Annotated bibliography: References examining assaults by women on their spouses/partners. In B. M. Dank & R. Refinette (Eds.), *Sexual harassment and sexual consent* (Vol. 1, pp. 273–286). New Brunswick, NJ: Transaction.

Fiebert, M. S., & Gonzalez, D. M. (1997). College women who initiate assaults on their male partners and the reasons offered for such behavior. *Psychological Reports, 80,* 583–590.

Foshee, V. A. (2004). *Safe dates: An adolescent dating abuse prevention curriculum.* Center City, MN: Hazelden Publishing and Educational Services.

Gelles, R. J., & Straus, M. A. (1988). *Intimate violence.* New York: Simon & Schuster.

Giles-Sims, J. (1983). *Wife battering: A systems theory approach.* New York: Guilford.

Greenblat, C. S. (1983). A hit is a hit is a hit . . . or is it? Approval and tolerance of the use of physical force by spouses. In D. Finkelhor, R. J. Gelles, G. T. Hotaling, & M. A. Straus (Eds.), *The dark side of families* (pp. 235–260). Beverly Hills, CA: Sage.

Hart, B. (1986). Preface. In K. Lobel (Ed.), *Naming the violence: Speaking out about lesbian battering* (pp. 9–16). Seattle, WA: Seal.

Holden, G. W., Geffner, R., & Jouriles, E. N. (Eds.). (1998). *Children exposed to marital violence: Theory, research, and applied issues*. Washington, DC: American Psychological Association.

Hornung, C. A., McCullough, B. C., & Sugimoto, T. (1981). Status relationships in marriage: Risk factors in spouse abuse. *Journal of Marriage and the Family, 43*, 675–692.

Jaffe, P. G., Wolfe, D. A., & Wilson, S. K. (1990). *Children of battered women*. Newbury Park, CA: Sage.

Jurik, N. C., & Gregware, P. (1989). *A method for murder: An interactionist analysis of homicides by women*. Tempe: Arizona State University, School of Justice Studies.

Kaufman Kantor, G., & Straus, M. A. (1990). Response of victims and the police to assaults on wives. In M. A. Straus & R. J. Gelles (Eds.), *Physical violence in American families: Risk factors and adaptations to violence in 8,145 families* (pp. 473–487). New Brunswick, NJ: Transaction.

Langan, P. A., & Innes, C. A. (1986). *Preventing domestic violence against women*. Washington, DC: U.S. Department of Justice, Bureau of Justice Statistics, Special Report NCJ 102037.

Makepeace, J. M. (1989). Dating, living together, and courtship violence. In M. A. Pirog-Good & J. E. Stets (Eds.), *Violence in dating relationships* (pp. 94–107). New York: Praeger.

Mann, C. R. (1990). Black female homicide in the United States. *Journal of Interpersonal Violence, 5*, 176–201.

Mills, L. (2003). *Insult to injury: Rethinking our responses to intimate abuse*. Princeton, NJ: Princeton University Press.

Moffitt, T. E., Caspi, A., Rutter, M., & Silva, P. A. (2001). *Sex differences in antisocial behavior*. Cambridge: Cambridge University Press.

Molidor, C., & Tolman, R. M. (1998). Gender and contextual factors in adolescent dating violence. *Violence against Women, 4*(2), 180–194.

O'Leary, K. D., Malone, J., & Tyree, A. (1994). Physical aggression in early marriage: Prerelationship and relationship effects. *Journal of Consulting and Clinical Psychology, 62*(3), 594–602.

Pirog-Good, M. A., & Stets, J. E. (1989). *Violence in dating relationships: Emerging social issues*. New York: Praeger.

Rennison, C. M. (2000). *Intimate partner violence*. Washington, DC: Bureau of Justice Statistics, Special Report NCJ 178247.

Scanzoni, J. (1978). *Sex roles, women's work, and marital conflict*. Lexington, MA: Lexington Books.

Sorenson, S. B., & Telles, C. A. (1991). Self-reports of spousal violence in a Mexican-American and non-Hispanic White population. *Violence and Victims, 6*(1), 3–15.

Stark, R., & McEvoy III, J. (1970). Middle-class violence. *Psychology Today, 4*, 52–65.

Stets, J. E., & Straus, M. A. (1990). Gender differences in reporting of marital violence and its medical and psychological consequences. In M. A. Straus & R. J. Gelles (Eds.), *Physical violence in American families: Risk factors and adaptations to violence in 8,145 families* (pp. 151–166). New Brunswick, NJ: Transaction.

Straus, M. A. (1974). Leveling, civility, and violence in the family. *Journal of Marriage and the Family, 36*, 13–29.

Straus, M. A. (1976). Sexual inequality, cultural norms, and wife-beating. In E. C. Viano (Ed.), *Victims and society* (pp. 543–559). Washington, DC: Visage.

Straus, M. A. (1980). Victims and aggressors in marital violence. *American Behavioral Scientist, 23*(May/June), 681–704.

Straus, M. A. (1986). Domestic violence and homicide antecedents. *Bulletin of the New York Academy of Medicine, 62*, 446–465.

Straus, M. A. (1990). Injury, frequency, and the representative sample fallacy in measuring wife beating and child abuse. In M. A. Straus & R. J. Gelles (Eds.), *Physical violence in American families: Risk factors and adaptations to violence in 8,145 families* (pp. 75–89). New Brunswick, NJ: Transaction.

Straus, M. A. (1991). Discipline and deviance: Physical punishment of children and violence and other crime in adulthood. *Social Problems, 38*, 101–123.

Straus, M. A. (1995). Trends in cultural norms and rates of partner violence: an update to 1992. In S. Stith and M. A. Straus, *Understanding partner violence: Prevalence, causes, consequences, and solutions, Families in Focus Series II:* 30–33.

Straus, M. A. (1999). The controversy over domestic violence by women: A methodological, theoretical, and sociology of science analysis. In X. Arriaga & S. Oskamp (Eds.), *Violence in intimate relationships* (pp. 17–44). Thousand Oaks, CA: Sage.

Straus, M. A., & Gelles, R. J. (1986). Societal change and change in family violence from 1975 to 1985 as revealed by two national surveys. *Journal of Marriage and the Family, 48*, 465–479.

Straus, M. A., & Gelles, R. J. (1990). *Physical violence in American families: Risk factors and adaptations to violence in 8,145 families.* New Brunswick, NJ: Transaction.

Straus, M. A., Hamby, S. L., Boney-McCoy, S., & Sugarman, D. B. (1996). The revised Conflict Tactics Scales (CTS2): Development and preliminary psychometric data. *Journal of Family Issues, 17*(3), 283–316.

Straus, M. A., & Hotaling, G. T. (Eds.). (1980). *The social causes of husband-wife violence.* Minneapolis: University of Minnesota Press.

Straus, M. A., Kaufman Kantor, G., & Moore, D. W. (1997). Change in cultural norms approving marital violence: From 1968 to 1994. In G. Kaufman Kantor and J. L. Jasinski (Eds.), *Out of the darkness: Contemporary perspectives on family violence.* Thousand Oaks, CA: Sage.

Straus, M. A., & Members of the International Dating Violence Research Consortium. (2004). Prevalence of violence against dating partners by male and female university students worldwide. *Violence Against Women, 10*(7), 790–811.

Sugarman, D. B., & Hotaling, G. T. (1989). Dating violence: Prevalence, context, and risk markers. In A. A. Pirog-Good and J. E. Stets (Eds.), *Violence in dating relationships: Emerging social issues* (pp. 3-31). New York: Praeger.

Tjaden, P., & Thoennes, N. (2000). *Full report of the prevalence, incidence, and consequences of violence against women: Findings from the National Violence against Women Survey.* Washington, DC: U.S. Department of Justice, Office of Justice Programs, NCJ 183781.

U.S. Department of Justice. (1976). *Dictionary of criminal justice data terminology.* Washington, DC: National Criminal Justice Information Service.

Vissing, Y. M., Straus, M. A., Gelles, R. J., & Harrop, J. W. (1991). Verbal aggression by parents and psychosocial problems of children. *Child Abuse and Neglect, 15,* 223–238.

Walker, L. E. (1984). *The battered woman syndrome.* New York: Springer.

5

Men's Violence Toward Women Is the Serious Social Problem

Donileen R. Loseke

Demie Kurz

O ur purpose in this chapter is to summarize, from a feminist perspective, differences in the two most important approaches to violence in heterosexual, marriage-type relationships. The *feminist* theoretical framework argues that violence must be located within the *gendered* context of men's and women's lives. Understanding violence as a gendered phenomenon leads to a focus on the problems of *violence against women*. In contrast, the *family conflict* approach (Straus, this volume) believes it is important to examine all violent behavior and argues that there is gender symmetry in the use of violence. In this chapter, we argue that the violence against women approach is best suited to understanding violence in heterosexual relationships.

Our task in this chapter is difficult for three reasons. First, when Straus is the spokesperson, major components of feminist theorizing can appear to be included in the family conflict perspective. Although Straus's inclusions of feminist understandings cannot easily be typified because they have changed over time (see Schwartz & DeKeseredy, 1993), he repeatedly has reminded his readers that men's violence creates more injuries than does women's violence, and that it is important to focus public attention on the problems faced by women victims. While these are central feminist understandings, we believe that the family conflict perspective is not feminist because it does not incorporate gender at the level of measurement, nor does it conceptualize violence as a gendered phenomenon.

Second, it is difficult to argue with Straus because we often agree with him. In particular, we do *not* dispute that more than 100 empirical studies using the research instrument called the Conflict Tactics Scale (CTS) consistently support the conclusions that women use as much violence as do men (see Kimmel, 2002, for a review of these studies). Because we do not dispute these findings, Straus's repeated claim that we are guilty of "suppressing evidence" about women's violence is *not* true. We also agree with him that the world would be a better place if there was no violence, that it is important to understand women's use of violence, and that it is nonsense to ignore women's use of violence while condemning violence by men. Yet even though we agree with Straus that women as well as men use violence, we dispute his characterizations of women's typical violence as motivated by their desire to "slap the cad." Such a characterization trivializes the complex meaning of violence and its impact on the lives of women. Furthermore, we are wary of the political implications of describing women's and men's violence as equivalent or symmetrical.

Third, and critically, our debate with Straus is difficult because he implicitly claims both more scientific expertise as well as a higher moral ground than feminist researchers. First, he claims greater scientific expertise when he characterizes the family conflict perspective as "scientific" while feminism is "advocacy" (Straus, 1999). We do not wish to engage in debate about the validity of feminist methodological assumptions and practices. We note only that feminist approaches to research have gained a prominent place among accepted research methodologies (see, for example, Dobash & Dobash, 1998; Reinharz, 1992). Second, Straus claims the moral high ground by referencing his goal of eliminating *all* violence, while feminism is concerned "only" with eliminating violence against women. We also are concerned with eliminating all violence, yet as we argue in this chapter, research emphasizing women's violence toward men is used as a justification to deny the seriousness of violence against women as well as to take resources away from battered women. Straus is aware of this and states in his chapter that "I am willing to accept the cost . . . because there is no way of avoiding it without suppressing the evidence on female violence." Perhaps *he* is willing to accept these consequences and perhaps *he* evaluates these as "bearable costs," yet *he* is not the one suffering the consequences. The very practical costs of advocating for *his* moral agenda are not experienced by *him*—they are experienced by real women victims of abuse.

Our argument proceeds in three parts. First, our comments focus on the family conflict perspective emphasis on how women's and men's use of violence is equivalent. Therefore, we examine the research methodologies leading to this claim. We do this briefly, because our goal is *not* to deny women's violence, *nor* is it to "suppress evidence," as Straus claims. Rather, we wish to challenge the claim that women's and men's use of violence is equivalent in sheer *counts* of violent acts. Second, we turn to a feminist theorizing of violence in order to argue that violence cannot be conceptualized as equivalent in terms of its *contexts, meanings,* or *consequences.* We conclude by addressing how the family conflict perspective is a political discourse used to disenfranchise women in general and individual battered women in particular.

❖ EXAMINING RESEARCH
PRODUCING GENDER SYMMETRY

Careful examinations of academic research spanning three decades does not yield a consistent picture of similarities or differences between women's and men's use of violence. Research on this topic is riddled with disagreements (see Kimmel, 2002, for a review of these issues). And, as Straus notes, different types of samples, even different types of question wording, produce vastly different data. Here we focus on exploring characteristics of the Conflicts Tactics Scale (CTS) and its administration. Developed by Straus and his colleagues, this research instrument is critical for two reasons.

First, the CTS is by far the most common research instrument used to study large, nationally representative samples that are the "gold standard" of scientific research. The CTS is a simple checklist of behaviors asking respondents to indicate whether or not they or their partners have used or have been the recipient of specific violent acts such as "slap," "push," and "shove" (classified on the CTS as "minor" assaults because they are not *statistically* associated with creating injury), or acts such as "kick, "throw something," or "choke" (classified on the CTS as "abusive" or "severe" assaults because such behaviors are *statistically* associated with creating injury). The ease and quickness of administrating the CTS are important because they make it ideal for large-scale research: Responding to the survey does not take long, and results (presence or absence of particular behaviors) are easily tabulated.

Second, and most critically for our purposes here, the CTS is important because, without exception, *all* research using the CTS finds that women's and men's rates of violence are more or less equivalent. And, with few exceptions, *only* research using the CTS yields such images of gender similarity. There is something special about the CTS, or the way it is administered, that constructs a view of the world not found through the feminist research methodology of in-depth interviewing that invariably finds women to be the overwhelming victims of violence.

Data gathered through the CTS that promote an image of gender equivalence in the use of violence are troublesome to feminists who want the public to remain focused on the problems of men's violence toward women, which causes far more harm and injury than does women's violence toward men. Given this, it is not surprising that there have been myriad critiques of the CTS (see, for example, Kimmel, 2002; Saunders, 2002; Dobash, Dobash, Wilson, & Daly, 1992; Langhinrichsen-Rohling, Neidig, & Thorn, 1995; Brush, 1990). Here we summarize only those characteristics of the CTS and its administration that lead to findings of gender equivalence in the use of violence.

- A basic lesson in research methodology surrounding research on family violence (or violence of any type) is that representative samples of the general population will not yield data showing a large amount of extreme violence, because, no matter how troublesome such violence is, extreme violence is not statistically common. This is a primary reason that CTS studies sampling the general population find so little extreme violence. The CTS also likely underestimates extreme violence in the general population because of the problem of "refusals to participate." When asked if they will participate in a survey, some people will decline. Survey results are not challenged if these refusals are random. Yet refusals to participate in the CTS survey likely are *not* random. Researchers from any perspective agree that it is overwhelmingly women who experience extreme violence, and, among cohabiting couples, abused women are much less likely than are non-abused women to agree to participate in general surveys about violence (Waltermaurer, Ortega, & McNutt, 2003). Given this, research based on representative samples will *underestimate* the amount of extreme violence experienced by women because severely abused women will not participate in the survey.

- There also is a likely gendered systematic reporting bias influencing CTS findings. In this volume, Straus notes the indications that men tend to *underestimate* their own use of violence. He attempts to control for this by examining only reports from women. Yet this does not correct the bias, because women *also* tend to underestimate men's use of violence. Furthermore, men and women alike tend to *overestimate* women's use of violence. Violence by men is expected, so it is not reported; violence by women is not expected, so it *is* notable and reported (Currie, 1998; also: Dobash et al., 1992; Kimmel, 2002; and Schafer, Caetano, & Clark, 2002). Given this, whether men *or* women are asked about their own *or* about their partner's violence, there will be a tendency for the CTS to *overestimate* violence done by *women* and *underestimate* violence done by *men*.

- Because the major CTS samples include only cohabiting couples, this research has missed violence by *former* partners. Violence by former partners is not symmetrical: Men are the aggressors in more than 90 percent of assaults involving former spouses (U.S. Department of Justice, 1998); National Crime Victimization Studies show that violence against separated women might be more than 8 times higher than rates for married women (Bachman & Saltzman, 1995). Again, the CTS *underestimates* violence experienced by women.

- Respondents must trust interviewers before they will talk about highly stigmatized and traumatic experiences such as assault (Brush, 1990; Schwartz, 2000). Yet in CTS surveys, respondents are asked only whether or not specific behaviors have occurred. Given that women are overwhelmingly the victims of extreme violence, and given that administrating the CTS does not allow respondents to develop trust or rapport with interviewers, the CTS will *underestimate* extreme violence experienced by women.

- In any version, the CTS contains a simple—and short—checklist of behaviors. Only in its most recent version has it included the behavior of "sexual assault" or "sexual coercion." This is important, because there is little disagreement that women are the overwhelming victims of such assaults. Indeed, national studies indicate that women might be 20 times more likely than men to be victims of sexual assault (Tjaden & Thoennes, 2000). Given this, the CTS *underestimates* violence experienced overwhelmingly by women.

Combined, these various characteristics of the CTS and its administration serve to overestimate the violence done by women while underestimating the violence done by men.

❖ THE GENDERED CONTEXTS, MEANINGS, AND CONSEQUENCES OF VIOLENCE

If such biases could be corrected, the CTS likely would measure *more* violence by *men* and *less* violence by *women* and hence, the rates of men's and women's violence no longer would seem so symmetrical. Yet certainly, CTS data still would show considerable violence by women. We continue to our next question: Is violence done by women the same as violence done by men? We move to a feminist perspective, with its primary belief that violence must be examined as a gendered phenomenon that is only understood when placed within the context of current male and female social positions in our society. We argue that when violence is examined in this way, it is not equivalent: It occurs within different contexts and has different meanings and consequences for women and for men.

The Gendered Context of Violence

Men's violence toward women and women's violence toward men are not the same, because these acts occur within the historical, cultural, political, economic, and psychological contexts of *gender*. Gender—views of proper roles and relationships for men and women—is a basic organizing principle for institutions and for the distribution of resources. Despite considerable social change in recent years, gender remains the overriding context of violence that cannot be ignored or trivialized.

This gendered context includes the history of tolerance of men's violence toward women (see Dobash & Dobash, 1979, for a review) that continues to be taught and reinforced in social institutions such as sports (Messner, 1989) and fraternities (Sanday, 1991). It includes the normalization of violence against women in heterosexual romantic relationships (Wood, 2001).

Notwithstanding considerable social change, our world remains separated into two spheres, each gender identified. The public sphere of work is associated with men and is valued more highly than the private sphere of family, which is associated with women. Of course, *Leave It to Beaver* families of the 1950s, where men went off to work and women stayed home, are increasingly rare. Many, indeed most, women now are employed. Yet despite changes, the gendered core of work and family remains and promotes gender inequality.

Consider how gender permeates women's employment. True, many women now are employed, yet more women than men are employed part-time rather than full-time, and far more women than men take time out of the labor force in order to dedicate themselves to their families (U.S. Department of Labor, 2000). While many women want to do this, this choice means that they have less income than their male partners as well as less job security and seniority. Gender inequality also explains differences in women's and men's median weekly earnings: Women who worked full-time in 2000 earned an average of $491 per week while men earned $647 (U.S. Statistical Abstracts, 2001). Women's work is devalued: A college degree in engineering, a field dominated by men, leads to much higher average pay than a college degree in social work or education, fields dominated by women. As a result, it is far more common for women to be economically dependent on their male partners than for men to be economically dependent on their female partners. Unfortunately, all too many women make a decision to stay in violent relationships because they cannot support themselves and their children without the abuser's income.

While women have become far more active in the labor force, men have become more active family members. Since the mid-1960s, married men have more than doubled the average number of hours each week they spend doing household chores or child tending. Yet men's average of 9.8 hours a week remains less than half of married women's average of 19.5 hours a week. The division of labor inside households is not gender equivalent (Bianchi & Spain, 1996).

While the consequences of gender can sometimes be measured in terms of dollars earned or hours of housework done, much of the gendered meaning of social life is immeasurable because it is so deeply woven into the identities and the everyday lives of women and men. Despite social change, women and men are socialized differently, have different expectations for themselves and for their partners, and often think about the world differently. Consider, for example, common patterns in partner selection. Statistically, most couples are people with similar levels of education and of similar ages, but when there are differences, it is likely that the man will have more education and/or be older than his partner. Because education and age are associated with economic advantage, patterns of partner selection can bring gender inequality into individual homes. Likewise, on a couple-by-couple basis, women and men continue conventional patterns of partner selection, with men choosing women partners who are smaller than they are and women choosing men who are taller and heavier than they are. On the average, then, men have a physical advantage over their female partners. The gendered nature of modern family life is perhaps the most obvious in parenting. While many men now are more actively engaged fathers than in the past, neither men or women think of "mothering" and "fathering" as similar. Fathering is something men do along with other things in their lives, mothering is something that often is an all-encompassing identity and set of responsibilities for women (Walzer, 1998).

To summarize, what happens inside homes, and the meaning of what happens inside homes, is different for women and for men. The gendered nature of coupling leads to the typical situation in which the woman has less income than her partner, he is bigger than she is, and she is more involved, in time as well as in psychological commitment, with her children and household than he is. These gendered characteristics of family life influence how women and men think about violence, how they can think about the possibilities of eliminating the violence or of "leaving home." We see the world through the lens of gender, and this is the context for violence.

The Gendered Meanings of Violence

Not surprisingly, given the gendered contexts of all social life, violence has typical gendered differences both in why it is used as well as in what it means to be a victim.

Why do people use violence? For certain acts of violence—those clustered at the lower end of violence severity, such as pushes, shoves, and slaps—the *rates* of women's and men's use of violence appear similar. However, it is critical to examine the *motives* for these acts. While both women and men use violence to express anger (see Kimmel, 2002, for further discussion), as compared to men, many more women say they use violence in self-defense (Dasgupta, 1999, 2002). In contrast, men rarely say they use violence in self-defense. As compared to women, men are far more likely to say they use violence in order to intimidate, coerce, or punish unwanted behavior. Much more so than for women, men's violence is about perceived challenges to their authority, honor, and self-esteem (see Saunders, 2002; Dasgupta, 1999; and Dobash et al., 1992, for references).

Motives for using violence are gendered. There also is a question about the meaning of violence experienced: What does it mean to be assaulted by a partner? Here again, there is little gender equivalence. The meaning of violence for women is *fear* (Cascardi, O'Leary, Lawrence, & Schlee, 1995). Many women—but not many men—who have experienced violence report fear (Langhinrichsen-Rohling et al., 1995). This meaning of violence as fear reflects women's perceptions of violence as male control. Rather than a "conflict tactic," implying mutuality of disagreements, or as "expressive violence" implying emotional upset, violence can be perceived by women as a tactic to control them. Indeed, it is not just women who perceive violence as a means of male control. Interviews with men who use violence show the distressing finding that men often believe they are *justified* in their use of violence; they believe it is their "right" as a man, particularly when their wives do not conform to their ideal of the "good wife" (Adams, 1988; Dobash & Dobash, 1979).

Violence used as self-defense is a complex topic, because it brings together motives for doing violence as well as the experiences of victimization. In her interview study of a random sample of divorced mothers, Kurz (1995) explored women's use of violence. Three-quarters of the women who experienced violence reported they used some type of violence—primarily the less severe forms—themselves. When women noted their own acts of violence, the interviewer would make statements such as "You seem to be describing mutual violence; he was violent and you were violent." Almost all women replied that they did *not* view the violence as mutual; rather, they understood their violence as being used in self-defense. Consider the responses of two of these women:

Respondent 1:   My husband did all those things on your list except use a gun. I did the first two—I threw something at him and I pushed him.

Interviewer: So, your violence was the same as his?

Respondent 1:   I used violence to protect myself when he came after me. (33-year-old woman, married 7 years, 1 child)

Respondent 2:   He did all those things on your list. . . . I did all those things, too.

Interviewer: So why did you do these things? You were angry at him?

Respondent 2:   I'm not a violent person. It was because he was violent. I had to protect myself. (29-year-old woman, married 8 years, 4 children)

In its most narrow legal sense, "self-defense" applies only when a person uses violence in order to protect against an immediate *physical* threat. Straus uses this narrow definition: He argues that women's violence is not in self-defense when women—and not their partners—use physical violence. Yet self-defense as a legal category often includes more than responding to an immediate physical threat (see Osthoff & Maguigan, this volume). Subjective evaluations of imminent threat are complex and inextricably related to the experience of prior abuse. Many studies of battered women show that, within the context of ongoing abuse, a verbal threat of more violence is very real. While Straus argues that such violence only leads to greater violence, it is morally troublesome to criticize women for responding to cues they have painfully learned signal an imminent assault (Kurz, 1993).

This gendered meaning of the use of violence is also necessary to understand women's use of lethal force. The U.S. Bureau of Justice (Langan & Dawson, 1995) conducted a study of 540 spouse abuse murder defendants in the United States. In sheer count, there was not a remarkable gendered difference—men committed 59 percent of these homicides and women committed 41 percent. Yet the picture of near-gender equivalence stops after noting simple counts. Only 10 percent of male defendants—but 44 percent of female defendants—had been assaulted by their spouses at or around the time of the murder. Other examinations of homicide reports show that homicides by women—but not by men—typically occur after a long period of abuse or during a violent assault (see Saunders, 2002, for a review of these studies).

The Gendered Consequences of Violence

While there are multiple consequences to violence, the most obvious is physical injury. In his chapter, Straus spends considerable time offering evidence for his conclusion that women's violence creates injury. We do not dispute his evidence, nor do we believe that men's injuries should be denied or ignored. Our argument is that—whether intended or not—emphasizing how women's violence can create injuries diverts attention from the main message: *All* researchers agree that women experience far *more* injuries, and far more *serious* injuries from violence than do men.

Families are, statistically speaking, very dangerous places for women but not for men: More than 40 percent of women's hospital emergency room visits arising from intentional violence were caused by their male intimates; violence by intimates caused fewer than 5 percent of visits by men (Greenfield et al., 1998); for every 1 man hospitalized for spousal assault, 46 women are hospitalized (Straton, 1994). When attention is focused on the most severe assaults—those coming to the attention of police—gender differences are the most striking: Rarely are men injured (see Saunders, 2002, for a review of injury studies).

Other consequences of violence are also gendered. For example, women report nearly double the problems of psychosomatic symptoms, stress, and depression than do men who have experienced an equivalent "level" of violence (as measured by the CTS). Likewise, clinical samples of people experiencing severe violence show much higher levels of psychological trauma and depression in women than in men (see Saunders, 2002, for a review of these studies).

In summary, within the feminist perspective, violence by men and by women are *not* the same: statistical counts of behaviors are meaningless unless they are understood in relation to their contexts, consequences, and meanings. From a feminist stance, the family conflict perspective *degenders the problem* and *genders the blame* (Berns, 2001). Simple counts of behaviors degender the problem: Women's violence and men's violence are conceptualized as the same. Arguing that women's violence toward men creates men's violence toward women genders the blame: Battered women are held responsible for the violence they experience.

Academic debates of any type often involve disagreements about proper research methodologies as well as differences in theoretical perspectives. The topic for this chapter so far has been one such academic debate. Now we move outside the world of academia, where research has practical consequences.

❖ FAMILY CONFLICT RESEARCH AND POLITICAL REALITIES

When research leaves the pages of academic journals and enters the ongoing world, it no longer focuses on debates about research methodology or appropriate theoretical approaches; most often it does not carry with it the hesitant language and often subtle distinctions made by academic researchers. In his chapter on women's violence toward men, Straus (this volume) offers an academic presentation and supports his arguments with a blizzard of statistics. Yet many of his readers likely will breeze through the statistics, ignore his disclaimers, and remember only four points: Women are as violent as men, women's violence creates injuries, women's violence toward men causes men's violence toward women, and women's violence must stop. These are the simple messages that have entered the public world. Just as feminist research led to increased public sympathy and added resources for battered women, family conflict research is used to blame women and reduce resources.

Family Conflict Perspectives, the Structure of Public Concern, and Victim Blaming

Of the many troubles people face, only some become matters of public attention. For example, why is there no general concern about the multiple problems faced by prostitutes? Or, why do people often ask rape victims questions such as "Where were you?" or "What were you wearing?" These examples show aspects of the very complicated logic surrounding how Americans in general think about problems and the people who have them. Although the details are complicated (see Loseke, 2003), the general theme is clear: In practice, many Americans do not take problems seriously unless they believe the people suffering these problems are "pure victims," people who are in no way responsible for their plights.

Because of this cultural logic, "North Americans are only interested in charity for the deserving, and violent women are not seen as deserving" (Schwartz, 2000, p. 817). Thus, research portraying women as "equally violent" as men reduces public sympathy for women victims. It is no wonder that advocates for abused women have a difficult time talking about women's violence:

It has been extremely difficult . . . to talk about women's use of violence. These discussions quickly career off into polemics about women being as violent or more violent than men, women's "participating in" or "provoking" their own victimization, and women not being "good" (or pure) victims, or even being victims at all. (Bible, Dasgupta, & Osthoff, 2002, p. 1269)

This cultural logic influencing what Americans worry about and take seriously is consequential for public images of battered women in general, and for individual battered women in particular. Research shows, for example, that judges and juries will not take women's victimization seriously if women have *any* history of violence (Ferraro, 2003). This reflects attitudes of the public in general who lose sympathy for battered women when they believe these women are even verbally assertive (Follingstad, Brondino, & Kleinfelter, 1996; Harris & Cook, 1994).

In their scholarly articles, family conflict researchers often argue that evidence of women's violence against men should not be used to excuse men's violence toward women. Yet their findings *are* used that way. Because it places such emphasis on women's violence, the family conflict perspective provides rhetorical support for judges and juries who acquit rapists and wife beaters with the justification that rape victims and battered women have provoked their own victimization, and that men therefore are not responsible. The family conflict perspective also provides rhetorical support for members of the public who will not offer sympathy or assistance to any woman evaluated as less than a "pure" victim. In the conclusion to his chapter, Straus recognizes this but states that *he* is "willing to accept certain costs to achieve a nonviolent society." We note only that *he* is not experiencing such costs.

Family Conflict Perspectives, Public Policy, and Social Resources

Family conflict researchers also argue that their findings of gender equivalence should not be used to justify taking resources away from battered women. Yet findings from these studies *are* used to achieve this purpose. In New Hampshire, for example, family conflict study findings were used to justify reducing resources for a women's shelter. Likewise, funding for a women's shelter in Chicago was blocked by referencing findings about women's violence (Currie, 1998).

Family conflict research also serves an important function for a variety of men's rights advocacy groups. The Men's Defense Association (www.mensdefense.org), for example, filed a lawsuit in June 2003, seeking to overturn the Minnesota Battered Woman's Act. Entered into the legal record were manuscripts from family conflict researchers. The logic of the litigation is that because such research by what they term the "best experts" shows that women are as violent as men, it is discriminatory to protect only women. Is the purpose of this lawsuit to shift resources to battered men? No, the suit explicitly states that it does *not* want resources to shift to men. The Men's Defense Association wants to achieve equality by reducing resources for women. Family conflict research is offered as a "scientific" justification to roll back protections for battered women.

Other men's rights advocacy groups use family conflict research to justify demands to reduce men's requirements to pay child support (www.mens-network.org) and to eliminate laws defining marital rape as a crime (the Equal Justice Foundation: www.ejfi.org). While again, Straus says *he* is "willing to accept the cost of radical male advocacy groups misusing the results of my research," any successes of these groups will not affect *him*. It is easy to accept costs when they are suffered by others.

❖ CONCLUSIONS

In this chapter we compared feminist and family conflict perspectives on violence between men and women in marital-type relationships. From a feminist perspective, focusing on the dire problems of battered women, the family conflict perspective *degenders the problem* of violence when it conceptualizes men's violence and women's violence as equivalent. In contrast, feminists argue that men's violence and women's violence differs in its contexts, its consequences, and its meanings. Because a great deal of women's violence is in self-defense, focusing on women's violence and training women that "no violence is allowed" have troublesome implications. Furthermore, the assertion that "women's violence creates men's violence" *genders the blame* for violence: Battered women become responsible for their own victimization. Within our cultural logic, if a woman is responsible she does not deserve sympathy and services.

Should women's violence toward men be ignored? Of course not. Should we deny that men, too, can be victims? Definitely not. However, we repeat what feminists have been saying for many years: Talking about "gender equivalence," equating women's and men's use of violence, and dramatizing women's violence quickly leads to polemics in which women's violence is used to justify men's violence, women are evaluated as not deserving of sympathy or support, and services for battered women are reduced. Thus, it is critical that we base our research on a thorough understanding of the gendered dynamics of control, self-defense, and power in male–female relationships. It is only through a gender perspective that we can accurately identify the causes and consequences of violence and develop effective strategies for reducing the unacceptably high rates of violence toward women and the toll this violence takes on women and their families.

❖ REFERENCES

Adams, D. (1988). Treatment models of men who batter: A profeminist analysis. In K. Yllö & M. Bograd (Eds.), *Feminist perspectives on wife abuse* (pp. 176–199). Newbury Park, CA: Sage.

Bachman, R. & Saltzman, L. (1995). *Violence against women: Estimates from the redesigned National Crime Victimization Survey.* Washington, DC: U.S. Department of Justice, Bureau of Justice Statistics.

Berns, N. (2001). Degendering the problem and gendering the blame: Political discourse on women and violence. *Gender & Society, 15,* 262–281.

Bianchi, S. M., & Spain, D. (1996). Women, work, and family in America. *Population Bulletin, 51,* 2–47.

Bible, A., Dasgupta S. D., & Osthoff, S. (2002). Guest editors' introduction. *Violence against Women, 8,* 1267–1270.

Brush, L. D. (1990). Violent acts and injurious outcomes in married couples: Methodological issues in the national survey of families and households. *Gender & Society, 4,* 56–67.

Cascardi, M. K., O'Leary, D., Lawrence, E. E., & Schlee, K. A. (1995). Characteristics of women physically abused by their spouses and who seek treatment regarding marital conflict. *Journal of Consulting and Clinical Psychology, 63,* 616–623.

Currie, D. H. (1998). Violent men or violent women? Whose definition counts? In R. K. Bergen (Ed.), *Issues in intimate violence* (pp. 97–111). Thousand Oaks, CA: Sage.

Dasgupta, S. D. (1999). Just like men? A critical view of violence by women. In M. E. Shepard & E. L. Pence (Eds.), *Coordinating community response to domestic violence: Lessons from Duluth and beyond* (pp. 195–222). Thousand Oaks, CA: Sage.

Dasgupta, S. D. (2002). A framework for understanding women's use of nonlethal violence in intimate heterosexual relationships. *Violence against Women, 9,* 1364–1389.

Dobash, R. P., & Dobash, R. E. (1979). *Violence against wives: A case against the patriarchy.* New York: Free Press.

Dobash, R. P., & Dobash, R. E. (1998). *Rethinking violence against women.* Thousand Oaks, CA: Sage.

Dobash, R. P., Dobash, R. E., Wilson, M., & Daly, M. (1992). The myth of sexual symmetry in marital violence. *Social Problems, 39,* 71–91.

Ferraro, K. J. (2003). The words change, but the melody lingers: The persistence of the battered woman syndrome in criminal cases involving battered women. *Violence against Women, 9,* 110–129.

Follingstad, D. R., Brondino, M. J., & Kleinfelter, K. J. (1996). Reputation and behavior of battered women who kill their partners: Do these variables negate self-defense? *Journal of Family Violence, 11,* 251–267.

Greenfield, L. A., Rand, M. R., Craven, D., Klaus, P. A., Perkins, C. A., et al. (1998). *Violence by intimates: Analysis of data on crimes by current or former spouses, boyfriends, or girlfriends.* Washington, DC: U.S. Department of Justice.

Harris, R. J., & Cook, C.A. (1994). Attributions about spouse abuse: It matters who the batterers and victims are. *Sex Roles, 30,* 555–565.

Kimmel, M. S. (2002). "Gender symmetry" in domestic violence: A substantive and methodological research review. *Violence against Women, 8,* 1332–1363.

Kurz, D. (1993). Physical assaults by husbands: A major social problem. In R. J. Gelles & D. R. Loseke (Eds.), *Current controversies on family violence* (1st ed., pp. 88–103). Thousand Oaks, CA: Sage.

Kurz, D. (1995). *For richer, for poorer: Mothers confront divorce.* New York: Routledge.

Langan, P. A., & Dawson, J. M. (1995). *Spouse murder defendants in large urban counties.* Washington, DC: U.S. Department of Justice, Office of Justice Programs, Bureau of Justice Statistics, NCJ-153256.

Langhinrichsen-Rohling, J., Neidig, P., & Thorn, G. (1995). Violent marriages: Gender differences in levels of current violence and past abuse. *Journal of Family Violence, 10,* 159–176.

Loseke, D. R. (2003). *Thinking about social problems: An introduction to constructionist perspectives* (2nd ed.). New York: Aldine DeGruyter.

Messner, M. (1989). When bodies are weapons: Masculinity and violence in sport. *International Review of Sociology of Sport, 25,* 203–220.

Reinharz, S. (1992). *Feminist methods of social research.* New York: Oxford University Press.

Sanday, P. R. (1991). *Fraternity gang rape: Sex, brotherhood, and privilege on campus*. New York: New York University Press.

Saunders, D. G. (2002). Are physical assaults by wives and girlfriends a major social problem: A review of the literature. *Violence against Women, 8*, 1424–1448.

Schafer, J., Caetano, R., & Clark, C. L. (2002). Agreement about violence in U.S. couples. *Journal of Interpersonal Violence, 17*, 457–470.

Schwartz, M. D. (2000). Methodological issues in the use of survey data for measuring and characterizing violence against women. *Violence against Women, 6*, 815–838.

Schwartz, M. D., & DeKeseredy, W. S. (1993). The return of the "battered husband syndrome" through the typification of women as violent. *Crime, Law, and Social Change, 20*, 249–265.

Straton, J. (1994). The myth of the "battered husband syndrome." *Masculinities, 2*, 79–82.

Straus, M. A. (1999). The controversy over domestic violence by women: A methodological, theoretical, and sociology of science analysis. In X. B. Arriaga & S. Oskamp (Eds.), *Violence in intimate relationships* (pp. 17–44). Thousand Oaks, CA: Sage.

Tjaden, P., & Thoennes, N. (2000). *Extent, nature, and consequences of intimate partner violence*. Washington, DC: National Institute of Justice and the Centers for Disease Control and Prevention.

U. S. Department of Justice. (1998). *Violence by intimates: Analysis of data on crimes by current or former spouses, boyfriends, and girlfriends*. Washington, DC: U.S. Department of Justice, Bureau of Justice Statistics.

U.S. Department of Labor. (2000). *Employment characteristics of families in 1999*. Washington, DC: U.S. Department of Labor, Bureau of Labor Statistics, USDL00–172.

U.S. Statistical Abstracts. (2001). *Statistical Abstract of the United States: 2001*. Washington, DC: U.S. Census Bureau.

Waltermaurer, E. M., Ortega, C. A., & McNutt, L. A. (2003). Issues in estimating the prevalence of intimate partner violence: Assessing the impact of abuse status on participation bias. *Journal of Interpersonal Violence, 18*, 959–974.

Walzer, S. (1998). *Thinking about the baby: Gender and transitions into parenthood*. Philadelphia: Temple University Press.

Wood, J. T. (2001). The normalization of violence in heterosexual romantic relationships: Women's narratives of love and violence. *Journal of Social and Personal Relationships, 18*, 239–261.

6

More Data Have Accumulated Supporting Date and Acquaintance Rape as Significant Problems for Women

Sarah L. Cook

Mary P. Koss

S ince the first edition of *Current Controversies on Family Violence* was published in 1993, mounting evidence has documented the nature and scope of date and acquaintance rape. Yet, critics continue to disparage empirical data that underscore this problem. When Koss, Gidycz, and Wisniewski (1987) published an epidemiological study of sexual assault on college campuses funded by the National Institute of Mental Health (NIMH), their findings startled the scientific community and the nation. Results indicated that, since their fourteenth birthdays, 27 percent of college women recalled an incident that met the legal definition of rape, including attempts. In a 12-month period, 76 per 1,000 college women experienced one or more attempted or completed rapes. Of these, 8 of 10 involved someone the victim knew, and more than half (57 percent) involved a date. Initially, many did not believe that this level of assault could exist without coming to the attention of police, parents, or institutional authorities. Today, rape and sexual assault are acknowledged serious problems with consequences that require responses at local, state, and federal levels. But University of California social welfare professor Neil Gilbert (this volume) continues to question whether rape could possibly be as common as researchers suggest without being known to justice authorities. In this chapter we summarize Gilbert's criticism of the NIMH study and present new evidence that the scope of rape remains widespread.

❖ DEFINITIONS OF RAPE

Studies of rape must begin by defining terms. The FBI defines *rape* as attempted or completed vaginal intercourse with a female, forcibly and against her will (Federal Bureau of Investigation, 1999). This definition is used only to collect federal crime statistics. State laws govern the adjudication of rape cases, unless the crime occurs on federal government property. Federal and state rape laws have been reformed since the 1970s and are more contemporary than the FBI definition because they (1) are gender neutral, meaning men and women can be victims; (2) cover oral and anal penetration, including object insertion as well as vaginal intercourse; and (3) extend to nonforcible assaults if intercourse is obtained with someone unable to consent due to mental illness, mental retardation, or intoxication (for example, Michigan Statutes Annotated, 1980). Social scientists distinguish several types of rape, including stranger rape, acquaintance rape, date rape, and marital rape. *Acquaintance rape* refers to assaults committed by anyone who is not a complete stranger. *Date rape* is a type of acquaintance rape that involves a victim and a perpetrator who have some level of romantic relationship. However, the essential meaning of *rape* is unaffected by relationships, except in states that still limit women's rights to charge husbands with rape.

❖ WHAT THE CRITICS CONTEND

Gilbert asserts that rape researchers practice "the craft of advocacy research" by promulgating inaccurate research findings into the policy realm as fact by sheer repetition (Gilbert, 1997, p. 236). Ultimately, Gilbert's criticism targets the U.S. Congress's use of Koss's study to establish the need for the Violence against Women Act of 1994 (P.L. 102–322). He claims that these data unduly influenced policy that resulted in inappropriate federal expenditures for campus sexual assault prevention. Gilbert objects to definitions of *rape* that he contends are overly broad and lead to inflated estimates of rape prevalence (Gilbert, 1993). Specifically, he disputes the inclusion of questions that ask about alcohol and drug involvement in nonconsensual sex, the process of defining rape in behavioral terms instead of relying solely on the victim's perspective, and definitions of consent. More recently, he questions using the scientifically accepted practice of using converging evidence from methodologically similar studies to support early prevalence estimates (Gilbert, 1997). Gilbert also alleges that advocacy research has created a climate on college campuses so conducive to reporting sexual assault that women should be able to freely report experiences of assault without concern for privacy and well-being (Gilbert, 1993). Let's examine each of the charges he levels.

❖ THE CRITICS REDEFINE RAPE

Gilbert thinks that "radical feminists have distorted the definition of rape and created a bogus epidemic" (quoted in Hendrix, 1991). He focuses mainly on definitions of rape and asserts that the scope of victimization found is so large because it is based on a new, radical, and elastic definition. Gutmann (1990) writes, "If, (as some researchers propose), we broadly define rape to include sex a woman subsequently regrets or even subjection to sexual innuendo, almost every woman has been raped" (p. 50). Although educational materials may promote broad interpretations of rape, critics err by assuming that these definitions undergird research. The NIMH survey definition of rape was consistent with the statutes in most North American jurisdictions; the rape rate included only instances of unwanted sexual penetration, perpetrated by force, threat of harm, or when the victim was intoxicated.

Moreover, the definition reflects how rape is treated in the 1999 Centers for Disease Control's *Uniform Definitions and Data Elements:*

> Sexual violence [involves] . . . use of physical force to compel a person to engage in a sexual act against his or her will, whether or not the act is completed [and includes an] attempted or completed sex act involving a person who is unable to understand the nature or condition of the act, to decline participation, or to communicate unwillingness to engage in the sexual act (e.g., because of illness, disability, or the influence of alcohol or other drugs due to intimidation or pressure. (Saltzman, Fanslow, McMahon, & Shelly, 1999, p. 12)

The Role of Intoxicants

Gilbert questions the item used to obtain information about unwanted penetration that occurred while women were intoxicated. Although rape when incapacitated is a legitimate part of legal definitions, for the sake of discussion it is helpful to examine prevalence when these instances are removed from consideration. Removing this item from the estimate among the 3,187 women students in the national sample lowers the attempted rape figure from 12 percent to 8 percent and the completed rape figure from 16 percent to 11 percent (Koss et al., 1987). Even when limited to instances where unwanted penetration was attempted or obtained forcibly, 20 percent of college women, or 1 in 5, qualified as rape victims since age 14.

By presenting prevalence estimates that omit victimization due to incapacitation, we do not intend to minimize problems associated with heavy alcohol use among college students, particularly sexual assault. Alcohol plays a complex role in date and acquaintance rape. The National Women's Survey, conducted by the National Crime Victims Research and Treatment Center, provides the strongest evidence to date that women's alcohol use does not cause victimization or revictimization (Kilpatrick, Acierno, Resnick, Saunders, & Best, 1997). This study examined physical and sexual assault, as well as alcohol and illicit drug use, in a national probability sample of 3,006 women. After accounting for age, education, and race, and prior sexual and physical assault experiences, previous alcohol use alone did not increase the likelihood that a woman experienced a new assault. Illicit substance use, however, alone or in combination with alcohol use, heightened chances of another assault. Because of the study's longitudinal design, the investigators confidently determined that although alcohol use came first, it did not influence the risk of rape. Similar findings from another study show that alcohol consumption during college did not predict new assaults among women who had been sexually victimized in adolescence (Gidycz, Hanson, & Layman, 1995). Rather than causing victimization, heavy alcohol use is a likely consequence (Kilpatrick et al., 1997).

Consent

Critics also take issue with definitions of consent. It would be outrageous to ask a car thief, "Well, you did take the car, but did you intend to steal it?" Nevertheless, Gutmann (1991) suggests that for a man to be guilty, he must have *intended* to rape. Using this logic, as long as a man interprets "No" as a part of foreplay, he can never be guilty of rape (Muehlenhard, Powch, Phelps, & Giusti, 1992). Gilbert (1991) criticizes a "radical feminist effort to impose new norms governing intimacy between the sexes" and complains that "the awesome complexity of human interaction is reduced to 'No means no'" (p. 61). "He believes that young men should reject a face-value interpretation of the word *No*. He characterizes as "inconvenient" Muehlenhard and Hollabaugh's (1988) findings that 39 percent of college women surveyed admitted to having said No when they meant Yes, but he failed to recognize the converse: The majority of women (61 percent) had never engaged in token resistance, a finding replicated by other studies (Muehlenhard & McCoy, 1991; Shotland & Hunter, 1995; Sprecher, Hatfield, Corese, Potapova, & Levitskaya, 1994). More important, two of these studies explode the myth that only women engage in token resistance. When explicitly defined, men and women use token resistance with equal frequency.

Gilbert (1991) also believes that women should label their experiences as "rape" to be included in prevalence estimates. But, failure to embrace the correct legal term for a crime does not mean the incident never happened. With this assertion, critics reveal unfamiliarity with victimization survey methodology. Survey experts have long known that the public is unaware of legal definitions for rape, larceny, burglary, robbery, and so on. Ideas of what constitutes rape are often based on rape myths conveyed by pornography, "dirty" jokes, movies, and rock music videos that do not accurately portray sexual assault. These myths are played out in women's experiences. College women, who were raped but did not define their experience as rape, were more likely than others to hold a "script" limiting rape to a violent blitz perpetrated by a stranger (Kahn, Mathie, & Torgler, 1994). More college women than ever before are viewing unwanted penetration as rape. A recent national survey found that approximately half of women whose experiences fit legal definitions acknowledged the word *rape* as describing their experiences (Fisher, Cullen, & Turner, 2000). And, although some women may not realize that their experiences match legal standards for rape, it does not follow that they view these incidents positively or even neutrally. In fact, half of rape victims in the national survey considered their experiences to be rape or some crime similar to rape. Only 10 percent of women contended that they did not feel victimized. Many women did not initially label their experiences as rape but later reported incidents to researchers they now understood as rape, after learning the legal definition. Regardless of whether they identified as rape victims, women whose experiences fit legal definitions suffered significantly higher levels of psychological distress than women who reported no unwanted sexual experiences (Frazier & Seales, 1997; Koss, Dinero, Seibel, & Cox, 1988; Layman, Gidycz, & Lynn, 1996).

Keeping Rape a Secret

Gilbert's suggestion that rape victims can make reports on college campuses without fear is utopian. In spite of more than a decade of campus and community education, national data continue to show that women are more likely to report when their experiences match stereotypical notions of rape by strangers than when they are raped by acquaintances (Pino & Meier, 1999). Moreover, in a representative sample of 4,009 adult women, recent rape victims had greater fear than women raped in earlier years about their names being made public (Kilpatrick, Edmunds, & Seymour, 1992). One-half of victims stated they would be more likely to report if laws prohibited name and address disclosure by the media. The reporting rate for rape in this study was only 16 percent (Kilpatrick et al., 1992). Victims are also concerned that police will discredit their allegations and blame them. Gilbert's own skepticism vividly illustrates the disclosure climate that victims fear. Women raped by men they knew often delayed telling anyone, and when they did, they experienced more negative reactions than women who were raped by strangers (Sudderth, 1998). And, sadly, some victims still encounter the same victim-blaming attitudes and behaviors from legal, medical, and mental health systems that were first documented 15 years ago (Campbell et al., 1999). From this perspective, women's decisions not to report are rational. In reality, prosecutors dismiss more than half of all rape cases, freeing perpetrators with absolutely no consequences (Koss, 2000). Is it really surprising that fewer than 5 percent of college rape victims reported their assaults to the police and almost half told no one at all (Koss et al., 1987)? Also note that an identical figure is reported in the National College Women Sexual Victimization survey, funded by the U.S. Department of Justice (Fisher et al., 2000), which is described later in the chapter.

Rape or Rapette?

The term "date rape" appears to be an oxymoron. *Date* connotes mutuality and pleasure, whereas *rape* implies powerlessness and humiliation. The juxtaposition of these words modifies the traditional sense of outrage associated with *rape,* and *date rape* comes to signify "rapette." It is viewed as something like rape, but certainly not as traumatizing as "real rape" perpetrated by a violent stranger. The truth is the thought that one will be killed or seriously injured is equally common among women who are raped by dates and by total strangers (Kilpatrick et al., 1992). And, although women in the national survey were sufficiently free of emotional impairment to function as students, evidence suggests that their rapes were traumatic. Afterward, 27 percent of victims thought about suicide to the point that they considered possible methods to use (Koss et al., 1988). Furthermore, scores on standard measures of psychological symptoms for rape victims averaged one standard deviation higher than those for nonvictimized women, and were similar to the scores of those who sought campus counseling services. Psychological distress generated by rape was equal whether the rapist was a stranger, casual acquaintance, or steady date. These findings have been replicated in 16 studies that examined depression, fear, anxiety, PTSD symptoms, and overall distress in rape victims (Frazier & Seales, 1997).

Another finding that suggests rapette to critics is that approximately 40 percent of the victims reported having sex again with the men who raped them (Koss et al., 1987). Unfortunately, the data did not allow us to differentiate between voluntary sexual contacts and additional rapes by the same perpetrator. Shotland (1992) theorizes that women's responses to date rape may depend upon the relationship's context. For example, women raped on first dates may be more likely to assume that their dates are totally responsible for the assault than women raped by steady dates who never aggressed before. Regardless, 87 percent of victims in the national study eventually ended their relationships with the men who raped them (Koss et al., 1988).

❖ THE BIGGER PICTURE

Critics seize on discrepant estimates of rape prevalence across studies as evidence that statistics are exaggerated. They fail to recognize that the risk of sexual assault varies with age and life circumstances and that one must assure that the rates being compared represent similarly aged and situated people. Most importantly though, the 15 percent completed rape prevalence rate from the 1987 national study of college students is only one part of a bigger picture of rape prevalence, and this is a story the critics don't tell.

The National Institute of Justice and the Centers for Disease Control and Prevention recently funded the Center for Policy Research to conduct the Violence against Women Survey (Tjaden & Thoennes, 2000). This study, a nationally representative telephone survey conducted between 1995 and 1996, questioned 16,000 women and men about experiences with stalking, physical violence, and rape. Results indicated that 14.8 percent of women and 2.1 percent of men reported a completed rape at some point in their lives, and these figures did not include rapes in which the victim was incapable of consent. Another study conducted in 1992, the National Victims Center National Women's Study, used a similar survey method and definition of rape and reported a prevalence rate of 14 percent for U.S. women generally (Kilpatrick et al., 1992).

The 1995 National College Health Risk Behavior Survey (NCHRBS), funded by the Centers for Disease Control and Prevention (Brener, McMahon, Warren, & Douglas, 1999), examined the prevalence of forced sexual intercourse in a national sample of 4,609 women college students. In all, 20 percent of respondents disclosed that they had been victims of a completed rape at some point in their lives. When the estimate was restricted to women raped since the age of 15, the prevalence rate was 15 percent. This figure is virtually identical to Koss et al.'s 1987 estimate even without explicitly asking about alcohol-related rapes or attempts where no penetration occurred.

Another series of college-based surveys were directed by Bonnie Fisher and colleagues (Fisher, Sloan, Cullen, & Lu, 1998; Fisher et al., 2000) including Crime in the Ivory Tower and the National College Women Sexual Victimization Study. The latter used a national sample of randomly selected 4,446 college women contacted by telephone between February and May 1997. Embedded within the survey was a mini-experiment comparing the rates of sexual victimization obtained using two different measurement strategies. The first presented the survey focus as "unwanted sexual experiences" and used behaviorally specific wording in sexual assault screening questions. The alternate version adopted the approach of the National Crime Victimization Survey (NCVS) and told respondents the survey focused on "increasing concern about criminal victimizations that that women may experience during college" and used the NCVS sexual assault screening questions (Bureau of Justice Statistics, 1997). The rates obtained using the NCVS questions are presented later. With specific questions about unwanted sexual experiences, the study reported the 6- to 9-month incidence rate for rape, including attempts for undergraduates, was approximately 3.1 percent, meaning that within just 7 months, 3 of every 100 college women was raped. Although this rate may sound low, the authors projected that 5 percent of college women were raped annually, and across the typical 5 years that it now takes to complete college, between 1 in 4 and 1 in 5 college women may be sexually assaulted. Fisher and colleagues (2000) omitted from their definition of rape consideration of rape when incapacitated, and its inclusion could have further elevated the rates obtained. Nevertheless, their estimation of the magnitude of rape on campus (1 in 4) is identical to the one based on the 1987 work that Gilbert attacks.

Critics have implied that college student populations may be over-sensitive to issues of victimization. But a recent survey demonstrates that college students may not be the group at highest risk. The U.S. Naval Recruit Health Study (Merrill et al., 1998) collected data from a representative sample of 3,776 male and female recruits. Naval recruits come from ethnically and economically diverse backgrounds, and they are in the same age group as college students. Five questions from the Sexual Experiences Survey (SES) screened for rape victimization at the start of basic training. Results indicated that 36.1 percent of women had been raped prior to enlistment. In addition, 14.8 percent of men reported perpetrating attempted or completed rape prior to military service. Women naval recruits reported victimization at rates 2.4 times higher than college women, and male recruits reported rates of perpetration 3.3 times higher than college men.

While the primary focus of the Harvard School of Public Health College Alcohol Study was on binge drinking and subsequent health risk behaviors, investigators also examined sexual assault as a second-hand effect of others' binge drinking (Wechsler, Dowdall, Maenner, Gledhill-Hoyt, & Lee, 1998). The study concerned changes in binge drinking between 1993 and 1997 in a nationally representative sample of 14,521 students at 130 colleges. In all, 2.2 percent of non-binge drinkers reported being the victim of sexual assault or date rape. These rates are for a 6–9 month period and cannot be compared to lifetime prevalence rates. The authors failed to ask those women who met criteria for occasional or frequent binge drinking whether they had been the victims of sexual assault or rape (Wechsler et al., 1998). These limitations notwithstanding, additional analyses with the same data support the contention that alcohol is the most widely used "date rape drug" on college campuses. Women from colleges with medium and high binge-drinking rates were more than one and a half times more likely to be raped while intoxicated than women from schools with low binge-drinking rates (Mohler-Kuo, Dowdall, Koss, & Wechsler, 2004).

The National Survey of Adolescents, funded by the National Institute of Justice, surveyed a probability sample of 4,023 adolescents aged 12–17 by telephone about victimization experiences and, in addition, about their own and their families' substance use. Thirteen percent of female adolescents reported that they had been victims of sexual assault in their lifetimes (Kilpatrick et al., 2000, p. 30). This finding resulted despite exclusion of adolescents whose parents did not grant permission for participation, who did not speak English, and/or who resided in institutional settings or households without parents or guardians and homes lacking telephones—all groups who might be expected to have average or higher rates of sexual assault.

Does a Gold Standard for Estimating Rape Prevalence Exist?

Although research strategies continually improve, identified levels of rape and attempted rape depend on methodological features of studies. Definitions, question context and specificity, inclusion and exclusion criteria, and incident classification rules form a context in which estimates must be presented and interpreted (Crowell & Burgess, 1996; Koss, 1993). Some rape prevalence studies do not define rape (for example, Brener et al., 1999; Wechsler et al., 1998). However, most recent studies define rape based on legal statutes that include forms of penetration other than penile-vaginal (Fisher et al., 2000; Koss et al., 1987; Tjaden & Thoennes, 2000). Many of these studies fail to measure rape while incapacitated and unable to consent (Brenner et al., 1999; Fisher et al., 2000; Tjaden & Thoennes, 2000). This omission is perplexing, especially in the context of a host of recent state laws imposing stiff sentences for rapes accomplished by the use of date rape drugs. Readers should be aware of this limitation in the coverage of all the recent rape estimates. Even when studies use consistent definitions, many variations in methodology exist, including sample composition, context of questioning (for example, whether questions are in crime, health, or sexuality surveys), number and type of screening questions, recall period, different age boundaries, and use of the terms "sexual assault" or "unwanted sexual experiences" as alternatives to "rape" (see Koss, 1992, 1993, 1996).

Is the methodology of the NCVS the gold standard, as Gilbert asserts? (See, for example, Bureau of Justice Statistics, 1997; Greenfeld et al., 1998.) Recent improvements in NCVS methods include expanding the definition of sexual assault, rewording screening questions, and providing a new introduction that attempts to dispel the mindset toward severe crime that is created by prior questions in the survey. However, it has long been acknowledged that the methods inherent in crime surveys undermine self-disclosure of sexual and physical assault by intimates (Harlow, 1991). The NCVS uses four questions for sexual assault. For example, the first reads,

> Other than any incidents already mentioned, has anyone attacked or threatened you in any of these ways: (a) With any weapon, for instance, a gun or knife? (b) With anything like a baseball bat, frying pan, scissors, or a stick? (c) By something thrown, such as a rock or bottle? (d) Include any grabbing, punching, or choking? (e) Any rape, attempted rape, or other type of sexual attack? (f) Any face-to-face threats? (g) Any attack or threat of use of force by anyone at all? (quoted in Tjaden & Thoennes, 2000, p. 24)

Clearly, expressions such as "sexual attacks" set up the expectation that the interviewer wishes to hear about unwanted but violent attacks that involve weapons, thrown objects, and baseball bats. These context and language choices may misguide respondents from recalling relevant experiences. Fisher and colleagues (2000) compared the use of methods such as those developed by Koss to the standard NCVS practice. They found that the incidence of rape was 10 times higher (1.7 percent versus 0.6 percent) when assessed by specific questions presented in an "unwanted sexual experiences" context compared to vague questions about sexual attacks presented in a context of crime. Contrary to Gilbert's assertions, the NCVS is not the gold standard for measuring rape. Under the imprimatur of the U.S. Department of Justice, Fisher and colleagues (2000) concluded, "It seems likely that NCVS underestimates the true incidence of rape victimization in the United States" (p. 33).

❖ RECOGNIZING PSYCHOSOCIAL AND ECONOMIC COSTS

Many women measure their exposure to crime in terms of the chances of being raped and take steps to reduce their risks. The effects of bypassed opportunities due to fear of rape on women's achievement of their potentials, health, and economic well-being are unknown, but the costs of a sexual assault are high for those women who are direct victims. Economically, rape exacts a toll in terms of dollars spent for health and mental health care plus time lost from work or school. Per rape, out-of-pocket costs for medical and mental health treatment average $5,100. When a victim's quality of life is considered, the average cost of rape skyrockets to $87,000, even when criminal justice system costs are excluded (Miller, Cohen, & Wiersema, 1996; estimated in 1993 dollars). In the aggregate, rape extracts from society $127 billion a year when lost quality of life and direct costs are included in the estimate (Miller et al., 1996).

Rape is considered to be one of the most severe of traumas, and its psychological impact has been extensively researched (for reviews, see Crowell & Burgess, 1996; Koss et al., 1994). Although women may be very resourceful and good at problem solving, persisting stigma about rape complicates healing and interferes with eliciting the social support that tides people through most other types of trauma. Acute and chronic depressive symptoms have been identified among women who were raped (Crowell & Burgess, 1996; Kilpatrick, Saunders, Veronen, Best, & Von, 1987; Koss et al., 1994). Published lifetime prevalence rates of PTSD have ranged from approximately 24 percent for women exposed to any trauma (Breslau, Davis, Andreski, & Peterson, 1991) to 65 percent for women who have experienced a complete rape (Rothbaum, Fao, Riggs, Murdock, & Walsh, 1992). Victimized women show more indications of risky sexual behaviors, smoke, use alcohol and other drugs more, and have higher weight and lower physical activity levels than nonvictimized women (Acierno, Kilpatrick, Resnick, Saunders, & Best, 1996; Kilpatrick et al., 1997). Likewise, there are increased risks of contracting sexually transmitted diseases (Irwin et al., 1995), sexual problems (Letourneau, Resnick, Kilpatrick, Saunders, & Best, 1996), and suicide attempts (Davidson, Hughes, George, & Blazer, 1996). These hazardous behaviors may be initiated or escalated as attempts to cope with rape-related distress.

Although women are less likely than men to be victims of all violent crimes, they are 25 times more likely to be raped (Tjaden & Thoennes, 2000) and 8 times more likely to be physically assaulted by an intimate (Greenfeld et al., 1998). Yet, college women still fear rape by strangers more than by acquaintances (Hickman & Muehlenhard, 1997), and a large number expect rape and attempted rape as an inherent feature of college dating situations (Cook, 1995). For young women, acknowledging the risk of rape is frightening and, at the very least, disconcerting. Women restrict their lives—socially, intellectually, recreationally, and spiritually—to protect themselves from date and acquaintance rape. The sexual roles and scripts that contribute to rape must be reexamined. We note with optimism that few college students find sexual aggression acceptable (Cook, 1995) and a majority defines rape as sexual intercourse that proceeded after objections were stated (cited in Muehlenhard et al., 1992).

❖ THE ROLE OF SCIENCE IN PREVENTION

Criticism leveled against sexual assault research also targets prevention efforts, which Gilbert (1993) labels "dysfunctional consequences of advocacy research" (p. 12). According to Gilbert, neither mutual respect nor reasonable discussion can occur because of the negative climate created by advocacy research. However, the evidence neither supports his assertions that the figures are inflated nor documents that a communication impasse exists. Gilbert's views about rape prevention are misdirected. The inadequacy in prevention efforts is not as much in program content as it is in intervention design, implementation, and evaluation. Colleges and universities are responding on a continuum from revising sexual assault policies to hiring education and prevention coordinators. Many prevention programs have been developed, but few reach most or all enrolled students, a minority are theoretically grounded, some are either too narrow or broad in their focus, and hardly any have been rigorously evaluated (Lonsway, 1996). Evidence of short-term reductions in rape-supportive attitudes is growing, but without parallel reductions in victimization incidence evidence is insufficient to conclude that sexual assault prevention programs on college campuses change behavior (Bachar & Koss, 2001; Breitenbecher, 2000). The next step for sexual assault prevention programs is critical assessment of intervention process, impact, and outcome, areas ripe for basic and applied research. Beyond answering questions of program effectiveness, preventive intervention research aids in developing greater understanding of the causes of sexual aggression.

❖ ACTION-ORIENTED RESEARCH

Psychological research can and should play an integral role in the development of public policy. At the same time, scientists have responsibilities when disseminating research results. Justice David L. Bazelon (1982) implores psychologists to focus less on broad summary statements and more on disclosure of underlying values, admitting uncertainties and divisions of opinion that may exist. The majority of sexual assault research, when held to these standards, fares well (for thoughtful discussions of these issues, see Muehlenhard et al., 1992; White & Sorenson, 1992). Nevertheless, research that is widely disseminated for the public's use runs the risk of being misused. No scientist can guarantee that his or her research will always be appropriately interpreted or applied, but the misuse of it does not invalidate original findings. Gilbert is wrong to fault a particular research study that used a legally based definition of rape because some prevention programs and educational efforts have arisen that incorporate broader definitions. This is like holding the car manufacturer responsible for a purchaser's driving habits.

Gilbert's final issue is that advocacy groups have inappropriately used sexual assault research to influence the passage of the Violence against Women Act of 1994 (P. L. 102–322) (VAWA), the first federal legislation to address domestic violence and sexual assault. Although Koss's testimony exemplified how social science research can inform congressional action, Gilbert fails to acknowledge the crucial role in the bill's passage played by the grassroots National Task Force on the Violence against Women Act. (In the NOW Task Force, sexual assault advocates were joined by domestic violence coalitions and 100 organizations, despite their drastically different agendas for federal policy—for example, the United Auto Workers, the AFL-CIO, the Association of Flight Attendants, the Leadership Council on Civil Rights, the Older Women's League, the National Association of Attorneys General, and organizations from national religious and ethnic minority communities such as Navajo Nation.) After considering research as well as testimony from citizens and organizations, Congress determined that expenditures for prevention interventions on college campuses were not only justified, they were imperative. Gilbert believes that Congress was not only misguided but also overly generous given the scope of the problem. He objects to spending $20 million for sexual assault programs on college campuses and suggests that this money translates into prevention costs of $20,000 per victim (Gilbert, 1997). However, the calculation he uses to produce this estimate is wrong. He took the total number of women victimized in the 1987 study as the denominator, but the correct method should use the total population of college women. Prevention efforts must be directed toward all women, because no evidence exists to predict who will be assaulted at a later point. Moreover, rape prevention efforts also aim to prevent perpetration by male students, who assault not only fellow students but also others in the community. Furthermore, Congress actually awarded only $8.1 million to colleges and universities to combat violence against women (Daniel S. Carter at www.campussafety.org; quoted in Fisher et al., 2000). It is more correct to place these prevention dollars in the context of the 14.9 million people who are enrolled as students in Title IV postsecondary institutions (National Center for Education Statistics, 1999). Doing so results in a per student expense of 54 cents. We assert that this expense is clearly justified by the potential benefits of rape prevention. We further believe that that sum is inadequate, given warnings about the urgency of the problem that have been issued by authors of all the major surveys who have examined rape on campus during the past 15 years, including reports issued in the name of the U.S. Navy, U.S. Centers for Disease Control and Prevention, and the U.S. Department of Justice.

❖ CONCLUSION

It is important to realize that the "question of advocacy can be raised about those claiming that virtually everyone has been victimized and about those arguing that 'real' violence is relatively uncommon" (Berliner, 1992, p. 121). And, just as scientists have responsibilities when disseminating research, so do those who critique research. The type of overgeneralized and emotional statements that are woven throughout Gilbert's commentary appear to be made by someone who objects to research findings rather than by someone involved in the scholarly dialogue aimed at improving understanding and response to social issues. Furthermore, he has too little faith in science's ability to self-correct by generating new data that eliminate weak or misleading data and conclusions (Lerch, 1999, on behalf of the American Association for the Advancement of Science). This chapter has placed the findings of the 1987 national study of rape among college students in the context of a large body of ongoing, relevant research to illustrate that the study's findings are not isolated or spurious. Instead, the march of science has demonstrated that it is the stance of Gilbert and his followers that has been blown over. When fiscal and human resources are limited, decisions must be made about when efforts should shift from understanding the scope of problems to preventing problems. Although science has yet to answer all critical questions about rape (for a research agenda, see Crowell & Burgess, 1996), more than sufficient evidence warrants a move to implement scientifically grounded preventive interventions.

❖ REFERENCES

Acierno, R., Kilpatrick, D. G., Resnick, H. S., Saunders, B., & Best, C. L. (1996). Violent assault, posttraumatic stress disorder, and depression: Risk factors for cigarette use among adult women. *Behavior Modification, 20*, 363–384.

Bachar, K., & Koss, M. P. (2001). From prevalence to prevention: Closing the gap between what we know about rape and what we do. In C. M. Renzetti, R. K. Bergen, & J. L. Edelson (Eds.), *Sourcebook on violence against women* (pp. 117–142). Thousand Oaks, CA: Sage.

Bazelon, D. L. (1982). Veils, values, and social responsibility. *American Psychologist, 37*, 115–121.

Berliner, L. (1992). Facts or advocacy statistics: The case of acquaintance rape. *Journal of Interpersonal Violence, 7*, 121–126.

Breitenbecher, K. H. (2000). Sexual assault on college campuses: Is an ounce of prevention enough? *Applied and Preventive Psychology, 9*, 23–52.

Brener, N. D., McMahon, P. M., Warren, C. W., & Douglas, K. A. (1999). Forced sexual intercourse and associated health-risk behaviors among female college students in the United States. *Journal of Consulting and Clinical Psychology, 67*, 252–259.

Breslau, N., Davis, G., Andreski, P., & Peterson, E. (1991). Traumatic events and posttraumatic stress disorder in an urban population of young adults. *Archives of General Psychiatry, 48*, 216–222.

Bureau of Justice Statistics, U.S. Department of Justice. (1997). *Criminal victimization in the United States, 1994 (NCJ-162126)*. Washington, DC: U.S. Government Printing Office.

Campbell, R., Sefl, T., Barnes, H. E., Ahrens, C. E., Wasco, S. M., & Zaragoza-Diesfeld, Y. (1999). Community services for rape survivors: Enhancing psychological well-being or increasing trauma? *Journal of Consulting and Clinical Psychology, 67*, 847–858.

Cook, S. L. (1995). Acceptance and expectation of sexual aggression in college students. *Psychology of Women Quarterly, 19*, 181–194.

Crowell, N. A., & Burgess, A. W. (1996). *Understanding violence against women*. Washington, DC: National Academy of Sciences.

Davidson, J. R., Hughes, D. C., George, L. K., & Blazer, D. G. (1996). The association of sexual assault and attempted suicide within the community. *Archives of General Psychiatry, 53*, 550–555.

Federal Bureau of Investigation. (1999). *Crime in the United States*. Washington, DC: Department of Justice.

Fisher, B. S., Cullen, F. T., & Turner, M. G. (2000). *The sexual victimization of college women*. Washington, DC: U.S. Department of Justice, Office of Justice Programs, National Institute of Justice.

Fisher, B. S., Sloan, J. J., Cullen, F. T., & Lu, C. (1998). Crime in the ivory tower: The level and sources of student victimization. *Criminology, 36*, 671–710.

Frazier, P. A., & Seales, L. M. (1997). Acquaintance rape is real rape. In M. D. Schwartz (Ed.), *Researching sexual violence against women: Methodological and personal perspectives* (pp. 54–64). Thousand Oaks, CA: Sage.

Gidycz, C. A., Hanson, K., & Layman, M. J. (1995). A prospective analysis of the relationships among sexual assault experiences: An extension of previous findings. *Psychology of Women Quarterly, 19*, 5–29.

Gilbert, N. (1991). The phantom epidemic of sexual assault. *Public Interest, 103*, 54–65.

Gilbert, N. (1993). Examining the facts: Advocacy research overstates the incidence of date and acquaintance rape. In R. J. Gelles & D. R. Loseke (Eds.), *Current controversies on family violence* (1st ed., pp. 120–132). Newbury Park, CA: Sage.

Gilbert, N. (1997). Advocacy research exaggerates rape statistics. In M. R. Walsh (Ed.), *Women, men and gender: Ongoing debates* (pp. 236–242). New Haven: Yale University Press.

Greenfeld, L. A., Rand, M. R., Craven, D., Klaus, P. A., Ringel, C., Warchol, G., et al. (1998). *Violence by intimates: Analysis of data on crimes by current or former spouses, boyfriends, and girlfriends* (No. NCJ-167237). Washington, DC: U.S. Department of Justice.

Gutmann, S. (1990). Date rape: Does anyone really know what it is? *Playboy, 48*–56.

Gutmann, S. (1991). "It sounds like I raped you!" How date-rape re-education fosters confusion, undermines personal responsibility, and trivializes sexual violence. In O. Pocs (Ed.), *Human sexuality* (16th ed., pp. 217–221). Guilford, CT: Dushkin.

Harlow, C. W. (1991). *Female victims of violent crime* (NCJ 126826). Washington, DC: U.S. Department of Justice.

Hendrix, K. (1991, July 9). Defining controversy: Professor raises furor by claiming date rape statistics are inflated. *Los Angeles Times*, p. 1.

Hickman, S. E., & Muehlenhard, C. L. (1997). College women's fears and precautionary behaviors relating to acquaintance rape and stranger rape. *Psychology of Women Quarterly, 21*, 527–547.

Irwin, K. L., Edlin, B. R., Wong, L., Faruque, S., McCoy, H. V., & Ward, C. (1995). Urban rape survivors: Characteristics and prevalence of human immunodeficiency virus and other sexuality transmitted infections. *Obstetrics and Gynecology, 85*, 330–336.

Kahn, A., Mathie, V. A., Torgler, C. (1994). Rape scripts and rape acknowledgements. *Psychology of Women Quarterly, 18*, 53–66.

Kilpatrick, D. G., Acierno, R., Resnick, H. S., Saunders, B. E., & Best, C. L. (1997). A 2-year longitudinal analysis of the relationships between violent assault and substance use in women. *Journal of Consulting and Clinical Psychology, 65*, 834–847.

Kilpatrick, D. G., Acierno, R., Saunders, B., Resnick, H. S., Best, C. L., & Schnurr, P. P. (2000). Risk factors for adolescent substance abuse and dependence: Data from a national sample. *Journal of Consulting and Clinical Psychology, 68*, 19–30.

Kilpatrick, D. G., Edmunds, C. N., & Seymour, A. K. (1992). *Rape in America: A report to the nation.* Arlington, VA: National Victim Center.

Kilpatrick, D. G., Saunders, B. E., Veronen, L. J., Best, C. L., & Von, J. M. (1987). Criminal victimization: Lifetime prevalence, reporting to the police and psychological impact. *Crime and Delinquency, 33*, 479–489.

Koss, M. P. (1992). The underdetection of rape: Methodological choices that influence the magnitude of incidence estimates. *Journal of Social Issues, 48*, 61–75.

Koss, M. P. (1993). Detecting the scope of rape: A review of prevalence research methods. *Journal of Interpersonal Violence, 8*, 198–222.

Koss, M. P. (1996). The measurement of rape victimization in crime surveys. *Criminal Justice and Behavior, 23*, 55–69.

Koss, M. P. (2000). Shame, blame, and community: Justice responses to violence against women. *American Psychologist, 55*, 1332–1343.

Koss, M. P., Dinero, T. E., Seibel, C. A., & Cox, S. L. (1988). Stranger and acquaintance rape: Are there differences in the victim's experience? *Psychology of Women Quarterly, 12*, 1–24.

Koss, M. P., Gidycz, C. A., & Wisniewski, N. (1987). The scope of rape: Incidence and prevalence of sexual aggression and victimization in a national sample of higher education students. *Journal of Consulting and Clinical Psychology, 55*, 162–170.

Koss, M. P., Goodman, L. M., Browne, A., Fitzgerald, L. F., Keita, G. P., & Russo, N. F. (1994). *No safe haven: Male violence against women at home, at work, and in the community.* Washington, DC: American Psychological Association.

Layman, M. J., Gidycz, C. A., & Lynn, S. J. (1996). Unacknowledged versus acknowledged rape victims: Situational factors and posttraumatic stress. *Journal of Abnormal Psychology, 105*, 124–131.

Lerch, I. (1999, November/December). Letter from Chair, AAAS Committee on Scientific Freedom and Responsibility, to Ray Fowler, Executive Director of the American Psychological Association. *Science Directorate Newsletter, 12*(6), 2–3.

Letourneau, E. J., Resnick, H. S., Kilpatrick, D. G., Saunders, B. E., & Best, C. (1996). Comorbidity of sexual problems and posttraumatic stress disorder in female crime victims. *Behavior-Therapy, 27*, 321–336.

Lonsway, K. A. (1996). Preventing acquaintance rape through education: What do we know? *Psychology of Women Quarterly, 20*, 229–266.

Merrill, L. L., Newell, C. E., Milner, J. S., Koss, M. P., Hervig, L. K., Gold, S. R., Rosswork, S. G., & Thornton, S. R. (1998). Prevalence of premilitary adult sexual victimization and aggression in a navy recruit sample. *Military Medicine, 163*, 209–212.

Michigan Statutes Annotated. (1980). 28.788 (1) (h) (Callaghan) (Cum. Supp.).

Miller, T. R., Cohen, M. A., & Wiersema, B. (1996). *Victim costs and consequences: A new look* (NCJ 155282). Washington, DC: National Institute of Justice.

Mohler-Kuo, M., Dowdall, G. W., Koss, M. P., & Wechsler, H. (2004). Correlates of rape while intoxicated in a national sample of college women. *Journal of Studies on Alcohol. 65*(1), 37-45.

Muehlenhard, C. L., & Hollabaugh, L. C. (1988). Do women sometimes say no when they mean yes? The prevalence and correlates of women's token resistance to sex. *Journal of Personality and Social Psychology, 54*, 872–879.

Muehlenhard, C. L., & McCoy, M. L. (1991). Double standard/double bind: The sexual double standard and women's communication about sex. *Psychology of Women Quarterly, 15*, 447–461.

Muehlenhard, C. L., Powch, I. G., Phelps, J. L., & Giusti, L. M. (1992). Definitions of rape: Scientific and political implications. In J. White & S. B. Sorenson (Eds.), *Special Issue Journal of Social Issues* (Vol. 48, pp. 23–44).

National Center for Education Statistics. (1999, November). *Fall enrollment in postsecondary institutions, 1997. US Department of Education, Office of Educational Research and Improvement (NCES99-162).* Washington, DC: U.S. Government Printing Office.

Pino, N. W., & Meier, R. F. (1999). Gender differences in rape reporting. *Sex Roles, 40,* 979–990.

Rothbaum, B. O., Fao, E. B., Riggs, D. S., Murdock, T., & Walsh, W. (1992). A prospective examination of posttraumatic stress disorder in rape victims. *Journal of Traumatic Stress, 5,* 455–475.

Saltzman, L. E., Fanslow, J. L., McMahon, P. M., & Shelly, G. A. (1999). *Intimate partner violence surveillance: Uniform definitions and recommended data elements.* Atlanta: Centers for Disease Control and Prevention.

Shotland, R. L. (1992). A theory of the causes of courtship rape: Part 2. *Journal of Social Issues, 48,* 127–143.

Shotland, R. L., & Hunter, B. A. (1995). Women's "token resistant" and compliant sexual behaviors are related to uncertain sexual intentions and rape. *Personality and Social Psychology Bulletin, 21,* 226–236.

Sprecher, S., Hatfield, E., Corese, A., Potapova, E., & Levitskaya, A. (1994). Token resistance to sexual intercourse and consent to unwanted sexual intercourse: College students' dating experiences in three countries. *Journal of Sex Research, 31,* 125–132.

Sudderth, L. K. (1998). "It'll come right back at me": The interactional context of discussing rape with others. *Violence against Women, 4,* 572–594.

Tjaden, P., & Thoennes, N. (2000). *Extent, nature, and consequences of intimate partner violence.* Washington, DC: U.S. Department of Justice.

Wechsler, H., Dowdall, G. W., Maenner, G., Gledhill-Hoyt, J., & Lee, H. (1998). Changes in binge drinking and related problems among American college students between 1993 and 1997. *Journal of American College Health, 47,* 57–68.

White, J. W., & Sorenson, S. B. (1992). A sociocultural view of sexual assault: From discrepancy to diversity. *Journal of Social Issues, 48,* 187–195.

7

Advocacy Research Overstates the Incidence of Date and Acquaintance Rape

Neil Gilbert

The *Ms.* magazine Campus Project on Sexual Assault directed by Dr. Mary Koss (Koss, 1988; Koss, Dinero, Seibel, & Cox, 1988; Koss, Gidycz, & Wisniewski, 1987) is one of the largest, most widely disseminated, and most frequently cited studies of rape on college campuses in the United States. Because it was funded by the National Institute of Mental Health, this research effort was endorsed by a respected federal agency. Often quoted in newspapers and journals, on

AUTHOR'S NOTE: An earlier version of this chapter appeared as "Realities and Mythologies of Rape" in *Society* (May/June 1992).

television, and during the 1991 Senate hearings on sexual assault, the study findings have gained a degree of authority by process of repetition. Most of the time, however, those who cite the research findings take them at face value, understanding neither where the numbers come from nor what they actually represent. This is, in part, because this study benefits from the powerful aura of scientific research. Prefaced by sophisticated discussions of the research methods, the findings are presented in a virtual blizzard of data supported by a few convincing case examples and numerous references to lesser-known studies. But footnotes do not a scholarly endeavor make, and the value of quantitative findings depends on how accurately the research variables are measured, how well the sample is drawn, and the analysis to which the data are subject. Despite the respected funding source, frequent media acknowledgment, and aura of scientific respectability, a close examination of this study reveals serious flaws.

The *Ms.* study, undertaken in 1985, involved a survey of 6,159 students at 32 colleges. As Koss (1988) operationally defines the problem, 27 percent of the female college students in the study had been victims of rape (15 percent) or attempted rape (12 percent) an average of two times between the ages of 14 and 21. Using the same survey questions, which she claims represent a strict legal description of the crime, Koss calculates that during a 12-month period, 16.6 percent of college women were victims of rape or attempted rape and that more than one-half of these victims were assaulted twice (Koss, 1988; Warshaw, 1988). There are several reasons for serious researchers to question the magnitude of sexual assault conveyed by these findings.

To begin, there is a notable discrepancy between Koss's definition of *rape* and the way most of the women she labels as victims interpreted their experiences. When they were asked directly, 73 percent of the students whom Koss categorizes as victims of rape did not think that they had been raped. This discrepancy is underscored by the subsequent behavior of 42 percent of these women, who had sex again with the men who supposedly raped them. Of those categorized as victims of attempted rape, 35 percent later had sex with their purported offenders (Koss, 1988; Koss et al., 1987).

Rape and attempted rape were operationally defined in the *Ms.* study (Koss, 1988) by five questions, three of which referred to the threat or use of "some degree of physical force." Two other questions, however, were asked: "Have you had a man attempt sexual intercourse (get on top of you, attempt to insert his penis) when you didn't want to by giving you alcohol or drugs, but intercourse did not occur?" and "Have you had sexual intercourse when you didn't want to because a man gave you alcohol or drugs?" Some 44 percent of all the women identified as victims of rape and attempted rape in the previous year were so labeled because they responded positively to these awkward and vaguely worded questions.

What does it mean to have sex "because" a man gives you drugs or alcohol? A positive response does not indicate whether duress, intoxication, force, or the threat of force was present; whether the woman's judgment or control was substantially impaired; or whether the man purposefully got the woman drunk in order to prevent her resistance to sexual advances. It could mean that a few drinks lowered the respondent's inhibitions and she consented to an act she later regretted. Koss assumes that a positive answer signifies that the respondent engaged in sexual intercourse against her will because she was intoxicated to the point of being unable to deny consent (and that the man had administered the alcohol for this purpose). The item could have been clearly worded to denote "intentional incapacitation of the victim," but as the question stands it would require a mind reader to detect whether any affirmative response corresponds to this legal definition of rape.

Unable to address this problem, Koss takes the question as originally reported, "Have you had sexual intercourse with a man when you didn't want to because he gave you drugs or alcohol?" (Koss, 1988; Koss et al., 1987) and adds the words "to make you cooperate." Rather than helping the case, however, this revised version suggests that instead of being too drunk to deny consent, the respondent actually cooperated in the act of intercourse after taking drugs or alcohol.

Finally, there is a vast disparity between the *Ms.* study findings and the rates of rape and attempted rape that come to the attention of various authorities on college campuses. The number of rapes formally reported to the police on major college campuses is remarkably low— on the order of two to five incidents a year in schools with thousands of women (or fewer than 1 per 1,000 female students). It is generally agreed that many rape victims do not report their ordeals because of the embarrassment and callous treatment frequently experienced at the hands of the police. Over the past decade, however, rape crisis counseling and supportive services have been established on virtually every campus in the country. Highly sensitive to the social and psychological violations of rape, these services offer a sympathetic environment in which victims may come forward for assistance without having to make official reports to the police. Although these services usually minister to more victims than are reported to the local police, the numbers remain very low compared with the incidence rate of rape and attempted rape on college campuses as Koss defines the problem.

For example, applying Koss's finding of an annual incidence rate of 166 in 1,000 women (each victimized an average of 1.5 times) to the population of 14,000 female students at the University of California at Berkeley, in 1990, one would expect about 2,000 women to have experienced 3,000 incidents of rape or attempted rape that year. Yet on the Berkeley campus, two rapes were reported to the police in 1990, and between 40 and 80 women sought assistance from the campus rape counseling service. Although this represents a serious problem, its dimensions (3–6 cases in 1,000) are a mere fraction of the number (166 cases in 1,000) we would expect from the *Ms.* study.

What accounts for these discrepancies? Koss offers several explanations, some of which appear to derive from new data or additional analysis. Therefore, it is important to distinguish between the data originally reported in 1987–88 and later versions of the findings. The findings from the *Ms.* study were originally described in three articles, one by Koss and two coauthors in a 1987 issue of the *Journal of Consulting and Clinical Psychology* (Koss et al., 1987); the second (an expanded version of that article) authored by Koss (1988) as a chapter in the 1988 book *Rape and Sexual Assault II*; and the third by Koss, Dinero, Seibel, and Cox (1988) in a 1988 issue of the *Psychology of Women Quarterly*. Also published in 1988 was Robin Warshaw's book *I Never Called It Rape: The Ms. Report on Recognizing, Fighting, and Surviving Date and Acquaintance Rape* (Warshaw, 1988), with an afterword by Koss describing the research methods used in the *Ms.* project on which the book was based.

Two of these articles (Koss, 1988; Koss et al., 1987) reported that only 27 percent of the students whom Koss classified as rape victims believed they had been raped; the third article (Koss et al., 1988) provided additional data on how these supposed victims labeled their experiences. The findings reported in the third article indicate that (1) 11 percent of the women said they "don't feel victimized"; (2) 49 percent labeled the experience "miscommunication"; (3) 14 percent labeled it "crime, but not rape"; and (4) 27 percent said it was "rape." Although there was no indication that other data might have been available on this question, three years later a surprisingly different distribution of responses was put forth. Koss (1991a) reported that the students labeled as victims viewed the incident as follows:

> One quarter thought it was rape, one quarter thought it was some kind of crime but did not believe it qualified as rape, one quarter thought it was sexual abuse but didn't think it qualified as a crime, and one quarter did not feel victimized. (p. 6)

In a later paper, the gist of these new findings was revised, with Koss (1991c) recounting, "One quarter thought it was some kind of crime, but did not *realize* it qualified as rape; one quarter thought it was *serious* sexual abuse, but did not know it qualified as a crime" (p. 9; emphasis added).

Finally, with lack of both accuracy and candor, Cook and Koss (this volume) report, "In fact, half the rape victims identified in the national survey considered their experience to be rape or some crime similar to rape." The lack of accuracy is reflected in the fact that, as noted previously, the data originally reported show not "half," but only 41 percent of respondents labeling their experience as rape or as "a crime, but not rape" (Koss et al., 1988). The lack of candor is reflected in the fact that Cook and Koss fail to tell the reader that 49 percent of the women labeled their experience as "miscommunication."

These inconsistencies in the reported findings aside, the additional data are difficult to interpret. If one-quarter thought their incidents involved a crime, but not rape, what kind of crime did they have in mind? Were they referring to illegal activity at the time, such as under-age drinking or drug use? Despite Koss's elaboration on the data originally reported, at least one version of the findings reveals that 60 percent of the students either did not feel victimized or thought the incident was a case of miscommunication. Although in the second version many more of the women students assessed these sexual encounters in negative terms, the fact remains that 73 percent did *not* think they were raped.

Concerning the 42 percent of labeled victims who had sex afterward with their supposed assailants, again new data have surfaced. Describing this finding in her chapter in *Rape and Sexual Assault*, Koss (1988) originally noted,

> 42% of the women indicated that they had sex again with the offender on a later occasion, *but it is not known this was forced or*

voluntary; most relationships (87%) did *eventually* break up subsequent to the victimization. (p. 16; emphasis added)

Three years later, in a letter to the *Wall Street Journal,* Koss (1991b) is no longer surprised by this finding and evidently has new information revealing that when the students had sex again with the offenders on later occasions they were raped a second time and that the relationships broke up not "eventually" (as do most college relationships), but immediately after the second rape. Referring to this group's behavior, Koss explains:

Many victims reacted to the first rape with self-blame and thought that if they tried harder to be clear they could influence the man's behavior. Only after the second rape did they realize the problem was the man, not themselves. Afterwards, 87% of the women ended the relationship with the man who raped them. (1991b, p. 21)

As a further explanation of the students' behavior, Koss (1991b) suggests that because many of the students were sexually inexperienced, they "lacked familiarity with what consensual intercourse should be like" (p. 21).

These explanations are not entirely convincing. It is hard to imagine that many 21-year-old college women, even if sexually inexperienced, are unable to judge whether their sexual encounters are consensual. As for the victims blaming themselves and believing they might influence the men's behavior if they tried harder the second time, Koss offers no data from her survey to substantiate this process of reasoning. Although research indicates there is a tendency for victims of rape to blame themselves (Craig, 1990), there is no evidence that this induces them to have sex again with their assailants. One might note that there are cases of battered wives who stay with their husbands under insufferable circumstances, but it is not apparent that the battered woman syndrome applies to a large proportion of female college students.

With regard to the operational definition of rape used in the *Ms.* study and described in the earlier reports, Koss (1990, 1991a, 1991b) continues to claim that the study measures the act of "rape legally defined as penetration against consent through the use of force, or intentional incapacitation of the victim" (Koss in Warshaw, 1988, p. 207). No explanation is offered for how the researcher detects the *"intentional* incapacitation of the victim" from affirmative answers to questions such as, "Did you have unwanted sex because a man gave you alcohol?"

In reviewing the research methodology for the *Ms.* study, Koss (1988; Koss et al., 1987) explains that previous reliability and validity studies conducted on the 10-item Sexual Experience Survey (SES) instrument showed that few of the female respondents misinterpreted the questions on rape. However, the instrument originally referred to (Koss & Oros, 1982) contained neither of the questions dealing with rape or attempted rape "because a man gave you alcohol or drugs."

Finally, Koss accounts for the vast discrepancy between *Ms.* study figures and the number of students generally seen by rape counseling services or reported to authorities on college campuses by the assertion that most college women who are sexually violated by an acquaintance do not recognize themselves as victims of rape. According to Koss (1991b), many people do not realize that legal definitions of rape make no distinctions about the relationship between victim and offender. Contrary to this claim, findings from the U.S. Bureau of Justice Statistics (1991) suggest that the crime of rape by an acquaintance may not be all that difficult to comprehend; in recent years 33–45 percent of the women who said they were raped identified their assailants as acquaintances.

In support of the findings from the *Ms.* project, Koss uses many additional studies as sources of independent verification. Yet there are problems: Some of these studies used different definitions of forced sexual behavior, involved small or nonrepresentative samples, or are referred to without explanation or critical examination. Claiming that the *Ms.* survey's estimates of rape prevalence "are well-replicated in other studies," Koss (1991c, p. 8) refers us to Craig's (1990) discerning review of the literature to confirm the consistency of prevalence data on college students. This is a curious citation, given that Craig is, in fact, of a different opinion. Analyzing the problems of definition, Craig notes that studies "vary from use of force to threat of force, to use of manipulative tactics such as falsely professing love, threatening to leave the woman stranded, or attempting to intoxicate the woman" (p. 403). Even when studies use the same general definitions, their authors often develop idiosyncratic measures to operationalize the terms, all of which leads Craig to conclude "that this lack of consistency limits the comparability of studies and makes replication of results difficult" (p. 403).

❖ ADVOCACY NUMBERS: WHAT DO THEY MEAN?

The *Ms.* study is a highly sophisticated example of advocacy research. Under the veil of social science, elaborate research methods are employed to persuade the public and policymakers that a problem is vastly larger than commonly recognized. This is done in several ways: (1) by measuring a problem so broadly that it forms a vessel into which almost any human difficulty can be poured; (2) by measuring a group highly affected by the problem and then projecting the findings to society at large; (3) by asserting that a variety of smaller studies and reports with different problem definitions, methodologies of diverse quality, and varying results form a cumulative block of evidence in support of current findings; and (4) by changing definitions and revising data when research is criticized in the hope that no one will examine the facts as originally reported.

Advocacy research is not a phenomenon unique to studies of rape on campus. It is practiced in a wide variety of substantive problem areas and supported by groups that, as Peter Rossi (1987) suggests, share an "ideological imperative" maintaining that findings politically acceptable to the advocacy community are more important than the scientific quality of research from which they are derived; playing fast and loose with the facts is justifiable in the service of a noble cause; and data and sentiments that challenge conventional wisdom are to be condemned or ignored. Denounced for expressing objectionable sentiments, for example, folk singer Holly Dunn's hit, "Maybe I Mean Yes (When I Say No)" was clearly out of tune with the feminist rhetoric, "No means no." The controversy over these lyrics ignored Muehlenhard and Hollabaugh's (1988) inconvenient findings that 39 percent of the 610 college women they surveyed admitted to having said "No" to sexual advances when they really meant "Yes."

Although advocacy studies do little to elevate the standards of social science research, they can serve a useful purpose in bringing grave problems to public attention. No matter how it is measured, rape is a serious problem that creates an immense amount of human suffering. One might say that even if the rape research magnifies this problem in order to raise public consciousness, it is being done for a good cause, and in any case the difference is only a matter of degree. So why make an issue of the numbers?

The issue is not that advocacy studies simply overstate the incidence of legally defined rape, but the extent to which this occurs and what it means. After all, the difference between boiling and freezing is "only a matter of degree." The tremendous gap between estimates of rape and attempted rape emerging from data collected annually by the U.S. Bureau of Justice Statistics (U.S. Bureau of Justice Statistics [BJS], 1991) and the figures reported in advocacy studies have a critical bearing on our understanding of the issue at stake.

The BJS surveys, actually conducted by the Census Bureau, interview a random sample of about 62,000 households every six months. The confidentiality of responses is protected by federal law, and response rates are about 96 percent of eligible units. The interview schedule asks a series of screening questions such as the following: Did anyone threaten to beat you up or threaten you with a knife, gun, or some other weapon? Did anyone try to attack you in some other way? Did you call the police to report something that happened to you that you thought was a crime? Did anything happen to you which you thought was a crime, but you did not report to the police? A positive response to any of these screening items is followed up by further questions: What actually happened? How were you threatened? How did the offender attack you? What injuries did you suffer? When, where did it happen, what did you do, and so forth.

BJS findings are that 1.2 women in 1,000 over 12 years of age were victims of rape or attempted rape. This amounts to approximately 135,000 female victims in 1989. No trivial number—that annual figure translates into a lifetime prevalence rate of roughly 5–7 percent, which suggests that as many as 1 out of 14 women is likely to experience an incident of rape or attempted rape sometime over the course of her life. As in other victimization surveys, there are problems of subject recall, definition, and measurement in the BJS studies that, as Koss (1991a) and others (Jencks, 1991; Russell, 1984) have pointed out, lead to a underestimate of the amount of sexual assault. Yet even assuming that the BJS survey underestimated the problem by 50 percent—missing 1 out of every 2 cases of rape or attempted rape in the sample—lifetime prevalence rate would rise to 10–14 percent. Although this is an enormous level of sexual assault, at that rate the BJS estimates would still be dwarfed by the findings of Koss (1988) and Russell's (1982) studies, which suggest that 1 in 2 women will be victimized an average of twice in her lifetime. This brings us to the crux of the issue, which is that the huge differences between federal estimates and advocacy research findings have implications that go beyond matters of degree in measuring the size of the problem.

If 27 percent of female college students suffer an average of two incidents of rape or attempted rape by the time they are 21, the lifetime prevalence rate of these offenses is so high that one is driven to conclude that rape occurs so frequently as to be almost a norm in sexual relations, and that most men are rapists. This is a view advanced by a small but vocal group of advocates. "The truth that must be faced," according to Russell (1984), "is that this culture's notion of masculinity—particularly as it is applied to male sexuality—predisposes men to violence, to rape, to sexually harass, and to sexually abuse children" (p. 220). In a similar vein, Koss (1988) notes that her findings support the view that sexual violence against women "rests squarely in the middle of what our culture defines as 'normal' interaction between men and women" (p. 23). Catherine MacKinnon (1991), one of the leading feminists in the rape crisis movement, offers a vivid rendition of the theme that rape is a social disease afflicting most men. Writing in the *New York Times,* she advises that when men charged with the crime of rape come to trial, the court should ask, "Did this member of a group sexually trained to woman-hating aggression commit this particular act of woman-hating sexual aggression?"

❖ SOME DYSFUNCTIONAL CONSEQUENCES OF ADVOCACY RESEARCH

Advocacy research not only promulgates the idea that most men are rapists, it provides a form of seemingly scientific legitimacy for the promotion of social programs and individual behaviors that act on this idea. When asked if college women should view every man they see as a potential rapist, a spokeswoman for the student health services at the University of California, Berkeley, told the *Oakland Tribune,* "I'm not sure that would be a negative thing" (quoted in Brydoff, 1991). This echoes the instruction supplied in one of the most popular college guidebooks on how to prevent acquaintance rape. "Since you can't tell who has the potential for rape by simply looking," the manual warns, "be on your guard with every man" (Parrot, 1988, p. 3). Experts on date rape advise college women to take their own cars on dates or to have a backup network of friends ready to pick them up, to stay sober, to inform the man in advance what the sexual limits will be that evening, and to prepare for the worst by taking a course in self-defense beforehand (Warshaw, 1988). These instructions imply that dating men is a dangerous affair.

Beyond taking courses in self-defense, the implications drawn from advocacy research sometimes recommend more extreme measures. During a public lecture titled *The Epidemic of Sexual Violence Against Women*, Russell (1991) was asked by a member of the audience whether, in light of the ever-present danger, women should start carrying guns to protect themselves against men. Russell stated that personal armament was a good idea for women, but that they should probably take lessons to learn how to hit their targets. Her response was greeted by loud applause.

But not all feminists, or members of the rape crisis movement, agree with the view that all men are predisposed to be rapists. Gillian Greensite (1991), founder of the Rape Prevention Education program at the University of California at Santa Cruz, for example, writes that the seriousness of this crime "is being undermined by the growing tendency of some feminists to label all heterosexual miscommunication and insensitivity as acquaintance rape" (p. 15). This tendency, Greensite observes, "is already creating a climate of fear on campuses, straining relations between males and females" (p. 68).

Heightened confusion and strained relations between men and women are not the only dysfunctional consequences of advocacy research that inflates the incidence of rape to a level indicting most men. According to Koss's data, rape is an act that most educated women do not recognize as such when it happens to them, and after which almost half of the victims continue their relationships with the alleged rapists. Characterizing this type of sexual encounter as rape trivializes the trauma and pain suffered by the all too many women who are truly victims of this crime, and may ultimately make it more difficult to convict their assailants. In exaggerating the statistics on rape, advocacy research conveys an interpretation of the problem that advances neither mutual respect between the sexes nor reasonable dialogue about assaultive sexual behavior.

It is difficult to criticize advocacy research without giving an impression of not caring about the problem. However, one may be deeply concerned about the problem of rape and still wish to see a fair and objective analysis of its dimensions. Advocacy studies have, in their fashion, rung the alarm. Yet before the rush to arms, a more precise reading of the data is required if we are to draw an accurate bead on this problem and resolve it successfully.

❖ REPLY TO COOK AND KOSS

In this second edition of *Current Controversies on Family Violence,* Cook and Koss are unable to answer the critical questions raised about the *Ms.* study, particularly the researchers' shifting definitions, inconsistent interpretations of data, and their immense disregard for the way college women interpreted their own experiences: How many college women reading this volume would not know if they had been raped? Instead, Cook and Koss (this volume) continue to employ the common tactic of advocacy research, deflecting criticism of the *Ms.* study with claims that the study's findings are replicated in other studies, which are cited without critical analysis. Cook and Koss begin their chapter with the claim that "in a 12-month period, 76 per 1,000 college women experienced one or more attempted or completed rapes." What they do not tell the reader is that initially, using the *Ms.* study definition, Koss reported this figure to be 166 per 1,000 college women (the 76 per 1,000 college women is based on applying a more restrictive definition to the *Ms.* study data). In remarkable contrast to these figures, FBI (Federal Bureau of Investigation, 1993) data reveal that at 500 major colleges and universities with an overall population of 5 million students, only 408 cases of rape and attempted rape were reported to the police. This number yields an annual rate of .16 per 1,000 female students, which is 475 times smaller than Koss's findings—and 1,000 times smaller if one uses the *Ms.* study definition. Although it is generally agreed that many rape victims do not report their ordeals because of the embarrassment and callous treatment often experienced in the process, no one to my knowledge publicly claims that the problem is 475 (or 1,000) times greater than the number of cases reported to the police.

❖ REFERENCES

Brydoff, C. (1991, May 30). Professor: Rape figures are inflated. *Oakland Tribune,* p. 1.

Craig, M. E. (1990). Coercive sexuality in dating relationships: A situational model. *Clinical Psychology Review, 10,* 395–423.

Federal Bureau of Investigation. (1993). *Crime in the United States: Uniform crime reports, 1992.* Washington DC: U.S. Government Printing Office.

Greensite, G. (1991, Fall). Acquaintance rape clarified. In *Student Guide, University of California at Santa Cruz.* Santa Cruz: University of California.

Jencks, C. (1991). Is violent crime increasing? *American Prospect, 4,* 98–109.

Koss, M. P. (1988). Hidden rape: Sexual aggression and victimization in a national sample of students in higher education. In A. W. Burgess (Ed.), *Rape and sexual assault II* (pp. 1–25). New York: Garland.

Koss, M. P. (1990). Testimony in Senate hearings on women and violence. In *Women and violence: Hearings before the Committee on the Judiciary, United States Senate, 101st Congress, Second Session, Part 2* (pp. 27–43). Washington, DC: Government Printing Office.

Koss, M. P. (1991a, July 17). Statistics show sexual assaults are more prevalent than many realize. *Los Angeles Daily Journal,* p. 6.

Koss, M. P. (1991b, July 25). [Letter to the editor]. *Wall Street Journal,* p. 21.

Koss, M. P. (1991c). *Rape on campus: Facing the Facts.* Unpublished manuscript.

Koss, M. P., Dinero, T. E., Seibel, C. A., & Cox, S. L. (1988). Stranger and acquaintance rape: Are there differences in the victim's experience? *Psychology of Women Quarterly, 12,* 1–24.

Koss, M. P., Gidycz, C. A., & Wisniewski, N. (1987). The scope of rape: Incidence and prevalence of sexual aggression and victimization. *Journal of Consulting and Clinical Psychology, 50,* 455–457.

Koss, M. P, & Oros, C. (1982). The sexual experiences survey: A research instrument investigating sexual aggression and victimization. *Journal of Consulting and Clinical Psychology, 50,* 455–457.

MacKinnon, C. (1991, December 15). The Palm Beach hanging. *New York Times,* p. 15.

Muehlenhard, C. L., & Hollabaugh, L. C. (1988). Do women sometimes say no when they mean yes? The prevalence and correlates of women's token resistance to sex. *Journal of Personality and Social Psychology, 54,* 872–879.

Parrot, A. (1988). *Acquaintance rape and sexual assault prevention training manual.* Ithaca, NY: Cornell University.

Rossi, P. (1987). No good applied social research goes unpunished. *Society, 25*(1), 73–79.

Russell, D. E. H. (1982). *Rape in marriage.* New York: Macmillan.

Russell, D. E. H. (1984). *Sexual exploitation: Rape, child sexual abuse, and workplace harassment.* Beverly Hills, CA: Sage.

Russell, D. E. H. (1991, November 25). *The epidemic of sexual violence against women: A national crisis.* Berkeley: University of California, Seabury Lecture.

U.S. Bureau of Justice Statistics. (1991). *Criminal victimization in the United States, 1989.* Washington, DC: U.S. Department of Justice.

Warshaw, R. (1988). *I never called it rape: The Ms. report on recognizing, fighting, and surviving date and acquaintance rape.* New York: Harper & Row.

8

Proper Socialization Requires Powerful Love and Equally Powerful Discipline

John Rosemond

"All of the arguments raging in America's culture war," says Professor Francis Fukayama of George Mason University, "lead back to the breakdown of the traditional family brought about by the movement of women into the workforce and the separation of sex from reproduction." Quite so. Since it is clearly part and parcel of our culture war, the argument over whether or not parents should be allowed to spank children is really about the breakdown of the traditional family.

When the traditional family reigned supreme, parental discretion in disciplinary matters was taken for granted. If you heard one of your next-door neighbors' kids being spanked, you might have disapproved, but you didn't call the Spanking Gestapo and make a secret report. When the traditional family began its slow, ongoing dissolve, so too did the cultural norms with which it was associated, and nature abhors a vacuum. Where the traditional family once stood, the bureaucracy stands today, and the weaker the traditional family, the stronger the bureaucracy. One of the bureaucracies in question is Child Protective Services, the strength of which is attested to by the fact that parental discretion in matters of discipline is no longer taken for granted in America. Today, America's parents are painfully aware that CPS is "watching" (or certainly trying to watch) how they discipline their children and stands ready to swoop down and intervene should it decide that a parent is violating the largely unwritten canons of "disciplinary correctness," one of which is "Thou shalt not spank."

At this point, let me make perfectly clear that I do not "believe" in spankings. Here is what I believe:

- Human nature, brought into the world by every child, is not a pretty thing. Humans are, by nature, inclined toward narcissistic, antisocial behavior. The child must learn how to share, tell the truth, and obey legitimate authority.
- Proper socialization requires a combination of powerful love and equally powerful discipline. When love is lacking, discipline is likely to be violent.
- To be powerful, corrective discipline must be punitive, but it does *not* have to ever be corporal. It must simply (a) cause emotional discomfort and (b) create a lasting memory. One cannot reason a child into abandoning his or her antisocial inclinations. On the other hand, one can persuade a child that it is in his or her best interest to respect the interests of others without ever spanking the child.
- The evidence strongly attests to what is commonsensical: The happiest children are also the best behaved. Notable in this regard is the fact that the rate of child and teen depression has risen sharply since 1965. In other words, today's child is not likely to be as happy as was the typical child of a generation past. In my estimation, this is the result of a general weakening of both parental love and parental discipline. Today, what often passes for "love" is nothing more than indulging, enabling, and rescuing. And, today's parents seem convinced it is possible to correct misbehavior without ever making a child feel bad. Ironically, in days gone by, when children were made to feel bad when they misbehaved, children were generally happier.

This brouhaha produces some incredible narrow-mindedness and some equally incredible hysteria. One of the more narrow-minded notions is that recently expressed to me by a well-intentioned clinical social worker, who had gotten herself worked up because, in her view, I was "sanctioning child abuse."

"There is always an alternative to spanking," she pleaded.

She's absolutely right, of course, but the broader question is whether or not any alternative, in a given disciplinary situation, will be as effective as a spanking in deterring future instances of the same misbehavior. My opinion is that at certain times and in certain situations, when a certain child behaves in a certain antisocial way, a spanking is the most effective deterrent. Because it is in the best interests of both the child and society that the misbehavior in question be deterred as effectively as possible, the child's parents would do well to spank.

❖ THE ANTI-SPANKING IDEOLOGUES

My opinion is distinguished from that of such eminently ideological individuals as Murray Straus (this volume) and his fellow anti-spanking ideologues who would have us believe that spanking causes violent behavior. The evidence—which one does not have to obtain a government grant to collect—is otherwise. Most baby boomers were spanked. Few now are anything other than law-abiding citizens. Straus's research, the results of which he "spins" to suit his personal bias on the subject, supports only what is, again, commonsensical: Violent discipline, as dispensed by parents who do not love their children powerfully, inclines a child toward either violence or depression.

Overall, the research leads to the following conclusion: The most well-behaved and, therefore, well-adjusted children are those whose parents give themselves permission to spank, but do so only occasionally, if ever at all. For example, research by Diana Baumrind (1996a, 1996b) and Robert Larzelere (1996, 2000) supports neither the idea that spankings per se are bad nor the equally ludicrous notion that they are necessary. The only sensible conclusion: Sometimes, a spanking is the best disciplinary alternative, but the "some times" in question are few and far between. But this does not mean that parents who choose not to spank will necessarily raise children who are less well-behaved or well-adjusted than parents who do so occasionally. The general rule does not predict specific outcomes.

"So," a passionate anti-spanker recently rejoined, "why spank at all?"

That is a red herring. The issue is not whether parents should or should not spank. The issue is whether the government or the individual parent should be allowed to decide this matter. I do not feel passionately about spankings either one way or the other. I do, however, feel passionately about government deciding how parents can and cannot discipline. Anyone who thinks that government, if given authority over this matter, will stop there is naive. The rule of bureaucracies, recognized by the founding fathers and verified historically, is they expand. If the state is permitted to disallow parental spanking, there will be no turning back. The state will begin to disallow other forms of discipline it arbitrarily deems "psychologically incorrect." Eventually, it will be impossible for parents to discipline children in any powerful (effective) fashion—a state of affairs that is clearly not in the best interest of children. Furthermore, when the state is allowed to make final determination in child-rearing matters, the autonomy of the family unit is at an end. Karl Marx was quite specific in this regard: The autonomy of the family unit was inimical to the realization of his utopian dream.

❖ THE PRO-SPANKING IDEOLOGUES

But then, much of the rhetoric on the other side of the Great Spanking Divide is equally disingenuous and dangerous. Witness Marvin Munyon, President of the Madison, Wisconsin-based conservative Family Research Forum. In late September 2000, Munyon told an audience of parents in Eau Clair, Wisconsin, that spanking was the most effective of all deterrents to misbehavior and that in designing a child's rear end, God had spanking at least partly in mind. Adding further disinformation to an issue that is already well past the point of disinformation overload, Munyon said that spanking builds self-esteem. Munyon is obviously not aware that research consistently finds that high self-esteem is associated with low self-control (Baumeister, 1999; Baumeister & Heatherton, 1996; Baumeister, Heatherton, & Tice, 1993).

What really bothered me the most, however, was Munyon's claim that parents should never use their hands to spank. Rather, they should use paddles and switches and the like. Why? Well, according to Munyon, because every intelligent human being knows that a child should associate only love with parents' hands, not discipline. I think it is reasonable to say Munyon also meant that a child should not be afraid of his parents' hands. Instead of contributing to a rational discussion of the pros and cons of spanking, he engages in hyperbole. Munyon is clearly no scientist. There is *no* evidence to support his contention that spankings promote good self-esteem. Nor is there evidence that spankings cause children to be afraid of their parents' hands. Furthermore, common sense will tell you that the hand is preferred over an object like a paddle for the simple reason that when a hand hits a bottom, both the bottom and the hand sting. Therefore, a parent using his or her hand is receiving important feedback concerning when "enough is enough."

Marvin Munyon is clearly unaware that the group of anti-spanking zealots, such as Straus (this volume), wants nothing more than for him to keep babbling to as many audiences as will have him.

❖ CONCLUSION

For Murray Straus and other anti-spanking lobbyists, operating within the free market of ideas, it is fine to try to *persuade* parents not to spank. But the intentions of the anti-spanking lobby are zealous. They are convinced they occupy the moral high ground and that those who disagree with them are hopelessly benighted. Their self-righteousness justifies their belief that the parent who cannot be *persuaded* to their point of view should be *forced* to submit to it, for the sake of his or her children. This argument is both disingenuous and dangerous.

The anti-spanking lobby is determined to see parental spanking made illegal, as it is in Sweden, where a follow-up study found that the problem of child abuse had significantly worsened since passage of that ill-advised law. If the anti-spanking lobby succeeds, parental discretion in disciplinary matters is in grave danger.

❖ REFERENCES

Baumeister, R. F. (1999). Low self-esteem does not cause aggression. *APA Monitor 1*, 7.

Baumeister, R. F., & Heatherton, T. F. (1996). Self-regulation failure: An overview. *Psychological Inquiry 7*, 1–15.

9

Children Should Never, Ever, Be Spanked No Matter What the Circumstances

Murray A. Straus

There are many reasons why children should never be spanked or subjected to any other kind of corporal punishment. Three of the most fundamental reasons:

1. Spanking has serious harmful side effects that parents have no way of seeing, because such effects do not show up until later.

2. Spanking is no more effective than other methods of correction and control, and it is therefore unnecessary to subject children to the risk of the harmful side effects.

3. Spanking contradicts the ideal of nonviolence in the family and society.

Progress is being made toward the goal of nonviolence in the family. Assaults on partners have decreased (Straus, 1995). Fewer and fewer parents and professionals who advise parents approve of spanking (American Academy of Pediatrics, 1998; Schenck, Lyman, & Bodin, 2000; Straus & Mathur, 1996). There has also been a large decrease in the percentage of parents who use corporal punishment (CP) with *school-age* children (Straus & Stewart, 1999).

No one is sure about the reasons for these important changes. In addition, there are some paradoxical aspects to the trend away from CP. One paradox is that, although only about half of American parents now believe that spanking is sometimes necessary (Straus & Mathur, 1996), 94 percent of parents still spank toddlers (Straus & Stewart, 1999). A second paradox is that although ever-larger percentages of professionals who provide information to parents are opposed to spanking, few directly advise parents not to spank. Even fewer advise parents to *never* spank.

Given these paradoxical discrepancies, one objective of this chapter is to draw on the research evidence to explain the discrepancy between what parents believe and what they actually do, and the discrepancy between what professionals who advise parents believe and what they actually advise.

A second objective is to identify the implications of the research evidence for advising parents about spanking and other forms of CP. A particular focus is on whether parents should be advised to *never* spank or to use other forms of CP under any circumstance. The analysis suggests a third paradox: Focusing almost exclusively on helping parents learn alternative strategies to CP unwittingly contributes to *perpetuating* CP.

❖   THE THREE PARADOXES

It is important to identify the conditions that explain why almost everyone spanks toddlers, because that can contribute to understanding disciplinary strategies used by parents and to developing methods to help parents shift to nonviolent discipline strategies. The three paradoxes about spanking provide a framework for explaining why almost everyone spanks toddlers, and what to do to change that.

Paradox 1: Approval of Spanking
Has Decreased, But Spanking Toddlers Has Not

Most aspects of CP have changed in major ways in the last generation. The percentage of parents who believe that CP is necessary dropped from 94 percent in 1968 to 55 percent in 1999 (Straus, 2004). The percentage of parents who hit adolescents has also dropped by about half—from about two-thirds in 1975 to one-third in 1995 (Straus & Stewart, 1999). Despite these major steps away from CP, 94 percent of the parents of toddlers in our most recent national survey used CP. Moreover, other studies show that parents who spanked toddlers did so an average of about three times a week (Giles-Sims et al., 1995; Holden, Coleman, & Schmidt, 1995). Obviously, we need to understand why parents who "don't believe in spanking" continue to hit toddlers and do it so frequently.

Paradox 2: Professionals Opposed to Spanking Fail to Advise Parents to Never Spank

• Many pediatricians, nurses, developmental psychologists, and parent educators are now opposed to CP, at least in principle. Yet when I suggest to these professionals that it is essential to tell parents to *never* spank or use any other type of CP, with rare exception, that idea has been rejected. Some object because they believe that it would turn off parents. Some object because they think parents would not know what else to do, and children would not receive proper direction and discipline (see Straus, 2001b). They argue for what some call a "positive approach," by which they mean teaching parents alternative disciplinary strategies, as compared to the "negative approach" of advising to never spank. As a result, the typical pattern is to say nothing about spanking.

• Both the movement away from spanking and an important limitation of that movement are illustrated by the publication of the "Guidelines for Effective Discipline" of the American Academy of Pediatrics (1998). This publication recommends that parents avoid CP. However, it carefully avoids saying *never* spank. The difference between advising parents to avoid spanking and advising them to never spank may seem like splitting hairs. However, the typical sequence of parent–child interaction that eventuates in CP (described later) suggests that, in the absence of a commitment to *never* spank, even parents who are against spanking are likely to continue to spank toddlers.

Paradox 3: Focusing Exclusively on Teaching Alternatives Results in Almost Everyone Spanking

• This paradox grows out of the combination of the high short-run failure rate of all methods of correcting and controlling the behavior of toddlers and the myth that spanking works when other things do not. As will be shown later in the chapter, when toddlers are corrected for a misbehavior (such as for hitting another child or disobeying), the "recidivism" rate is about 50 percent within two hours and about 80 percent within the same day. Consequently, on any given day, a parent is almost certain to find that so-called alternative disciplinary strategies such as explaining, deprivation of privileges, and time out, do not work. When that happens, because our culture teaches that spanking works when other things have failed, parents turn to spanking. The result is the infamous statistic "94 percent of parents spank toddlers."

Because these paradoxes are rooted in cultural myths about spanking, it is necessary to consider the research evidence on the two most directly relevant: the myth that spanking is harmless if done by loving parents, and the myth that spanking may sometimes be necessary because it works when other methods do not (see Straus, 2001b, for other myths about spanking).

❖ THE MYTH THAT SPANKING IS HARMLESS

In a meta-analysis of 88 studies, Gershoff (2002) located 117 tests of the hypothesis that CP is associated with harmful side effects such as aggression and delinquency in childhood, crime and antisocial behavior as an adult, low empathy or conscience, poor parent–child relations, and mental health problems such as depression. Of the 117 tests, 110, or 94 percent, found evidence of harmful effects of CP. This is an almost unprecedented degree of consistency in research findings. A number of these studies controlled for parental warmth, and showed that CP is harmful even when done by loving parents. However, because the reviewed studies were cross-sectional, it is just as plausible to interpret most of them as showing that misbehavior, delinquency, and mental illness cause parents to use CP in their attempts to deal with those problems.

That interpretation has become dramatically less plausible since 1997. Seven studies that mark a watershed change have become available since then. These are "prospective" studies that take into account the child's misbehavior at Time 1 as well as whether or not the parents used CP. They examine the *change* in behavior subsequent to the CP. These studies therefore provide evidence on whether responding to the misbehavior by spanking benefited the child in the sense of resulting in a better-behaved child as measured two or more years later (as most parents think), or harmed the child in the sense of *increasing* misbehavior and mental health problems three years later. *All* of these prospective studies found harmful, not beneficial, effects.

The first two of these studies found that, on average, spanked children had an *increase* in misbehavior two years later, whereas unspanked children had a *decrease* in misbehavior (Gunnoe & Mariner, 1997; Straus, Sugarman, & Giles-Sims, 1997). A study by Brezina (1999) found that CP was associated with a subsequent increase in the percentage of children who hit a parent. Simons, Lin, and Gordon (1998) found that, when children whose parents used CP were in high school, they were more likely to hit a dating partner than were children whose parents had not spanked at the start of the study.

Three of my studies (Straus, 2004) found that, after controlling for many other variables, CP use at the start of the study was associated with:

- A slower rate of cognitive development than children who were not spanked
- Lowered scores on a test of educational achievement
- An increased probability of crime as an adult

❖ THE MYTH THAT SPANKING WORKS WHEN OTHER METHODS FAIL

The idea that spanking works when other methods fail may be the most prevalent myth about spanking. Even people who do not believe in spanking on philosophical grounds or because of the evidence of harmful side effects tend to think that spanking works when other methods have failed. For example, Dr. Lewis R. First of Children's Hospital, Boston, said he was opposed to CP, but he also said, "If a child repeatedly runs into traffic, for example, you may want to play the big card" (Lehman, 1989). This seeming contradiction probably occurred because, for Dr. First, protecting the safety of the child was even more important that avoiding CP. But it is based on the mistaken assumption that spanking works when other things do not.

If it is true that spanking is effective when other methods have failed, eliminating spanking would be a questionable goal. Fortunately there is excellent evidence on this issue from rigorous experiments and also from a carefully done short-term prospective study. There is also a great deal of less definitive evidence on the effectiveness of spanking relative to other discipline techniques. For example, a large body of experimental research on animals shows that punishment, including corporal punishment, is not more effective than other modes of training, especially reward.

To adequately examine the effectiveness of spanking, it is important to distinguish between effectiveness in three time periods: in the immediate situation, in the short run (the next few hours or days), and in the long run (months or years subsequent to the misbehavior that was corrected).

Immediate-Situation Effectiveness

Spanking for Breaking Time Out. The most definitive evidence that spanking is no more effective than other modes of discipline is from experimental studies that randomly assigned spanking as one of the means of correcting a child who leaves the time-out chair before the time is up. Experiments by Roberts and colleagues (Day & Roberts, 1983; Roberts, 1988; Roberts & Powers, 1990) demonstrated that spanking was no more effective than other methods of training a child to remain in time out for the specified time. An example of an alternative to spanking for breaking time out is what they call the "escape-barrier" method. For the escape-barrier method, a child who breaks time out is placed in a room with a waist-high piece of plywood held across the open door for a period of only one minute. The barrier method required an average of eight repetitions before the child was trained to stay in time out by himself, but so did spanking. On average, it took 8.3 spankings to secure compliance. In addition, the spanked children engaged in more disruptive behavior (such as yelling and whining) before achieving compliance. In short, spanking had the same failure rate as the barrier method. If repeated enough times, spanking also had the same success rate as other methods. The key is that, with toddlers, on average, nothing works without repetition, including spanking.

Spanking for Disobedience and Fighting. Larzelere, Schneider, Larson, and Pike (1996) studied the discipline techniques used by mothers of 40 children ages 2–3. They asked the mothers to use a "discipline record" form to write down each misbehavior for a sample of days. The mothers entered the nature of the misbehavior and the type of corrective

Figure 9.1   The Number of Hours Until a Toddler Repeats a Misbehavior
Is About the Same No Matter What the Parents Do to Correct
the Misbehavior (2,853 Instances of Disobedience and 785
Instances of Fighting by 40 Children Age 2–3).

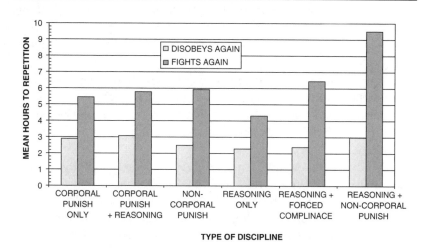

SOURCE: Larzelere & Merenda, 1994, Tables 2 & 3.

measure that was used. The results were similar to the experiments on
teaching children to observe time out. They showed that *all* methods
of discipline had a high short-term failure rate as measured by the
number of hours until the child repeated the misbehavior. The "recidivism rate" for misbehavior by the toddlers was about 50 percent within
two hours. A few children repeated the misbehavior within two minutes.
By the end of the day, 80 percent had repeated the misbehavior.

Figure 9.1 compares six discipline scenarios in the average number
of hours until a repetition of the misbehavior occurred. An effective
discipline method is one that not only stops the behavior, but also teaches
the child to not do it again. Therefore, the longer the time before the
misbehavior reoccurs, the more effective the method. Using this measure
of effectiveness, Figure 9.1 shows that the six discipline types had
about the same degree of effectiveness.

CP, either alone or in combination with reasoning, worked no
better than reasoning alone, noncorporal punishment alone, reasoning
and CP, and so on. However, there was one combination of discipline
methods that does seem to be more effective. It is the right-hand bar in
Figure 9.1. It shows that children whose mothers used "reasoning and

*non*corporal punishment" avoided fighting again longer than the children of mothers who used other methods, but the difference was not large enough to be statistically reliable.

Other Studies. Another study that contradicts the idea that spanking teaches a lesson that children won't forget comes from interviewing a representative sample of 1,002 mothers in two Minnesota counties (Straus & Mouradian, 1998). The mothers were asked what was the last misbehavior for which they had spanked their child. They were then asked if they had previously spanked for that misbehavior. Seventy-three percent said they had previously spanked for that misbehavior. This can be interpreted as showing that spanking had a 73 percent failure rate.

A study by Fower and Chapieski (1986) observed 18 mothers interacting with their 14-month-old children. They recorded the children's response to requests by the mother. Given the age of the children, all of these had to be relatively simple requests, such as "Come here" and "Put than down." The children whose mothers rarely or never spanked failed to comply with the mother's requests in 31 percent of the interactions, whereas the children whose mothers relied on spanking did not comply in 49 percent of the interactions observed. This means that spanking was associated with a 58 percent *greater* rate of misbehavior. Thus CP was, on average, less effective in teaching a lesson the child will not forget than were noncorporal disciplinary strategies.

Although this study involved only 18 children, and neither this study nor the Minnesota study were experimental or prospective studies, when combined with the experimental and longitudinal studies the weight of the evidence strongly indicates that it is a myth that spanking works when other methods fail. Spanking is no more effective than noncorporal modes of correction and control, as the longitudinal studies show, and in the long run is less effective or counterproductive.

❖ WHY SPANKING IS NO MORE EFFECTIVE—AND
    PROBABLY LESS EFFECTIVE—THAN OTHER METHODS

The Short Run

There is little doubt that spanking will, on average, stop misbehavior, at least at that moment. But why is such a strong step no more effective than nonviolent discipline in "teaching a lesson" that lasts even a few hours or days? A main reason is that, as shown in Figure 9.1, with toddlers, *every* mode of discipline has a high short-term failure rate. With spanking, however, at least two other things interfere with it working better than other methods of correction and control.

Spanking Interferes With Cognitive Functioning. Being slapped or spanked is a frightening and threatening event that arouses strong negative emotions such as humiliation, sadness, and anger. Children also experience CP as highly stressful (Turner & Finkelhor, 1996). Fright, stress, and other strong negative emotions can result in cognitive deficits such as erroneous or limited coding of events and diminished elaboration (Heuer & Reisberg, 1992; Meerum Terwogt & Olthof, 1989). To the extent that spanking arouses such emotions, it interferes with learning. Moreover, it can evoke resentment and defiance, which further impede learning and may be part of the explanation for the long-term boomerang effect of spanking.

Spanking Does Not Provide an Explanation of the Problem. The effectiveness of spanking is also limited because toddlers and infants may not understand the reason for being hit. Imagine a toddler who is pushing food off a highchair tray. The parent says "Stop that!" When the child does it again, the parent slaps the child's hand. Toddlers do not understand that pushing food off the tray creates a mess and therefore do not understand why they are being hit. The same principle applies, and perhaps more strongly, to being spanked for doing something that is potentially dangerous, such as touching a food mixer while watching a parent prepare dinner. The child who is spanked for doing that may come away with the idea that the danger is the parent, because the child does not understand the idea of "potential danger." The learning from these situations comes from the parent also *explaining* what is wrong with pushing food off a tray or touching a mixer and probably occurs despite the CP rather than because of it.

The Long Run

The research evidence clearly shows that, in addition to being no more effective in the short run, in the long run, spanking is *less* effective. What could account for the lower effectiveness of spanking compared to other methods of correction and control?

Less Well-Developed Conscience. One of the earliest hints of the long-run problems with spanking was in a study by Sears, Maccoby, and Levin (1957) of 379 five-year-old children. They found that spanking was associated with a less adequately developed conscience. Spanking teaches a child to avoid misbehavior if a parent is watching, or will learn about it, rather than avoiding misbehavior because the parents have explained why some things are right and others wrong. When parents explain, children gradually understand and accept these standards, and they are likely to remain in effect in situations when no parent is present, and probably also for life. Proponents of spanking, of course, believe that this is what spanking accomplishes, but Sears, Maccoby, and Levin (1957) and many others since then (see Gershoff, 2002) have found the opposite.

Feasibility of External Control Diminishes With Age. The long-term effectiveness of spanking is also low because, from school age on, children are increasingly out of sight of the parents. Hence, reliance on external controls such as spanking puts a child at an increased risk of misbehavior because, as a child grows older, the feasibility of external controls diminishes.

Weakens Child-to-Parent Bond. Although most children accept the legitimacy of parents spanking, they also resent it and feel angry with their parents for doing it. Many even say they hated their parents for doing it (Straus, 2001a, p. 154). Because spanking or other legal CP typically continues for 13 years (Straus & Stewart, 1999), bit by bit, this anger and resentment chips away at the bond between parent and child (Straus & Hill, 2004). A strong child-to-parent bond is important because children are more likely to accept parental restrictions and follow parental standards if there is a bond of affection with the parent. A strong bond facilitates internalizing the rules for behavior and developing a conscience. Many empirical studies, starting with Hirschi (1969), have found a link between a weak parent–child bond and juvenile delinquency (Hindelang, 1973; Rankin & Kern, 1994; Wiatrowski & Anderson, 1987).

Decreased Opportunity to Acquire Cognitive and Social Skills. When parents explain *why* they are spanking, the adverse effect of spanking is reduced but not eliminated (Larzelere, 1986). More generally and also more importantly, to the extent that a parent decides, either as a first resort or a last resort, that they have to spank, it denies the child an opportunity to observe and participate in conflict resolution strategies that are important in many life situations. Children of parents who do not spank and whose parents enforce the rules by explaining, negotiating, and creating appropriate alternatives and compromises are to that extent more likely to themselves acquire and use these vital skills.

❖ WHY IS CORPORAL PUNISHMENT PERCEIVED AS MORE EFFECTIVE THAN IT IS?

Research showing that CP is no more effective than other discipline techniques, even as a last resort, fly in the face of what almost everyone thinks, including people who do not believe in spanking. Why just about everyone think this, despite the evidence of their own experience with having to spank repeatedly, and despite the research evidence, cries out for an explanation. If these are the scientific facts and the facts of daily experience, why do parents believe that spanking is so effective? A number of different processes probably come together to produce this belief.

Selective Perception of Effectiveness

Even though every parent can observe the short-run high failure rate of spanking, few perceive it. The selective perception results from the cultural belief and expectation that spanking is effective. When a child misbehaves and the parent explains and the child does it again, the repetition is attributed to the ineffectiveness of reasoning with a young child. But, as explained previously, when a parent spanks and the child does it again, it is not perceived as indicating the ineffectiveness of spanking, but as indicating the need to spank again. As the time-out experiments show, repetition of spanking does result in compliance, but these same experiments also show that the repetition of just putting the child back in the time-out chair is equally effective and is accompanied by less disruptive behavior such as crying, yelling, and whining.

Confusion With Consistency and Perseverance. The studies reviewed previously show that all methods of discipline, including spanking, have a high failure rate with toddlers. It takes a great deal of time and many repetitions for a young child to internalize standards of behavior.

When non-spanking methods are used, and the child repeats the misbehavior, parents give up after a few tries and turn to spanking as a presumably more effective solution. They do not know the results of the research that shows that *all* methods, including spanking, have a high short-run failure rate. Ironically, when parents turn to spanking, or when they use spanking in the first place, they will spank over and over again, until the child does learn. They then attribute the success to the spanking, not the consistency and persistence of the discipline.

The consistency and persistence displayed by spanking parents in doing it over and over again is exactly right, but unfortunately, applied to the wrong method. When parents are as consistent and persistent in the use of other methods of discipline, they are as or more successful than spanking, but without the increased risk of the serious harmful side effects.

Emotional Gratification

Another part of the explanation may be that, when a child misbehaves and repeats the misbehavior and the parent is angry and frustrated, hitting the child may be emotionally rewarding in the sense that it can be experienced as relieving frustration over the child's misbehavior.

Confusion With Retribution

Part of the reason for spanking despite the evidence that it is not an effective form of punishment is the idea of "just deserts" or retribution. The belief that children should "pay" for their misbehavior is a moral principle, not an indication of change in the behavior of the child. However, when a child is made to pay for his or her misbehavior, it is probably often confused with effectiveness.

Long-Term Effects Are Not Observable

Finally, spanking is perceived as more effective than it is because parents cannot see the long-term harmful effect. If an effect such as delinquency or depression is going to occur, it rarely does so until months or years down the road. Moreover, when there is delinquency or depression, the possibility that it is the result of CP is so inconsistent with the cultural myth that spanking by loving parents is harmless that it is almost unimaginable. The only way parents can know about these links is by being informed of the results of the research showing that spanking increases the probability of delinquency, depression, and other maladaptive behaviors.

❖ BENEFICIAL VERSUS HARMFUL SIDE EFFECTS

Table 9.1 summarizes the evidence on the effectiveness of spanking as compared to other discipline strategies. The last row of the table on side effects, and especially the lower right cell, requires additional comment.

All methods of discipline are likely to have side effects, that is, to result in behaviors by the child that were not necessarily part of the behavior the parent intended to influence. The side effects of spanking are overwhelmingly to produce behaviors that the parents would not want if they had been able to choose, as shown by 110 of the 117 studies reviewed by Gershoff (2002). The side effects of other modes of discipline, while not the direct focus of much research, are beneficial. Take as an example one of the pioneer studies of CP by Sears, Maccoby, and Levin (1957), which found that noncorporal methods of discipline have the side effect of the child developing a stronger conscience and being less physically aggressive.

When parents use hitting as a method of discipline, the side effect is a child who does a lot of hitting. Similarly, when parents consistently use explanation and reasoning as a means of correcting and influencing the child, the side effect is likely to be a child who uses and insists on a lot of explanation and reasoning. Ironically, this is a side effect that

Table 9.1   Effectiveness and Side Effects of Corporal Punishment Compared to Noncorporal Discipline

Effectiveness and Side Effects	Corporal Punishment	Noncorporal Discipline
Immediate Effectiveness	High	High
Short-Term Effectiveness (hours, days)	Low	Low
Long-Term Effectiveness (months, years)	Makes worse	High
Side Effects	Harmful	Beneficial

in the short run can be a problem, because a child who uses and expects a reason and an explanation for everything can be exasperating, even infuriating. However, while that behavior may be exasperating from a child, it represents exactly the kind of behavior that most parents want to see in their child as an adult.

❖ WHY "NEVER SPANK" MUST BE THE ADVICE TO PARENTS

Spock (Spock & Rothenberg, 1992) and many others now advise parents to "avoid spanking if you can." That seems like sensible advice. However, as noted earlier, within the same day 80 percent of toddlers will repeat a misbehavior for which they were corrected, no matter what the mode of discipline. This means that almost all parents who follow the advice to "avoid spanking if you can" will conclude that they can't avoid it because they have seen with their own eyes that the alternatives did not work. They fall back on the myth that spanking works when other methods have failed, not realizing that *all* methods of discipline have a high failure rate with toddlers. Because of this set of circumstances, reliance on teaching alternative disciplinary techniques by itself is not sufficient. They must be advised to *never* spank.

Unless child psychologists, parent educators, pediatricians, and others who advise parents communicate an unambiguous "Never spank" message, almost all toddlers will continue to be spanked.

Professionals Need to Be Informed

In order to effectively communicate a "Never spank" message, professionals who advise parents must themselves be informed about the research evidence and its implications. The key points to cover are the research evidence that:

- All methods of correction and control have a high failure rate with toddlers. Therefore, noncorporal discipline strategies will be experienced as "not working."
- CP is not more effective than other modes of correction and control.
- CP has harmful side effects.

This evidence makes it necessary to advise parents to never, ever, under any circumstance, hit a child. Professionals need be informed about the research evidence that makes it necessary to unambiguously advise parents to never spank. The success of the never-spank approach in Sweden has shown that such an approach is not only necessary in principle but that it has been very effective.

Since the passage of the no-spanking law and the steps to inform every parent, *and every child,* in Sweden that CP is wrong and is contrary to national policy, use of CP has decreased from rates that were about the same those as in the United States to a small minority of parents. So have the rates of crime, drug abuse, and suicide by youth decreased (Durrant, 1999). The Swedish experience shows that an absolute never-spank approach has worked to reduce use of CP. It has also shown that the disaster foreseen by the critics of the Swedish law—that without the ability to spank "when necessary," parents would lose control and Sweden would become a nation of kids running wild—has not occurred.

Once child psychologists, pediatricians, and other professionals have been informed about the research and accept the implication that parents must be advised to never spank (as compared to advising parents to "avoid it if you can"), the key steps are relatively inexpensive, and given a desire to do so, relatively easy to implement. Some examples of these steps:

- Parent education programs, such as STEP, which are now silent on spanking, can be revised to include the evidence that spanking does *not* work better than other disciplinary tactics, even in the short run; and specifically to say *"Never* spank."
- The Public Health Service can follow the Swedish model and sponsor no-spanking public service announcements on TV and on milk cartons.
- A "Never Spank" poster and pamphlets can be displayed in pediatrician's offices and hospital maternity departments.
- A warning notice can be put on birth certificates such as:

WARNING: SPANKING HAS BEEN DETERMINED TO BE DANGEROUS TO THE HEALTH AND WELL-BEING OF YOUR CHILD—*DO NOT EVER, UNDER ANY CIRCUMSTANCES, SPANK OR HIT YOUR CHILD.*

The research cited in this chapter shows that there are many harmful effects of CP and many benefits of avoiding CP, but they are virtually impossible for parents to perceive by observing their children. The situation with spanking is parallel to that of smoking. Smokers in the past could perceive the short-run satisfaction from a cigarette, but had no way to see the adverse health consequences down the road until they were informed about the research. Similarly, parents can perceive the beneficial effects of a slap. However, it is difficult for them to perceive the equal effectiveness and equal short-term failure rate of alternatives. Most important, like smokers, they have no way of looking a year or more into the future to see if there is a harmful side effect of having hit their child to correct misbehavior. The only way parents can know this is through a major effort to inform all parents about the scientific evidence emphasizing two key points:

1. Spanking increases the risk of many behavior problems that parents want their children to avoid.

2. There is no need to put a child at risk for these problems because other methods of discipline are just as effective in the short run and more effective in the long run.

The Ethics of Advising Parents Never to Spank

Some defenders of CP argue that it is unethical to advise parents to never spank until there is absolutely conclusive evidence on the two key issues just mentioned (Larzelere, Baumrind, & Polite, 1998). The evidence from the experimental and prospective studies summarized in this book, although extremely strong, is not absolutely conclusive. Nevertheless, it *requires* informing and advising parents to never spank. For example, imagine a drug for which there is evidence of harmful side effects, but not conclusive evidence. Imagine that a new drug becomes available that is equally effective and that is known not to have the side effects of the old drug. A pediatrician would ordinarily advise parents to change to the new drug. CP is like the old drug. Alternative modes of correction and control are like the new drug. Consequently, the abundance of evidence indicating that CP has many harmful side effects, in combination with the evidence that other discipline responses are just as effective or more effective, creates an ethical *requirement* to advise parents to "switch to the new drug"—to never spank.

❖ JOHN ROSEMOND'S GIFT
    TO THE EFFORT TO END SPANKING

Rosemond's chapter (this volume) begins by condemning "the separation of sex from reproduction" and by condemning "the movement of women into the workforce." This is a worldview that denies a central aspect of human expression (sexuality) and that denies half of humanity the right to choose their occupations. It is therefore not surprising that Rosemond also denies children the right to be free of physical attacks by their parents.

Perhaps one reason Rosemond can hold such a fossilized worldview, is that, despite academic credentials, he pays no attention to scientific evidence and does not even bother to check out ordinary facts. For example, he says that Child Protective Services is a "Spanking Gestapo" and disregards "parental discretion in matters of discipline." On the contrary, the child abuse statues of almost all states make a clear distinction between spanking and child abuse. Ironically, these "child protection" laws actually reinforce the right of parents to hit children because they include a disclaimer that says that the statute should not be construed as prohibiting or interfering with the right of parents to spank. In addition, the criminal laws of every state of the United States exempt parents from prosecution for the crime of assault if they use "reasonable force" in the form of spanking. Because of these legal directives and because they are typically understaffed, Child Protective Services will not even investigate reports about spanking unless it is "extreme," unless there are indications that it is malicious rather than disciplinary, or unless the child is injured.

In addition to Rosemond's fossilized worldview and his ignoring of both scientific evidence and the law of his own and every other U.S. state, there are the deceptions. Rosemond says, "Let me make perfectly clear that I do not 'believe' in spankings," but then he proceeds to advocate spanking. For example, he says that other modes of discipline are not as effective as spanking, and that "because it is in the best interests of the child and society that the misbehavior in question be deterred as effectively as possible, the child's parents would do well to spank." My interpretation of these contradictory statements is that the "I don't believe in spankings" preface was to ease the concerns of readers who are uneasy about spanking. Then, when their concern has been neutralized, the real message—that spanking is sometimes necessary—is presented. This may be good rhetoric, but it is bad science because it ignores the research showing that other modes of discipline are just as effective as spanking in the short run and more effective in the long run. Moreover, there is a great deal of other research showing that in the long run, spanking is *less* effective or counterproductive.

Rosemond's chapter may set a record for false statements, deceptions, and contradictions per page. Here are some of the others:

- "Most baby boomers were spanked. Few now are anything other than law-abiding citizens." While correct, it does not show that spanking is harmless, just as the fact that two-thirds of heavy smokers do *not* die of a smoking-related disease (Mattson, Pollack, & Cullen, 1987) does not show that smoking is harmless.
- "Violent discipline, as dispensed by parents who do not love their children powerfully, inclines a child toward either violence or depression." At least in this sentence when Rosemond refers to spanking as "violent discipline" he is calling a spade a spade. But the sentence also falsely implies that, if parents "love their children powerfully," spanking will not increase the probability of the child being violent. There have been many studies that controlled for parental warmth and love and still found that spanking is related to violence by the children and also later as adults.
- "In Sweden . . . the problem of child abuse . . . significantly worsened since passage of [the no-spanking law]." The research shows just the opposite. Joan Durrant (1999), who has studied the Swedish law and its effects in detail, found that Sweden has *not* become a nation of kids running wild. In fact, the rates of juvenile crime, drug and alcohol use, and suicide have all *decreased* (Durrant, 2000). There is no way of knowing if these improvements in the well-being of Swedish youth occurred because of the decrease in spanking. However, it can be said with certainty that ending spanking has not had the dire consequences for children feared by opponents of the no-spanking law. In addition, it can also be said with certainty that no one has gone to jail or been fined for spanking, because the Swedish law is entirely for purposes of education and helping parents. It contains no provisions for penalties.
- John Rosemond's chapter is guided by a view of human life and family relations that is so unrealistic and inhumane, and is

so full of errors, contradictions, and deceptions, that it will probably make an unintended contribution to the effort to end what Rosemond himself calls "violent discipline."

❖ REFERENCES

American Academy of Pediatrics. (1998). Guidance for Effective Discipline (RE9740). *Pediatrics, 101*(4), 723–728.

Brezina, T. (1999). Teenage violence toward parents as an adaptation to family strain: Evidence from a national survey of male adolescents. *Youth and Society, 30*(4), 416–444.

Day, D. E., & Roberts, M. W. (1983). An analysis of the physical punishment component of a parent training program. *Journal of Abnormal Child Psychology, 11*(1), 141–152.

Durrant, J. E. (1999). Evaluating the success of Sweden's corporal punishment ban. *Child Abuse and Neglect, 23*(5), 435–448.

Durrant, J. E. (2000). Trends in youth crime and well-being since the abolition of corporal punishment in Sweden. *Youth and Society, 31*(4), 437–455.

Fower, T. G., & Chapieski, M. L. (1986). Childrearing and impulse control in toddlers: A naturalistic investigation. *Developmental Psychology, 22*(2), 271–275.

Gershoff, T. E. (2002). Corporal punishment by parents and associated child behaviors and experiences: A meta-analytic and theoretical review. *Psychological Bulletin, 128*(4), 539–579.

Giles-Sims, J., Straus, M. A., & Sugarman, D. B. 1995. Child, maternal and family characteristics associated with spanking. *Family Relations, 44,* 170–176.

Gunnoe, M. L., & Mariner, C. L. (1997). Toward a developmental-contextual model of the effects of parental spanking on children's aggression. *Archives in Pediatric Adolescent Medicine, 151*(August), 768–775.

Heuer, F., & Reisberg, D. (1992). Emotion, arousal, and memory for detail. In S. A. Christianson (Ed.), *The handbook of emotion and memory: Research and theory* (pp. 151–180). Mahwah, NJ: Erlbaum.

Hindelang, M. J. (1973). Causes of delinquency: A partial replication and extension. *Social Problems, 20*(4), 471–487.

Hirschi, T. (1969). *The causes of delinquency.* Berkeley: University of California Press.

Holden, G. W., Coleman, S. M., & Schmidt, K. L. (1995). Why 3-year-old children get spanked: Parent and child determinants as reported by college-educated mothers. *Merrill-Palmer Quarterly, 41,* 431–452.

Larzelere, R. (1986). Moderate spanking: Model or deterrent of children's aggression in the family? *Journal of Family Violence, 1*(1), 27–36.

Larzelere, R. E., Baumrind, D., & Polite, K. (1998). The pediatric forum: Two emerging perspectives of parental spanking from two 1996 conferences. *Archives of Pediatrics and Adolescent Medicine, 152,* 303.

Larzelere, R. E., & Merenda, J. A. (1994). The effectiveness of parental discipline for toddler misbehavior at different levels of child distress. *Family Relations, 43,* 480–488.

Larzelere, R. E., Sather, P. R., Schneider, W. N., Larson, D. B., & Pike, P. L. (1998). Punishment enhances reasoning's effectiveness as a disciplinary response to toddlers. *Journal of Marriage and the Family, 60*(2), 388–403.

Larzelere, R. E., Schneider, W. N., Larson, D. B., & Pike, P. L. (1996). The effects of discipline responses in delaying toddler misbehavior recurrences. *Child and Family Therapy, 18,* 35–37.

Lehman, B. A. (1989, March 13). No spanking doesn't mean no discipline, parents told. *Boston Globe,* p. 31.

Mattson, M. E., Pollack, E. S., & Cullen, J. W. (1987). What are the odds that smoking will kill you? *American Journal of Public Health, 77*(4), 425–431.

Meerum Terwogt, M., & Olthof, T. (1989). Awareness and self regulation of emotion in young children. In C. Saarni & P. L. Harris (Eds.), *Children's understanding of emotion* (pp. 209–237). New York: Cambridge University Press.

Rankin, J. H., & Kern, R. (1994). Parental attachments and delinquency. *Criminology, 32*(4), 495–515.

Roberts, M. W. (1988). Enforcing timeouts with room timeouts. *Behavior Modifications, 4,* 353–370.

Roberts, M. W., & Powers, S. W. (1990). Adjusting chair timeout enforcement procedures for oppositional children. *Behavior Therapy, 21,* 257–271.

Rosemond, J. K. (1994). Should the use of corporal punishment by parents be considered child abuse?: Response. In M. A. Mason & E. Gambrill (Eds.), *Debating children's lives: Current controversies on children and adolescents* (pp. 215–216). Thousand Oaks, CA: Sage.

Schenck, E. R., Lyman, R. D., & Bodin, S. D. (2000). Ethical beliefs, attitudes, and professional practices of psychologists regarding parental use of corporal punishment: A survey. *Children's Services: Social Policy, Research, and Practice, 3*(1), 23–38.

Sears, R. R., Maccoby, E. C., & Levin, H. (1957). *Patterns of child rearing.* New York: Harper & Row.

Simons, R. L., Lin, K.-H., & Gordon, L. C. (1998). Socialization in the family of origin and male dating violence: A prospective study. *Journal of Marriage and the Family, 60*(2), 467–478.

Spock, B., & Rothenberg, M. B. (1992). *Dr. Spock's baby and child care.* New York: Pocket Books.

Straus, M. A. 1995. Trends in cultural norms and rates of partner violence: An update to 1992. In S. Stith & M. A. Straus (Eds.), *Understanding partner violence: Prevalence, causes, consequences, and solutions,* pp. 30-33 vol. II, Families in focus series. Minneapolis, MN: National Council on Family Relations.

Straus, M. A. (2001a). *Beating the devil out of them: Corporal punishment in American families and its effects on children* (2nd ed.). New Brunswick, NJ: Transaction.

Straus, M. A. (2001b). Ten myths that perpetuate corporal punishment. In M. A. Straus (Ed.), *Beating the devil out of them: Corporal punishment in American families and its effects on children* (2nd ed, pp. 149–164). New Brunswick, NJ: Transaction.

Straus, M. A. (2004). *The primordial violence: Corporal punishment by parents, cognitive development, and crime.* Walnut Creek, CA: Alta Mira Press.

Straus, M. A., & Hill, K. A. (2004). The child-to-parent bond and delinquency. In M. A. Straus (Ed.), *The primordial violence: Corporal punishment by parents, cognitive development, and crime.* Walnut Creek, CA: Alta Mira Press.

Straus, M. A., & Mathur, A. K. (1996). Social change and the trends in approval of corporal punishment by parents from 1968 to 1994. In D. Frehsee, W. Horn, & K.-D. Bussmann (Eds.), *Family violence against children: A challenge for society* (pp. 91–105). New York: Walter deGruyter.

Straus, M. A., & Mouradian, V. E. (1998). Impulsive corporal punishment by mothers and antisocial behavior and impulsiveness of children. *Behavioral Sciences and the Law, 16,* 353–374.

Straus, M. A., & Stewart, J. H. (1999). Corporal punishment by American parents: National data on prevalence, chronicity, severity, and duration, in relation to child, and family characteristics. *Clinical Child and Family Psychology Review, 2*(2), 55–70.

Straus, M. A., Sugarman, D. B., & Giles-Sims, J. (1997). Spanking by parents and subsequent antisocial behavior of children. *Archives of Pediatric and Adolescent Medicine, 151*(August), 761–767.

Turner, H., & Finkelhor, D. (1996). Corporal punishment as a stressor among youth. *Journal of Marriage and the Family, 58*(February), 155–166.

Wiatrowski, M., & Anderson, K. L. (1987). The dimensionality of the social bond. *Journal of Quantitative Criminology, 3*(1), 65–81.

SECTION III

Controversies in Cause

E xamining causation is the nexus of research, theory, and social intervention for all social problems, including family violence. Of course, the types of causal connections that are of interest are determined by conceptual frameworks: Chapters in Section I showed how psychological frameworks focus on examining how individual characteristics lead to violent behavior; feminist frameworks conceptualize the conditions and characteristics associated with gender as the cause of violence by men toward women; and sociological frameworks stress how social forces, social processes, and social structures set the stage for violence.

While psychology, feminism, and sociology offer general conceptual frameworks for examining questions about the causes of violence, Section III focuses on two particular controversies. The first involves the relationship between alcohol or other drug use and violence. Jerry Flanzer asserts that alcohol and other drugs *cause* violence; Richard Gelles and Mary Cavanaugh maintain that while alcohol and other drugs are *associated* with violence, they are not its cause. The second controversy is about adult children who abuse their elderly parents. Suzanne Steinmetz believes that these abused elderly people are dependent on their adult children who abuse them, while Karl Pillemer argues the reverse: Adult children who abuse their elderly parents suffer from problems with alcohol or mental illness. Because of this, the abusive adult children are dependent on the elderly whom they abuse.

Both of these controversies share the characteristic that one side of each reflects what many members of the public accept as common knowledge. In the popular imagination, the causal connection between alcohol and violence often is simply assumed, so Flanzer's chapter can be read as offering empirical support for this popular understanding. Likewise, in the popular imagination, the relationship between elder abuse and dependence seems fairly straightforward, and this is the argument of Steinmetz, who maintains that the "stress, frustration, and feelings of burden experienced by caregivers who are caring for dependent elders can result in abusive and neglectful treatment."

The authors of the opposing viewpoints are well aware that they are fighting an uphill battle against folk understandings. In asserting that alcohol does *not* cause violence, Gelles and Cavanaugh talk about the historical and continuing popularity of the "demon rum" explanation for violence. Pillemer, in turn, complains that assertions about the "dependence of elderly people" have been repeated so frequently that "they have come to be widely believed, despite the lack of evidence."

Although the chapters in this section demonstrate disagreements about the causes of violence, they also illustrate how controversies can be fueled by failures to agree on how important concepts should be defined and measured. At times, these are differences between how researchers define concepts and how these concepts are generally understood by members of the public. For example, although the public's interest is in the *immediate* effects of alcohol on the *abuser,* Flanzer's definition of alcohol use includes "the alcohol intake of all family members" and the "intergenerational and developmental consequences of living in a home with a family culture of alcoholism and violence." Part of the reason why he can claim simply that alcohol causes violence is that he includes a great deal in his definition of alcohol use. In the same way, definitional disagreements can arise between researchers who study violence and practitioners who attempt to do something about this violence. Steinmetz argues that the "term *elder abuse* is ambiguous because the legal and social service definitions do not necessarily correspond to definitions used by researchers."

As with all controversies in this volume, questions and complaints about research loom large in this section. Gelles and Cavanaugh comment that although there is a considerable literature linking alcohol and family violence, there are many methodological problems with the research that even undermine the claim that alcohol or other drugs are highly associated with violence. They also challenge Flanzer's assertion that alcohol causes violence by noting that Flanzer never defines such key concepts as *alcoholism, substance abuse,* or *alcohol intake,* and that studies about alcohol typically and inappropriately generalize information from nonrepresentative samples to the general population.

Failures to define important concepts or disagreements about how concepts should be defined lead to problems for readers attempting to evaluate the soundness of arguments. Steinmetz, for example, offers support for her belief that abused elderly people are dependent on their abusive adult children by discussing her own research as well as the conclusions from "a rich body of literature covering more than three decades of research." In turn, Pillemer also cites many research studies that, according to him, provide "substantial evidence that elder abusers are often not primary caregivers at all, but are instead deeply troubled individuals who depend heavily on the people they abuse." Readers might well wonder how Steinmetz and Pillemer both are able to muster so many examples of research supporting their arguments when these arguments are diametrically opposed. This is a major lesson: Research *will* come to different conclusions depending on initial conceptualizations and on the characteristics of study samples.

The controversies in this section also indirectly or directly raise questions about social interventions. What should be done to stop violence? Issues of intervention are implicit in the controversy about relationships between violence and alcohol or drugs. Flanzer's assertion that alcohol causes violence leads to social interventions that would eliminate alcohol use. In comparison, Gelles and Cavanaugh assert that the culprit is not alcohol per se; it rather is how we *think* about alcohol. Their argument points to a need to change the system of ideas that lead Americans to accepting alcohol and other drug use as an excuse or rationalization for violence.

The arguments of Steinmetz and Pillemer also point the way to different forms of social intervention. If the perception of stress created by caring for dependent elderly family members creates abuse, then it is logical that there should be more programs to reduce caregiver stress. But if adult children are abusive because they are alcoholic or otherwise deviant, then other interventions, such as assistance programs for elderly people and perhaps legal action against their abusive caregivers, are called for.

Of course, it is logical that each of these opposing views contains at least a grain of truth and, given this, that all routes to problem resolution should be pursued simultaneously. Indeed, Steinmetz concludes her chapter by admitting that Pillemer also is correct: Some elderly people are abused by their disabled adult children. Given this, the population of abused elderly people includes distinct subgroups. Steinmetz does not believe this is a problem, because in a "society as rich as ours, the issue should not be which population is in greatest need of limited resources, but rather how we can best meet the needs of all at-risk elders and their families." Unfortunately, our real world is one of tradeoffs. Attention to, and thus money for, some types of research and social services diverts resources from other types of research and services. Pillemer therefore notes that the power of the image of "stressed caregivers" and "dependent elderly" has led to the reality that the "most frequently recommended programs to reduce elder abuse are those that treat caregiver stress."

Controversies over the cause of violence are not simply academic debates. Who wins—and who loses—these arguments has very practical implications.

10

Alcohol and Other Drugs Are Key Causal Agents of Violence

Jerry P. Flanzer

A lcoholism causes family violence. Just as high alcohol intake leads to cirrhosis of the liver, brain damage, and heart failure, so does high alcohol intake lead to violence in the family. At first glance, the reader may be shocked at this assertion, even outraged. Certainly one knows of alcoholics who are not prone to be abusive in the family, and certainly one knows of violent families where alcohol does not appear to be in the picture. Nevertheless, I remind the reader that there are other causes for cirrhosis of the liver, brain damage, and heart failure—but alcohol is certainly high on the list. Similarly, I agree that

AUTHOR'S NOTE: The views expressed in this paper are the views of the author and should not be necessarily construed as the views of the National Institute on Drug Abuse.

family violence has other causes. However, alcoholism, in its varying forms, is very high on the list.

In this volume, Cavanaugh and Gelles argue that cultural or social context dictates responsive behavior to alcohol use, and thereby they attempt to minimize the "alcohol-cause" argument. The following should serve to negate or, at the very least, to question their premise.

Substance abuse—alcohol abuse in particular—frequently emerges as the prominent risk factor contributing to myriad family problems. Despite media attention, alcoholism (alcohol dependence and abuse) continues to account for the overwhelming majority of substance abuse problems in the United States and, not surprisingly, remains the most frequently mentioned form of substance abuse contributing to family problems in general and family violence specifically (for documentation, see Ackerman, 1988, who reports a higher incidence of all types of abuse occurring in alcoholic families). Although the folklore across centuries and cultures refers to the link between alcoholism and family violence in all its forms (child abuse and severe neglect, sibling abuse, spouse abuse, and elder abuse), social scientists have begun to investigate the link between alcoholism and family violence seriously only in the past few decades. The link is becoming clear, whether one refers to the actual occurrence of violence in the home or to the intergenerational and developmental consequences of living in a home with a family culture of alcoholism and violence. In this chapter I take the broad view of the intergenerational effect of alcoholism on family violence, going beyond the specific concern of the immediate effects of alcohol to the more general concern of long-term effects. Similarly, I take into account the alcohol intake of all family members, not just that of the perpetrator of the abuse.

My task in this chapter is to focus on the intermeshed behaviors of family violence and alcoholism. First, let's look at the common interactive behaviors among and between the alcoholic-abusive perpetrator, the victim, and resultant dynamic function within the family. And then let's look at the how these and other factors lead to support for my argument of a causal connection.

Similar clinical portraits are noted by numerous authors. Table 10.1 represents an attempt to portray the commonalties of behavioral responses and purposes that alcoholism and family violence both share for the perpetrator, the victim, and the family as a whole. The responses may be broadly defined as defense mechanisms, issues of parenting, tolerance levels, projection, loyalty, communication patterns, control or mastery

Table 10.1   Commonalities of Behavioral Response among Family
Members Experiencing Alcoholism and Family Violence

Response	Perpetrator	Victim	Family Function
Defense Mechanisms	Denial of the problem, minimizing, rationalizing, isolating	Denial of the problem, minimizing, rationalizing, isolating	Denial of the problem, rationalizing, isolating
Parenting	Autocratic	Enmeshed, infantilized	Parentification
Tolerance	Low frustration, increasingly aggressive, controlling	High frustration, increasingly hurt	Increasing tolerance
Projection	Blaming others	Accepting blame, feeling shame	Family inferiority
Loyalty	Secretive	Secretive, loyal	Keeping the family intact
Communication	Decreasing empathetic communication	Distancing to avoid abuse	Minimizing pain through rigidifying communication patterns
Control	Solidifying power	Decreasing power	Unequal power relationship
Affection	Less intimate	Less intimate	Rigidify affectionate relationships to avoid pain
Stress	Increasingly provocative, restrictive	Increasingly alarmed, timid	Stress reduction
Depression	Defending against depression, low self-esteem	Building depression, lowering self-esteem	Depression, eventual destabilization
Thought patterns	Increasing impulsivity	Increasing magical thinking	External rescue fantasies

over others, affection needs, responses to stress, depression, and thought patterns.

Repeated clinical observations of the behaviors of abusers and their victims have led to a consensus among experts about the behavioral sets of the participants. Universally, all abusers, whether hitters or drinkers, project blame onto others: "It's not my fault"; "She deserves that." Universally, all perpetrators (alcoholics and abusers) tend to be jealous and possessive of targeted victims. The slightest suspicion of a spouse's relationship with another, for example, brings tirades and recriminations. Often, abusers expect children to behave as their parents do, or expect spouses to take care of everything. These role expectations are impossible to meet. If one questions an abuser about a critical incident, one finds that he or she does not always remember the details and may even "black out" the incident altogether. Regardless, the abuser is not abusive all the time. In fact, he or she might otherwise be a model citizen.

Victims tend to be socially isolated, ashamed to show their physical and emotional scars, and unwilling to expose their plight to others. Part of this social isolation is caused by the victim's internalization of blame. The victim mistakenly agrees with the abuser: "I deserve it." Invariably, the victim believes strongly in family loyalty. Family secrets are guarded to an extreme; maintenance of family integrity is desired at all costs. The perpetrator's violent and alcoholic behavior blocks the development of intimacy and masks the abuser's frightening feelings of low self-esteem. These deleterious behaviors also block feelings of dependency and the extreme fear of being "swallowed up" that is linked to concerns of losing one's identity. The perpetrator maintains the illusion of superiority and control over his or her own life and that of the victim and, in so doing, actually creates the opposite effect.

All parties become more disoriented. At first, they must structure time to maintain functional family relationships. But they generally find themselves losing identity, first through the total enmeshment and then the total lack of involvement, or disengagement, with one another. Some families, having lived only with drinking and violence, have accepted this as the norm for family life, and even when they want to change, they do not know the truly "normal" ways to act. They pretend, and act as they have observed others to be. Thus, as is observed with crisis-prone individuals, they appear rigid and adhere strictly to authority.

Children growing up in violent homes evidence many of the same symptoms as children growing up in alcoholic homes. Clinicians have reported similar portraits among and between these two groups of children: emotional triangulations, secrets and isolation, stressed relationships, failing finances, and hopelessness. Children in alcoholic homes appear to have the same litany of maladaptive behaviors as child abuse victims, including juvenile delinquency, low self-esteem, suicide attempts, overrepresentation among clients of psychotherapists, sexual dysfunction, and marital difficulties (Berry & Boland, 1977; Edwards, 1982; Flanzer, 1981, 1982; Flanzer & Sturkie, 1987; Polch, Armor, & Braiker, 1981).

Given the string of clinical similarities, one may wonder if we are dealing with the same population. Are these essentially the same families, looked at from a different angle, if you will? Could it be that one abuse is contributing to or causing the other? Or are these two abuses mutually exclusive, but only by chance frequently occur among the same families? Or are these two forms of abuse symptomatic of yet a third factor? I believe it is plausible that alcoholism and other addictive drugs may be a primary cause of violence in families.

I am aware, as is the reader, that there are many families in which alcoholism or some form of family violence appears to occur without the appearance of the other. Not all alcoholic families appear to include physical, sexual, or emotional abuse, and not all violence in families appears to be triggered by drinking or the taking of drugs. But with further exploration of the history of the family, I suggest that this mutually exclusive occurrence is rare and is not the norm. So the question may be: How can it happen that family violence occurs without drinking or drug use? I maintain that the pattern of effects of alcoholism or drug abuse on increasing family violence emerges with clarity when one broadens the definition of alcoholism and drug abuse. If researchers would examine the periods and cycles of abuse, abstinence and withdrawal, cognitive and neurological damage to individual family members, the frequency of alcohol or other drug (AOD) use, and AOD effects on family interaction and development, they would see that they have missed the presence of AOD in the preponderance of their studies. In other words, alcoholism, or other substance dependence or abuse, may be more than a contributory factor to family violence; it may actually be one of the primary causes of violence in the family.

In trying to prove a causal relationship, three properties must be demonstrated (Denzin, 1980, p. 213):

1. *Association.* Proof of significant associations or correlations of the key variable must be shown. The researcher must show that the causal variables in the "symptom" produced variations in the dependent variable.

2. *Time.* A clear temporal relationship, wherein one factor precedes the other, must be shown. The researcher must show that the causal variable occurs before the dependent variable.

3. *Intervening variables.* An explanation of the relationship of intervening factors as catalysts or products must show that this causal system is not spurious—not the product of other variables.

❖ ASSOCIATION

Byles (1978) was among the first to report alcoholism as highly associated with spouse battering among 139 persons appearing in family court. Similar alcohol-spouse abuse associations were found by Cleek and Pearson (1985) in their divorce study; Wilson and Orford (1978) in their review; and Stewart and DeBlois (1981) in their study of abused mothers of children in psychiatric settings. Alcoholism and child abuse and neglect have been shown to appear together in a host of studies and clinical reviews. Studies of child-abusing families similarly have shown varying rates of alcoholism among family members.

These studies have used a variety of clinical and research methodologies. They also have been inconsistent in their definitions of key variables, such as the actual definitions of the levels or degrees of child abuse and neglect, spouse abuse, and alcohol abuse and dependency. These differences make comparisons across studies and subsequent clinical reviews difficult. Still, the trends are evident. The correlations between alcohol and child abuse increase when we include the drinking patterns of all family members and not just those of the perpetrators. Samples of incestuous fathers have been shown to have a range of associations between alcoholism and incest of from 20–25 percent (Gebhard, Gagnon, Pomeroy, & Christenson, 1965; Meiselman, 1978) to 50 percent (Virkunnen, 1974). Samples of perpetrators of physical abuse show a range of associations between alcoholism and physical abuse of 23 percent (Black & Mayer, 1980) to 42–65 percent (Behling, 1971). Positive correlations—the greater amount of alcohol abuse correlated with greater severity of child abuse and neglect—have been found in a DWI sample (Spieker & Mousakitis, 1977) and in an adolescent abuse sample (Flanzer, 1980). Such associations might even be underestimates: Both of these studies also note that many of the most severe drinkers no longer have the opportunity to be perpetrators or victims, as they have lost their families. Evidence of a curvilinear relationship between levels of abuse exists. Downs and Miller (1986) found that having an alcoholic father might be related to being a victim of sexual abuse by a significant other. This finding seems to "delink" alcoholism as a direct cause, allowing speculation about a "secondary" relationship, but it strengthens the argument that the presence of alcoholism in a system supports an abusive relationship.

❖ TIME

Two timing issues need to be addressed: First, was there any drinking *before, during,* or *instead* of the violence incident? Second, is there any pattern connecting drinking and abuse viewed over long periods of time?

Several researchers report timing variables that link drinking to the abusive event. For example, Glazier (1971) and Gil (1973) found 13 percent of their abusing sample to be intoxicated during the abusive events. In a study of adolescent-abusing parents, I found nearly half to be drinking instead of hitting their children, and most of the others to be drinking after abusive events (Flanzer, 1982). The examination of the relationship between the two abuses over a long period of time helps us to realize that either a continuous or a delayed effect may be occurring over years within families, and timing may be different during different phases of the life cycle or between generations. Many researchers have reported intergenerational findings, in which abused children grew up to be alcoholic adults, with varying samples. Black and Mayer (1980) found 47 percent of their sample had been abused as children; Covington (1986) reports similar findings. Miller, Downs, and Gondoli (1987) have reported that the alcoholic women in a population of women sexually abused in childhood tended to have been sexually abused as children over longer periods of time than did the nonalcoholic women in that population. Researchers also have found that being raised in alcoholic homes is related to becoming a perpetrator of child abuse (Famularo, Stone, Barnum, & Wharton, 1986). So, in these studies, one abuse appears to precede the other intergenerationally, thus supporting the broader definition of a relationship between alcohol and violence.

❖ INTERVENING VARIABLES

There are a number of intervening variables to be considered, including the following:

- Alcohol as an instigator of violence
- Alcohol as a disinhibitor of social control
- Alcohol's destruction of the normal growth and development of the individual and the family system
- Alcohol as a rationalization for violence
- Alcohol's alteration of brain functioning

Alcohol can *instigate* violence. Violent behavior results from a combination of the situation, the drug, and the individual's personality (Niven, 1986; Miller & Potter-Efron, 1990). Miller and Potter-Efron (1990) suggest that psychological disorders or reactions to environmental stressors may cause the aggressive behavior more than the actual physiological effects of the abused drugs. For the aggression-instigating condition, an imbibing individual may be physiologically unable to attend to the ambiguous cues and complexity of behaviors that normally mediate social behavior. This individual, who in effect has tunnel vision, sees only immediate and limited cues that in themselves might instigate aggressive behavior (Miller & Potter-Efron, 1990). In some cases, the individual's ability to distinguish between aggressive-instigating and aggressive-inhibiting cues becomes impaired, and the vulnerability to engage in aggressive behavior increases.

Alcohol causes *disinhibition* that can lead to violence. Much of the literature suggests that alcohol reduces inhibitions, which results in a higher likelihood of aggressive behavior. An individual harboring intense underlying anger that has been contained by psychological defense mechanisms can become physically aggressive and intimidating as a result of the disinhibiting effects of alcohol. Miller and Potter-Efron (1990) also support a major contention, as do I, that the abused drugs act as disinhibitors of pent-up underlying anger. This disinhibition can cause the drinking or drug-abusing person to do things that he or she would not ordinarily do were he or she not abusing drugs or alcohol.

Alcohol *destroys normal growth and development* of the individual and the family system. Steinglass, Bennett, Wolin, and Reiss (1987) pay particular attention to the regulatory and central organizing functions of alcoholism and alcohol-related behaviors on the structure of family life. The alcohol-involved family life is skewed toward short-term stability at the expense of long-term growth. The family accommodates to the demands of alcoholism, and distortions occur that shape family growth and development. This restructuring of family life establishes a milieu that tolerates and accommodates to violence.

Alcohol may serve as a *rationalization* for violence, allowing the perpetrator to avoid taking responsibility for his or her actions. Intense drinking by the perpetrator or the victim (spouse) often leads to increased marital conflict, the drinking party's lack of responsibility, and other environmental (often employment or financial) stressors.

Alcohol *alters brain functioning*. The ingestion of alcohol over time results in the laceration of brain matter. The changes in the brain and neurotransmitter system as a result of drinking may be a causative agent in the relationship between alcohol and violent behavior, especially during periods of withdrawal. "Withdrawal syndrome" is the brain's reaction to the absence of alcohol. Withdrawal symptoms include increased irritability, quick temper, and anger. Being in a hyper-irritable state, the drinker does not need much stimulus to react with anger.

❖ CONCLUSION

In the matter of alcohol and family violence, the case for causality rests on evidence of association, timing, and the presence of intervening variables. The high frequency of association is strengthened by the expansion of the definition to include clinical relationships over time. As researchers take more careful clinical histories, they find evidence of AOD involvement in families prior to their presentation as "violent families." At the present state of knowledge, the strongest case for the causative relationship between AOD and violence are the five intervening variables presented earlier in the chapter.

Well-functioning people have greater capacity for autonomy than do malfunctioning people. Individuals living under the intense anxiety of double abuse are likely to be less autonomous, less differentiated, less able to process perceptions on an objective level, more enmeshed, and governed by their abusive relationships and perceptions. Thereby, they are also more at risk for the occurrence of any dysfunctional, invasive behaviors of others. Stated in other terms, they are vulnerable to accepting external others' (the predominant culture's) belief systems and norms, and are less able to govern their behavior by their own internal, moral, and self-worth or integral beliefs. This may account for abusive behaviors surrounding drinking within the violent pervasive American culture, and for less provocative behavior surrounding drinking in more "depressed" and/or less violence-tolerating cultures. The violent perpetrator, stressed by AOD, is less likely to be able to manage anxiety in the external world and, supported by the external world's acceptance of violence, is more likely to exacerbate his or her dysfunctional behavior. He or she will drink more and hit more. The "context"—the "culture"—is the catalyst, the condition in which the cause, alcoholism, operates. I contend that AOD intake, abuse, and dependency are key causal agents for violence in the family. Although this position is in opposition to current mainstream thinking, the clinical experience of many therapists, as well as the evidence presented here, certainly warrants further testing of this position.

❖ REFERENCES

Ackerman, R. J. (1988). Complexities of alcohol and abusive families. *Focus on Chemically Dependent Families, 11*(3), 15.

Behling, D. W. (1971). *History of alcohol abuse in child abuse cases reported at Naval Regional Medical Center.* Paper presented at the National Child Abuse Forum, Long Beach, CA.

Berry, R. E., & Boland, J. P. (1977). *The economic cost of alcohol abuse.* New York: Free Press.

Black, R., & Mayer, J. (1980). Parents with special problems: Alcoholism and opiate addiction. In C. H. Kempe & R. E. Helfer (Eds.), *The battered child* (3rd ed.). Chicago: University of Chicago Press.

Byles, J. A. (1978). Violence, alcohol problems and other problems in the disintegrating family. *Journal of Studies on Alcohol, 39,* 551–553.

Cleek, M. G., & Pearson, T. A. (1985). Perceived causes of divorce: An analysis of interrelationships. *Journal of Marriage and the Family, 47,* 179–183.

Covington, S. S. (1986). Facing the clinical challenges of women alcoholics: Physical, emotional and sexual abuse. *Focus on Family, 9*(3), 10–11, 37, 42–44.

Denzin, N. K. (1980). *Sociological methods: A sourcebook.* Chicago: Aldine.

Downs, W., & Miller, B. (1986). *Childhood abuse and alcohol histories.* Paper presented at the annual meeting of the American Society on Criminology, Atlanta, GA.

Edwards, G. (1982). *The treatment of drinking problems.* New York: McGraw-Hill.

Famularo, R., Stone, K., Barnum, R., & Wharton, R. (1986). Alcoholism and severe child maltreatment. *American Journal of Orthopsychiatry, 56*(3), 481–485.

Flanzer, J. P. (1980). Alcohol-abusing parents and their battered adolescents. In M. Galanter (Ed.), *Currents in alcoholism* (Vol. 3, pp. 529–538). New York: Grune & Stratton.

Flanzer, J. P. (1981). The vicious circle of alcoholism and family violence. *Alcoholism, 1*(3), 30–32.

Flanzer, J. P. (1982). *The many faces of family violence.* Springfield, IL: Charles C. Thomas.

Flanzer, J. P., & Sturkie, D. K. (1987). *Alcohol and adolescent abuse.* Holmes Beach, FL: Learning Publications.

Gebhard, P. H., Gagnon, J., Pomeroy, W., & Christenson, C. (1965). *Sex offenders.* New York: Harper & Row.

Gil, D. (1973). *Violence against children: Physical child abuse in the United States.* Cambridge, MA: Harvard University Press.

Glazier, A. E. (1971). *Child abuse: A community challenge.* Buffalo, NY: Henry Stewart.

Meiselman, K. C. (1978). *A psychological study of causes and effects of child sexual abuse with treatment recommendations.* San Francisco: Jossey-Bass.

Miller, B. A., Downs, W. R., & Gondoli, D. M. (1987). Childhood sexual abuse incidents for alcoholic women versus a random household sample. *Violence and Victims, 2,* 157–172.

Miller, M. M., & Potter-Efron, R. T. (1990). Aggression and violence associated with substance abuse. In R. T. Potter-Efron & P. S. Potter-Efron (Eds.), *Aggression, family violence, and chemical dependency* (pp. 1–36). New York: Haworth.

Niven, R. (1986). Adolescent drug abuse. *Hospital and Community Psychiatry, 37,* 6596–6607.

Polch, J. M., Armor, D. J., & Braiker, H. B. (1981). *The course of alcoholism.* New York: Wiley.

Spieker, G., & Mousakitis, C. (1977). *Alcohol abuse and child abuse and neglect.* Paper presented at the 27th annual meeting of the Alcohol and Drug Problems Association of North America, New Orleans, LA.

Steinglass, P., Bennett, L., Wolin, S., & Reiss, D. (1987). *The alcoholic family.* New York: Basic Books.

Stewart, M. A., & DeBlois, S. C. (1981). Wife abuse among families attending a child psychiatric clinic. *Journal of the American Academy of Child Psychiatry, 20,* 845–862.

Virkunnen, M. (1974). Incest offenders and alcoholism. *Medicine Science and Law, 14,* 124–128.

Wilson, C., & Orford, J. (1978). Children of alcoholics: Report of a preliminary study and comments on the literature. *Journal of Studies on Alcohol, 39,* 121–142.

11

Association
Is Not Causation

*Alcohol and Other Drugs Do
Not Cause Violence*

Richard J. Gelles and Mary M. Cavanaugh

The "demon rum" explanation for violence and abuse in the home is one of the most pervasive and widely believed explanations for family violence in the professional and popular literature. Addictive and illicit drugs, such as cocaine, crack, heroin, marijuana, and LSD, are also considered causal agents in child abuse, wife abuse, and other forms of family violence.

That alcohol and substance abuse may be related to, or may directly cause, family violence is not a new idea. William Hogarth's etching *Gin Lane*, done in the early 1700s, presents a graphic visual portrayal of the abuses and neglect that befall children whose parents abuse alcohol (for a copy of this etching, see Radbill, 1974). Not surprisingly, Hogarth's etching also implies that only certain types of alcohol, in this case gin, which was used primarily by the lower classes, are related to abuse and neglect. Social workers in the United States in the 1800s believed alcohol was the cause of child maltreatment, and the prohibition movement in the United States in the 1920s was partially based on the assumption that drinking led to the mistreatment of children (Gordon, 1988).

Both conventional wisdom and scholarly presentations, such as the chapter by Jerry Flanzer (this volume), argue not only that there is a substantial association between alcohol and drug use and violence in the home, but that the substances themselves are direct causal agents. The key to the argument that alcohol causes violent behavior is the proposition that alcohol acts as a *disinhibitor* to release violent tendencies. The proposition is based on a causal link between alcohol and the human brain. Alcohol is viewed by many as a "superego solvent" that reduces inhibitions and allows violent behavior to emerge. Crack, cocaine, heroin, LSD, and marijuana have also been postulated as direct causal agents that reduce inhibitions, unleash violent tendencies, and/or directly elicit violent behavior.

There is substantial support for the notion that alcohol and drug use is related to violence in general, and to family violence in particular. Research on homicide, assault, child abuse, and wife abuse all find substantial associations between alcohol use and abuse and violence (for example, Bennett, 1995; Boles & Miotto, 2003; Coleman & Straus, 1983; Gelles, 1974; Kaufman Kantor & Straus, 1989). In his chapter, Flanzer reviews a number of studies that demonstrate an association between alcohol use and misuse and family violence. Research on drug use and abuse is much more suggestive and anecdotal than is the research on alcohol and violence. In our own survey of violence in American families, we found that parents who reported "getting high on marijuana or some other drug" at least once a year also reported higher rates of violence and abusive violence toward their children (Wolfner & Gelles, 1993).

❖   ALCOHOL AND VIOLENCE: ARGUMENTS AND
    EVIDENCE AGAINST THE THEORY OF DISINHIBITION

It is our contention that, with the exception of the data we discuss in the following section on amphetamines and violence, there is little empirical evidence to support the claim that alcohol and drugs act as disinhibitors and are of primary importance in explaining family violence. Stated another way, there is little scientific evidence to support the theory that alcohol and drugs such as cocaine and crack have chemical and pharmacological properties that directly produce violent and abusive behavior. Evidence from cross-cultural research, laboratory studies, blood tests of men arrested for wife beating, and survey research all indicates that although alcohol use may be *associated* with intimate violence, alcohol is not a primary *cause* of the violence. Indeed, as Bennett (1995) suggests, the majority of men who use alcohol and drugs are not violent toward their female partners, and most episodes of violence do not involve substance abuse.

Evidence From Cross-Cultural Research

The best evidence against the disinhibitor theory of alcohol comes from cross-cultural studies of drinking behavior. Craig MacAndrew and Robert Edgerton (1969) reviewed the cross-cultural evidence on how individuals react to drinking. If the pharmacological properties of alcohol are the direct causes of behavior after drinking, then there should be very little variation in drinking behavior across cultures; if alcohol acts chemically on the human brain, then it should have the same general behavioral consequences across societies. Contrary to what one would expect using a pharmacological explanation, MacAndrew and Edgerton found that drinking behavior varies greatly from culture to culture. In some cultures, individuals drink and become passive; in others, individuals drink and become aggressive. What explains the cross-cultural variation? The differences in drinking behavior appear to be related to what people in each society *believe* about alcohol. If the cultural belief is that alcohol is a disinhibitor, then people who drink tend to become disinhibited. If the cultural belief is that alcohol is a depressant, drinkers become passive and depressed.

Because in our society the belief is widespread that alcohol and drugs release violent tendencies, according to MacAndrew and Edgerton (1969) people are given a "time out" from the normal rules of social behavior. They assert that alcohol and drug use occur in a cultural context in which an individual's behavior can be attributed to the admission of being "loaded." Because family violence is widely considered deviant and inappropriate behavior, there is a desire to "hush up" or rationalize abusive behavior in families. The desire of both offenders and victims to cover up family violence and the belief that alcohol is a disinhibitor combine to provide a socially acceptable explanation for violence. "I didn't know what I was doing, I was drunk" is a frequent explanation for wife beating and sometimes child beating. Victims of family violence often explain the perpetrator's actions by noting, "My husband is a Dr. Jekyll and Mr. Hyde—when he drinks he is violent, but when he is sober, he is no problem." In the end, the social expectations about drinking and drinking behavior in our society teach people that if they want to avoid being held responsible for their violence, they can either drink before they are violent or at least say they were drunk.

Evidence From Laboratory Experiments

MacAndrew and Edgerton's (1969) cross-cultural findings about alcohol, disinhibition, and violence have been put to an experimental test. If drinking behavior is learned, then it follows that a researcher could manipulate a situation to produce "drunken behavior" even if the people involved were not actually drinking alcohol. Lang and his colleagues performed an experiment in which college student subjects were assigned randomly to one of four groups (Lang, Goeckner, Adesso, & Marlatt, 1975). Two groups received tonic water, and the other two groups received tonic water and vodka. Vodka was selected as the alcoholic beverage because the taste of vodka could not be differentiated from "'decarbonated" tonic water. Subjects in two groups— one receiving tonic water only and one receiving vodka and tonic—were accurately told what they were drinking. Subjects in the other two groups were misled—the tonic water-only drinkers believed they were drinking vodka and tonic, and the vodka and tonic drinkers believed they were drinking only tonic water that had been decarbonated. Aggression was measured by assessing the intensity and duration of shocks subjects believed they were administering to Lang's associates. Subjects were told they were going to be in a learning experiment and they were "teachers" responsible for teaching "students." Experimental confederates acted as if they were shocked, but no actual shock was administered. Fine motor skills were measured by having subjects try to place shaped objects into shaped holes.

The researchers found that although drinking (whether the subjects correctly knew they were drinking alcohol or not) was related to fine motor skills, drinking was related to aggression only as a function of expectancy. In other words, the most aggressive subjects—the ones who gave the most and strongest shocks—were those who *thought* they were drinking alcohol, regardless of whether their glasses actually contained alcohol. It is *expectancy* that determines how people behave when they are, or even believe they are, drinking.

Evidence From Blood Tests of Men Arrested for Wife Beating

A third type of evidence disputing the association between alcohol and violence comes from the work of Morton Bard and Joseph Zacker (1974), who trained police officers to observe, record, and intervene in cases of domestic assault. In 1,388 cases of domestic assault, one or both partners were drinking in 56 percent of the incidents. Drinking was as common in cases of verbal disputes as in physical assaults. However, although nearly half of the assaultive men *said* they were drinking at the time of the assaults, blood alcohol tests found that fewer than 20 percent of the men were legally intoxicated (Bard, personal communication, 1974). Thus, although alcohol was *associated* with the violence, there is less than compelling evidence that the men were actually physically affected by alcohol they had consumed. One drink can affect motivation and coordination, but it usually takes two drinks in an hour to bring about a blood level of .10—the general legal limit of intoxication.

Evidence From Survey Research

Additional evidence disputing the link between drinking and violent behavior comes from survey research. Murray Straus and his colleagues examined data from two national surveys of family violence. The first survey found that there was a strong relationship between alcohol use and family violence (Coleman & Straus, 1983). However, extreme levels of alcohol use were *not* related to high levels of violence. In fact, that analysis found that men who never drank alcohol were violent more often than were men who drank infrequently. Physical violence in families actually declined for those who reported the highest incidence of being drunk.

Glenda Kaufman Kantor and Murray Straus (1987) examined data from the second National Family Violence Survey and found that, contrary to the earlier study, excessive drinking was associated with higher levels of wife abuse. The rate of husband-to-wife violence was highest among binge drinkers; next highest among those reporting they drank alcohol from three times a week up to daily and who had three or more drinks each time they drank; and lowest among those who reported that they abstained from drinking alcohol. While these data seem to provide support for at least the theory that drinking is associated with violence, Kaufman Kantor and Straus also examined drinking behavior *at the time of the violent incident*. Their analysis of the data clearly demonstrates that alcohol was not used immediately prior to the violent conflict in the majority (76 percent) of the cases. One or both partners were drinking at the time of the violent episode in 24 percent of the cases. The violent male was drinking at the time of the incident in 14 percent of the cases, the victimized female in 2 percent of the cases, and both were drinking in 8 percent of the cases.

Thus, although the survey research demonstrates a substantial association between drinking and violence, alcohol use per se is not a necessary or sufficient cause of family violence.

❖ DRUGS AND VIOLENCE

Drugs other than alcohol also have been implicated as direct causes of violent behavior. The issue of a possible link between drug use and abuse and violence is emotion laden, and fact often is mixed with myth. The majority of studies examining relationships between illicit drugs and violence tend to group all illicit drugs together; therefore it is difficult to make an empirical or theoretical distinction between the association of a particular illicit drug and violent behavior (Parker & Auerhahn, 1998). With regard to family violence, research on child or wife abuse rarely includes information on the use of drugs, other than alcohol (Kaufman Kantor & Straus, 1989). Another problem is that there are many different drugs that have been implicated in acts of violence, and each of these has a different physiological effect. The drugs implicated include marijuana, phencyclidine (PCP), cocaine, opiates, hallucinogens such as LSD, stimulants, and sedative-hypnotics (Miller & Potter-Efron, 1990). The available research on the different types of drugs and their possible effects on violent behavior has found some consistent evidence.

Cannabis or marijuana use is frequent among juvenile offenders and violent juvenile offenders, and some investigators attribute fearfulness, panic, and intense aggressive impulses to marijuana use (Nicholi, 1983). On the other hand, marijuana is generally classified as a drug producing a euphoric effect, and it may actually reduce rather than increase the potential for violent behavior. Some researchers have found that the higher the dose of marijuana, the lower the likelihood of violent behavior (Taylor & Leonard, 1983). Reiss and Roth (1993) suggest that marijuana in moderate doses inhibits violent behavior in both animals and humans.

Research studies provide evidence that hallucinogen use, particularly LSD, does not actually trigger violent behavior, but may aggravate the effects of preexisting psychopathology, including violent episodes (Reiss & Roth, 1993).

Opiates such as heroin also have been linked to criminal and violent acts. Crime rates for opiate users are unusually high, and violence may often be part of the criminal act. In fact, Roth (1994) asserts that the withdrawal from opiates tends to heighten aggressive responses to provocation. In some cases, individuals addicted to opiates may commit crimes to pay for its use rather than experience the severe withdrawal symptoms associated with this drug (Senay, 1999).

Cocaine is an extremely volatile drug with a short and intense effect. Although the intensity of the cocaine or crack rush is substantial and the effects varying, there appears to be little evidence that cocaine or crack is actually causally related to aggressive behavior (Johnson, 1972; Miller & Potter-Efron, 1990). However, cocaine use is associated with the perpetration of violent crimes (Kosten & Singha, 1999).

One drug does stand out as a possible cause of violent behavior: amphetamines. Amphetamine use has been associated with increased crime and violence. In fact, if used frequently, it is more closely related to violent behavior than any other psychoactive drugs (Kosten & Singha, 1999). Amphetamines raise excitability and muscle tension, and this may lead to impulsive behavior. The behavior following amphetamine use is related to both the dosage and the pre-use personality of the user. High-dosage users who already have aggressive personalities are likely to become more aggressive when using this drug (Johnson, 1972). Interestingly, studies of nonhuman primates, in this case stump-tailed macaques, have found that monkeys do become more aggressive when they receive dosages of d-amphetamine (Smith & Byrd, 1987). Based on research with monkeys, as many as 5 percent of instances of physical child abuse may be related to amphetamine use and abuse (Smith & Byrd, 1987).

❖ METHODOLOGICAL ISSUES

Despite the evidence to the contrary, some researchers and clinicians, such as Flanzer (this volume), continue to assert that alcohol and drugs cause violence. Although the literature linking alcohol and drug use and abuse to various forms of family violence appears abundant and consistent, there are a number of important methodological limitations that both undermine the claim for a strong and consistent association between alcohol and drug use and violence and, more important, limit the ability to make causal inferences about the link between alcohol and other drug use and violent behavior.

Definitions

The main concepts in studies linking alcohol and drug use to family violence are often inadequately defined. The majority of investigators who study the relationship between substance use and abuse and family violence fail to appreciate the problems that arise in defining *family violence, child abuse, child maltreatment, wife abuse, spouse abuse,* and *elder abuse.*

Abuse and Violence. The terms *violence, abuse, domestic violence, intimate violence,* and *family violence* are often used interchangeably in research on alcohol or drugs and violence. In many cases, the terms are used without definitions at all. In addition, investigators examining the association between drinking and/or drug use and child abuse often examine more than one form of maltreatment—physical abuse, sexual abuse, and/or neglect. Because each specific form of maltreatment has a relatively low base rate, and because the forms of abuse overlap— some children are both physically and sexually abused—many researchers use *child abuse* or *child maltreatment* as a global construct and include various forms of maltreatment under the general term. When physical abuse and neglect are combined under the same term, it is impossible to know whether an association between alcohol and/or drug use and maltreatment is the result of alcohol and drugs producing disinhibition and thus violent behavior, whether the alcohol and drug abuse is itself considered a sign of neglect, or whether the alcohol and drug use led to neglect because of the debilitating effects of chronic or excessive alcohol and/or drug use.

Most studies of alcohol use and child maltreatment cannot be compared with one another because of the wide variation of nominal definitions of *maltreatment* employed by investigators. Some researchers study violence toward children, others focus on sexual abuse, and still others examine the full range of acts of commission and omission under the concept of child maltreatment. The varying definitions of abuse and neglect result in wide variations in the associations reported between drinking and drug use and child abuse and neglect. To a lesser extent, the same definitional problems affect the study of spouse abuse, woman abuse, and domestic violence. Definitions of *woman abuse* typically focus on acts of damaging physical violence directed toward women by their spouses or partners. Some investigators broaden the definition to include sexual abuse, marital rape, and even pornography.

Violence, the core concept in studies that attempt to test the hypothesis of a causal relation between alcohol and violence, has also proven to be difficult to define. The word *violence* is frequently used interchangeably with *aggression*, although *violence* refers to a physical act, while *aggression* refers to any malevolent act intended to hurt another person. The hurt may be emotional injury or material deprivation. Second, because of the negative connotation of the term *violence*, some investigators try to differentiate between hurtful violence and acts that may be evaluated as legitimate. Thus, William Goode (1971) tries to distinguish between legitimate acts of force and illegitimate acts of violence. Spanking a child who runs into the street might be considered "force," whereas beating the same child would be "violence." Attempts to clarify the concept of violence have demonstrated the difficulty of distinguishing between legitimate and illegitimate acts. Offenders, victims, bystanders, and agents of social control often accept and tolerate many acts between family members that would be considered illegitimate if committed by strangers.

Measuring Abuse and Violence. Although there is considerable variation in the nominal definitions of *abuse* and *violence*, there is quite a bit of similarity in the way researchers operationally define these terms. Abuse and violence are typically seen as taking place in those instances in which the victim becomes known and labeled by a professional or official agency. Thus, studies examining the relationship between alcohol and child abuse typically obtain a sample of abused children or abusive parents from clinical caseloads or official reports of child maltreatment. Studies focusing on wife assault most often obtain samples from clinical caseloads, programs for battered men, or shelters for battered women.

The major problem with operationally defining *violence* and *abuse* through the use of clinical cases or official report data is that the operational definitions overlook the systematic biases in the process by which cases of abuse are either officially labeled or come to clinical attention. For example, Newberger and his colleagues (1977) argue that poor and minority children with injuries seen in public hospitals are more likely to be labeled "abused" than are middle- or upper-class children seen in physicians' private practices.

A significant limitation of using clinical cases or official reports of abuse as the means of operationalizing the variables *maltreatment, abuse,* or *violence* is that the strength of the association between alcohol or other drug use and violence may be artificially increased by a selective labeling process. Physicians, social workers, police officers, and other social service and criminal justice personnel who believe that alcohol and drug abuse *cause* family violence may be susceptible to labeling an incident "child abuse" or "woman abuse" if alcohol or another substance is involved. If alcohol or substance use is absent, the same incident or injury may well be labeled an "accident." Sarah Fenstermaker Berk and Donileen Loseke (1980) found that police were more likely to make arrests in cases of domestic violence when the offender was drinking than when he was not drinking. Thus, studies using police records, court cases, social service records, and official registry data of child abuse and domestic violence probably overrepresent incidents in which alcohol and drugs were involved. These are the types of samples used in the majority of research studies cited by Flanzer (this volume). As noted earlier, if the study is examining child neglect and cases are drawn from official registries, the alcohol and drug use may have been the defining factor that led the caretaker to be reported for neglecting his or her child.

Alcohol and Drug Use. There are similar problems with the nominal and operational definitions of *alcohol* and *drug use* and *abuse.* The terms *alcohol use, alcohol abuse, alcoholism, drug use, drug dependency,* and *excessive use* are often used interchangeably, and the terms are often either not precisely defined or not defined at all. Flanzer himself (this volume) uses these terms interchangeably and never actually defines what he means by *alcoholism, substance abuse,* or *alcohol intake.* Paul Roman (1991) points out that an overarching problem with all research on alcohol use and abuse is that the jargon of *alcoholism, alcohol abuse, responsible drinking, problem drinking,* and all other such concepts are not effectively and consensually defined and measured. Just as some studies use the general term *child maltreatment,* some studies use the general term *substance abuse* to encompass use and abuse of a range of substances—alcohol, cocaine, marijuana, heroin, and so on. The use of a general construct for substance use and abuse ignores the differing pharmacological properties of the substances.

Furthermore, when studies actually do attempt to define and measure alcohol or drug use and abuse, they tend to use a single-item measure. Some studies use a single self-report measure of drinking, drug use, drinking problems, or drug problems—for instance, an item that asks whether the respondent has an alcohol problem. In other studies, it is not at all clear how the diagnoses of alcoholism or alcohol problems were made. Kenneth Leonard and Theodore Jacob (1988) note that it appears that someone—the offender, his or her spouse, or some social agency—simply categorizes the offender with respect to drinking habits.

Few studies attempt to distinguish between the amount of alcohol or a drug that is consumed and the frequency of consumption. Very few studies actually collect direct data on alcohol or drug use, such as using blood or saliva tests to assess the presence of alcohol or drugs in the body. Thus, because self-reports or classifications of alcohol or drug use are not validated against an objective measure, the validity of these classifications in many studies is questionable.

An additional measurement dilemma is that some studies assess history of alcohol and drug use and correlate this with violence; other studies measure alcohol or drug use for a specific period of time, for instance, the past six months or year; still other studies measure alcohol or substance use at the time of a violent incident.

When data are obtained on drinking or drug use at the time of the violent incident, researchers rarely obtain a measure of whether the perpetrator has a pattern of drinking or substance use. Conversely, some studies focus on the alcohol or drug problem, but do not measure whether the offender actually was using the substance at the time of the violent incident. This latter shortcoming is especially important, because such studies can shed no light on the disinhibition hypothesis about alcohol, drugs, and violence.

Research Designs

Flanzer (this volume) explains that there are three criteria that must be satisfied in order to demonstrate a causal relationship. He also argues that the research linking alcohol, drugs, and violence satisfies the criteria of causality. We believe that research not only fails to satisfy the three criteria, it fails to satisfy the fourth criteria of "theoretical rationale" as well.

1. *Association.* Research design problems in many of the studies examining drinking, drugs, and family violence limit the ability to determine whether significant associations exist. The main limitation of many studies is that the investigators fail to use a control or comparison group, or, if a comparison group is employed, it is not appropriate. Numerous studies simply collect data on the alcohol or drug use of a clinical population of abusers or abused. These studies identify the proportion of offenders who have alcohol problems or drug problems. Even if the proportions are quite high—greater than 50 percent—it is impossible to know whether these proportions are higher than would be found among other individuals in the clinical population who do not use violence against family members. When comparison groups are employed, investigators often fail to establish baseline measures of family violence. Thus, a study comparing alcohol use in a sample of individuals seen in therapy for domestic violence to a sample of individuals seen in therapy for marital distress cannot establish a valid association unless there is a baseline measure of domestic violence obtained from the presumed nonviolent distressed couples. Even when baseline data on violence are collected from a comparison group, the group itself may be inappropriate for comparison because of variations in significant social, demographic, or psychological variables.

Even when the studies employ control or comparison groups, the actual associations between alcohol and family violence are quite variable. Flanzer (this volume) asserts that estimates of the association of alcoholism and incest range from 20 percent to 50 percent. The relationship between alcohol use and domestic violence is similarly variable, depending on the study methodology. Thus, although the available evidence *does* demonstrate an association, it does *not* demonstrate a uniformly strong association between substance use and family violence.

2. *Time Order.* Because the vast majority of studies of drinking, drugs, and family violence are cross-sectional, where data are collected at only one point in time, investigators have difficulty in meeting the time order condition of causality. In brief, this means that the investigators

cannot demonstrate that the alcohol or drug use preceded the violent or abusive behavior. It is at least plausible that the drinking or drug use that is correlated with violence commenced *after* the onset of the violent behavior. Unless investigators examine the pattern of drinking and drug use over time, they cannot determine whether or not the drinking or drug use preceded the violent or abusive behavior.

3. Intervening Variables or Spuriousness. Few studies attempt to rule out spuriousness in the relationship between drinking or other drug use and family violence. As noted previously, one plausible spurious variable is that drinking may be the determining factor in whether a case is identified as child maltreatment or whether an arrest is made in the case of wife abuse. Another plausible source of spuriousness is that a social factor, such as poverty or marital conflict, may be simultaneously related to the likelihood of both substance abuse and violent and abusive behavior. Finally, the relationship between drinking and drug use and family violence may be spurious; it may be simply a function of expectancy effects. Because individuals in our culture assume that alcohol and drugs reduce inhibitions and increase the likelihood of violent or untoward sexual behavior, the cultural expectancy, rather than the chemical properties of the substances, may explain the association between drinking or drug use and family violence.

4. Theoretical Rationale. The final threat to the validity of the claim for a causal relationship between alcohol or other drug use and family violence is the inadequacy of the theoretical rationale. The key theoretical link used to explain the purported relationship is that alcohol and some drugs chemically affect the brain and break down or reduce inhibitions, and thus cause violent behavior. Yet the body of research just reviewed undermines this claim.

❖ CONCLUSION

It is clear that there is no simple link between substance use and family violence. The relationship cannot be explained simply by stating that alcohol or certain drugs "release inhibitions" and cause violent behavior. Even in the case of amphetamines, which have the most direct psychopharmacological relationship to violence, the effect depends on dosage and pre-use personality (Goldstein, 1985). The use of alcohol and/or drugs is not the sole determinant of whether or not an individual exhibits violent behavior. The influence of substances on the likelihood of violence is mediated by social factors, such as income, education, and occupation; cultural factors, such as attitudes about violence, drugs, alcohol, and the effects of alcohol; and personality factors.

Except for the evidence that appears to link amphetamine use to family violence, the portrait of the alcohol-and-drug-crazed partner or parent who impulsively and violently abuses a family member is a distortion. There is no conclusive, empirical evidence to support a causal relationship between abuse and alcohol or other drug use or abuse. The relationship between substance abuse and violence is complex and mediated by a myriad of individual, situational, and social factors.

❖ REFERENCES

Bard, M., & Zacker, J. (1974). Assaultiveness and alcohol use in family disputes. *Criminology, 12,* 281–292.

Bennett, L. (1995). Substance abuse and the domestic assault of women. *Social Work, 40,* 760–771.

Berk, S., & Loseke, D. (1980). "Handling" family violence: The situated determinants of police arrest in domestic disturbances. *Law and Society Review, 15,* 317–346.

Boles, S. M., & Miotto, K. (2003). Substance abuse and violence: A review of the literature. *Aggression and Violent Behavior, 8,* 155–174.

Coleman, D. H., & Straus, M. A. (1983). Alcohol abuse and family violence. In E. Gottheil, K. Druley, T. Skoloda, & H. Waxman (Eds.), *Alcohol, drug abuse and aggression* (pp. 104-124). Springfield, IL: Charles C. Thomas.

Gelles, R. J. (1974). *The violent home: A study of physical aggression between husbands and wives.* Beverly Hills, CA: Sage.

Goldstein, P. J. (1985). The drugs/violence nexus: A tripartite conceptual framework. *Journal of Drug Issues, 15,* 492-506.

Goode, W. J. (1971). Force and violence in the family. *Journal of Marriage and the Family, 33,* 624-636.

Gordon, L. (1988). *Heroes of their own lives: The politics and history of family violence.* New York: Viking.

Johnson, R. (1972). *Aggression in man and animals.* Philadelphia: W. B. Saunders.

Kaufman Kantor, G., & Straus, M. A. (1987). The drunken bum theory of wife beating. *Social Problems, 34,* 213-230.

Kaufman Kantor, G., & Straus, M. A. (1989). Substance abuse as a precipitant of wife abuse victimizations. *American Journal of Alcohol Abuse, 15,* 173-189.

Kosten, T. R., & Singha, A. K. (1999). Stimulants. In M. Galanter & H. D. Kleber (Eds.), *Textbook of substance abuse treatment* (2nd ed., pp. 183–193). Washington, DC: American Psychiatric Press.

Lang, A. R., Goeckner, D. J., Adesso, V. J., & Marlatt, G. A. (1975). Effects of alcohol on aggression in male social drinkers. *Journal of Abnormal Psychology, 84*, 508-518.

Leonard, K. E., & Jacob, T. (1988). Alcohol, alcoholism, and family violence. In V. B. Van Hasselt, R. L. Morrison, A. S. Bellack, & M. Hersen (Eds.), *Handbook of family violence* (pp. 383-406). New York: Plenum.

MacAndrew, C., & Edgerton, R. B. (1969). *Drunken comportment: A social explanation.* Chicago: Aldine.

Miller, M. M., & Potter-Efron, R. T. (1990). Aggression and violence associated with substance abuse. In R. T. Potter-Efron & P. S. Potter-Efron (Eds.), *Aggression, family violence, and chemical dependency* (pp. 1-36). New York: Haworth.

Newberger, E. H., Reed, R. B., Daniel, J. H., Hyde, J. N., Jr., & Kotelchuck, M. (1977). Pediatric social illness: Toward an etiologic classification. *Pediatrics, 60*, 178-185.

Nicholi, A. (1983). The non-therapeutic use of psychoactive drugs. *New England Journal of Medicine, 308*, 925-933.

Parker, R. N., & Auerhahn, K. (1998). Alcohol, drugs, and violence. *Annual Review of Sociology, 24*, 291–311.

Radbill, S. (1974). A history of child abuse and infanticide. In R. E. Helfer & C. H. Kempe (Eds.), *The battered child* (2nd ed., pp. 3-21). Chicago: University of Chicago Press.

Reiss, A. J., & Roth, J. A. (1993). Alcohol, and other psychoactive drugs and violence. In A. J. Reiss & J. A. Roth (Eds.), *Understanding and preventing violence* (pp. 182–220). Washington, DC: National Academy Press.

Roman, P. M. (1991). Preface. In P. M. Roman (Ed.), *Alcohol: The development of sociological perspectives on use and abuse* (pp. 1-18). New Brunswick, NJ: Rutgers Center on Alcohol Studies.

Roth, J. A. (1994). *Psychoactive substances and violence.* Washington, DC: National Institute of Justice, Office of Justice Programs (February).

Senay, E. C. (1999). Opioids: methadone maintenance. In M. Galanter & H. D. Kleber (Eds.), *Textbook of substance treatment* (2nd ed., pp. 271–279). Washington, DC: American Psychiatric Press.

Smith, E. O., & Byrd, L. (1987). External and internal influences on aggression in captive group-living monkeys. In R. J. Gelles & J. Lancaster (Eds.), *Child abuse and neglect: Biosocial dimensions* (pp. 175-199). Hawthorne, NY: Aldine de Gruyter.

Taylor, S., & Leonard, K. E. (1983). Alcohol and human physical aggression. In R. Green & E. Donnerstein (Eds.), *Aggression: Theoretical and empirical reviews, Vol. 2* (pp. 77–111). New York: Academic Press.

Wolfner, G., & Gelles, R. J. (1993). A profile of violence toward children: A national study. *Child Abuse and Neglect, 17*, 197-212.

12

Elder Abuse Is Caused by the Perception of Stress Associated With Providing Care

Suzanne K. Steinmetz

C onsiderable research in the gerontology literature has documented the impact of stress associated with providing care to an elder. "Caught in the middle," "the sandwich generation" (E. Brody, 1966, 1970), and "generationally inverse families"(Steinmetz, 1988; Steinmetz & Amsden, 1983) are phrases used to describe middle-aged caregivers who simultaneously are providing some level of care for aging parents as well as caring for their own children. As the caregiving responsibility for an elderly family member increasingly takes over the life of the caregiver, it is not unrealistic to expect some

AUTHOR'S NOTE: Support for this project was provided by Public Health Service grant D31AH65033.

negative consequences. The title selected for a book describing the difficulties faced by families caring for individuals with Alzheimer's disease, *The 36-Hour Day* (Mace, 1981), illustrates the feelings experienced by caregivers. A 55-year-old daughter who was providing care to both her 74-year-old mother and 89-year-old aunt described her feelings in a similar fashion:

> DON'T DO IT, DON'T EVER, EVER DO IT! Do whatever you can. You can give them so much more of yourself when you go to visit them if they are not living with you. It is so easy to be loving and to carry them to the doctor's office when they don't live with you. . . . I could give her more moral support and a lot more loving attention if I didn't have to physically care for her. . . . I could go get her and say "Oh your hair is so pretty and let's go here and let's go there." I don't feel like taking her to Longwood Gardens on Sunday when I've had her 6 days a week besides. . . . I would have a much better relationship, [if we were] separate. The way it is now, all I want to do is to get away from her. (Steinmetz, 1988, p. 137)

While Pillemer (this volume) argues that it is the dependent family member who is abusing the caregiving elder, my challenge in this chapter is to provide evidence that the stress, frustration, and feelings of burden experienced by caregivers who are caring for dependent elders can result in abusive and neglectful treatment. Based on a growing number of studies, it is clear that both situations occur. Because the availability of resources to address this problem is limited, an attempt to evaluate the relative need of each group is needed. If the goal of this debate is to provide guidance for policymakers and social planners, then it is critical to analyze the elder's risk of abuse by spouse, by adult caregiving child, and by dependent adult child.

❖ THE IMPORTANCE OF DEFINITIONS

The label placed on a phenomenon greatly influences our perception of, and the attributes associated with, the phenomenon. The term *elder abuse* is ambiguous because the legal and social service definitions do not necessarily correspond to definitions used by researchers. Thus it is not surprising that noncomparable and often contradictory findings result. Although the generally accepted definition of *family violence*, "the intentional use of physical force on another person" (Steinmetz & Straus, 1974, p. 4), is suitable for designing academic studies of family violence, this definition is incongruent with legal definitions used by law enforcement, Adult Protective Services (APS), and social service agencies. Such a definition would include not only acts of physical abuse, but also verbal abuse, emotional or psychological abuse (such as threats, insults), medical abuse (such as overmedicating, refusal to give medicine or to follow medical orders), resource or material abuse, and neglect. These categories of abuse and neglect are consistent with APS legislation as well as the basis for many studies (Fulmer & O'Malley, 1987; Phillips, 1983; Steinmetz, 1988).

It also is important to consider findings based on caregivers' self-reported fear of becoming violent (Pillemer & Suitor, 1992) or self-reported threats to commit violent acts (Steinmetz, 1988), as they provide indicators of situations that, without intervention, might easily develop into physical abuse. In fact, Pillemer and Suitor (1992) note that in their study of caregivers, "those who were only fearful of becoming violent differed little from those respondents who actually became violent" (p. S170).

Defining the Actors

In other forms of domestic violence, the dyad or participating members define the behavior. For example, *child abuse* is defined as neglect or physical, emotional, or sexual abuse or exploitation of a child by a parent or caretaker. *Spouse, partner,* or *courtship violence* is defined in terms of the participants and their relationship to one another. *Elder abuse,* on the other hand, is defined primarily by the age of the victim—an age that varies from state to state based on eligibility for services—rather than the relationship of victim to perpetrator (for a discussion of differences in states' definitions of elder abuse and resultant rates of elder abuse and maltreatment, see American Public Welfare Association and National Association for State Units on Aging, 1986). Spousal or partner violence has been documented to be the most prevalent form of family violence in national or regional random samples, regardless of the age of the spouses (Gelles & Straus, 1988; Pillemer & Finkelhor, 1989; Straus, Gelles, & Steinmetz, 1980).

This raises the issue of whether we are measuring elder abuse or simply relabeling behaviors when they occur among those over 60 or

65 years of age. In other words, is *elder abuse* a distinct category of family violence, or is it simply an adjective denoting the age of the victim and modifying a variety of categories of family violence? Unfortunately, when elder abuse is based on the age of the participants, the critical dimension of *dependency* is not considered. To determine if the 35-year-old child is dependent on the elderly parent or is providing care to the 65-year-old parent requires an examination of the sociodemographic characteristics of the individuals involved and the social roles they have assumed.

Defining the Act

Adult protective service agencies serve the needs of all adults over 18 years of age, not just individuals over 65 years of age. The focus of these agencies is on identifying and protecting the adult who is experiencing abuse; the perpetrator or form of abuse is secondary. Furthermore, the relationship between the abused and the perpetrator is not clearly defined and includes family, other informal caregivers, nursing home attendants, neighbors, and those targeting the elderly for consumer fraud.

One of the most comprehensive surveys of agency-based data was conducted by the American Public Welfare Association and National Association of State Units on Aging (1986). Data were compiled on reported, suspected, or alleged elder abuse for 1983 and 1984 from the state agencies mandated to collect these data. Although data were collected from all but six states, nationwide comparisons are problematic. For example, only 29 states had categorized their data by age. Of these, 13 states included self-abuse/neglect as well as abuse and neglect perpetrated by informal caregivers, and 7 states included institutional abuse as well as that perpetrated by informal caregivers and self-abuse/neglect.

Data based on APS statistics present a picture of dependent, frail elders, predominantly women, in their late seventies or early eighties, who are experiencing maltreatment at the hands of informal caregivers—primarily immediate family members. The argument could be made, of course, that APS statistics underestimate the actual amount of elder abuse because they represent the most severe cases—those who have come to the attention of the authorities.

Although the research of Pillemer and his colleagues represents a major contribution to our understanding of physical violence against people over 65 years old, the findings based on responses to the Conflict Tactic Scales (CTS; see Straus et al., 1980) bear little resemblance to the cases received by Adult Protective Services. For example, Pillemer and Finkelhor (1989) note that individuals were categorized as experiencing physical abuse if they experienced any of the physical violence categories on the CTS. Yet, in another article discussing the use of the CTS for obtaining measures of verbal and physical abuse, Pillemer and Prescott (1989) state, "No claim is made here that the concept of elder abuse and neglect should be defined for the purpose of social policy in the same way as for this study" (p. 69). The classification of neglect also was problematic. On one hand, individuals could be classified as experiencing neglect if the elder "reported that a caregiver had failed to provide needed care 10 or more times in the preceding year." This is a very rigorous test for neglect and one that assumes that the elder person has a calendar-like mind with a remarkable ability to recall events. However, elders also could be classified as experiencing neglect if they "termed the lack of care as 'somewhat' or 'very serious'" (Pillemer & Finkelhor, 1989, p. 182). It is not possible to determine which method of classification was used most frequently.

❖ THE IMPORTANCE OF SAMPLES

As in all research, the sample selected and the questions posed define the results. For more than 30 years we have debated the differences in findings from studies based on interviews with battered women and those from large representative samples of men and women. If one wants to study the characteristics of battered women, the circumstances leading up to the battering incident, or the processes involved in the decision to leave a relationship characterized by violence, then in-depth interviews with women who have come to shelters for battered women is an appropriate way to do so. However, these findings will not be comparable to large, representative samples of women and men designed to produce incidence or prevalence rates of spousal violence. Similarly, data compiled from caseloads of APS agencies portray self-neglect and self-abuse as constituting the majority of elder abuse cases handled (American Public Welfare Association and National Association for State Units on Aging, 1986); yet this is not the picture portrayed in either Pillemer and Finkelhor's (1989) study or my own work (Steinmetz, 1988).

Three distinct characteristics distinguish the adult children and elders in Pillemer and Finkelhor's (1989) study and those in my most recent study (Steinmetz, 1988) of informal caregivers of elders. First, with a mean age of 82, the dependent elders were considerably older in my sample than were the dependent elders in Pillemer and Finkelhor's random sample (mean age of about 74). Because there is evidence that both dependency and conflict between younger caretakers and "elderly" parents increase with age, one would expect that Pillemer and Finkelhor's sample would not show the same patterns of dependency and abuse.

Second, nearly 3 in 4 of the adult children in Pillemer and Finkelhor's study had never married, and nearly two-thirds of the adult children had never left home. Clearly, some of the conflict found could result from parental perceptions that their children were not fulfilling normative adult roles—growing up, moving out, and setting up their own households—as well as the adult children's resenting their parents' reminders that they have not yet obtained full independence. In contrast, with few exceptions, the elders in my study resided in the *adult child's* household. Therefore, it was the middle-aged (or older) child, and his or her family's lifestyle, that had to accommodate the elder. In the exceptions, the elderly parent had refused to move in with the adult child even though it was evident that the parent no longer was able to live independently. The solution, in these families, was for the child and his or her family to move into the elder's home. Unfortunately, conflicts over home ownership, which was considered to be synonymous with being the boss of the household, resulted.

Third and finally, the adult children in Pillemer and Finkelhor's study were fairly young, with a mean age of 38. For comparison, the mean age of adult children in my study was 52.

❖ THE IMPORTANCE OF RESEARCH DESIGN

Comparability across studies is also hindered by differences in the types of samples (random, convenience, quota) and methods of data collection (observation, questionnaire, personal interview) as well as by differences in the instruments used. Elder abuse research has used third-party reporting by professionals, victimization data collected by law enforcement and APS agencies, and interviews with caretakers and elders (for a review of these studies, see Steinmetz, 1987, 1988). Given the range of methodologies for collecting the data, as well as the diversity of samples, it is not surprising that there is little congruence among the studies.

It is important to recognize that the criteria for selecting the individuals to be interviewed define the parameters of the findings. For example, Sengstock and Liang (1982) selected only verified cases of abuse; therefore, the high levels of physical abuse they report, when compared with other studies, are not unexpected. Pillemer and Finkelhor (1989) interviewed a random sample of individuals 65 years or older and found that the abusive family member was often dependent on the elder, and in nearly 60 percent of the cases, this abusive family member was a spouse. Their findings are inconsistent with those from other studies based on samples of informal caregivers that correlated increasing dependency to increasing stress (S. J. Brody, 1978; Kosberg, 1983) and abuse (Cicirelli, 1983; Fulmer & O'Malley, 1987; Phillips, 1983; Pillemer & Suitor, 1992; Steinmetz, 1983, 1988; Steinmetz & Amsden, 1983).

Pillemer and Finkelhor (1989) administered the CTS to individuals over 65 years of age by telephone and in person; the researchers note that they were not likely to tap those most vulnerable—the frail elderly with physical and mental impairments. Because the sampling procedure identified households headed by independent elders, when a 65-year-old or older individual was dependent, he or she was likely to be a spouse. It is not surprising, then, that in this study 58 percent of the perpetrators of abuse were spouses. Although in some families the spousal abuse represented lifelong abusive marital relationships, in other families both the elderly spouse's physical and emotional dependency on the caregiver and abusive behavior most likely resulted from Alzheimer's disease or other age-related illnesses, such as strokes. Pillemer (1985) provides examples of this problem:

A frail woman . . . had a stable relationship with her husband. He developed Alzheimer's disease and needed constant supervision. "He would beat me pretty bad, choke me. He grabbed me and said 'I'll kill you. . .'"

An elderly woman was the primary caretaker for her wheelchair-bound husband. He was totally incontinent. In the preceding few months, he had become violent. He ripped his diapers off and would not let her change them. He threatened her with his walker and hit her when she tried to take care of him. (p. 154)

A problem faced by APS workers is how to ascertain the credibility of the information provided by the elder alleging abuse. This is accomplished by observing the elder and asking a series of questions to assess his or her cognitive functioning. Unfortunately, in a one-time, relatively brief telephone interview, it may not be possible to adequately screen out elderly people who might be suffering from paranoia or the early stages of dementia. The report of a 53-year-old daughter who had been caring for her 93-year-old mother for eight years illustrates this problem:

> You don't know what I went through! She got on my nerves so bad that my niece came and got her. . . . She kept her for a while and got on her nerves so bad that I had to go down south and get Mamma and bring her back. . . . I put her in a foster home and had to go and get her. . . . She didn't fit in. If I said 'mamma, here's your dinner,' she'd say 'I don't want it.' She broke her hip and told the doctor that I threw her down and broke her hip. (Steinmetz, 1988, p. 20)

If we had interviewed this elder, could we report with confidence that the adult child had thrown her mother down the stairs? Another caregiver, a 47-year-old daughter who had been caring for her 84-year-old mother for five months, described her mother's paranoia and inability to deal with reality:

> One day she called us up and said that she had been shot. Several times in the middle of the night she would come to our bedroom door and she would want to know . . . where her [dead] sister Helen was now. (Steinmetz, 1988, p. 20)

Without corroborating data, the validity of the responses is problematic, especially in view of the complexity of the CTS when administered by phone to an elderly person. Interviewing the caregiver should not be interpreted as a lack of sensitivity to the elder's perception of the situation. Caregivers often make it quite clear that their views of events probably differ from their parents' perceptions of the same events. Just as family therapists have long recognized that there is the wife's marriage, the husband's marriage, and the couple's marriage, there is the adult child caregiver's view of parent–child interaction as well as the elder's view. However, a symbolic interaction perspective suggests that the caregiver's perception of reality would strongly influence his or her behavior. I have found that if caregivers *perceive* caregiving to be stressful, they are more likely to resort to abuse, regardless of the actual degree of dependency of the elder on the caregiver (Steinmetz, 1988).

❖ EXAMINING THE FINDINGS ON ELDER DEPENDENCY AND ABUSE BY CAREGIVERS

Pillemer (this volume) notes that I am the leading proponent of the view that increased dependency is linked to abuse. He states that this view is not supported by his data. He suggests that we should refocus our research on the characteristics of the abuser, rather than the victim. Clearly, more scientific data are needed on all participants who play a role in elder abuse. However, focusing on one member of an interacting pair (caregiver–elder) and assuming that we can obtain an adequate picture of elder abuse and recommend appropriate prevention and/or intervention programs are not prudent approaches and do not reflect the complexity of the elder–caregiver relationship.

Many of the studies that have examined elders' dependency and the impact on the caregiving family, a rich body of literature covering more than three decades of research, carefully articulate the relationships among dependency, stress, and burden. More recently, this literature has been linked to elder abuse.

In studies I have conducted, caregivers were asked how frequently they had to provide a series of modified activity of daily living (ADL) tasks for an elderly person and how much it bothered them to do so (Steinmetz, 1983, 1988; Steinmetz & Amsden, 1983). They were also asked questions about the problems and associated stress resulting from feeling totally responsible for the elder's well-being and sharing a residence with the elder. A moderate relationship was observed between elder abuse and *objective* levels of elder's impairment or caregiver's need to provide dependency-related tasks. However, a much stronger relationship was observed between elder abuse and the *subjective* feelings of stress and burden as a result of need to assist the elder.

Similar findings are provided by Fulmer and O'Malley (1987) in their comparison of 107 cases referred to an elder abuse assessment team with 147 cases of the same age group who were not referred to the abuse assessment team. They used a five-point Likert scale to rate a variety of forms of dependency (administration of medication, physical mobility, continence, feeding, maintenance and hygiene, and management of finances). The elder's dependency on the caregiver was found to be an important predisposing factor for elder abuse and neglect. Fulmer and Ashley (1989) conducted a factor analysis on data generated from the Elder Assessment Instrument. They found that level of dependency on the care provider was an important variable in predicting elder abuse and neglect.

Phillips (1983) categorized families into "abusive" and "good relationships." This procedure was somewhat problematic because the nurses who interviewed the families were unable to assign 12 of the 63 families into one category or the other, so independent judges made the final assignment. This may account for the lack of significant findings between physical functioning and abuse. However, the strongest direct relationship in Phillips's causal model was that between "family members in the house also available to help" and abuse. Based on her data, it is clear that the availability of others to assist with providing care, thus reducing the responsibility and dependency of the elder's care on a single caregiver, reduces the likelihood of abuse.

Brown (1989) interviewed one-third of the Native Americans over 60 years old residing at the Oljato Chapter of the Navajos in Arizona. An additional close member of the family (spouse, child, grandchild) also was interviewed. This study found that dependency patterns provided an important abuse indicator. Caregivers who lived with an elder and who had total responsibility for his or her care (indicators of dependency) were more likely to be physically abusive. These findings were consistent when reported by either the elder or the other family member.

Finally, Pillemer and Suitor's (1992) research on caregivers of elders with Alzheimer's disease examined the effect of dependency on abuse. Using a combined measure of actual violence and fear of violence, they report that violent caregivers tended to live with the elders, provide care for more functionally impaired elders, and provide help with a greater number of activities. These findings are contrary to the large number of articles in which Pillemer and colleagues have forcefully stated that elder dependency as measured by functional impairment does *not* result in being abused by the caregiver (see Pillemer, this volume). Given that Cicirelli (1983), Phillips (1983), and I (Steinmetz, 1988) used causal modeling to distinguish the relative impact of a variety of factors related to dependency that contributed to elder abuse, Pillemer and Suitor's (1992) statement that their findings "stand in contrast to the simplistic view propounded in the elder abuse literature that the dependency of the care recipient leads directly to violence" (p. S171) is most curious.

If one defines *dependency* in terms of ability to perform ADLs, then a relationship between dependency and abuse is limited. However, if one defines *dependency* in terms of the number of responsibilities that the caregiver has to fulfill and the inability to be relieved of these responsibilities (such as when the elder lives with the caregiver, or when others are unavailable to assist in this care), then a relationship between dependency and abuse is found. If the research findings are to be useful in preventing or ameliorating elder abuse, policymakers and social service providers would be well advised to focus on the dynamics in these families rather than on a specific definition of dependency based exclusively on the elder's level of functional impairment.

An interesting example is provided by Greenberg, McKibben, and Raymond (1990) in their analysis of 204 abused elders and their adult children. Of this group, 51 percent of the elders were described as "frail" and 20 percent were "homebound." Therefore, 71 percent of this group of abused elders were substantially dependent on their adult children for care and assistance. However, 25 percent of their adult children were financially dependent on the elderly parents. In these families, were the adult children abusive caregivers or abusive dependent adult children? The answer depends on the definition of *dependency* used.

Although setting up a straw person with the goal of systematically knocking down the myths is a useful approach for presenting one's arguments, one needs to have a viable straw person. Pillemer's is lacking. Although he expends considerable effort on presenting data to refute the simplistic notion that elders' level of impairment leads to abuse, none of the recent literature and few studies in the past have proposed this limited relationship between dependency defined as functional impairment and abuse.

Stone, Cafferata, and Sangl (1987), using data from the 1982 long-term care survey, found that primary caregivers of the elderly were most likely to be immediate family members. Adult daughters were caregivers in 29 percent, wives in 23 percent, and husbands in 13 percent of the families. As the number of frail elderly increases, we can expect the problem of elder abuse to also increase. It is important that high-quality, inexpensive, continuum-of-care facilities are available to meet the needs of this increasingly larger population of vulnerable elderly. With more women in the workforce (who are likely to continue working until age 70 unless they are experiencing serious medical problems), we need to ask, Who will care for our elderly parents? Given their own unfortunate experiences, many adults who have cared for an elderly parent have told their children that when they can no longer maintain their independence they want to be institutionalized. A 58-year-old daughter who had cared for her mother for eight years reported:

> I didn't have anyone to go to. . . . I was so deeply depressed. She [the 93-year-old mother] told me she didn't want to go into a home. What can I do? I told my son "If I get disabled I don't want you to hesitate. I don't want to be a burden on you. Put me in a home, I won't mind it. I've been through it. I know what it is." (Steinmetz, 1988, p. 227)

In a similar vein, a 66-year-old daughter who had been caring for her 86-year-old father for four years noted in a discussion with her daughter:

> I want you to promise me that when I get like this that you will please put me someplace. She said, "I couldn't do that." I said, "I want you to do it because I don't want to wreck someone's life, and that is exactly what it is. . . . Please put me someplace. Let me maintain my sense of dignity. I don't want to be in somebody's home and I don't want to feel that I am a burden—that's what it is, a burden." (Steinmetz, 1988, p. 176)

Intervention also is necessary for elderly parents who are being abused by their dependent, often disabled, adult children for whom they are providing care. Deinstitutionalization has resulted in the burden of caring for emotionally, mentally, and chronically ill children being placed on the family. As the parents age, we can anticipate that this problem will continue to increase.

Likewise, spouses need assistance in caring for partners who have become abusive as the result of Alzheimer's disease or a stroke—or are simply continuing with patterns of spousal abuse established earlier in the marriage. With increasing life expectancy, higher costs of living, and inadequate Social Security and pensions, we can assume that the responsibility of caring for an elderly parent, for a large percentage of families, will ultimately fall on an adult child. Even if an elderly spouse had provided care for his or her dependent partner, it is still likely that he or she will also eventually require assistance from other family members.

As the cost of institutional care continues to rise, family members, especially adult children, will continue to be a major source of care for elderly parents. These informal caregivers, tackling an around-the-clock job with no training and limited resources, will increasingly be at risk of abusing elders unless we are able to provide education, resources, and home-based assistance.

It is important to identify the caregiving situations and characteristics of elders and caregivers that are likely to result in the use of abusive techniques to gain or maintain control. In my studies based on a sample of dependent elders, as well as those of other researchers, level of dependency (primarily emotional and mental health) was positively correlated with abuse. However, an even stronger predictor of abuse was the *caregiver's perception of the stress* associated with providing the care. Thus the expressed feeling of burden and stress from having to perform tasks for the elder provided a more accurate prediction of abuse than did the duration of caregiving or the actual level of care needed. This suggests that families and social service agents need to consider the caregiver's subjective feeling about providing care as well as the level of care that will need to be provided when an elder can no longer live independently and alternative arrangements need to be made.

Three distinct populations have been identified in which elders are at risk: An elder may be abused by adult children who are caring for him or her, by an elderly spouse, or by adult children who are physically, mentally, or emotionally disabled and are dependent on the elder. In a society as rich as ours, the issue should not be *which* population is in greatest need of limited resources, but rather how we can best meet the needs of *all* at-risk elders and their families.

❖ REFERENCES

American Public Welfare Association and National Association of State Units on Aging. (1986). *A comprehensive analysis of state policy and practice related to elder abuse: A focus on legislation, appropriations, incidence data, and special studies.* Washington, DC: Author.

Brody, E. (1966). The aging family. *Gerontologist, 6,* 201–206.

Brody, E. (1970). The etiquette of filial behavior. *Aging and Human Development, 1,* 87–94.

Brody, S. J. (1978). The family caring unit: A major consideration in the long-term support system. *Gerontologist, 18,* 556–561.

Brown, A. S. (1989). A survey on elder abuse at one Native American tribe. *Journal of Elder Abuse and Neglect, 1,* 17–37.

Cicirelli, V. C. (1983). Adult children's attachment and helping behavior to elderly parents: A path model. *Journal of Marriage and the Family, 45,* 815–825.

Fulmer, T., & Ashley, J. (1989). Clinical indicators which signal elder neglect. *Applied Nursing Research Journal, 2,* 161–167.

Fulmer, T., & O'Malley, T. (1987). *Inadequate care of the elderly: A health care perspective on abuse and neglect.* New York: Springer.

Gelles, R. J., & Straus, M. A. (1988). *Intimate violence: The causes and consequences of abuse in the American family.* New York: Simon & Schuster.

Greenberg, J. R., McKibben, M., & Raymond, J. A. (1990). Dependent adult children and elder abuse. *Journal of Elder Abuse and Neglect, 2,* 73–86.

Kosberg, J. I. (Ed.). (1983). *Abuse and maltreatment of the elderly: Causes and interventions.* Littleton, MA: John Wright, PSG.

Mace, N. L. (1981). *The 36-hour day: A family guide to caring for persons with Alzheimer's disease, related dementing illness, and memory loss in later life.* Baltimore: Johns Hopkins University Press.

Phillips, L. R. (1983). Abuse and neglect of the frail elderly at home: An exploration of theoretical relationships. *Journal of Advanced Nursing, 8,* 379–39.

Pillemer, K. (1985). The dangers of dependency: New findings on domestic violence against elderly. *Social Problems, 33,* 146–158.

Pillemer, K., & Finkelhor, D. (1989). Causes of elder abuse: Caregiver stress versus problem relatives. *American Journal of Orthopsychiatry, 59,* 179–187.

Pillemer, K., & Prescott, D. (1989). Psychological effects of elder abuse: A research note. *Journal of Elder Abuse and Neglect, 1,* 65–73.

Pillemer, K., & Suitor, J. J. (1992). Violence and violent feelings: What causes them among family caregivers. *Journal of Gerontology, 47,* S165–S172.

Sengstock, M. D., & Liang, J. (1982). *Identifying and characterizing elder abuse.* Detroit, MI: Wayne State University Press.

Steinmetz, S. K. (1983). Dependency, stress and violence between middle-aged care-givers and their elderly parents. In J. I. Kosberg (Ed.), *Abuse and maltreatment of the elderly: Causes and interventions* (pp. 134–139). Littleton, MA: John Wright, PSG.

Steinmetz, S. K. (1987). Family violence: Past, present and future. In M. B. Sussman & S. K. Steinmetz (Eds.), *Handbook of marriage and the family* (pp. 725–765). New York: Plenum.

Steinmetz, S. K. (1988). *Duty bound: Elder abuse and family care.* Newbury Park, CA: Sage.

Steinmetz, S. K., & Amsden, D. J. (1983). Dependent elders, family stress, and abuse. In T. H. Brubaker (Ed.), *Family relationships in later life* (pp. 173–192). Beverly Hills, CA: Sage.

Steinmetz, S. K., & Straus, M. A. (Eds.). (1974). *Violence in the family.* New York: Harper & Row.

Stone, R. C., Cafferata, C. L., & Sangl, J. (1987). Caregivers of the frail elderly: A national profile. *Gerontologist, 27,* 616–626.

Straus, M. A., Gelles, R. J., & Steinmetz, S. K. (1980). *Behind closed doors: Violence in the American family.* Garden City, NY: Anchor/Doubleday.

13

Elder Abuse Is Caused by the Deviance and Dependence of Abusive Caregivers

Karl Pillemer

W hy do people abuse elderly family members? As with other forms of family violence, this question is as critically important to answer as it is difficult to do so. Some of the difficulties are methodological: Obtaining information on a hidden—and, for many people, shameful—topic is a daunting task at best. The search for risk factors has also been clouded by elder abuse's 30-year history as a social problem: Early assertions, founded on faulty data (or no data at all) have

AUTHOR'S NOTE: This chapter was prepared with support from the Florence V. Burden Foundation and the Ittleson Foundation. It is adapted from Wolf and Pillemer (1989).

been repeated so frequently that they have come to be widely believed, despite the lack of evidence. Research has yet to move creatively beyond some of these mistaken assumptions about elder abuse.

In some ways, an examination of what has been written to date on elder abuse has a certain Alice-in-Wonderland feel to it. This is a field in which review articles outnumber actual research reports; in which most of the researchers use health and human service professionals, rather than victims and their families, as their subjects; and in which such basic research tools as random sample surveys and case-control studies are rarely used. State laws and intervention programs have been founded on this shaky information, with little or no scientific evaluation.

An appropriate example of the problems in developing a body of knowledge about elder abuse is the issue of *dependency*. Since the earliest writings about maltreatment of the aged, dependency has been postulated as a major risk factor. Two views have been juxtaposed (see Fulmer, 1990): one that emphasizes the increased frailty and dependence of elders on caregivers, and an alternative view that focuses on the deviance and dependence of abusive relatives on their victims. Suzanne Steinmetz (this volume) offers a thoughtful and cogent review of the former perspective.

In contrast, in this chapter I present an argument that deemphasizes the role of the dependency of the victim and highlights instead the pathology and dependency of the *abuser*. I do so based on an evaluation of the available scientific evidence. To be sure, the empirical evidence is flawed to some degree. However, a review of the most reliable and valid studies conducted to date calls for a refocusing on characteristics of the abuser—rather than of the victims—as major risk factors for elder abuse.

What are the criteria by which we should evaluate the issue of dependency and elder abuse? There appear to me to be several crucial questions to be addressed. First, what are the origins of the view that the dependency of the victim leads to abuse? Second, is there evidence that abused elders are especially likely to be ill or impaired? Third, is there evidence that victims are especially dependent on their abusive relatives? Finally, what about the reverse proposition: Is there evidence that abusers are dependent on their victims?

In the remainder of this chapter, I address these questions in turn. While I focus my discussion on physical violence, it is impossible to restrict the analysis entirely to physical abuse, because many of the studies discussed in this chapter include victims of several types of maltreatment, including psychological and material abuse (for example, Bristowe & Collins, 1989; Phillips, 1983; Pillemer & Finkelhor, 1989).

❖   "PITY THE PERPETRATOR": VICTIM
     DEPENDENCY AS THE CAUSE OF ABUSE

In this volume, Steinmetz argues that few studies have proposed a limited relationship between dependency defined as functional impairment and abuse. On this point, I strongly disagree. In fact, if there can be a "traditional" view in a field that is now three decades old, it is that elder abuse can be summed up in the following way: Elderly people become sick, frail, dependent, and difficult to care for. They cause stress for their caregivers. As a result of this stress, these otherwise responsible and well-meaning relatives lose control and become abusive toward the elders. In this view, elder abuse is seen as essentially a natural outgrowth of the aging process that leads to the need for family care.

This view has been described succinctly by Baumann (1989), who notes that, as with many social problems, "claims-makers" developed a view of the issue designed to bring it quickly to national attention and to garner resources to treat it. In this case, advocates used analogies with child abuse to call attention to elder abuse. As Baumann notes, statements about the dependency of the elderly were a major way to justify allocating resources to elder abuse. Assertions that the elderly are abused because of their increased needs for care provided a rationale for assistance; our society is seen as morally obligated to provide for these elders, because they—like children—cannot fend for themselves.

Indeed, much early writing on elder abuse emphasized the dependency of the elder in precisely this way. For example, from their survey of professionals, Hickey and Douglass (1981) claim:

The sudden or unwanted dependency of parents is a key factor in understanding neglect and abuse. . . . To the extent that dependent individuals must rely on others for care, protection, and sustenance, they are at-risk of being hurt, unprotected, etc. (p. 174)

Similarly, Davidson (1979), in an early report, tied abuse directly to the "crises" created by the needs of an elderly parent for care:

Yet just as the child is abused by his parent who resents the dependency of the child because the parent himself lacks satisfaction of needs, the adult child who must assume a caretaker role to his own parents may become abusive as a result of his parents' dependency and the lack of need satisfaction. (p. 49)

Steinmetz (1988) was another early proponent of this view. She argued that families undergo "generational inversion," in which the elderly person becomes dependent upon his or her children. This places the caregiver under severe stress.

This view has been so pervasive that many have come to consider elder abuse exclusively a problem of family caregiving. In a number of articles, abusers are referred to as "caregivers," and abuse is defined as actions by caregivers. For example, O'Malley, O'Malley, Everitt, and Sarson (1986) suggest that all elder abuse be subsumed under the term "inadequate care." As such, the definition of *abuse* they propose is "active intervention by a caretaker such that unmet needs are created with resultant physical, psychological, or financial injury"(p. 26). Many individuals have adopted this view in designing interventions, so much so that probably the most frequently recommended programs to reduce elder abuse are those that treat caregiver stress (see Douglass, 1988; Scoggin et al., 1989).

Baumann (1989) points out that there are several related themes in the literature on elder abuse that reinforce the notion that the *victim's* characteristics are the most important factors leading to abuse. Old people are usually characterized as "frail" and "vulnerable." The abused elderly are frequently referred to as "incompetent" and unable to care for themselves. The literature argues that these characteristics both lead to additional family stress and to greater risk for the victims, who are assumed not to be able to seek help for abuse on their own. There is more than a trace of ageism in this view. The situation of elderly persons is equated with that of children, in that they are seen as being in need of protection simply because of their age status.

❖ VICTIM DEPENDENCY: THE RESEARCH EVIDENCE

To paraphrase the famous expression: Nothing is so sad as a wonderful theory punctured by a few facts. Indeed, it is difficult to find firm research results that support the claim that physical abuse results directly from the elder's ill health and dependency. The available evidence shows instead that the analogy between elder abuse and child abuse is a false one, and that the widely held view that elder dependency and the demands for care are the major causes of elder abuse is, in fact, a fallacy.

What is the contrary evidence? Let us begin with a simple point. It is clear from the gerontology literature that a large number of elderly people are dependent on relatives for some degree of care (Rabin & Stockton, 1987). However, findings about the prevalence of elder abuse indicate that only a small minority of the elderly (3–4 percent) are abused. Because abuse occurs in only a small proportion of families, no direct correlation can be assumed between dependency of an elderly person and abuse. In fact, a recent study that included only caregivers to Alzheimer's disease victims (a high-risk situation for caregiver stress) found that only 5 percent of these caregivers became abusive (Pillemer & Suitor, 1992).

In order to determine the importance of elder dependency, our best source of information is the few studies that have used case-control designs. Most studies of elder abuse have involved case studies of victims identified through service agencies, with no comparison group. For this reason, the generalizations made from these studies are necessarily suspect. In the present instance, we are examining the assertion that the abused elderly tend to be physically and/or mentally impaired. Many of the aged, however, suffer from chronic conditions, and a substantial proportion have some form of dementia, especially among those over the age of 85 (Evans et al., 1989). Without a comparison group, it is impossible to know if abuse victims are more or less impaired than other people in their own age group.

Over the past few years, several researchers have begun to use case-control designs to understand risk factors for elder abuse. Although these studies all have weaknesses (owing in part to the difficulty of the phenomenon under study), they have at least attempted to compare abuse victims with non-abused elders. I provide only a brief description of the methods here; readers are referred to the original studies for more information.

Bristowe and Collins (1989) wished to compare abusive families with families where appropriate care was provided to elderly relatives. Four categories of maltreatment were included: passive neglect, active neglect, verbal abuse, and physical abuse. Most of the cases came from a homemaker agency, in which the staff identified clients as in either appropriate care or abusive situations. To augment the sample, requests were made in the media for additional cases of abuse.

In my own research, I obtained data on victims of physical abuse from the caseloads of three model projects on elder abuse (Pillemer, 1985, 1986). These people were individually matched on gender and living arrangement with non-abused clients of the agencies sponsoring the projects. A comparison relative in each of the comparison group families was matched with the abuser.

Homer and Gilleard (1990) studied clients who were receiving respite care or who had been referred for respite care during a six-month period. Caregivers were asked about three types of maltreatment: physical abuse, verbal abuse, and neglect. The study compared the caregivers who reported that they had been abusive with those who did not.

Phillips (1983) selected respondents from social service agencies, who were then assigned to abuse and non-abuse groups by service providers. Phillips's study is unique in that she used a "blind" interview technique, in which the interviewers were not aware of whether the respondent was or was not an abuse victim.

In a study I conducted with David Finkelhor, a general population survey of people 65 and older in the greater Boston area was conducted to determine the prevalence of elder abuse (Pillemer & Finkelhor, 1989). Victims of physical abuse, verbal aggression, and neglect were compared with non-abused control cases randomly selected from the larger sample.

Finally, data from a large-scale study of caregivers to Alzheimer's disease victims were used to examine violence in those relationships (Pillemer & Suitor, 1992). Cases in which the caregiver reported he or she had been violent were compared with those in which the caregiver had not reported violence. In addition, the fear of becoming violent toward the care recipient was examined.

None of these studies using case-controlled designs found support for the notion that elder abuse results from the excessive dependency of the victim. Instead, these studies uniformly failed to find important differences in health and functional status between victims and non-victims. Three of the studies in fact found the abuse victims to be *less* impaired than the controls (Bristowe & Collins, 1989; Pillemer, 1985; Wolf & Pillemer, 1989). *None* of these studies found abused elders to have other characteristics that might point toward greater activity limitations, such as advanced age or cognitive impairment.

Regarding the 1992 article I cowrote with Suitor, Steinmetz's statement that we found that violent caregivers "provided care for more functionally impaired elders, and provided help with a greater number of activities" is simply incorrect. Differences between violent and nonviolent caregivers on the Activities of Daily Living Scale and on a helping scale were not statistically significant. Further, initial differences on these two variables between caregivers who feared becoming violent and those who did not disappeared in a multivariate analysis (see Pillemer & Suitor, 1992, Tables 2–3).

The unanimity of the results from these case-controlled studies is striking in light of the divergent methods used. Several of the studies have included only caregivers (Homer & Gilleard, 1990; Phillips, 1983; Pillemer & Suitor, 1992), whereas others (Bristowe and Collins, 1989) included both caregivers and non-caregivers. The Pillemer and Finkelhor (1989) study compared abuse victims with the general population, and the Pillemer (1985, 1986) and Wolf and Pillemer (1989) studies compared identified cases with non-abused agency subsamples. Despite the divergence in methods, these comparison group studies provide *no* evidence that abuse victims are significantly more impaired than non-victims.

In light of the findings from these studies, the predominance of the view that elder impairment in itself leads to abuse is somewhat remarkable. In a different context, Ethel Shanas (1979) likened a myth about old age to a "hydra-headed monster," referring to the legendary beast that grew two heads for each one that was cut off, and was thus impossible to kill (at least until Hercules came along). In using this image, Shanas wished to convey the persistence of the myth— regardless of the number of scientific studies to refute a popular view, it reappeared again and again in public opinion. A similar phenomenon appears to exist in this popular view of the causes of elder abuse. As I have asserted elsewhere, in the absence of new case-comparison evidence, the notion that physical abuse results from the health problems of the elder should be rejected and alternative hypotheses explored (Pillemer & Finkelhor, 1989).

Even if poor health is not a major risk factor for abuse, it is possible that abused elders are nevertheless more dependent on their relatives. In the few studies that have addressed this issue, however, no evidence has appeared that this is the case. In both the Pillemer (1985, 1986) and Wolf and Pillemer (1989) studies, the abuse victims were distinctly *unlikely* to rely on the abuser for assistance with activities of daily living. For example, in the first study, respondents were asked to identify their most likely helpers. Those in the abuse group were much less likely than those in the non-abuse group to name their abusers as the persons they would be most likely to rely upon for help (26 percent versus 63 percent).

In the Wolf and Pillemer (1989) study, respondents were asked who the person was who would be most likely to help them if they became more sick or disabled. Only 20 percent said that this person was the abuser. In the same study, caseworkers were asked to name the person who each abuse victim could call in a crisis; in only 6 percent of the cases was this the abuser. Even in cases where the abuser lived with the victim, someone else was usually named as the person most depended upon.

As another measure of the dependency of the victim on the abuser, respondents in both of these studies were asked directly, "People depend on each other for many things. How much do you depend on [the abuser or a comparison relative] in each of the following areas?" Respondents were asked to answer whether they were dependent or independent in six areas: housing, financial support, cooking or cleaning, household repair, companionship/social activities, and transportation. In both the Pillemer (1985, 1986) and Pillemer and Wolf (1989) studies, abuse victims were not found to be more dependent in any of these areas. In the first study, no significant differences were found in five of the six areas. A difference was found in financial dependency, with the abuse group more likely to be independent than the comparison group. Wolf and Pillemer (1989) found that in five areas, the abuse group was significantly less dependent on the abuser than the non-victims were on the comparison relatives; in the sixth, financial dependency, the abuse group was less dependent, but not significantly so.

In sum, the available research evidence does not support the notion that the illness or dependency of an elderly person places him or her at special risk of becoming an abuse victim. To be sure, additional replication studies are necessary to verify this statement. However, in the absence of any comparison group data to the contrary, it seems misguided to continue asserting that elder dependency and caregiver stress lead to elder abuse. I now turn to the question of whether it is more appropriate to focus on characteristics of the abuser rather than of the victim in the search for causes of elder abuse.

❖ ABUSER DEPENDENCY: THE RESEARCH EVIDENCE

Interestingly, findings were available early on indicating that elder abusers were themselves dependent individuals. In a study published in 1982, Wolf, Strugnell, and Godkin surveyed community agencies in Massachusetts regarding elder abuse cases they had encountered. The authors identified a "web of mutual dependency" between abuser and abused. In two-thirds of the cases in that study, the perpetrator was reported to be financially dependent on the victim.

Several other studies have confirmed this profile of the abuser as dependent on the victim. In the Pillemer (1985, 1986) study, respondents were asked a dependency index (identical to that described in the previous section), with the questions reversed. That is, they were asked, "How much does [the abuser or comparison relative] depend on you in each of the following areas?" Abusers were found to be significantly more dependent on the elders in four areas: housing, household repair, financial assistance, and transportation. Another study (Wolf & Pillemer, 1989) inquired only about two forms of abuser dependency: finances and cooking and cleaning. A statistically significant difference was found for financial dependency, with abusers much more likely to be dependent.

In the Pillemer and Finkelhor (1989) analysis of cases from a random-sample survey, nearly identical results emerged. Abusers were significantly more likely to be dependent financially for household repairs, for transportation, for housing, and for cooking and cleaning than were the relatives of non-abused comparison cases. Although not including control groups, other studies also have found substantial percentages of financially dependent abusers (Anetzberger, 1987; Greenberg, McKibben, & Raymond, 1990).

The question then arises: Why are the abusers dependent? All studies addressing this issue have been unequivocal in their assessment: Rather than being healthy, stable, well-intentioned caregivers, elder abusers tend to suffer from a variety of mental health, substance abuse, and stress-related problems. Overwhelmingly, the studies indicate that the abusers have a range of such problems playing a major role in the abuse situation.

It is interesting to note that these results occur both in studies of caregivers and in those including all relatives. In the Pillemer and Finkelhor (1989) study, discriminate function analyses demonstrated that abuser deviance and dependence were the strongest predictors of abuse. Homer and Gilleard (1990) found greater alcohol consumption on the part of abusive caregivers to be related to physical abuse, whereas caregivers' depression and anxiety led to verbal abuse. Bristowe and Collins (1989) also found alcohol consumption by the abuser to be the major distinguishing factor between the abusive and non-abusive groups. Greenberg et al.'s (1990) analysis of predictors of dependency among abusive adult children found similar results: Substance abuse was the major factor. Qualitative data from the same study indicated that chronic psychological problems are characteristic of dependent abusers.

Further, all studies seeking such information have found that abusers are overwhelmingly more likely to have been violent in other contexts, to have been arrested, or to have been hospitalized for psychiatric reasons (see Pillemer & Finkelhor, 1989; Wolf & Pillemer, 1989). It is impossible to contrast these findings with the Steinmetz study because this type of question was simply not asked. Items relating to deviance and dependency on the part of the caregivers were not included in the study, so it was impossible to evaluate the relative strength of the abuser-dependency and victim-dependency hypotheses.

❖ DISCUSSION

Our knowledge about the problem of elder abuse may no longer be in its infancy, but it has certainly not progressed much beyond the toddler stage. It is interesting to note that there has been the most debate over the one issue on which we have the clearest data. Simply put, all of the more rigorous studies of elder abuse have failed to find dependency of the victim to be a primary characteristic of maltreatment situations. They have, on the other hand, found substantial evidence that elder abusers are often not primary caregivers at all, but are instead deeply troubled individuals who depend heavily on the people they abuse.

By no means do I intend to imply that this issue is entirely resolved. Readers familiar with research methods will have noted many flaws in the available research. Further, we are just now becoming aware of the complex, multifaceted nature of the problem we have labeled "elder abuse." For example, many of the studies did not differentiate among different types of abuse and neglect; it may be that the pattern described here holds more strongly for physical abuse and less so for other types of maltreatment (see Wolf & Pillemer, 1989, for preliminary data supporting this possibility). Further, the samples in the studies cited were almost exclusively white; the dynamics of abuse involving African Americans, Asian Americans, and Hispanics may differ from the findings presented here. Clearly, there is fertile ground for additional research.

Based on existing studies, however, it seems we must conclude that the hypothesis that caregiver stress is a major cause of elder abuse is incorrect. One might then ask, Why is this an important issue? In fact, the question of who is depending on whom in families where elder abuse exists has several major implications.

Those who argue that elder abuse results from problematic characteristics of elderly people have—unintentionally, I believe—blamed the victim. In the same way that some writers held that "spoiled" children were more likely to be abused, or that nagging, demanding wives were more likely to be battered, the elderly themselves have been cited as the cause of abuse. Focusing on caregiver stress normalizes the problem; it relieves the abuser of much of the blame because, after all, the elderly are demanding, hard to care for, and sometimes even downright unpleasant.

The research data argue that we should refocus on the *abuser*. We must begin to examine how people come to depend on elderly relatives, and the ways in which that dependency sometimes results in abuse. Other explanations should not be excluded; as I have argued elsewhere (Pillemer, 1985), in some cases caregiver stress may play a role in elder abuse. But the dominance of the view that abusers are caregivers who are pushed to their limits has tended to keep researchers from focusing on a more promising explanation: the deviance and dependency of abusers.

Practice and policy can also benefit from this refocusing. Based on the hypothesis that dependency of victims leads to abuse, supportive services have been offered to caregivers, such as home care services, housekeeping, meal preparation, and support groups. Although such services may play some role in preventing or ameliorating elder abuse, the research findings summarized in this chapter point to a need for other services.

A focus on the abuser suggests that either the rewards of dependency on the victim can be decreased or the costs of abusing the victim can be increased. To achieve the former goal, unhealthy dependence of a relative on an older person could be reduced through psychotherapy, employment counseling, and financial support for the abuser while he or she establishes an independent household. In some cases, the change in living situation may be nursing home placement for a dependent, abusive spouse.

The costs of abusing an elderly person can be raised in a variety of ways. One option is to offer victim assistance services to the abused elderly. For example, the battered women's movement has had great success with support groups for victims. Such groups convey to victims that they have a right to be free from abuse, and help them to develop strategies to resist it. Another possibility is the development of "safe houses" or emergency shelters for elder abuse victims. A shelter can help a victim escape from abuse and then provide support so that the victim can make a decision about whether to live independently or return to the abuser, who now is aware that the victim no longer will tolerate being mistreated.

Another alternative is legal action. When elder abuse was conceived of as occurring because of caregiver strain, involving the police rarely seemed necessary. In the framework proposed here, elder abuse (especially physical violence) has parallels with spouse abuse: relatively independent people sharing a residence with physically stronger ones who victimize them. Using legal sanctions against abusers may deter future victimization.

Let me conclude with an exhortation to do two things. First, let us continue to expand the research base on elder abuse, using more complex multivariate models of maltreatment, and resist relying on monocausal explanations such as caregiver stress. Second, as we await further research findings, let us begin to base our policy and practice on the knowledge that many abusers are not caregivers and many victims are not cared for (at least by their abusers). Such a view will allow new and creative solutions to the problem to emerge.

❖ REFERENCES

Anetzberger, G. J. (1987). *Etiology of elder abuse by adult offspring.* Springfield, IL: Charles C. Thomas.

Baumann, E. A. (1989). Research rhetoric and the social construction of elder abuse. In J. Best (Ed.), *Images of issues: Typifying contemporary social problems.* New York: Aldine deGruyter.

Bristowe, E., & Collins, J. (1989). Family mediated abuse of noninstitutionalized frail elderly men and women in British Columbia. *Journal of Elder Abuse and Neglect, 1,* 45–64.

Davidson, J. L. (1979). Elder abuse. In M. R. Block & J. D. Sinnott (Eds.), *The battered elder syndrome: An exploratory study* (pp. 49–55). College Park: University of Maryland, Center on Aging.

Douglass, R. L. (1988). *Domestic maltreatment of the elderly: Towards prevention.* Washington, DC: American Association of Retired Persons.

Evans, D., et al. (1989). Prevalence of Alzheimer's disease in a community population of older persons. *Journal of the American Medical Association, 262,* 2551–2554.

Fulmer, T. (1990). The debate over dependency as a relevant predisposing factor in elder abuse and neglect. *Journal of Elder Abuse and Neglect, 2,* 51–58.

Greenberg, J. R., McKibben, M., & Raymond, J. A. (1990). Dependent adult children and elder abuse. *Journal of Elder Abuse and Neglect, 2,* 73–86.

Hickey, T., & Douglass, R. (1981). Neglect and abuse of older family members: Professionals' perspectives and case experiences. *Gerontologist, 21,* 171–176.

Homer, A. C., & Gilleard, C. (1990). Abuse of elderly people by their carers. *British Medical Journal, 301,* 1359–1362.

O'Malley, T., O'Malley, H. C., Everitt, D. E., & Sarson, D. (1986). Categories of family mediated abuse and neglect of elderly persons. *Journal of the American Geriatrics Society, 32,* 362–369.

Phillips, L. R. (1983). Abuse and neglect of the frail elderly at home: An exploration of theoretical relationships. *Journal of Advanced Nursing, 8,* 379–392.

Pillemer, K. (1985). The dangers of dependency: New findings on domestic violence against elderly. *Social Problems, 33,* 146–158.

Pillemer, K. (1986). Risk factors in elder abuse: Results from a case-control study. In K. Pillemer & R. S. Wolf (Eds.), *Elder abuse: Conflict in the family* (pp. 236–263). Dover, MA: Auburn House.

Pillemer, K., & Finkelhor, D. (1989). Causes of elder abuse: Caregiver stress versus problem relatives. *American Journal of Orthopsychiatry, 59,* 179–187.

Pillemer, K., & Suitor, J. J. (1992). Violence and violent feelings: What causes them among family caregivers. *Journal of Gerontology, 47,* S165–S172.

Rabin, D. L., & Stockton, P. (1987). *Long-term care for the elderly: A factbook.* New York: Oxford.

Scoggin, E., Beall, C., Bynum, J., Stephens, C., Grote, N. P., Baumhover, L. A., & Bolland, J. M. (1989). Training for abusive caregivers: An unconventional approach to an intervention dilemma. *Journal of Elder Abuse and Neglect, 1*(4), 73–86.

Shanas, E. (1979). The family as a social support system in old age. *Gerontologist, 19,* 169–174.

Steinmetz, S. K. (1988). *Duty bound: Elder abuse and family care.* Newbury Park: CA: Sage.

Wolf, R. S., & Pillemer, K. (1989). *Helping elderly victims: The reality of elder abuse.* New York: Columbia University Press.

Wolf, R. S., Strugnell, C. P., & Godkin, M. A. (1982). *Preliminary findings from three model projects on elder abuse.* Worcester: University of Massachusetts Medical Center, University Center on Aging.

SECTION IV

Controversies in Social Intervention

The focus of this volume so far has been on the disagreements among experts about how family violence should be conceptualized, defined, or measured; nor do the experts agree about the causes of family violence. While such controversies certainly inform and shape the practical world, they are, in many ways, academic debates about how family violence should be *studied.* Family violence, however, also is a practical problem to be *resolved.* What should the public do about this violence? In an ideal world, social interventions would be based upon agreements about proper conceptualizations, definitions, and measurements. In an ideal world, interventions would be based upon agreements about the causes of violence. Our world is not ideal. Questions about social intervention cannot wait until the underlying controversies are resolved. This final section contains four specific controversies about social interventions.

One of these debates is about victims of wife abuse. Many interventions to assist victims—shelters for battered women, police arrest of abusers, and special counseling—currently are surrounded by relatively few controversies, except the need for more such interventions. Controversy does swirl, however, around another issue: What should be the legal defense for abused wives who kill their abusive partners? Sue Osthoff and Holly Maguigan believe such women are most helped by allowing juries and judges to hear expert testimony about "battering and its effects." In contrast, Donald Downs and James Fisher argue that such testimony about the "battered woman syndrome" can hinder the jury's ability to understand the reasonable nature of women's use of deadly force. Furthermore, they believe the indiscriminate use of such testimony can lead to "vigilante justice" in which it is too easy for women to be excused for murdering their partners.

The other controversies in this section all revolve around child victims. The first involves an issue of *primary* intervention, a type of program designed to prevent violence from happening. While primary intervention might not seem controversial, child sexual abuse education programs have been surrounded by controversy since their beginning. Is child sexual abuse education appropriate for young children? Do these programs prevent this abuse? Carol Plummer argues that while educating children should not be the only effort to stop child sexual abuse, these programs are both appropriate and effective. In their opposing chapter, N. Dickon Reppucci, Jeffrey Haugaard, and Jill Antonishak raise many questions about the appropriateness of these programs and maintain there is no evidence that such education actually prevents child sexual abuse.

The next controversy involves a question of *secondary* intervention to stop abuse that is happening: Are current laws and procedures for reporting child abuse effective, efficient, and fair? Douglas Besharov contends there are "twin" reporting problems: Too many severe cases are not reported to child abuse hotlines, but too many trivial cases are brought into the system, and these divert resources from severe cases. In contrast, David Finkelhor believes that overreporting is not a problem; the continuing problem, he argues, is that too few critical cases reach the attention of authorities.

The final controversy surrounds *tertiary* intervention: What should be done to repair the damage of violence? We conclude this volume with the most far-ranging and difficult public policy question about services for abused or neglected children: Should services focus on changing abusive or neglectful parents so that children can remain in their own homes, or should children be taken from their abusive homes and placed in foster care? Richard Wexler argues that most children, most of the time, benefit when they remain in their own homes while their parents receive considerable social service support and oversight. Conversely, Richard Gelles maintains that such "family preservation" programs work to preserve families at the unacceptable cost of further harm to children.

The controversies addressed in this section illustrate how, regardless of disagreements, spokespersons might well be working toward the same goal. For example, when controversies are about interventions for child victims, concern is with the well-being of children. Besharov clearly is troubled by the overreporting of suspected cases of child abuse because he believes that children who are in real danger are getting lost in the press of inappropriate cases. Finkelhor's opposing argument is that we need more reporting because "large numbers of seriously abused and neglected children are still not coming to the attention of child protective authorities." In the same way, Plummer supports child sexual abuse educational programs because they can help "make the world safer for children," while Reppucci and his colleagues call for more research on program effectiveness because "our children deserve no less."

While authors of opposing chapters are concerned with achieving the same goals, they simultaneously see negative consequences of supporting the "other side" of the controversy. For example, Downs and Fisher believe that while abused women accused of killing their abusive partners do benefit from expert testimony in court about the consequences of abuse, they also assert that making such testimony the centerpiece of a defense can backfire and actually hurt women. Likewise, Reppucci and his colleagues believe that child sexual abuse education programs "may actually retard the development of other programs . . . that might be more effective." In turn, Besharov maintains that Finkelhor's plan to increase reporting of child abuse is "unrealistic" and "harmful to children," while Finkelhor argues that Besharov's call to reduce inappropriate cases disguises an underlying attitude that stopping child abuse is not worth the inefficiency and intrusion in family life. Finally, in supporting family preservation programs, Wexler dramatizes the horrors of life in the foster care system, with "children sleeping on office floors. Epidemics of abuse in substitute care. Increases in child abuse deaths." Gelles, in turn, believes that family preservation efforts "are not widely successful" and "compromise children's safety, well-being, and opportunity to be raised in a safe and permanent home."

As with other controversies in this volume, the real or perceived problems in research supporting an opponent's arguments are a critical component in each chapter. For example, Reppucci and his colleagues question the appropriateness and effectiveness of child sexual abuse education programs by pointing to the lack of rigorous scientific evaluations of these programs. According to them, without such research, such programs are based merely on a series of unproven assumptions. Likewise, Gelles complains that there were "major methodological and design limitations of the early evaluations of IFPS [intensive family preservation services]" and that the "empirical case that abusive and neglectful families can be preserved . . . has yet to be made."

Although the controversies in this section have much in common with others in this volume, debates about social interventions differ from others in two ways. First, unlike some controversies for which "sides" were chosen long ago and where the evidence supporting the perspectives does not change much over time, debates about social interventions tend to be more dynamic. Some of this fluidity comes from the fact that we know even less about what to do to stop violence than we know about its meaning or its causes. Controversies are fueled when so little is known. Disagreements about social interventions also are dynamic because what we know constantly changes. So, while Dutton and Fisher maintain that the core of the "battered woman defense" is the "battered woman syndrome," a large part of the argument by Osthoff and Maguigan is that testimony of "battering and its effects" has changed radically over time. Whether it has changed enough to challenge Dutton and Fisher's complaints therefore is the underlying issue requiring evaluation.

These chapters differ from others in this volume in a second way: Because the topic here is social *intervention,* each directly illustrates how efforts to do something about family violence can involve balancing the rights of victims, offenders, families, and the public in general. As such, and perhaps more so than with other controversies, these particular debates raise a host of distinctly ethical questions: How easy—or difficult—should it be for a woman to claim she was justified in killing her partner because he abused her? How easy—or difficult— should it be to investigate a family accused of child abuse? How easy— or difficult—should it be to remove children from abusive homes? Should children—or adults—bear the responsibility for stopping child sexual abuse? Such are the controversies swirling around attempts to do something about family violence.

14

Explaining Without Pathologizing

Testimony on Battering and Its Effects

Sue Osthoff and Holly Maguigan

I n 1978, a coalition of social scientists, trial consultants, legal workers, and attorneys formed the Women's Self-Defense Law Project in order to help attorneys provide effective representation to women who had been forced to defend themselves against violent attacks (Bochnak, 1981). That was also the year that Dr. Lenore Walker first offered expert testimony in support of a battered woman's self-defense claim (Walker,

AUTHOR'S NOTE: The authors are grateful for the assistance of Ruth Cionca, Melissa Eve Dichter, and Heather Lipa-Fuentes, and for the financial support of the Filomen D'Agostino and Max E. Greenberg Faculty Research Fund at New York University School of Law. Portions of this chapter appeared as "A Review Essay: It's Time to Move Beyond 'Battered Woman Syndrome,'" *Criminal Justice Ethics*, 17, 50–57 (1998, Winter/Spring). That essay is adapted here with the permission of the editors of *Criminal Justice Ethics*.

1989). In the intervening 25 years, many advocates, researchers, and lawyers—including the authors of this chapter—have joined the effort to demonstrate what these early practitioners seemed to understand so clearly: Like others who defend themselves against imminent harm, battered women who kill their abusers can, and in many circumstances should, argue *self-defense*. Instead of viewing battered women who kill as insane or otherwise incapacitated (as many attorneys and jurors had done in the past), these pioneers in the field argued that the battered women they represented had been reasonable and justified when they defended themselves against their abusers.

In the late 1970s, expert testimony about what came to be known as "battered woman syndrome" (BWS) was introduced to help jurors understand more fully a battered woman's experiences, because this background information was necessary to their evaluation of her reasonableness and self-defense claim. Unfortunately, it did not take long for some scholars and practitioners to mischaracterize this BWS testimony as creating a new and novel defense. Such an interpretation was frequently based on the mistaken belief that testimony on behalf of battered women defendants focused on their pathology, incapacity, or lack of reason. Reverting to the stereotype of battered women as damaged human beings can be particularly problematic for women who kill their abusers, because *reasonableness* is central to their self-defense claims.

The past quarter-century has witnessed the dogged persistence of these misconceptions about battered women who kill and their legal defenses. There are five categories of *mistaken notions* regarding battered women's legal defenses:

1. Battered women charged with homicide invoke a separate "battered woman's defense" or "battered woman syndrome defense."

2. The basis of this so-called special defense is either vigilantism or a version of the insanity defense.

3. The most important evidence in support of a woman's legal defense is expert testimony.

4. The expert testimony is only about "battered woman syndrome" (BWS).

5. BWS testimony is based on a victimization analysis that denies women's capacity, responsibility, and agency.

These errors result from a disconnect between the reality of what goes on in the courtroom and the political and philosophical issues that arise in cases involving battered women who kill. The reality is straightforward:

- There is no separate defense for battered women anywhere in the country.
- Most battered women who are charged with homicide against abusive partners use the traditional law of self-defense. Self-defense is a justification. Under criminal law, it is the claim that the act was not a crime because it was necessitated by the circumstances.
- Expert testimony is not introduced in every battered woman's case. When it is offered, it is generally one of many pieces of evidence introduced to support a woman's defense claim.
- In the overwhelming majority of cases where expert testimony is used, this testimony addresses a range of social and psychological issues related to the reasonableness of a defendant's use of force to protect herself. It does not focus on the woman's incapacity or lack of reason.

We begin this chapter with a review of developments in social science and in the law over the past 25 years. We turn next to the current use of social science testimony in battered women's homicide trials. We conclude with a discussion of the central question: How can we explain the impact of intimate violence without pathologizing battered women and denying their reason and capacity?

❖ HISTORICAL REVIEW

Until the past quarter-century, many battered women accused of homicide or assault had been encouraged by their lawyers to plead guilty, or, if they went to trial, to claim the excuse of insanity rather than the justification of self-defense (Bochnak, 1981; Maguigan, 1991; Jones, 1996). This pattern changed in the late 1970s, when there were several high-profile cases of women who defended themselves or their children against domestic violence and argued that they acted in self-defense (Jones, 1996; McNulty, 1980; Schneider & Jordan, 1981). These cases received considerable attention in the popular press, in part because, by fighting back against abusers, "[the defendants] challenged historically accepted notions of women's roles" (Schneider & Jordan, 1981, p. 3). Many, but certainly not all, of these women eventually were acquitted (Schneider & Jordan, 1981).

It was in trials involving traditional self-defense law that experts like Dr. Lenore Walker and, a year later, Dr. Julie Blackman began testifying in cases of battered women who killed their abusers. The expert evidence was introduced to help juries assess the reasonableness of the defendants' belief in the necessity of using deadly force to defend themselves. In the earliest trials, the testimony was often offered "on the subject of battered women" (Blackman, 1989; Walker, 1989).

❖ FROM BATTERED WOMAN SYNDROME TO BATTERING AND ITS EFFECTS

In her 1979 book, *The Battered Woman*, Walker (1979) introduced the BWS concept when she described a psychological profile of women living with intimate violence. She further developed the theory and coined the term "battered woman syndrome" in 1984 (Walker, 1984, 1993). Walker identified two key phenomena of BWS: (1) "learned helplessness," a concept she adapted from the work of Martin Seligman and which, in this context, she described as the loss of belief in the ability to predict the effectiveness of particular responses to achieve safety; and (2) the "cycle of violence"—a three-phase pattern of violence and abuse. In her early work, Dr. Walker also described characteristics that she suggested were common to all battered women: low self-esteem, belief in the myths about battering relationships, traditionalist views about the home, and acceptance of responsibility for the batterer's actions (Walker, 1979, 1984, 1993). In her later work, Walker described BWS as "part of a recognized pattern of psychological symptoms called post-traumatic stress disorder (PTSD), reported in the psychological literature as produced by repeated exposure to trauma" (Walker, 1993, p. 133) and as "a group of usually transient psychological symptoms that are frequently observed in a particular recognizable pattern in women who report [being abused]" (Walker, 1993, p. 135).

BWS has been depicted in several ways in the 20 years since its identification (Bradfield, 2002). Some have considered BWS as a way of describing the women's psychological responses to battering and rationalizing why battered women fail to leave violent relationships. Others use BWS as "a shorthand term" to encompass either the variety of conditions experienced by women who live with intimate violence or the mass of social science literature on the impact of battering (for example, Bowker, 1993; Hatcher, 2003; Mangum, 1998–99).

Contemporaneous with the development and popularization of BWS in social science literature were changes in legal strategies. In the late 1970s, battered women defendants began resorting less to guilty pleas and insanity defenses and making more use of traditional self-defense law. By doing so they were employing legal principles that were already well established in criminal courts throughout the country.

Criminal courts had long held that *any* defendant was entitled to have the jury consider a claim of self defense if evidence (disputed or not) was offered at trial that (1) the decedent had behaved in a way that the defendant interpreted as posing an imminent threat of death or serious bodily injury; (2) the defendant was not the initial aggressor; (3) the defendant did not have a duty to retreat; and (4) the force used was proportional to the perceived threat (Maguigan, 1991). In the early 1970s, BWS testimony was offered to support battered women's traditional self-defense claims and to corroborate the reasonableness of the defendant's belief that the use of defensive force was necessary.

Over the years, experiences in criminal courts persuaded advocates, lawyers, and researchers to move beyond the "battered woman syndrome" formulation to more comprehensive testimony. They came to understand that BWS fails to capture the full experience of battered women, and that it risks subjecting women who are battered to labels that deny their diversity and that portray them as helpless and incapacitated (Allard, 1991; Ammons, 1995; Dutton, 1993, 1997a). Donald Downs and James Fisher (this volume) follow others (Dutton, 1997a, 1997b; Parrish, 1996; Schneider, 1986) when they recognize that expert testimony couched only in terms of battered woman syndrome stigmatizes and pathologizes battered women because the terminology implies a mental illness.

The "syndrome" label may encourage jurors to perceive the defendant as pathological. Such a perception is at odds with a defense argument that the woman's actions were actually reasonable in light of the circumstances (Dutton, 1996, 1997a; Osthoff, 2001; Parrish, 1996; Schneider, 2000). Additional possible negative implications of labeling battered women as suffering from a syndrome are relevant for women involved in custody cases, tort actions, clemency or parole actions, or in other situations where credibility and rationality are at issue.

The "learned helplessness" language that Walker used in her early work to describe one component of BWS presents similar problems with negative associations. Critics have argued that this phrasing misleadingly focuses too much attention on battered women's passivity (Schuller & Rzepa, 2002) and creates new stereotypes for battered women (Crocker, 1985; Schneider, 1986).

Additional criticisms about the shortcomings of BWS include that while it had been "a useful construct as a focus for women's self-defense work . . . it is now outmoded" because it does not adequately reflect the state of knowledge and practice (Stubbs & Tolmie, 1999, p. 713), "shifts the blame for intimate violence away from the perpetrator and onto the woman" (Schneider, 2000, p. 123), and misrepresents battering in a way that is "inaccurate, reductionist, and potentially demeaning" (Stark, 1995, p. 975).

There are others who focus on the scientific reasons to move beyond BWS, reasons distinct from, but consistent with, the concerns about the impact of the formulation in court and on public opinion. They have critiqued Dr. Walker's methodology (Bradfield, 2002; Burke, 2002; Faigman & Wright, 1997), arguing that the "battered woman syndrome" research includes a self-report bias, lacks a rigorous statistical analysis, and that the data do not fully support the conclusions (Schopp, Sturgis, & Sullivan, 1994).

Certainly many of the criticisms are valid, but unfortunately, even today, too much critical discussion focuses on Walker's earliest book and ignores her own further development of the theory in later important works. The utility of commentary based only on Walker's early formulations is weakened because it is so dated (Downs, 1996; Downs & Fisher, this volume; Faigman, 1987; Faigman & Wright, 1997). Since Walker published her first book about battered women, she and other researchers and clinicians have made huge strides in developing our knowledge about women who have been battered.

More recent work has made it clear that BWS is no longer the appropriate term to describe either the state of our knowledge or the content of expert testimony. The phrase "testimony on battering and its effects" more accurately describes the expert evidence because it focuses on battered women's experiences, moves their social context to the foreground, emphasizes the diversity of their range of reactions to trauma, and highlights the utility of expert testimony to explain the psychological sequelae of living with violence (Dutton, 1996; Schneider, 2000). Testimony about "battering and its effects" is a more accurate representation of the range of issues relevant to a battered woman's legal defense, including the nature and dynamics of battering, the effects of violence, battered women's responses to violence, and the social and psychological context in which domestic violence occurs (Dutton, 1996).

As was the situation in the early cases, today most experts testify both about the social and practical experiences of battered women, and about the psychological impact of being battered. Their testimony is usually much more comprehensive than many critics, including Donald Downs and James Fisher (this volume), have suggested. Even in early cases when most testimony was described as about BWS, expert testimony rarely focused solely on the psychological consequences of being battered. Nor did they offer what might appear to be a version of insanity defense evidence. Rather, from the earliest cases, expert testimony has included discussion of the practical realities of having an abusive partner and what is today called testimony about battering and its effects. There is a continuum between Dr. Walker, who emphasizes the psychological framework but includes the social context, and many other researchers who emphasize the social context but recognize the significance of the psychological impact of the violence (Blackman, 1989; Dutton, 1993, 1997a; Gondolf, 1988).

❖ INCORPORATING EXPERT
    TESTIMONY INTO EXISTING SELF-DEFENSE LAW

Battered women were not departing from traditional defense strategy when in support of their self-defense claims they began asserting their right to introduce evidence that they had been beaten in the past by the men they were accused of killing. Evidence of the nature of a prior relationship between defendant and decedent has been routinely accepted in courts for as long as the law has recognized claims of self-defense. That evidence has always been considered relevant to defendant's subjective perception of danger, and to the question of whether that perception was reasonable (whether a reasonable person in the defendant's circumstances would have shared the belief) (Maguigan, 1991). Courts have recognized that past violence by an aggressor toward the defendant influences the defendant's assessment of the current danger posed by the aggressor's actions. The evidence is routinely received in murder trials, because most homicides involve people who were either acquainted with each other or in family relationships. A defendant in such a circumstance uses his or her experience with the decedent as a basis for evaluating whether the decedent posed an imminent threat of serious injury (Browne, Williams, & Dutton, 1999; Fox & Zawitz, 2002; Goetting, 1988; Rennison, 2003; Websdale, 1999; Zahn & Sagi, 1987).

Evidence about the context in which an incident occurred is frequently introduced in a variety of criminal cases (Maguigan, 1991, 1995; Mosteller, 1996; Walker & Monahan, 1987). This testimony, which includes the history of past violence, is often called "social framework evidence":

> The purpose of "social framework evidence" . . . is to provide the factfinder, usually a jury, with information about the social and psychological context in which contested adjudicative facts occurred. It is presumed that knowledge about the context will help the factfinder interpret the contested adjudicative facts. (Walker & Monahan, 1987, p. 560)

Trial judges and juries often have been resistant, however, to accepting this traditionally received social framework testimony when it is offered by a woman accused of killing her husband or intimate partner. When men offered evidence of *past* violence to support their self-defense claims against other men, courts understood that the history was relevant to the defendant's claim that he was reasonable to fear his attacker and to use self-defensive force on the *present* occasion. Yet when women offered exactly the same kind of evidence, it was frequently misinterpreted as being offered to support the premise that past violence *excused* present illegal retaliation. The history of violence serves to *support* a self-defense claim, not to *replace* it.

❖ SOCIAL SCIENCE IN THE
   COURTROOM: THE CURRENT SITUATION

In some jurisdictions, expert evidence is still sometimes described as "battered woman syndrome" testimony. It is more properly character-ized as testimony about "battering and its effects," and it is a form of social framework testimony that is now admissible in every jurisdiction in the United States (Maguigan, 1991; Parrish, 1996). In this part of the chapter we analyze the interplay in court between the expert testimony and the traditional law of self-defense.

Relying on self-defense law as a justification represents the current, as well as the historic, reality of most battered women's homicide charges: there is strong evidence that between 70 and 90 percent of battered women's homicide cases involve killings in what are called "confrontational" situations (Browne, 1987; Downs, 1996; Maguigan, 1991; Parrish, 1996; Wolfgang, 1958). A confrontational case is one in which there is evidence that would require that the judge tell the jury to consider self-defense. In other words, there is documentary or live-witness evidence that the necessary elements were present (fear of imminent harm, no initial aggression from the defendant, no duty to retreat, and use of force proportional to the threat from the decedent), and self-defense is a question for the jury to resolve.

Non-confrontation cases, those in which the evidence shows that the killing took place during a lull in the violence or was committed by someone else at the battered woman's request, are unusual. In some of these uncommon cases, especially those in which the evidence demonstrates that the defendant was held hostage, the claim may still be self-defense. In others, a traditional criminal law defense of excuse (like insanity) may be more appropriate. Lay and expert evidence are also important in these atypical cases to provide the context for evaluating the woman's defense.

In the last decade, many critics have focused on this small minority of non-confrontational battered women's homicide charges. They often misconstrue what is happening in the trials and believe the same inaccurate assertion described earlier in the chapter: that the history of abuse by itself is an excuse for the battered woman's actions, and that this so-called abuse excuse (Dershowitz, 1994; Downs, 1996) gives battered women a "license to kill." They allege that courts are excusing battered women who kill in non-confrontational circumstances and therefore encouraging vigilantism. This phenomenon exists nowhere but in the minds of these observers.

It is telling that the vast majority of the atypical non-confrontation cases that critics discuss actually were ones in which the defendants entered guilty pleas or were convicted after trial (Maguigan, 1998). These unusual cases are described as "common" examples of widespread and successful efforts to create a free-standing victimization defense. By emphasizing uncommon cases and by neglecting to discuss their real-life outcomes, these authors reinforce a false opposition between a so-called battered woman's defense of total incapacity and a traditional claim of reasonable self-defense. In a way, they are forced to place non-confrontation cases in the foreground in order to bolster their argument that expert testimony on battered woman syndrome necessarily supports a special defense like an "abuse excuse" rather than a generally applicable defense like justification. By doing so, they distort the actual trial contexts in which most such testimony is offered (Maguigan, 1998).

Even when they discuss the confrontation cases that make up the majority of battered women's homicide trials, many critics claim that current defense strategies represent an erosion of the notions of responsibility and of self-defense standards. They argue that the effect of social science testimony is to shift the focus from a woman's responsibility for her act to the victim of the killing. Donald Downs's work (1996) provides one example. Using the word *victim* in two ways, he argues that the shift is part and parcel of both a tendency to "blame the victim" (referring here to the decedent) and a proliferation of "victimization" defenses (referring here to the woman victimized by the batterer). He chastises lawyers and experts for creating a "psychoscientific version of the classical 'son of a bitch' defense" (p. 108), which he sees as equivalent to saying that the victim (decedent) caused his own death (p. 24). Arguing that the decedent caused his own death is, of course, nothing new. It is the classical core of any self-defense claim: The justification asserted for the killing is that it was the only thing to do because the attacker left the defendant no reasonable alternative to using defensive deadly force.

That core principle provides the context for the real interplay between social science and law in most trials of battered women. The claim is self-defense. The defendant offers evidence that she used deadly force because the batterer left her no alternative. The evidence includes testimony about the incident itself, about the history of abuse, and about battering and its effects. Some, but by no means all, of the evidence may be offered by a social scientist.

Evidence regarding the incident itself and the history of the abuse may come from a variety of sources. Sources of evidence about the actual incident include witnesses (including the defendant if she chooses to testify), calls to the police, records of the decedent's and defendant's injuries received during the confrontation, and police descriptions and photographs of the scene. The self-defense issues that are raised by this evidence, especially the questions of the defendant's fear of her partner and the reasonableness of the fear, are often best understood in the context of their history together.

To help the jury understand this context, it is important to introduce evidence about the history of abuse. Like the evidence about the incident, it comes from a variety of sources: lay witnesses (the defendant, friends, coworkers, and family who saw the abuse or her injuries afterward), records and photographs, and, when appropriate, expert testimony. Social science evidence often can help jurors understand the evidence of past abuse and its relationship to the defendant's fear that she was in imminent danger at the time of the killing. The testimony assists jurors in their evaluation of the reasonableness of the fear and of the defendant's actions. Social science testimony is not offered merely to focus on her psychological makeup. Although a woman's psychological reactions may sometimes be critical pieces of information, psychology is clearly not the whole story.

In addition, expert evidence can help explain the larger social context within which the defendant experienced and responded to her abuser's violence. Social science testimony has been introduced to describe the common patterns found in battering relationships (Schuller & Rzepa, 2002). Such testimony addresses both the general dynamics of battering and common responses to being abused and the particular dynamics of the relationship in a specific case. On the one hand, the expert describes the fact that there are certain common characteristics that battered women share. On the other, the witness acknowledges the great diversity of individual characteristics and experiences of battered women (Mahoney, 1994; Schneider, 1992). It is essential that this social framework testimony take account of differences based on individual characteristics of the defendant and decedent like race, ethnicity, class, immigration status, physical ability, and sexual orientation. Sometimes the defendant's individual characteristics include some not shared by the jurors. The differences between them can create a "social distance" across which an expert can serve as a bridge or translator (Macpherson, Ridolfi, Sternberg, & Wiley, 1981). Elizabeth Schneider (2000) has described the function of the evidence this way:

> Expert testimony on battered woman syndrome was developed to explain the common experiences of repeated assault on battered women, and its impact. The goal was to assist the jury and the court in fairly evaluating the reasonableness of the battered

women's action. The notion of expert testimony was predicated on an assumption that battered women's voices either would not be understood or were not strong enough to be heard alone in the courtroom. (p. 80)

Jurors come to the courtroom with their own biases about battered women that often create barriers to hearing or understanding a defendant's voice. An expert can explain the prevalence of and reasons for phenomena that might otherwise appear unreasonable to an outside observer: failure to call the police, failure to tell hospital personnel the real cause of injuries, failure to tell friends and family about the abuse. Probably the most significant among the phenomena that need explication, and where an expert can help the jury assess the defendant's testimony, is the question why she did not leave the relationship (Macpherson et al., 1981; Schneider, 2000). Very common among the public and therefore among jurors is an inability to comprehend how any woman who stays with a man who hurts her could be reasonable about anything (see Yllö and Loseke & Kurz, this volume).

❖ CONCLUSION: EXPLAINING WITHOUT PATHOLOGIZING

In social science research and in court, the move beyond the limitations of BWS testimony is significant. It does much to help solve the dilemma that has confronted scholars, advocates, and criminal defense lawyers who have sought to use social science to illuminate a battered woman's situation and behavior: how to explain the impact of intimate violence without appearing to pathologize battered women and deny their reason and capacity. This dilemma is at the core of Donald Downs's work about battered women (Downs, 1996, Downs & Fisher, this volume). As many social scientists, advocates, lawyers, and other practitioners agree, we must continue to grapple with the best way of explaining to jurors the rationality of battered women's actions, reactions, and behaviors that may appear at first to be unreasonable.

One reason to have an expert help educate jurors about the reasonableness of battered women's actions is that jurors tend to have a difficult time reconciling battered women's victimization on the one hand and their agency on the other. In trials of battered women who kill, this difficulty is compounded by widely held stereotyped beliefs that the defendants must be either totally passive victims or very aggressive women who could not possibly have been battered (Mahoney, 1994; Schneider, 2000). Expert testimony can help bridge this divide by describing a woman's victimization as well as her active survival strategies.

It is important that scholars and practitioners alike shift their attention from Lenore Walker's earliest work, acknowledge subsequent social science developments, and look at the actual current uses of expert testimony in battered women's criminal trials. They will see that expert testimony today is far from focusing solely on a woman's pathology or passivity. Testimony about battering and its effects includes information about a woman's active survival strategies and about her acute understanding of her partner's violence (what Downs calls "heightened perception"). The expert gives the jury information about what the defendant did to try to stop, reduce, resist, cope with, and escape from her abuser's violence. Rather than emphasize a woman's pathology or mental failings, the testimony helps the jurors see her often creative responses to very difficult circumstances in the past. It provides jurors with needed contextual information so that they can evaluate the reasonableness of her decision to use deadly force in the final incident. Evidence about battering and its effects is one important aspect of the self-defense claims of battered women.

❖ REFERENCES

Allard, S. A. (1991). Rethinking battered woman syndrome: A black feminist perspective. *University of California at Los Angeles Women's Law Journal, 1*, 191–207.

Ammons, L. L. (1995). Mules, madonnas, babies, bathwater, racial imagery and stereotypes: The African-American woman and the battered woman syndrome. *Wisconsin Law Review, 1995*(5), 1004–1080.

Blackman, J. (1989). *Intimate violence: A study of injustice.* New York: Columbia University Press.

Bochnak, E. (Ed.). (1981). *Women's self-defense cases: The theory and practice.* Charlottesville, VA: Michie.

Bowker, L. H. (1993). A battered woman's problems are social, not psychological. In R. J. Gelles & D. R. Loseke (Eds.), *Current controversies on family violence* (1st ed., pp. 154–165). Newbury Park, CA: Sage.

Bradfield, R. (2002). Understanding the battered woman who kills her violent partner: The admissibility of expert evidence of domestic violence in Australia. *Psychiatry, Psychology and Law, 9*(2), 177–199.

Browne, A. (1987). *When battered women kill.* New York: Free Press.

Browne, A., Williams, K. R., & Dutton, D. D. (1999). Homicide between intimate partners: A 20-year review. In M. D. Smith & M. A. Zahn (Eds.), *Homicide: A sourcebook of social research* (pp. 149–164). Thousand Oaks, CA: Sage.

Burke, A. S. (2002). Rational actors, self-defense, and duress: Making sense, not syndromes, out of the battered woman. *North Carolina Law Review, 81,* 211–314.

Crocker, P. L. (1985). The meaning of equality for battered women who kill men in self-defense. *Harvard Women's Law Journal, 8,* 121–153.

Dershowitz, A. M. (1994). *The abuse excuse: And other cop-outs, sob stories, and evasions of responsibility.* Boston: Little, Brown.

Downs, D. A. (1996). M*ore than victims: Battered women, the syndrome society, and the law.* Chicago: University of Chicago Press.

Dutton, M. A. (1993). Understanding women's responses to domestic violence: A redefinition of battered woman syndrome. *Hofstra Law Review, 21*(4), 1191–1242.

Dutton, M. A. (1996). Impact of evidence concerning battering and its effects in criminal trials involving battered women. In *The validity and use of evidence concerning battering and its effects in criminal trials* (sec. 1). Washington, DC: U.S. Department of Justice, National Institute of Justice, U.S. Department of Health and Human Services, & National Institute of Mental Health. Retrieved April 28, 2004, from www.ncjrs.org/pdffiles/batter.pdf

Dutton, M. A. (1997a). Battered women's strategic response to violence: The role of context. In J. L. Edleson & Z. C. Eisikovits (Eds.), *Future interventions with battered women and their families* (pp. 105–124). Thousand Oaks, CA: Sage.

Dutton, M. A. (1997b). *Critique of the "battered woman syndrome" model.* Applied Research Paper Series: VAWnet, a project of the National Resource Center on Domestic Violence (Harrisburg, PA). Retrieved April 28, 2004, from http://www.vawnet.org/vnl/library/ general/AR_bws.html

Faigman, D. L. (1987). The battered woman syndrome and self-defense: A legal and empirical dissent. *Virginia Law Review, 72,* 619–647.

Faigman, D. L., & Wright, A. J. (1997). The battered woman syndrome in the age of science. *Arizona Law Review, 39,* 67–116.

Fox, J. A., & Zawitz, M. W. (2002). *Homicide trends in the United States.* Washington, DC: US Department of Justice, Office of Justice Programs, Bureau of Justice Statistics.

Goetting, A. (1988). Patterns of homicide among women. *Journal of Interpersonal Violence 3,* 3–19.

Gondolf, E. W. (1988). *Battered women as survivors: An alternative to learned helplessness.* Washington, DC: Lexington Books.

Hatcher, G. R. (2003). Note: The gendered nature of the Battered Woman Syndrome: Why gender neutrality does not mean equality. *New York University Annual Survey of American Law, 59,* 21.

Jones, A. (1996). *Women who kill* (Rev. ed.). Boston: Beacon.

Macpherson, S., Ridolfi, K., Sternberg, S., & Wiley, D. (1981). Expert testimony. In E. Bochnak (Ed.), *Women's self-defense cases: The theory and practice* (pp. 87–105). Charlottesville, VA: Michie.

Mahoney, M. (1994). Victimization or oppression? Women's lives, violence, and agency. In M. A. Fineman & R. Mykitiuk (Eds.), *The public nature of private violence: The discovery of domestic abuse.* New York: Routledge.

Maguigan, H. (1991). Battered women and self-defense: Myths and misconceptions in current reform proposals. *University of Pennsylvania Law Review, 140*(2), 379–486.

Maguigan, H. (1995). Cultural evidence and male homicide: Are feminist and multiculturalist reformers on a collision course in criminal courts? *New York University Law Review, 70,* 36–99.

Maguigan, H. (1998, Winter/Spring). A review essay: It's time to move beyond "battered woman syndrome." *Criminal Justice Ethics, 17,* 50–57.

Mangum, P. F. (1998–99). Reconceptualizing battered woman syndrome evidence: Prosecution use of expert testimony on battering. *Boston College Third World Law Journal, 19,* 593–620.

McNulty, F. (1980). *The burning bed.* New York: Harcourt Brace Jovanovich.

Mosteller, R. P. (1996). Syndromes and politics in criminal trials and evidence law. *Duke Law Journal, 46,* 461–516.

Osthoff, S. (2001). When victims become defendants: Battered women charged with crimes. In C. M. Renzetti & L. Goodstein (Eds.), *Women, crime, and criminal justice* (pp. 232–242). Los Angeles: Roxbury.

Parrish, J. (1996). Trend analysis: Expert testimony on battering and its effects in criminal cases. *Wisconsin Women's Law Journal, 11,* 75–173.

Rennison, C. M. (2003). Intimate partner violence, 1993–2001. *Crime data brief.* Washington, DC: U.S. Department of Justice, Office of Justice Programs, Bureau of Justice Statistics.

Schneider, E. M. (1986). Describing and changing: Women's self-defense work and the problem of expert testimony on battering. *Women's Rights Law Reporter, 9,* 191–222.

Schneider, E. M. (1992). Particularity and generality: Challenges of feminist theory and practices in work on woman-abuse. *New York University Law Review, 67,* 520–568.

Schneider, E. M. (2000). *Battered women and feminist lawmaking.* New Haven, CT: Yale University Press.

Schneider, E. M., & Jordan, S. B. (1981). Representation of women who defend themselves in response to physical or sexual assault. In E. Bochnak (Ed.),

Women's self-defense cases: The theory and practice (pp. 1–39). Charlottesville, VA: Michie.

Schopp, R. F., Sturgis, B. J., & Sullivan, M. (1994). Battered woman syndrome, expert testimony, and the distinction between justification and excuse. *University of Illinois Law Review, 1994,* 45–113.

Schuller, R. A., & Rzepa, S. (2002). Expert testimony pertaining to battered woman syndrome: Its impact on jurors' decisions. *Law and Human Behavior, 26,* 655–673.

Stark, E. (1995). Re-presenting woman battering: From battered woman syndrome to coercive control. *Albany Law Review, 58,* 973–1026.

Stubbs, J., & Tolmie, J. (1999). Falling short of the challenge? A comparative assessment of the Australian use of expert evidence on the battered woman syndrome. *Melbourne University Law Review, 23,* 709–748.

Walker, L. E. (1979). *The battered woman.* New York: Harper & Row.

Walker, L. E. (1984). *The battered woman syndrome.* New York: Springer.

Walker, L. E. (1989). *Terrifying love: Why battered women kill and how society responds.* New York: Harper & Row.

Walker, L. E. (1993). The battered woman syndrome is a psychological consequence of abuse. In R. J. Gelles & D. R. Loseke (Eds.), *Current controversies on family violence* (1st ed., pp. 133–153). Newbury Park, CA: Sage.

Walker, L., & Monahan, J. (1987). Social frameworks: A new use of social science in law. *Virginia Law Review, 73,* 559–598.

Websdale, N. (1999). *Understanding domestic homicide.* Boston: Northeastern University Press.

Wolfgang, M. E. (1958). *Patterns in criminal homicide.* Philadelphia: University of Pennsylvania Press.

Zahn, M. A., & Sagi, P. C. (1987). Stranger homicides in nine American cities. *Journal of Criminal Law and Criminology, 78,* 377–397.

15

Battered Woman Syndrome

Tool of Justice or False Hope in Self-Defense Cases?

Donald A. Downs

James Fisher

For at least 25 years, lawyers and advocates of battered women have striven to make the legal system responsive to the dangerous plights of battered women who kill or commit other illegal acts. "Battered woman syndrome" (BWS) has emerged as a primary tool to accomplish this end. BWS has had many positive effects. It can be used to counter certain myths that prejudice defendants, such as the belief that battered women enjoy being beaten or that their failures to leave their relationships mean that they were not "really" abused. And

AUTHOR'S NOTE: Much of the analysis of this article is based on Donald Alexander Downs's book, *More Than Victims: Battered Women, the Syndrome Society, and the Law* (1996).

it can be a component in the construction of a narrative of abuse that compels the jury to appreciate the defendant's unique situation and perspective.

Advocates resorted to BWS because of the belief that the traditional standards of self-defense law are inadequate to account for the actual dangers that battered women confront. BWS can be used to show that danger in abusive relationships is ongoing, thereby stretching the time frame for justifiable self-defense. The standards of traditional self-defense law are rather demanding (for men as well as women). The law of self-defense requires that deadly force be used only when the threat of death or serious bodily harm is *imminent* (about to happen) or when the defendant *reasonably believes* that such force is necessary under the circumstances. Preemptive acts (such as threatening a sleeping person) are not allowed. Finally, the use of deadly force must be proportionate to the threat: Deadly force may be used only to repel the threat of death or serious bodily harm.

It is indeed necessary to pay careful attention to the special dangers often confronted by battered women. Tormentors in the most violent and coercive relationships essentially hold battered women captive, and many women know (because they have been told or shown) that they will receive severe beatings—or worse—if they exercise their simple right to leave the relationship. The law of self-defense must be cognizant of these special dangers.

It is time, however, to reassess the long-term pros and cons of BWS. Despite its uses, has BWS ultimately proved to be more harmful than beneficial for battered women and the legal system? We argue that BWS can undermine the valid self-defense claims of battered women, and that it is inconsistent with the basic principles of criminal law and a political system that values equal citizenship and freedom. It carries unnecessary baggage into the criminal law when there are more direct, unencumbered ways of achieving the goals to which it aspires.

❖ WHAT BWS IS

The concept of BWS arose with the pioneering work of psychologist Lenore Walker, whose first book, *The Battered Woman*, was published in 1979. Within 10 years, BWS was used in criminal defenses across the land. A species of "post-traumatic stress disorder" (PTSD), BWS is a "victimization syndrome," along with such syndromes as rape trauma syndrome, hostage syndrome, battered child syndrome, and Vietnam veteran's syndrome. Such victimization syndromes attempt to establish that a person's mental state has been affected, and impaired, by the pressure of prolonged and extensive trauma due to some form of oppression or violence. Victims of battering tend to display symptoms associated with PTSD, such as intrusive thoughts, avoidance responses, difficulty sleeping and concentrating, hyper-vigilance, depression, suicidal inclinations, substance abuse, and somatic problems. Battered women often feel a pervasive sense of fear and loss of the sense of security and support that is normally an expectation of family life (Dutton, 1992; Herman, 1992).

In Walker's hands, BWS paints a singular portrait of the dynamics of battering relationships. Its key tenets are the "cycle theory of violence," "learned helplessness," and hyper-vigilance. The cycle theory depicts the battering relationship as a recurring cycle of three distinct phases: a period of tension build-up, a period of explosive rage accompanied by an acute battering incident, and a subsequent period of contrition. If this characterization is accurate, then traditional self-defense law is seemingly inadequate because it envisions danger in terms of specific incidents rather than a cumulative, ongoing process.

After the cycle has repeated itself a few times, the victim falls into the state of learned helplessness, which is the most important and controversial tenet of BWS. Walker derived this theory from behavioral psychologist Martin Seligman's work with dogs and rats (Seligman, 1975). Seligman subjected dogs to electric shocks in cages from which they could not escape. Eventually, the animals "learned" to be helpless, and stopped trying to escape, even when the doors to their cages were opened. According to Walker (1979), battered women fall into the same trap because

> repeated beatings, like electric shocks (in animal experiments), diminish the woman's motivation to respond. She becomes passive. . . . Her cognitive ability to perceive success is changed. She does not believe that her response will result in a favorable outcome, whether or not it might. . . . [Ultimately], the battered woman does not believe anything she does will alter [her situation]. (pp. 49–50)

Walker portrays learned helplessness as a form of mental incapacity or impairment. According to her, "the process of learned helplessness results in a state with *deficits* in three specific areas: in the area where battered women think, in how they feel, and in the way they behave" (Walker, 1989, p. 36, emphasis added). In the criminal law, such logic normally supports a form of *excuse,* such as insanity or diminished responsibility. Excused actions are wrong, but the defendant is deemed less blameworthy because of her impaired reasoning ability. Excuses are to be contrasted with *justifications,* in which actions that are usually criminal (such as using deadly force against another person or breaking and entering private property without the owner's consent) are deemed acceptable under the special circumstances at hand, such as the necessity of defending one's self against an attack or saving one's life from a deadly storm. Unlike excuse defenses based on mental deficiency or incapacity, justification defenses require the defendant to have acted reasonably and responsibly under the circumstances. Self-defense is typically a *justification* because the defender has a right to defend herself, and because the law usually requires her to act reasonably under the circumstances. Excuses are generally less worthy of respect than justifications because, as feminist lawyer Shirley Sagaw (1987) remarks, "Excuse connotates personal weakness and implies that the defendant could not be expected to function as would a 'normal' person" (p. 256, n. 21; see also Fletcher, 1978, p. 759).

Walker and her supporters present the cycle theory and learned helplessness as the two lynchpins of BWS. But the theory also contains another element, which we believe holds a key to a better approach to cases of battered women who kill: *hyper-vigilance.* Though battered women often develop mental incapacities associated with sustained trauma, this very trauma can also engender a mental state that seems to be a strange combination of impairment and a heightened form of reason. As Thomas Szasz (1990, pp. 256–267) has written, sometimes what appears to be diminished capacity in some respects is also "increased capacity" in other respects. Studies of battered women and other victims of captive situations indicate that captives often develop a heightened awareness of their captors' emotional states and actions. Such hyper-vigilance is essential to survival. Nora Cashen (personal interview), a former battered woman and a leader in the Wisconsin shelter movement, noted that

> battered women often exhibit a lot of hyper-vigilant behavior, monitoring his behavior to know all the time what he is up to. They become experts on his cues, very externally motivated, they

don't think of themselves. They monitor their own behavior to see what they can do to maintain control over the situation. . . . I wouldn't phrase it as diminished capacity. It is someone whose survival has been so focused on maintaining peace, their energy is so channeled, they lose their ability to have perspective. It's like anything else—a job with long hours, you lose your social skills. So there is diminished capacity in this sense.

Thus, the trauma of domestic abuse can actually *sharpen* the victim's ability to detect impending danger. But note that this logic is the logic of a *special kind of reason* (attuned to the special circumstances of captivity or violence), not a form of "impaired" reason. It fits the logic of justification, not excuse—a point with special meaning if we are dealing with the law of self-defense, which is a justification, not an excuse. This fact is pivotal, for the most perceptive advocates of battered women depict how battered women can only be understood by taking such reason into consideration. Julie Blackman (1986) talks about

an alternative form of reasonableness . . . reasonable in a relational framework and with a sense of history that is quite explicitly different from the traditional, legal standard of reasonableness. . . . Careful attention to the battered woman's past experiences with her husband's or partner's violence enhances one's capacity to understand her attack against him as reasonable or not. (p. 231)

❖ POSITIVE ASPECTS OF BWS

By presenting an explanation of why battered women do not always leave violent relationships, BWS helps to counter unfair myths about battered women that can undermine valid defenses—though, as we will see, this end can be accomplished by an approach that carries less baggage. An equally important function of BWS's role is in informing the jury of the special understanding battered women possess of their batterers' behavioral cues. Juries informed of "heightened capacity" are more likely to credit a battered woman's claim that an attack was imminent in cases where imminence would not be apparent to an untrained eye (such as certain statements or body gestures, the "look in his eye").

In addition, advocates maintain that BWS is a "hook" that creates a legal basis for introducing more evidence of abuse than previously legally allowed. One reason is that it is similar to such psychological excuses as insanity or diminished capacity, defenses that traditionally have opened the evidentiary door to a consideration of the defendant's past and relationships. Furthermore, BWS can contribute to the construction of a "narrative of abuse," which connects the defendant's plight in a dramatic way to the jury's fundamental sense of justice. In our age, juries often are torn between sympathy for victims of abuse and a commitment to the standards of criminal responsibility. Accordingly, they are more likely to be sympathetic when they can link a story of victimization to traditional standards of criminal law. BWS can connect these dots by providing a telling narrative of abuse that at the same time ostensibly ties the narrative to criminal law standards. The letter of the law can be stretched, but not openly forsaken. BWS's scientific gloss enhances this effect.

A legal narrative is not likely to succeed without attaching itself to prevailing cultural norms. An example is the *Bobbitt* case (1993–94), in which Lorena Bobbitt sliced off her husband's penis while he slept. The defense won an acquittal by portraying Ms. Bobbitt as a traditional, nonthreatening Catholic wife who passively suffered under her husband's abuse. As one analyst observed, "By creating an atmosphere of support in the press and in the courtroom, the defense let the jury know that a not-guilty verdict would be acceptable" (Wiesselberg, 1994, p. 6). The jury found Bobbitt not guilty by reason of temporary insanity.

❖ NEGATIVE EFFECTS OF BWS

Inflexibility, Stereotyping, and Indivisibility. In the final analysis, however, when it comes to self-defense claims, the problems of BWS outweigh its benefits. First, standard self-defense law is not as inflexible as many critics claim, as the law of evidence in virtually every state now permits the defense to introduce evidence of prior abuse and the nature of the relationship, and accounts for differences in power and strength (Maguigan, 1991). Second, BWS is disturbingly inflexible as a concept. By *Webster's Dictionary* definition, *syndromes* denote uniformity rather than individuation: "a group of signs and symptoms that occur together, and characterize a disease." In essence, BWS creates a stereotype of battered women that impairs the ability of women outside the stereotype from advancing legitimate self-defense claims. As Sharon Angella Allard (1991) asserts:

[BWS] incorporates stereotypes of limited applicability concerning how a woman would, and, indeed, should react to battering. . . . [A] battered woman needs to convince a jury that she is a "normal" woman—weak, passive, and fearful—[Otherwise], the jury may not associate her situation with that of the typical battered woman. . . . Race certainly plays a role in the cultural distinction between "good" and "bad" woman. The passive, gentle white woman is automatically more like the "good" fairy princess stereotype than a black woman, who as the "other" may be seen as the "bad" witch. . . . [BWS] provides no means for assessing the reasonableness of the woman's act of killing unless she is given the "excuse" of learned helplessness. (pp. 193–194)

The relative inflexibility of syndrome logic is inconsistent with the normally detail-oriented nature of self-defense law and the variety of battering relationships (some are more abusive or violent than others). In self-defense law, the devil properly lies in the details. For example, while intentional homicides are committed for a variety of motives, BWS tends to reduce the abuse victim's motivation to kill to simplistic terms. Though fear of an attack and a sense of futility about escaping are predominant, other motives can also enter the picture. Battered women may kill because they desire to *prevent themselves* from falling into learned helplessness, or because of a basic desire to achieve independence. Other motives include anger over finding out about the abuse of their children, jealousy, and simple greed. Anyone who has studied cases in this area has encountered all of these motives for homicide. Battered women are human beings like the rest of us, and the use of BWS should not obscure the fact that battered women, despite the sympathy they deserve for their plights, sometimes kill for reasons that the criminal law cannot excuse or justify.

While the self-defense claims of battered women need to be taken seriously, we must critically examine the circumstances of each case. Uncritical application of BWS may ultimately provoke a backlash and call into question the legitimacy of entirely valid claims. It is instructive to note that Walker has never, to our knowledge, provided an example of a battered woman who attacked her batterer and was culpable. One suspects that the use of BWS represents overcompensation for the fact that we have failed as a society in adequately holding batterers responsible for their actions.

Scholars have noted how the portrayals of defendants in trials can "label" them in ways that have implications for their rights and treatment as citizens (Schneider, 1992). A defendant "diagnosed" with BWS is labeled as having a form of mental incapacity, possessing "deficits" in reason and will, in Walker's words. When a commitment to personal responsibility is an important legal condition, using BWS can "boomerang" against its purported beneficiaries. Responsibility in law is often indivisible: Evidence of a lack of responsibility in one context can be used as evidence of nonresponsibility in another context. BWS puts too much emphasis on battered women *as* battered women, making it their very status. Presenting BWS as a psychological disorder in effect cements this characterization, which may then bleed over into other areas of the law or policy.

For example, insurance companies have attempted to deny coverage to abuse victims on the grounds that such a status is a psychiatric "preexisting condition." In addition, BWS diagnoses have affected the disposition of custody cases because battered women are seen as too helpless, passive, and prone to violence to protect their children from abusers and other harms. Judicial and legislative responses to these problems have been promising, but this misuse of BWS will always lurk beneath the surface wherever BWS, with its logic of incapacity and nonresponsibility, is advocated (Downs, 1996, pp. 129–136).

Learned Helplessness. Seligman's dogs proved quite resistant to being trained to regain a measure of self-will. One wonders, then, how the theory of learned helplessness can explain the agency exhibited by a battered woman who finally strikes back against her oppressor. Acts of self-defense are simply inconsistent with the theory of learned helplessness, so a jury that accepts the theory is more likely to disregard a valid self-defense claim than a jury that does not buy it. At the very least, the theory can confuse matters along these lines.

Equally troublesome, learned helplessness asserts that battered women in large lack self-will, thereby reducing battered women to doglike status and stripping them of their dignity. BWS labels women with the same incapacity for agency that modern feminism attempts to transcend. Walker consistently analogizes battered women to dogs, a problematic analogy given the fact that battered women heroically manage to maintain a sense of dignity, cognitive choice, and skills to survive that dogs do not. There is no scholarly or professional consensus on the validity of learned helplessness, and the concept is contradicted by the views of many practitioners that women develop hyper-vigilant awareness of their batterers' behavior (see Gondolf, 1983). In an interview, Nora Cashen remarks, "I don't like the phrase 'learned helplessness.' I have seen women in extremely abusive relationships who still scheme after 50 years! They are still active problem solvers, which, by definition, is not learned helplessness."

Another problem arises from the fact that Seligman's experiments are analogous only to women in situations of *absolute captivity*. Thus, cases in which opportunities to leave are reasonably present do not conform to the BWS model. Accordingly, learned helplessness opens the door to invalidating a self-defense claim on the grounds that the jury may believe that the abuse victim had opportunities to leave (was not absolutely captive), and therefore does not conform to the BWS model. But this point should be *irrelevant* to a valid self-defense claim. Nowhere in the law can one find any authority for the proposition that one surrenders his or her right to self-defense because he or she has not left a violent relationship. Ironically, BWS's logic implicitly reintroduces to the jury the very myth that BWS was designed to counteract.

Problems of the Cycle Theory. Walker does not demonstrate that most battering relationships exhibit the cycle theory. Indeed, in her 1984 book, *The Battered Woman Syndrome,* she says that 65 percent of her sample experienced the tension-building stage, while 58 percent experienced a period of contrition. This means that only 38 percent experienced both stages. Two-thirds of the women in her own sample therefore did *not* experience the full cycle.

In addition, cycle theory is not a meaningful tool for resolving exacting questions about the nature of the danger present at the time of an act of alleged self-defense. The notion that the battering relationship produces a cumulative terror is legitimate, but it can be abused to justify violence against a batterer at any time, any place, by any method—in other words, it can amount to a license to kill that is not allowed in any other domain of self-defense law. To our knowledge, neither Walker nor any other BWS experts have provided an example of a battered woman overreacting, either in apprehending deadly harm or in using disproportionate force (such as countering non-deadly danger with deadly force).

Indeed, Walker's writings show that she is willing to stretch the definition of *battering* to the breaking point. Researchers (including Walker) typically—and reasonably—consider a battered woman to be a woman who is physically and/or psychologically abused by her partner without any concern for her personhood or rights. Referring to one woman's situation, however, Walker (1989) concluded, "It is also clear from the rest of her story that Paul had been battering her *by ignoring her and by working late,* in order to move up the corporate ladder, for the entire five years of her marriage" (p. 98, emphasis added). Declaring such absence and neglect a form of battering does a real disservice to those women who heroically deal with being held captive by their abusers, who refuse to allow them any independence—the paradigm case of abuse that the law must address. Walker's analysis of battered women does not resolve the difficult questions of differing levels of responsibility and culpability among battered women with any subtlety. Her treatment suggests that BWS is a defense *in itself.*

An example of such application is Walker's proposed testimony in *Burhle v. Wyoming* (1981). Ms. Burhle suffered through an 18-year marriage marked by episodes of sometimes-mutual physical abuse. In 1979, her husband initiated divorce proceedings and sought a restraining order *against her.* The next day she threatened him with a shovel, and he retaliated by beating her with a pair of work boots. Then he moved into a hotel. A week later, she showed up at the hotel with a rifle, and they argued through the door about money. He kept the chain on the door secured fast. After 45 minutes of arguing, Ms. Buhrle let loose and shot her husband dead. Then she hid the rifle, took his wallet, and "began shouting that someone had shot her husband."

In pretrial motions, the defense presented an offer of proof indicating that Lenore Walker would testify that Ms. Burhle "was in a state of learned helplessness resulting in loss of free will"; that "because of learned helplessness, Ms. Burhle's ability to walk away from a situation or escape was impaired"; that Ms. Burhle perceived herself to be acting in self-defense *(Burhle v. Wyoming,* 1981, p. 1377). Because Ms. Burhle's actions in no way resembled a battered woman plagued by learned helplessness and trapped by her tormentor, the court properly refused to let Walker testify (also see Downs, 1996, pp. 145–148).

Implications for Equal Citizenship. BWS, therefore, can slide into "victim ideology," which is the reluctance on the part of advocates to assign personal responsibility to a person who has been victimized in some profound way. Feminist Susan Brownmiller (1989) pinpoints the problem in her critique of the famous New York case in the 1980s in which authorities gave leniency to Hedda Nussbaum, who failed to do anything to save her daughter's life at the hands of her violently abusive husband, Joel Steinberg:

> The movement to aid battered women does the cause of feminism a disservice when it supports unquestionably the behavior and actions of all battered women. The movement must drop its simplistic attitude toward batterers, and cease to view them as giant suction machines with the power to pull in any woman who crosses their path. It must also cease to excuse every battered woman who engages in criminal behavior, with the argument that she is, after all, merely a victim of patriarchy. The point of feminism is to give women the courage to exercise free will, not to use the "brainwashed victim" excuse to explain away the behavior of a woman who surrenders her free will. (p. 349)

BWS's logic undermines claims of equal citizenship and treatment. Rights and responsibilities are interdependent. Historically, men have been privileged—and burdened—with what Simone de Beauvior (1989) calls "transcendence": the power and accountability that comes from sublimating one's desires into social and cultural achievements that benefit others. One of the lynchpins of sexism and racism is the belief that women and racial minorities do not possess the capacity to accept the responsibilities of citizenship. Claims of equal treatment, then, are also implicit claims that groups "on the outside" are *capable* of being transcendent. To claim equality, therefore, is to claim equal responsibility. As Catharine MacKinnon (1982) remarks concerning the unintended consequences of double standards in law, "double standards have often been a legal means for disadvantaging women, as well as for rationalizing women's social exclusion and denigration" (pp. 724–735). Elizabeth Rapaport (1991) makes a similar point regarding the lower incidence of death penalty verdicts for women compared to men:

> The reputed leniency that women receive with respect to death sentencing supports the view widely held in our society that women are incapable of achieving, nor are they in fact held to, the same standards as are men. . . . Equal democratic citizenship can proceed from no other premise than of equal personal responsibility for decisions and actions. (p. 367)

The "syndromization" of the criminal law stands in tension with the discourse of personal responsibility that lies at the heart of a society striving for equal citizenship. The question of justice is how to balance the empathy that should exist for women who have endured abusive relationships with the need to assume that those women possess a capacity for responsibility. In legally empathizing with victims of abuse, we must be careful not to compromise their claims to equal treatment under the law, the demands of equal treatment for women generally, and, ultimately, the system of constitutional freedom we currently possess.

This is *not* to say that gender differences are irrelevant to individual cases of self-defense. For example, size and power differences and women's fear of rape (which can be a grounds for the use of deadly force) should always be taken into consideration. Equally important, the difficulties and dangers the defendant faced must be factored into the judgment concerning self-defense. What is needed in the practice of self-defense is a type of "practical reasoning" and "individualized" justice that incorporates general understanding of the special dangers battered women often face along with a commitment to ultimately relying on the actual facts in the case at hand. The "general" must appropriately inform the "particular" (Bartlett, 1990, p. 829; Schneider, 1992). General knowledge of the nature of battering relationships can prepare the jury and society to be on the lookout for certain dangers that might justify the resort to deadly force (such as the special danger that often arises when the woman threatens to leave the relationship), and the defendant's ability to read the cues of his intentions. But the ultimate test must be the actual presence of such legally relevant facts in the case at hand.

Vigilante Justice. Indiscriminating use of BWS opens the door to vigilante justice, as it sanctions the use of deadly force outside accepted parameters based on society's dislike of a certain class of people. The key problem with vigilante justice is that it rests on claims about the *character* of the victim or the perpetrator of a crime. It focuses on the *status* of the person: Is he or she *worthy* of state protection against the violence of another? Such logic is dangerous for a society dedicated to equal protection of the law, especially for individuals belonging to minority groups. In *Robinson v. California* (1962), the Supreme Court rightly rejected state punishment of people merely for their status or moral judgments about their character. Indeed, judgments about battered women's character once provided a reason for the state to refrain from intervening in domestic disputes.

Though it is perhaps counterintuitive, it must be acknowledged that batterers have rights, too. While victims must have the right to defend themselves from violence, batterers must be allowed to defend themselves when unjustifiably attacked. If one group's rights are not secure because of judgments (however accurate) about their character, then no one's rights are secure, for fickle public opinion can turn against any group or individual given the right historical conditions. Constitutional freedom depends upon the principle that every group and individual deserves equal rights regardless of their character or beliefs.

❖ ALTERNATIVES TO BWS

Fortunately, there are alternative ways to achieve empathy and justice for battered women who kill that are more consistent with these principles and traditional criminal law. The solution lies in focusing on the unique dynamics and patterns of each battering relationship, particularly battered women's capacity to monitor the moods, behavior, and cues of their batterers. Each relationship is unique, but each also often possesses its own distinctive patterns of interaction. Battered women are able to pick up signals of impending danger that might not be obvious to a person uninformed of the nature of the particular relationship in question. Mary Ann Dutton (1992) notes that

> many battered women describe a certain "look in the eye" that signals extreme danger. . . . Unless one were to understand the patterning within previous incidents, when 'that look' preceded the violent rape, the choking to unconsciousness, or the severe beating, it would make little sense why a woman might respond with such terror at simply a "look in the eye." (pp. 4, 6)

This type of testimony by an expert and the defendant—along with expert testimony about the nature of the dangers that battered women often confront and why leaving the relationship is often dangerous and difficult for reasons other than learned helplessness—would refocus the question of self-defense on whether, in the context at hand, the defendant reasonably perceived harm to be impending or imminent. Assuming the facts merited such a determination, this type of testimony would make it more likely that the jury would see the situation from the battered woman's perspective rather than that of an uniformed outsider, making it more open to seeing imminent danger than would otherwise be the case.

This approach would be based on more valid psychological theory than learned helplessness, and would be predicated upon the unique patterns and circumstances of each particular relationship rather than a theory that inflexibly portrays all battering relationships as fundamentally alike.

Finally, this type of testimony does not rely on portraying the victims of abuse as incapacitated. It focuses on survivor skills grounded in reason and agency that the victim has developed in trying circumstances. Incorporating this type of testimony into self-defense law more directly deals with battered women's situations of danger, and is more respectful of their status as responsible citizens and persons than a syndrome defense that relies on portraying the victim of abuse as a "woman without a will"—the words Walker (in *U.S. v. Gordon*, 1986, p. 1148) once used before a court.

❖ REFERENCES

Allard, S. (1991). Rethinking battered woman syndrome: A black feminist perspective. *U.C.L.A. Women's Law Journal, 1*, 193–194.

Bartlett, K. B. (1990). Feminist jurisprudence, *Harvard Law Review, 103*, 829.

Blackman, J. (1986). Potential uses for expert testimony: Ideas toward the representation of battered women who kill. *Women's Rights Law Reporter, 9*, 231.

Brownmiller, S. (1989). *Waverly Place.* New York: Signet.

Burhle v. Wyoming, 627 P. 2d 1374 (1981).

de Beauvoir, S. (1989). *The second sex.* New York: Vintage.

Downs, D. A. (1996). *More than victims: Battered women, the syndrome society, and the law.* Chicago: University of Chicago Press.

Dutton, M. A. (1992). *Empowering and healing the battered woman: A model for assessment and intervention.* New York: Springer.

Fletcher, G. (1978). *Rethinking criminal law.* New York: Little, Brown.

Gondolf, E. W. (1983). *Battered women as survivors: An alternative to treating learned helplessness.* New York: Lexington Books.

Herman, J. (1992). *Trauma and recovery: The aftermath of violence—From domestic abuse to political terror.* New York: Basic Books.

MacKinnon, C. (1982). Toward feminist jurisprudence. *Stanford Law Review, 34*, 724–725.

Maguigan, H. (1991). Battered women and self-defense: Myths and misconceptions in current reform proposals. *University of Pennsylvania Law Review, 140,* 379.

Rapaport, E. (1991). The death penalty and gender discrimination. *Law and Society Review, 25,* 367.

Robinson v. California, 370 U.S. 660 (1962).

Sagaw, S. (1987). A hard case for feminists: People v. Goetz. *Harvard Women's Law Journal, 10,* 256, n. 21.

Schneider, E. (1992). Particularity and generality: Challenges of feminist theory and practice in work on woman-abuse. *New York University Law Review, 67,* 520.

Seligman, M. (1975). *Helplessness: On depression, development, and death.* New York: W. H. Freeman.

Stark, E. (1988). *Woman battering.* New York: Garland.

Szasz, T. (1990). *Insanity: The idea and its consequences.* New York: Wiley.

U.S. v. Gordon, 638 F. Supp. 1120 (W. D. La. 1986), p. 1148.

Walker, L. (1979). *The battered woman.* New York: Harper & Row.

Walker, L. (1984). *The battered woman syndrome.* New York: Springer.

Walker, L. (1989). *Terrifying love: Why battered women kill and how society responds.* New York: Harper Collins.

Wiesselberg, C. (1994, January 22). U.S.C. Law School, *Boston Globe,* p. 6.

16

Child Sexual Abuse Prevention Is Appropriate and Successful

Carol A. Plummer

C hild sexual abuse is an ancient phenomenon, but neither the public nor the professional community had significant awareness of it until the 1970s. Prior to then, child sexual abuse was vastly underreported and misunderstood by the public and minimized in the professional literature. The recognition of child sexual abuse led to both the public and professionals attempting to identify abuse in the present generation of children as well as seeking ways to end and prevent it in future generations.

In the 1970s, prevention programs already flourished for problems such as drug abuse, suicide, and unwanted pregnancy. Yet because we knew so little about child sexual abuse, preventing it demanded that we learn a great deal. First, in order to prevent abuse, it was imperative to determine what caused it, or at least what factors contributed to it.

Second, the pattern of abuse dynamics (how children are selected, coerced, sworn to secrecy, and plagued with silencing guilt) needed to be carefully studied to determine how best to intervene.

In 1980, the U.S. government's National Center on Child Abuse and Neglect encouraged child sexual abuse prevention efforts through grants to six communities. Other programs, most notably the Child Assault Prevention Program, began with no federal funding yet expanded quickly because of requests from schools. As with other newly discovered social issues, public demand sometimes did push practice ahead of theory. However, early leaders used emerging theory to justify selected interventions. Although the programs were experimental, they were *not* haphazard in design or implementation.

Newly emerging prevention programs sought input from education, law enforcement, social services, and child development experts. They sought and used ongoing feedback from parents and students (Kent, 1982; Plummer, 1999). Despite budget and expertise limitations, significant energy was spent in the earliest years on program evaluations. Although funding and staff limitations made elaborate large-scale research simply not possible, formative and summative evaluations were consistently undertaken, and programs improved as a result. While few of these earliest evaluation studies were submitted for publication, concern about and encouragement of research always have been hallmarks of prevention programs. Therefore, some of the harsher criticisms of prevention programs, including that they are well intentioned but naive, may stem from critics' lack of knowledge of prevention's history and process.

❖   WHAT IS CHILD ABUSE PREVENTION?

Prevention is a tricky business. By definition, *primary prevention* occurs prior to the problem in order to prevent it. Consequently, proving that intervention prevented a specific event (an event that did not occur) is impossible, because the event may not have occurred anyway. Likewise, it is nearly impossible to prove that preventive intervention did *not* prevent the unwanted outcome. Proving prevention's effectiveness is a difficult task; proving its ineffectiveness is equally problematic.

When examining the effectiveness of prevention programs, a major concern is a definition of terms. What constitutes "abuse," "prevention," or a "program" are all open to debate. The prevailing theories regarding prevention approaches reflect the unique components operating when sexual abuse occurs. As Finkelhor (1984) shows in his "four preconditions" model, for abuse to occur there must be (1) a proclivity to abuse in the offender, inadequate (2) internal and (3) external controls of that behavior, and (4) access to children. Given that all preconditions must be present for abuse to occur, intervention in any of the four arenas theoretically could prevent abuse. Yet unlike cases of physical abuse or neglect, which are likely to be discovered by a concerned adult, sexual abuse is often shielded by secrecy and/or threats, with usually only the offender and victim aware of the behavior. This means that it is important to lower children's risk of sexual abuse by educating them. While educating children to identify and respond to sexual abuse is a component of prevention programs, prevention *never* was conceptualized by program developers as solely aimed at making children responsible for keeping themselves safe. As I have noted in earlier work (Plummer, 1986):

> If we inform children about sexual abuse and ways to prevent it we adults believe children can be empowered to HELP avoid or interrupt their own victimization SOMETIMES. This limitation must be acknowledged. We cannot always prevent sexual abuse or exploitation of children by giving them information or skills. (p. 4)

A comprehensive child sexual abuse prevention program has multiple essential components: community awareness, parent education, teacher training, age-appropriate and culturally sensitive programming for children, ongoing evaluation, and necessary updates (Plummer, 1986). Optimally, all parts will be strong. They will be aimed at strengthening behavioral controls of offenders, restricting access to victims, and altering the societal factors that create offenders. Regardless of program ideology or location, these components were evident from the inception of all major child sexual abuse prevention programs (Cooper, 1991; Tobin & Kessner, 2002). And, in recent years, prevention components have expanded. New approaches include promoting healthy images of sexuality (considering not only what we are working against, but what we are aiming for), peer education, bystander responses, and messages about dealing with bullies. Others challenged us to include juvenile and adult sex offender prevention. All of these have greatly expanded the meanings and intents of child sexual abuse prevention.

While teaching children should be the last line of defense (Plummer, 1986), and while comprehensive programs have multiple components, the news media—and critics of prevention—always have been most intrigued by the idea of children being told about "sex" or "saying No" to adults. Despite what programs accomplished in their totality, the image of prevention was reduced to an image of children being taught to "Say No and tell someone." This focus has neither done justice to prevention programs nor has it informed people of the breadth and depth of prevention's scope.

❖ CRITICISMS OF CHILD SEXUAL ABUSE PREVENTION PROGRAMS

Criticisms of child sexual abuse prevention almost entirely have centered on the components of programs focusing on educating children. Some criticisms (such as most of those made by Reppucci, Haugaard, & Antonishak, this volume) have challenged programs to improve by raising questions regarding program effectiveness. Yet other criticisms seem motivated by a desire to hamper prevention efforts. Although it is reasonable to expect some objections to prevention programs, the intensity of the opposition to child sexual abuse prevention can be shocking. Although such programs were briefly the darling of the media in the early 1980s, by 1990 there were serious critics. This media turnaround powerfully influenced the public's view of child sexual abuse prevention. It included media stories chastising overzealous child protective interventions and warning of epidemics of false allegations. Sunday magazine covers depicted drawings of large children looming over small fathers who were being ruined by their own children's fabrications. Recently, one prevention program has even reported having opponents harass staff and their families (Plummer, 2001).

In this context, child sexual abuse prevention work has been judged more harshly than other types of prevention. After all, drug and alcohol abuse prevention programs have not been discontinued because some are arguably ineffective. When such programs fail, the outcry often is to improve them. Even child sexual abuse treatment and intervention programs, which often have less than successful track records, have not been subject to the scrutiny that child sexual abuse prevention programs have undergone. There have not been calls for those treatment programs to be closed because they didn't get everything right on the first try. Ironically, some attacks on child sexual abuse prevention may be related to its *effectiveness*, reflected in a predictable backlash to challenging some core values of our present culture. More than treatment, intervention, or research, child sexual abuse prevention undeniably is about social change: altering the conditions that allow sexual abuse to occur. Perhaps that ultimately is the issue most disturbing to the most vocal critics. It will take more than simply watching children more carefully to stop sexual abuse. Preventing abuse necessitates changing attitudes in a society where often children are seen as property, women as sex objects, pornography as harmless, sexual crimes as uncontrollable, the effects of abuse as negligible, the extent of abuse as insignificant, and unwanted touch as a normal part of life. Preventing sexual abuse calls into question many of our unexamined values.

Ideological Criticisms

In *With the Best of Intentions: The Child Sexual Abuse Prevention Movement* (Berrick & Gilbert, 1991), the authors make various claims about prevention advocates who are "overwhelmingly female," "include many sexual abuse victims," and who are linked by a common "feminist ideology" (p. 9). Although some prevention proponents do operate out of a feminist perspective, many do not—some are in the tradition of "child protection" (Crisci, 1983), others have advocated for "children's rights" (Tobin & Kessner, 2002). But that is not the issue. The question for these most extreme critics is why does belief in equality between the sexes, being a survivor, or even being female make a prevention advocate suspect? By arguing that advocates seek to "gain public funds" for the "feminist cause" (Berrick & Gilbert, 1991, p. 18), these authors use prejudicial buzzwords that are both unfair and untrue. Although critics claim prevention professionals are "opportunistic" (Berrick & Gilbert, 1991, p. 20), the fact is that professionals working in prevention programs traditionally have earned about half as much as those working in treatment programs, and prevention programs are allocated much smaller budgets than treatment programs. Like many social service professions, our field is largely female.

Criticisms of Program Effectiveness

For many reasons, it is difficult to examine the effectiveness of child sexual abuse prevention programs. Programs range in duration from one day to several weeks; they are presented by teachers or outside instructors and may or may not have follow-up sessions to reinforce initial lessons. There also are questions about how "effectiveness" should be defined. Should effectiveness be defined as programs doing what they claim (educating children about sexual abuse), or as children implementing what they learn (using skills to avoid abuse)? Are prevention programs effective only if there is a *decrease* in reported abuse, or are programs effective if they *increase* reports, as both adults and children identify abuse and take action more quickly, with less shame or confusion? In a promising new study, the hope that programs would actually prevent abuse was examined. Gibson and Leitenberg (2000) studied 825 females at a state university and found that those who had participated in a child-education prevention program were significantly less likely to later experience sexual abuse.

Examining program effectiveness also is difficult because the goals of most prevention programs are broad and include the following:

1. Raise the awareness of the general public.

2. Educate parents about abuse, its prevention, and early intervention.

3. Train professionals to understand abuse dynamics, symptoms, and reporting responsibilities.

4. Teach children factual information about sexual abuse.

5. Develop skills in children that may help them to avoid sexual abuse.

6. Work toward ending child sexual abuse in our communities.

Given such multiple goals, it is not reasonable to examine effectiveness by focusing on only what children learn in these programs and how they apply their knowledge.

Studies must consider all components of a sexual abuse prevention program, not only the training for children, since children were never meant to accomplish prevention single-handedly. Longitudinal studies will be necessary, because most advocates suggest a graduated training, with reinforcements and more sophisticated concepts as the child matures. Finally, consideration must be given to what constitutes effectiveness in training for children: knowledge or attitude change, increased assertiveness, skill acquisition, increased reporting, more immediate reporting, and so on. Acceptable standards of effectiveness need to be determined. Granted, all children do not need to have significant gains, but is 25 percent—or 50 percent or 75 percent—sufficient?

I, and others working in the area of preventing child sexual abuse, agree with the argument of Reppucci, Haugaard, and Antonishak (this volume), who argue that prevention programs must be held accountable and that their effectiveness needs to be seriously examined. Prevention programs need to be researched and improved; ineffective programs should be eliminated and replaced with more effective ones. However, while these critics repeatedly acknowledge that evaluation research is costly, they do not consider the meaning of that cost in the real world of prevention programs. Funding for prevention programs never has been sufficient; such programs typically are the first to suffer funding cuts. Prevention employees are low paid, resulting in frequent turnover (Plummer, 2001). Program workers, often volunteers, do what they can despite knowing that they need to do more. Yes, evaluation studies conforming to the state-of-the-art scientific methodology "should" be done, but the real world of prevention programs does not include the money, the time, nor the trained personnel to conduct such studies. Prevention programs therefore are being criticized for not doing *what it is not possible to do.*

Criticisms of Educating Children

While child sexual abuse prevention programs have multiple audiences, most critics target their criticisms on the content and outcomes of components seeking to educate children. While attitudes based on societal myths or beliefs (such as that offenders are strangers or that victims are partially at fault) have been found difficult to alter, even the most adamant critics acknowledge that most children learn some of the information presented without suffering ill effects. No fewer than 40 studies (with sample sizes ranging from 24 to 3,500) have documented that elementary, junior high, and high school students learn the main concepts taught in prevention programs (Rispens, Aleman, & Goudena, 1997). Information regarding what sexual abuse is and what should be done to prevent it are the messages most easily learned by children (Finkelhor &

Strapko, 1992). The older the child and the more concrete the information, the more learning occurs (Daro & McCurdy, 1994). Comparative research has found that programs actively involving children result in greater grasp of concepts (Carroll, Miltenberger, & O'Neill, 1992). Programs lasting longer and including follow-up sessions also are associated with more information retention (Wurtele & Miller-Perrin, 1992).

Prevention program organizers are well aware that children's increased knowledge and attitude change do not automatically translate to skills acquisition, or, critically, to using skills in dangerous situations. Some studies examining skills acquisition through role plays or responses to video situations have shown children can learn to tell what they will do. Yet even this does not definitely establish what children would do in a real situation. Yet, simulation studies have shown that children receiving prevention training are less likely to go with strangers than are children without such training (Fryer, Kraizer, & Miyoshi, 1987). These findings are encouraging; however, there are ethical issues inherent in pretending that children are being potentially abducted, which makes it very difficult to answer questions about children's actual use of skills taught. Given the particular challenges in the field of child sexual abuse, clear and convincing evidence of children's ability and willingness to use prevention skills in real situations may not be possible. Few adults, even those with self-defense training, can be certain how they would respond during an attempted rape. To focus *only* on using skills as a measure of prevention success will frustrate practitioners by continually circling us around to unanswerable questions: Will these skills be used? And, if so, will that use be effective? The answers, almost assuredly, are that sometimes they will be used and sometimes they will be effective.

For this reason, prevention advocates often suggest a blanket approach: less concern with which particular intervention prevented the assault as long as a combination of efforts keeps children safe. This suggests an approach along the lines of reducing cigarette usage: package warnings and school programs and smoke-outs and TV spots and doctors' advice, and so on. To be certain, researchers need to be much more exacting in discovering what works *best* with which children, yet the bottom line is that we protect children from child sexual abuse.

In the focus on prevention's effectiveness in educating children, critics have ignored the overwhelming success of prevention efforts in *adult* education. Prevention programs, including public awareness campaigns, have raised community awareness dramatically. A recent Vermont study showed that between 1995 and 1999, adults' willingness to report abuse had increased from 65 percent to 80 percent (Tabachnick & Dawson, 2000). Parents indisputably have gained new information and likewise give high ratings to the programs designed for their children (Elrod & Rubin, 1993; Nibert, Cooper, & Ford, 1989). Professionals have gained more information about the problem, improved their ability to detect possible abuse, and refined their skills in dealing with prevention presentations and disclosures. In examining program effectiveness, it is critical that we not lose sight of all that programs are doing, including efforts aimed at adult awareness.

Criticisms About the Content of Programs Educating Children

For some, rethinking prevention efforts has less to do with *whether* children should be informed than it does with *how* they should be informed. Trudell and Whatley (1988) have argued that programs should not inadvertently insinuate that children should or must use prevention skills, or else they are partially to blame for abuse. Debate continues regarding the use of formal anatomical terms versus "private parts." Research has documented the need for more interactive teaching, practice sessions for children, and at least yearly repetitions at the elementary level. Kolko (1988) makes an argument for not limiting discussion to touch discrimination, but including personal safety, assertiveness, and problem solving. Finkelhor and Strapko (1992) point out that sexual abuse prevention may be a child's first introduction to the topic of sexuality, so care must be taken not to present sex negatively. Wurtele (1987) encourages more attention to developmental issues. These issues are being addressed differently in each distinctive program, but they are being addressed. Prevention proponents ourselves take this question of how children should be educated very seriously.

Outcome data on preschool sexual abuse prevention programs show the least definitive results and are the most controversial. Critics have stated that certain concepts, such as that good or liked people can do bad or disliked behaviors, are incomprehensible to the youngest preschoolers. Most prevention advocates long have argued that preschoolers should not bear the burden of protecting themselves, but that adults must supervise and protect them (Plummer, 1986). Prevention programs for preschoolers emphasize *adult responsibility* and include considerations such as how to select baby-sitters and screen day care providers, facility design issues, policies in day care, and teaching parents about abuse. Undeniably, many programs need to enhance the adult-focused components of their prevention programs for preschoolers. Still, given the risk for abuse between ages three and six, it could be argued that some preschoolers can learn the concepts and skills and that to withhold this information is to rob them of their last defensive option against abuse. Withholding useful information from the vulnerable also raises ethical issues.

Past research shows a wide variation in learning by preschool children. More than 20 studies (some with random assignment) have shown that children can learn basic prevention concepts even if they do not learn all of the messages taught (Cooper, 1991; Daro & McCurdy, 1994; Finkelhor & Strapko, 1992; Wurtele & Owens, 1997). If 50 percent of the children learn, there is a strong argument that this is effective, especially when children's abilities vary so widely among three- to five-year-olds. Were negative outcomes shown to be a major risk, perhaps prevention education could wait until first grade. However, because some studies show that 30–50 percent of sexual abuse victims are under the age of seven (Wurtele & Miller-Perrin, 1992), the discomfort of adults with the loss of children's "innocence" should not weigh more heavily than actual risk to the youngest victims. Expanding adult involvement and creating developmentally appropriate programs are important challenges. Yet research does justify continuing to educate even very young children as part of a broader program (Harvey, Forehand, Brown, & Holmes, 1988).

The Criticism of Unanticipated Outcomes

It is important to examine the extent to which programs accomplish what they set out to do. Equally important is to consider the unintentional results of programs. Such outcomes can be either positive or negative. To date, most studies have found no negative impact of prevention programs on most children (Taal & Edelaar, 1997). Indeed, at least three studies have shown that children report *less* fear and *more* confidence as a result of certain programs (Lutter & Weisman, 1985). Studies asking parents about the negative effects of programs on their children also have found few or no negative consequences, such as fear, nightmares, anxiety, or bed-wetting (Wurtele & Miller-Perrin, 1987). Despite Reppucci and his colleagues' concerns (this volume), there is no evidence that parents are less protective if they know their children have been exposed to in-school prevention. In fact, some researchers have documented evidence that parents and children often increase discussion of safety after such a program

(Finkelhor & Dziuba-Leatherman, 1995). A few studies have shown an increase in anxiety after program participation. While "anxiety" is an unintended outcome, it is not necessarily negative, because anxiety might indicate heightened awareness in children, and thus more readiness to ward off attacks. As Finkelhor and Strapko (1992) report, the research on fearfulness and anxiety is "fairly reassuring." Of course, even a small number of children negatively affected cannot be ignored. Prevention professionals are well aware of the importance of unintended consequences and thus support further study.

❖ PREVENTION: THE SUCCESS STORY

While advocating for better research on prevention with children, we must also base our definitions of effectiveness on other criteria. Sexual abuse prevention has been effective already, even without a universal scientific stamp of approval from rigorous research. Success can be claimed because we have accomplished several objectives on the way to the ultimate goal of reducing or ending sexual abuse. Although reaching our goal will take decades of commitment and action, these accomplishments justify our continued striving:

- Prevention efforts have educated millions about sexual abuse and ways it can be prevented.
- Prevention programs have educated millions of children about sexual abuse prevention, breaking the silence and eroding the ignorance that makes children vulnerable.
- Parents have become better protectors of their children as a result of their education regarding sexual abuse prevention.
- Negative consequences of prevention education for children are nil to minimal, and there is reason to believe that unanticipated outcomes have been more positive than negative.
- Some studies have shown the ability of children to utilize prevention skills in order to avoid potentially dangerous situations.
- Prevention programs often have resulted in increased reporting of abuse, perhaps stopping abuse more readily than if no information had been given to children.
- Teachers and other professionals who come into contact with children frequently have been trained to create more protective environments and to respond more helpfully if abuse is suspected.

- Prevention programs have addressed the special needs of children of a variety of ages, ability levels, and cultural groups to prevent abuse more adequately.
- The most recent studies are showing less abuse among those females who participated in a prevention program compared with those who did not participate.

Preliminary results are promising. Programs aimed at preventing child sexual abuse have made significant strides in a little over 20 years. These efforts have not been perfect and have been much easier to criticize than to create, but prevention has proven itself in each category of its endeavors. Despite political opposition, financial onslaughts, and even programmatic imperfections, prevention is desired by the public and supported by research; it deserves a chance to get the work done to make the world safer for children.

By increasing and improving research methods, it is possible to learn much more about prevention's overall impact. Several constraints have kept this from occurring rapidly and thoroughly. Whether there will be research money and who will receive the money are primary concerns. Both research academicians and prevention practitioners should participate in framing the relevant questions and interpreting results. Currently there are few dollars allocated for such research and, at the same time, a cry for more "proof."

Given the sensitive topic, the issue of access to children, the age of the subjects, and ethical considerations, studies are inherently difficult, even with adequate funding. While we need valid and reliable testing instruments, control groups, and longitudinal data collection in order to examine program effectiveness, the major question facing prevention programs is one of survival: Given funding cuts, will we have programs to evaluate—programs with the quality and longevity needed to make possible a fair evaluation of prevention?

Methodological issues continue to pose challenges for researchers of prevention programs. However, pointing to research and shouting, "Inadequate!" should not be a substitute for preventive efforts to protect children from a real and present danger.

Prevention professionals must listen carefully to legitimate concerns about the problems with current prevention efforts. For example, Reppucci, Haugaard, and Antonishak (this volume) raise legitimate points. Certainly, prevention advocates agree that there is a need to conduct more research, improve weak programs, place more responsibility on adults, examine possible negative effects, and deal with the fact that knowledge gain does not necessarily translate to skill usage. Yet the flaw in their argument stems from their basing their analysis on premises gathered from Berrick and Gilbert's (1991) faulty conclusions about prevention programs. Prevention proponents must ask of our critics: Are your criticisms really about the specifics of our programs, or are they about the concept of prevention itself? And, what are *you* doing to try to prevent abuse? Answers to these questions can help us to sort out valid from invalid criticisms.

❖ REFERENCES

Berrick, J. D., & Gilbert, N. (1991). *With the best of intentions: The child sexual abuse prevention movement.* New York: Guilford.

Carroll, L., Miltenberger, R., & O'Neill, K. (1992). A review and critique of research evaluating child sexual abuse prevention programs. *Education and Treatment of Children, 15,* 335–354.

Cooper, S. (1991). *New strategies for free children: Child abuse prevention for elementary school children.* Columbus, OH: National Assault Prevention Center.

Crisci, G. (1983). *Personal safety curriculum.* (Available from the Franklin/Hampshire Community Mental Health Center, 76 Pleasant St., Northampton, MA 01060)

Daro, D., & McCurdy, K. (1994). Preventing child abuse and neglect: Programmatic intervention. *Child Welfare, 73*(5), 405.

Elrod, J. M., & Rubin, R. H. (1993). Parental involvement in sexual abuse prevention education. *Child Abuse and Neglect, 17,* 527–538.

Finkelhor, D. (1984). *Child sexual abuse: New theory and research.* New York: Free Press.

Finkelhor, D., & Dziuba-Leatherman, J. (1995). Victim prevention programs: A national survey of children's exposure and reactions. *Child Abuse and Neglect, 19,* 125–135.

Finkelhor, D., & Strapko, N. (1992). Sexual abuse prevention education: A review of evaluation studies. In D. J. Willis, E. Holden, & M. Rosenberg (Eds.), *Prevention of child maltreatment: Developmental and ecological perspectives* (pp. 150–167). New York: Wiley.

Fryer, G., Kraizer, S., & Miyoshi, T. (1987). Measuring actual reduction of risk to child abuse. *Child Abuse and Neglect, 11,* 173–185.

Gibson, L. E., & Leitenberg, H. (2000). Child sexual abuse prevention programs: Do they decrease the occurrence of child sexual abuse? *Child Abuse and Neglect, 24*(9), 1115–1125.

Harvey, P., Forehand, R., Brown, C., & Holmes, T. (1988). The prevention of sexual abuse: Examination of the effectiveness of a program with kindergarten-age children. *Behavior Therapy, 19,* 429–435.

Kent, C. A. (1982). *Illusion theater impact study: Phases in developing a child sexual abuse prevention education program.* (Available from Illusion Theater, 28 Hennepin Ave., Minneapolis, MN 55403)

Kolko, D. (1988). Educational programs to promote awareness and prevention of child sexual victimization: A review and methodological critique. *Clinical Psychology Review, 8,* 195–209.

Lutter, Y., & Weisman, A. (1985). *Sexual victimization prevention project.* Final Report to the National Institute of Mental Health, Grant R18MH39549.

Nibert, D., Cooper, S., & Ford, J. (1989). Parents' observations of the effect of a sexual abuse prevention program on preschool children. *Child Welfare, 68,* 539–546.

Plummer, C. (1986). Prevention education in perspective. In M. Nelson & K. Clark (Eds.), *The educator's guide to preventing child sexual abuse* (pp. 1–5, 69–79). Santa Cruz, CA: Network.

Plummer, C. (1997). *Preventing sexual abuse: Activities and strategies for those working with children and adolescents.* Holmes Beach, FL: Learning Publications.

Plummer, C. (1999). The history of child sexual abuse prevention: A practitioner's perspective. *Journal of Child Sexual Abuse, 7*(4), 77–95.

Plummer, C. (2001). Prevention of child sexual abuse: A survey of 87 programs. *Violence and Victims, 16*(5), 2001.

Rispens, J., Aleman, A., & Goudena, P. P. (1997). Prevention of child sexual abuse victimization: A meta-analysis of school programs. *Child Abuse and Neglect, 21*(10), 975–987.

Taal, M., & Edelaar, M. (1997). Positive and negative effects of a child sexual abuse prevention program. *Child Abuse and Neglect, 21,* 399–410.

Tabachnick, J., & Dawson, E. (2000). Stop it now! Vermont: A four year program evaluation, 1995–1999. *Offender Programs Report 1,* p. 49.

Tobin, P., & Kessner, S. L. (2002). *Keeping kids safe: A child sexual abuse prevention manual* (2nd ed.). Alameda, CA: M. S. Hunter House.

Trudell, B., & Whatley, M. (1988). School sexual abuse prevention: Unintended consequences and dilemmas. *Child Abuse and Neglect, 12,* 103–113.

Wurtele, S. K. (1987). School-based sexual abuse prevention programs: A review. *Child Abuse and Neglect, 11,* 483–495.

Wurtele, S. K., & Miller-Perrin, C. L. (1987). An evaluation of side effects associated with participation in a child sexual abuse prevention program. *Journal of School Health, 57,* 228–231.

Wurtele, S. K., & Miller-Perrin, C. L. (1992). *Preventing child sexual abuse: Sharing the responsibility.* Lincoln: University of Nebraska Press.

Wurtele, S. K., & Owens, J. S. (1997). Teaching personal safety skills to young children: An investigation of age and gender across five studies. *Child Abuse and Neglect, 21*(8), 805–814.

17

Is There Empirical Evidence to Support the Effectiveness of Child Sexual Abuse Prevention Programs?

N. Dickon Reppucci

Jeffrey J. Haugaard

Jill Antonishak

I n the 1970s, child advocates and feminist groups helped make the public and professionals aware of the prevalence of child sexual abuse (Finkelhor, 1986). Even the most conservative estimates suggested that 10 percent of female children are subjected to some form of child sexual abuse (Haugaard & Reppucci, 1988). The problem was brought to center stage in the media with the sensational 1984 court case of the McMartin Day Care Center in Los Angeles, in which the center's owner and six teachers were accused of systematically abusing hundreds of children over 10 years. The publicity resulted in a national obsession with child sexual abuse. The ongoing efforts to create child sexual abuse prevention programs received added emphasis through this surge in public awareness. Millions of children have now been exposed to these programs.

The widespread documented incidence of child sexual abuse, especially the disturbing data that 25–30 percent of all sexually abused children are under the age of seven (Finkelhor, 1986) and that the modal age for such abuse is 10 years (Melton, 1992), has highlighted the pressing need for effective prevention programs. The National Committee to Prevent Child Abuse (cited in Daro, 1994) conducted a survey in 1990 of 400 elementary school districts and found that 85 percent of the districts had offered a child sexual abuse prevention program in the past year; 64 percent of the districts had mandated such programs. Despite widespread dissemination and implementation of child sexual abuse prevention programs, it is still unclear if the children exposed to such programs have the cognitive, emotional, or physical capabilities to protect themselves. In the past decade, researchers have placed greater emphasis on evaluating child sexual abuse prevention programs, but evidence is still too ambiguous to conclude that the programs are effective. Targeting children as their own protectors may be misguided, and advocates' faith in these programs may actually retard the development of other programs targeting parents, other adults, and the community that might be more effective. We question the efficacy of child-focused sexual abuse prevention programs, not to advocate for abolishing prevention efforts, but to encourage developing effective ones.

We first describe the concepts, goals, and research requirements of prevention programs in general. We then turn to concerns that typical child sexual abuse prevention programs may not be well attuned to the developmental levels of the children receiving them. Finally, we examine assumptions upon which programs are based and conclude that caution is warranted regarding widespread use of these programs. We argue that the major research action goals should be developing new and better programs.

❖ PREVENTION PROGRAMS AND EVALUATION

Three types of prevention—primary, secondary, and tertiary—are generally identified in analyses of preventive practice. *Primary* preventions are interventions to prevent a problem from ever happening; *secondary* prevention suggests early identification and intervention to stop the problem from continuing; *tertiary* prevention aims to reduce the effects of the problem after it has occurred. Primary prevention has been the goal of public health practice for the past 200 years, and several successes have been recorded, including the development of vaccines to eliminate several infectious diseases and the fluoridation of drinking water to combat tooth decay. However, the focus on preventing psychological, behavioral, and social disorders began in earnest only with the emergence of the community mental health movement in the 1960s; documented successes of such endeavors have appeared only recently (Price, Cowen, Lorion, & Ramos-McKay, 1988), and conclusive documentation of effectiveness remains elusive.

Reasons for this state of affairs include the complexity of what these programs are trying to accomplish, the research designs necessary to provide the documentation, the lengthy time periods needed to demonstrate primary prevention, and the often enormous costs involved in evaluating such projects. Nevertheless, it does not lead us to Plummer's conclusion (this volume) that positively proving the effectiveness of prevention is an impossible task.

Muehrer and Koretz (1992, pp. 109–110) provide a list of seven fundamental methodological issues that must be addressed to accurately determine the impact of preventive interventions:

1. Adverse outcomes to be prevented and desired outcomes to be promoted must be specified.

2. A theoretical framework for intervention design must be articulated.

3. Process measures to ensure that the intervention was implemented as planned must be included.

4. Target populations must be identified and sample selection procedures justified.

5. Pilot data must be used to determine whether the proposed sample size will be large enough to detect an intervention effect.

6. An experimental research design should be used to examine potential causal relationships between the risk and protective factors and the outcomes.

7. Participants need to be followed longitudinally to determine whether the intervention has a lasting impact.

To date, no evaluation of any child sexual abuse prevention program has accounted for more than a few of these concerns.

Why Question the Effectiveness of Sexual Abuse Prevention?

Given the importance of preventing child sexual abuse, why would anyone want to question prevention programs? As a way of answering, we turn to the field of medicine. Suppose that someone claimed to have discovered a vaccine that would prevent the spread of AIDS. If the vaccine worked, it would reduce the incidence of AIDS. If, however, the vaccine only appeared to work but was *ineffective*, then it could result in the *increased* spread of AIDS. This would occur if those taking the vaccine believed it would work and stopped using sexual practices that are known to be effective in stopping the transmission of AIDS.

The same concern is appropriate for all types of prevention programs. If adults assume child sexual abuse prevention programs are effective, they may believe that children participating in these programs are protected from abuse. The adults may then become less protective of children. If prevention programs are not effective, then children may be at greater risk for being abused than if programs had not been presented at all.

Why Evaluate?

Program evaluation can be complex, time consuming, and costly. In a social environment in which the need for sexual abuse prevention is clear, but only limited funds are available, it is tempting to use all of the funds to provide prevention programs so that more children can be reached. Because we are looking for the long-term protection of our children, we must commit to undertaking the short-term costs; despite the costs, a good evaluation will help show which parts of a program are achieving their goals and which are not. Evaluation also can show with which audience a program is most effective. For example, in comparing gains in knowledge among first, third, and sixth graders who participated in a child sexual abuse prevention program, Tutty (1994) found younger children had more difficulty than older children in learning concepts.

The Complexity of Sexual Abuse Prevention

The complexity of the process that a child must engage in to repel or report an abusive approach can be highlighted by separating this process into three parts: First, a child must recognize that he or she is in an abusive situation; then, the child must believe that he or she can and should take some sort of action; finally, the child must possess and use specific self-protective skills. To be effective, prevention programs must focus on all of these three parts. Providing a child with skills in only one or two is likely to drastically reduce program effectiveness.

Prevention programs must first inform children about what sexual abuse is. Most have done this by trying to teach the concept of "good," "bad," and "confusing" touches. However, young children are very poor at making such distinctions, so teaching these concepts may be very difficult (Berrick & Gilbert, 1991; Haugaard & Reppucci, 1988). Indeed, even adults are not clear about what is and is not sexual abuse (Melton, 1992). Although most adults may agree that certain acts always entail sexual abuse (such as a parent having intercourse with a child), considerable disagreement exists about other acts (such as whether or not it is sexually abusive for a parent to clean a seven-year-old child's genitals during a nightly bath).

Assuming a child is able to label a certain experience as sexual abuse, the child must then understand that he or she should report or repel it. Many programs attempt to teach children that they do not have to allow other people to touch them (under most circumstances) and that they have the right to say No to anyone who tries to touch them in an unacceptable fashion. However, children at different cognitive levels often find it difficult to decide when an action should or should not be taken. For example, young children are much better at following broad and general rules (for example, "Do not let anyone touch your private parts") than they are at following rules that require making distinctions (for example, "Doctors or nurses can touch your private parts, and your parents can touch you if they are helping you clean yourself or if you are hurt there, but no one, not even your parents, can touch you there at other times"). Such rules may be incomprehensible to many children.

If a child understands that a certain act is sexual abuse and that something should be done to stop it, then the child must feel empowered and competent to implement a plan of action. The typical plan taught is that the child should not keep the abuse a secret, should tell adults until someone believes the child, and should run away if possible. However, such a strategy may not give the child enough information, especially if the child is fearful of threatened or imagined punishments. Most adults have been in situations where they know that something should be done, but if they are unprepared or afraid, they prefer to do nothing in order to avoid a wrong or ineffective action. It seems unreasonable to expect that children, who usually are not as cognitively or emotionally competent or as powerful as adults, will be able to engage in these complex behaviors in emotionally delicate and sometimes frightening situations.

Most existing prevention programs are based on the idea that they can teach children enough information in a very short time to enable children both to understand the issues and to protect themselves. Given the cognitive complexity of the issues and the emotionally charged situation in most abusive encounters, it seems highly unlikely that most young children could learn to apply the skills necessary to prevent their own abuse.

Prevention Programs for Schoolchildren

Although a few programs focus on junior and senior high school students, most target children are under age 10 and are taught in elementary schools or day care centers. Classroom programs involving lectures and discussions are most widespread, partly because of intimacy and convenience; children participate in small groups in a situation usually allowing time for questions (for a review of program content, see Daro, 1994). Two very different goals are usually emphasized: primary prevention and detection. The success of neither of these goals has been investigated systematically.

Programs for children generally address the following topics: educating children about what sexual abuse is; broadening their awareness of possible abusers to include people they know and like; teaching that each child has the right to control access to his or her body; describing a variety of "touches" that a child can experience; stressing actions a child can take in potentially abusive situations; teaching that some secrets should not be kept and that a child is never at fault for sexual abuse; and stressing that the child should tell a trusted adult if touched in an inappropriate manner (Finkelhor, 1986). However, in order to avoid controversy and increase the number of schools willing to accept the programs, most child sexual abuse prevention is approached from a protective, rather than sexual, standpoint. For example, discussions of bullies or relatives who forcefully try to kiss a child are frequently used to illustrate good and bad touching. More intimate or long-term types of sexual abuse, specific discussions of molestation by parents, and information that some "bad" touches can actually "feel" good tend to be ignored. Such modifications of content in order to increase schools' acceptance of the programs may reduce their preventive influence.

Many prevention programs involve only one or two presentations, whereas a much smaller number include 25–30 short sessions. A few sessions may be enough for detection, because some abused children will identify themselves after even brief exposure to the topic of sexual abuse. However, little evidence exists to suggest that primary prevention can be accomplished in very few sessions.

Prevention educators generally agree that the instructors of the programs should be authority figures such as teachers, specially trained volunteers, or mental health professionals. The program formats should be entertaining, of high interest, and nonthreatening. Movies, slides, videotapes, plays, discussions, and role-play situations, as well as printed materials such as coloring books or comic books are used. Unfortunately, neither the validity nor the efficacy of the formats or instructors is known (Roberts, Alexander, & Fanurik, 1990).

Although most prevention advocates emphasize that parental involvement is critical (Plummer, this volume), few programs implement components including parents. Prevention educators lament this lack of participation, but tend to accept it rather than use scarce resources to develop innovative programs targeting parents.

Outcome Research

The most common and consistent finding among the few programs that have been evaluated is a statistically significant, yet often slight, increase in knowledge about sexual abuse following participation in a prevention program (see Daro, 1994; MacMillan, MacMillan, Offord, Griffith, & MacMillan, 1994; Rispens, Aleman, & Goudena, 1997). Moreover, many children answer a high percentage of the questions accurately even *before* they participate in a prevention program (Berrick & Gilbert, 1991).

A 1996 report by the U.S. Government Accounting Office concluded that the efficacy of child sexual abuse prevention programs is inconclusive because of limitations in both the design and the outcome measures used in evaluation. Kohl (1993), for example, surveyed school-based prevention programs across the United States and found that although 114 of 126 individual programs reported that their programs were evaluated, most programs did not specify an evaluation design. Prevention programs with any sort of systematic evaluation deserve praise because only a very few have made any attempt to evaluate their effectiveness. However, the evaluations conducted so far all have had basic design flaws, and none has come close to meeting the seven basic methodological criteria for evaluating prevention programs spelled out by Muehrer and Koretz (1992). Although a few have used non-treatment control groups matched for such variables as age, gender, and socioeconomic status, and a repeated measures design, most have not. Therefore, there is no way to determine whether the programs caused any changes that might have occurred. Other design problems include small samples, lack of attention to the reliability and validity of the measuring instruments, no pretesting to establish a baseline of knowledge, and short-term follow-up assessments, usually after less than three months.

Critical Assumptions

Most child sexual abuse prevention programs are developed from anecdotal clinical information and are based on six critical assumptions, discussed in turn next.

Assumption 1: Increasing children's knowledge about sexual abuse will increase their ability to prevent abuse. Although prevention educators, parents, and others would like to believe this assumption is correct, no empirical evidence supports it (Reppucci, Land, & Haugaard, 1998). Some program evaluators have incorporated behavioral measures (such as hypothetical vignettes or role-play situations), but the results remain inconclusive. For example, although Hazzard, Webb, Kleemeier, Angert, & Pohl (1991) found a significant increase in knowledge about child sexual abuse in their experimental group relative to their control group, they did not find a significant difference between the two groups in knowledge of prevention skills. Kraizer, Witte, & Fryer (1989), however, did find a correlation between knowledge and behavior change in scripted role-play situations. In sum, there is no adequate basis for concluding that knowledge gleaned from a sexual abuse prevention program enables children to protect themselves.

Assumption 2: Prevention educators know what type of skills will make a child less susceptible to sexual abuse, and these skills are being taught. Sexual abuse comes in many forms. Skills useful for preventing one type of abuse might not be useful for preventing another type, and some skills may be useful for children of one age but not for children of another. Although this would suggest that developmentally sensitive curricula are imperative, current sexual abuse prevention programs "generally have failed to consider cognitive-developmental factors" and "look remarkably similar across age groups" (Melton, 1992, p. 182). Some research has examined developmental differences in comprehension of concepts presented in sexual abuse programs. Tutty (1994) and Wurtele and Owens (1997) have examined the effects of a sexual abuse prevention program on younger (as compared to older) children and found that there are differences in understanding important concepts. Younger children had more difficulty with concepts such as saying No to authority figures, trusting familiar adults, and reporting an abusive situation.

Clarity as to specific skills and behaviors that prevention programs should teach is needed in order to allow researchers to develop means of measuring their acquisition. Kraizer et al.'s (1989) program, based on what actually happens in abusive situations, is a step in the right direction. However, such programs are very difficult to construct because there are real questions surrounding the ethics of subjecting children to fictional sexual abuse situations in order to assess what prevention behaviors they exhibit. Moreover, studies of offenders suggest that they tend to fear only detection (Burdin & Johnson, 1989; Conte, Wolf, & Smith, 1989), thus teaching young children strategies such as when to say No, fight, yell, or run may be relatively useless because of the superior knowledge, strength, and skill of adult perpetrators. Such actions by children may even put them in more jeopardy.

Assumption 3: Prevention programs have no negative effects, or possible negative effects are so minor that they are insignificant when compared with the positive outcomes. Investigators have found mixed results regarding this issue. Some report no evidence of negative effects as measured by children's increased anxieties and fears (Hazzard et al., 1991; Wurtele & Miller-Perrin, 1987), while others report such effects for at least a small proportion of program participants (Gilbert, Berrick, LaProhn, & Nyman, 1989). For example, Finkelhor and Dziuba-Leatherman's (1995) survey findings suggest that 8 percent of children who were exposed to prevention programs worried a lot and 53 percent worried a little about being abused. They interpret these results as positive and adaptive, which may be the case. However, with no systematic follow-up, we do not know the amount of anxiety that is helpful versus harmful.

Assumption 4: Primary prevention is an achievable goal of existing prevention programs. No evidence exists that primary prevention ever has been achieved by existing prevention programs. Although we recognize that demonstrating effectiveness of primary prevention programs is a time-consuming and expensive affair, the fact that there is not even one published case study of a child using what he or she was taught to prevent an incident of abuse is troubling, especially because there are reports that children who had been participants in prevention programs still become victims. In a survey of 2,000 children, Finkelhor, Asdigian, and Dziuba-Leatherman (1995) found that children who had participated in comprehensive prevention programs reported using prevention strategies significantly more than did children who had participated in less comprehensive or no prevention programs. However, they found no significant differences in the number of completed incidents of sexual abuse as a percentage of all attempted and completed incidents.

Assumption 5: Detection of ongoing abuse has been achieved. This assumption appears to be on a solid foundation, in that many individual cases of ongoing or past abuse have been discovered as a result of these interventions. Unfortunately, no systematic information is available regarding what percentage of children is likely to disclose abuse or how many of the disclosures are confirmed. Most evaluations do not include documentation of the number of founded disclosures in an experimental group in comparison to a control group. In MacMillan et al.'s (1994) review of 19 published evaluations, only three collected disclosure data. Still, Finkelhor and Strapko's (1992) claim that detection is the "most important and unambiguous finding" of the prevention programs may be accurate, and their suggestion to rename them "disclosure" programs may be a positive step toward clarifying their true benefit.

Assumption 6: Children are the appropriate targets of sexual abuse prevention. Parental and community involvement would be valuable but are not crucial to the success of child abuse prevention efforts. Based on concerns regarding the issue of developmental readiness raised earlier (see Berrick & Gilbert, 1991; Piaget & Inhelder, 1969), as well as findings suggesting that neither self-defense techniques nor a child saying No would be a powerful deterrent to an offender (Conte et al., 1989), targeting children alone appears unlikely to be an effective strategy for preventing child sexual abuse. Moreover, as Melton (1992) states, "The primary focus on changing behavior of potential child abuse victims is not only unfair but also unrealistic. Telling children they have control over their bodies makes them no more powerful" (p. 181). As is done in programs to prevent physical child abuse and neglect, it may be more appropriate to target parents.

Little research examines the potential role parents can play in child sexual abuse prevention. Burgess and Wurtele (1998) evaluated a program for parents and found that after a training program, parents had significantly more discussions about child sexual abuse with their children than did parents who had participated in a general home safety program. Finkelhor et al. (1995) found that children who had received prevention instruction from parents were more likely to have disclosed sexual victimization.

Several surveys have evaluated parents' desire to participate in child sexual abuse prevention programs. Elrod and Rubin (1993) surveyed 101 parents of children attending either preschool or day care centers, and found that more than 90 percent of them rated themselves or their spouses as the person they most preferred to educate their child about sexual abuse. However, only 56 percent of these parents knew that abusers are more likely to be familiar people rather than strangers. Wurtele, Kvaternick, and Franklin (1992) found that the majority of parents discussing sexual abuse with their children focus on danger from strangers, not from acquaintances or intimates. Wurtele et al. (1992) caution that if prevention educators fail to coordinate the skills and information taught in school-based prevention programs with what is believed and taught at home, children could become confused, and conflict between children and parents could result. This research suggests that sexual abuse prevention programs should focus on parents as targets of intervention (see Reppucci, Jones, & Cook, 1994, for a review of parental involvement in child sexual abuse prevention programs).

❖ CONCLUSIONS

More definitive information about the six critical assumptions and more thorough evaluations of ongoing prevention programs are necessary if we are to determine their influence on children. Extensive investigations of the full range of prevention programs must be undertaken. Because the safety of children is the ultimate goal, we need to know much more about which programs work to teach which skills to which children. We need more sophisticated research regarding the process that a child must go through to repel or report abuse and determine how this process is experienced by children at various levels of cognitive and emotional development and in various ecological contexts. Furthermore, innovative forms of prevention focusing on parents must be developed. The low participation rates by parents in current school-based programs are cause for alarm. Educators and mental health professionals should try providing programs targeting parents and other adults through places of employment, churches, and community service groups, such as the Lions Club and Kiwanis, and through small discussion groups in local homes. Although all of these approaches would be time consuming, they would undoubtedly increase parental involvement and heighten awareness of the problem among adults. Targeting parents and other adults also would eliminate the inappropriate burden of children being responsible for preventing their own sexual exploitation.

Even though child sexual abuse prevention programs focusing on environmental and social change have not yet been developed, attention should be paid to such approaches. As Melton (1992) points out, the history of public health strongly suggests that prevention programs designed to change the risky behavior of individuals are not very successful. Eliminating or reducing the opportunities for risky behaviors has produced greater increases in safety in other areas than teaching or persuading people to avoid risky behaviors themselves. For example, childproof caps and lead-free paints are much more effective at reducing poisonings than are programs aimed at increasing parents' vigilance and children's avoidance behaviors. In other words, we need to consider alternative approaches to sex abuse prevention that do not target the child and may prove to be more effective.

In this chapter, we have not meant to be unduly critical of efforts to empower young children. However, we do feel that it is reasonable to question whether this relatively exclusive focus on children as their own protectors is appropriate, to emphasize that children's developmental capacities must be considered, and to encourage more rigorous evaluations of both positive and negative effects of every prevention program. By questioning these past and current efforts, we do not denigrate them. Nevertheless, our current state of knowledge regarding the best paths toward prevention requires a questioning stance of current approaches. Advocates must recognize that only by questioning these interventions can we sharpen them and develop new and more effective ones. Given the enormity of the problem, innovative programs must be developed, implemented, and evaluated. Our children deserve no less!

❖ REFERENCES

Berrick, J. D., & Gilbert, N. (1991). *With the best of intentions: The child sexual abuse prevention movement.* New York: Guilford.

Burdin, L. E., & Johnson, C. F. (1989). Sex abuse prevention programs. Offenders' attitudes about their efficacy. *Child Abuse and Neglect, 13,* 77–87.

Burgess, E. S., & Wurtele, S. K. (1998). Enhancing parent-child communication about sexual abuse: A pilot study. *Child Abuse and Neglect, 22,* 1167–1175.

Conte, J. R., Wolf, S., & Smith, T. (1989). What sexual offenders tell us about prevention strategies. *Child Abuse and Neglect, 13,* 293–301.

Daro, D. A. (1994). Prevention of child sexual abuse. *Future of Children, 4*(2), 198–223.

Elrod, J. M., & Rubin, R. H. (1993). Parental involvement in sexual abuse prevention education. *Child Abuse and Neglect, 17,* 527–538.

Finkelhor, D. (1986). Prevention: A review of programs and research. In D. Finkelhor & Associates (Eds.), *A sourcebook on child sexual abuse* (pp. 224–254). Beverly Hills, CA: Sage.

Finkelhor, D., Asdigian, N., & Dziuba-Leatherman, J. (1995). The effectiveness of victimization prevention instruction: An evaluation of children's responses to actual threats and assaults. *Child Abuse and Neglect, 19,* 137–149.

Finkelhor, D., & Dziuba-Leatherman, J. (1995). Victim prevention programs: A national survey of children's exposure and reactions. *Child Abuse and Neglect, 19,* 125–135.

Finkelhor, D., & Strapko, N. (1992). Sexual abuse prevention education: A review of evaluation studies. In D. J. Willis, E. Holden, & M. Rosenberg (Eds.), *Prevention of child maltreatment: Developmental and ecological perspectives* (pp. 150–167). New York: Wiley.

Gilbert, N., Berrick, J., LaProhn, N., & Nyman, N. (1989). *Protecting young children from sexual abuse: Does preschool training work?* Lexington, MA: Lexington Books.

Haugaard, J. J., & Reppucci, N. D. (1988). *The sexual abuse of children: A comprehensive guide to current and intervention strategies.* San Francisco: Jossey-Bass.

Hazzard, A., Webb, C., Kleemeier, C., Angert, L. & Pohl, J. (1991). Child sexual abuse prevention: Evaluation and one-year follow-up. *Child Abuse and Neglect, 15,* 123–138.

Kohl, J. (1993). School-based child sexual abuse prevention programs. *Journal of Family Violence, 8,* 137–150.

Kraizer, S., Witte, S. S., & Fryer, G. E., Jr. (1989, September-October). Child sexual abuse prevention programs: What makes them effective in protecting children? *Children Today,* 23–27.

MacMillan, H. L., MacMillan, J. H., Offord, D. R., Griffith, L., & MacMillan, A. (1994). Primary prevention of child sexual abuse: A critical review. Part II. *Journal of Child Psychology and Psychiatry, 35*(5), 857–876.

Melton, G. (1992). The improbability of prevention of sexual abuse. In D. J. Willis, E. Holden, & M. Rosenberg (Eds.), *Prevention of child maltreatment: Developmental and ecological perspectives* (pp. 168–189). New York: Wiley.

Muehrer, P., & Koretz, D. S. (1992). Issues in preventive intervention research. *Current Directions in Psychological Science, 1,* 109–112.

Piaget, J. & Inhelder, B. (1969). *The psychology of the child.* New York: Basic Books.

Price, R., Cowen, E., Lorion, R., & Ramos-McKay, J. (Eds.). (1988). *Fourteen ounces of prevention: A casebook for practitioners.* Washington, DC: American Psychological Association.

Reppucci, N. D., Jones, L. M., & Cook, S. L. (1994). Involving parents in child sexual abuse prevention programs. *Journal of Child and Family Studies, 3,* 137–142.

Reppucci, N. D., Land, D., & Haugaard, J. J. (1998). Child sexual abuse prevention programs that target young children. In P. K. Trickett & C. J. Schellenbach, (Eds.), *Violence against children in the family and the community* (pp. 317–337). Washington, DC: American Psychological Association.

Rispens, J., Aleman, A., & Goudena, P. P. (1997). Prevention of child sexual abuse victimization: A meta-analysis of school programs. *Child Abuse and Neglect, 21,* 975–987.

Roberts, M. C., Alexander, K., & Fanurik, D. (1990). Evaluation of commercially available materials to prevent child sexual abuse and abduction. *American Psychologist, 45,* 782–783.

Tutty, L. M. (1994). Developmental issues in young children's learning of sexual abuse prevention concepts. *Child Abuse and Neglect, 18,* 179–192.

Wurtele, S. K., Kvaternick, M., & Franklin, C. F. (1992). Sexual abuse prevention for preschoolers: A survey of parents' behaviors, attitudes, and beliefs. *Journal of Child Sexual Abuse, 1,* 113–128.

Wurtele, S. K., & Miller-Perrin, C. L. (1987). An evaluation of side effects associated with participation in a child sexual abuse prevention program. *Journal of School Health, 57,* 228–231.

Wurtele, S. K., & Owens, J. S. (1997). Teaching personal safety skills to young children: An investigation of age and gender across five studies. *Child Abuse and Neglect, 21,* 805–814.

18

Overreporting and Underreporting of Child Abuse and Neglect Are Twin Problems

Douglas J. Besharov

C hild protective agencies are plagued simultaneously by the twin problems of under- and overreporting of child abuse and neglect. On one hand, many abused and neglected children go unreported because they are afraid to come forward on their own and they are overlooked by informed professionals. The price is great: Failure to report exposes children to serious injury and even death. On the other hand, a large proportion of reports are dismissed after investigations find insufficient evidence upon which to proceed. Variously called "unfounded," "unsubstantiated," or "not indicated," these cases divert resources from already understaffed agencies, thus limiting their ability to protect children in real danger. In addition, such reports trigger what may be deeply traumatic experiences for all members of the families involved.

These two problems are linked and must be addressed together before real progress can be made in combating child abuse and neglect. In this chapter, I argue that public child protective agencies should take two parallel steps: They should enhance the public and professional education they provide, and they should upgrade their ability to screen inappropriate reports.

❖ SUCCESSES IN CHILD ABUSE AND NEGLECT REPORTING LAWS

Reporting begins the process of protection. Adults who are attacked or otherwise wronged can go to the authorities for protection and redress of their grievances. But the victims of child abuse and neglect often are too young or too frightened to obtain protection for themselves; they can be protected only if concerned adults recognize the danger and report it to the proper authorities. Thus all states now have child abuse reporting laws. Over the past years, the scope of these laws has greatly broadened in two ways. First, reporting laws initially mandated only that physicians report "serious physical injuries" or "non-accidental injuries." In the ensuing years, however, these laws have been expanded so that almost all states now require any form of suspected child maltreatment to be reported (physical abuse, sexual abuse and exploitation, physical neglect, and emotional maltreatment), and they require reports from a wide variety of professionals (physicians, nurses, dentists, mental health professionals, social workers, teachers, and other school officials, child care workers, and law enforcement personnel). About 20 states require all citizens to report, regardless of their professional status or relationship to the child. All states allow any person to report.

These reporting laws, and associated public awareness campaigns, have been strikingly effective in encouraging reporting. In 1963, about 150,000 children came to the attention of public authorities because of suspected abuse or neglect (U.S. Children's Bureau, 1966, p. 13). In 1997, nearly 3 million children were reported, more than 20 times the number reported in 1963 (Wang & Daro, 1997). See Table 18.1.

All states now have specialized child protective service (CPS) agencies to receive and investigate reports, and treatment services for

Table 18.1   Child Abuse and Neglect Reporting, 1976–1999

Year	Total Children Reported	Confirmed Victims	Substantiation Rate*
1976	669,000	314,430	47.0
1977	838,000	445,816	53.2
1978	836,000	334,400	40.0
1979	988,000	291,460	29.5
1980	1,154,000	415,440	36.0
1981	1,225,000	539,000	44.0
1982	1,262,000	517,420	41.0
1983	1,477,000	731,115	49.5
1984	1,727,000	727,000	42.0
1985	1,928,000	732,000	40-43
1986	2,086,000	737,000	40-42
1987	2,178,000	686,000	37-40
1988	2,265,000	N/A	N/A
1989	2,435,000	N/A	N/A
1990	2,557,000	997,230	39.0
1991	2,474,000	862,639	39.3
1992	2,900,000	993,000	41.0
1993	2,900,000	1,018,692	38.1
1994	2,900,000	1,011,628	37.1
1995	3,000,000	1,000,000	35.8
1996	3,000,000	970,000	34.4
1997	3,000,000	984,000	33.3
1998	2,806,000	903,000	29.2
1999	2,974,000	826,000	29.2

*Terminology varies across studies and years, and includes "substantiated," "indicated," "open for protective services," "protection services provided," and "reason to suspect."

SOURCE: Data for 1976–87, American Association for Protecting Children (1989); for 1988–90, McCurdy & Daro (1994); for 1991–99, U.S. Department of Health and Human Services, Child Maltreatment Series (1992–2001). Although these three studies used somewhat different methodologies and, in early years, incomplete data from the states, a generally consistent trend line exists through 1996, when it appears that the U.S. Department of Health and Human Services effort captures a more complete picture of official reporting.

maltreated children and their parents have been expanded substantially. As a result, many thousands of children have been saved from serious injury or even death. The best estimate is that over the past 30 years, child abuse and neglect deaths have fallen from more than 3,000 a year—and perhaps as many as 5,000—to about 1,100 a year (Sedlak,

1989, p. 2). Yet child maltreatment remains the sixth largest cause of death for children under 14 years of age (U.S. Department of Health & Human Services, 1980).

Despite this very positive change, large numbers of obviously endangered children still are not reported to the authorities. One study from the National Study of the Incidence and Severity of Child Abuse and Neglect estimated that in 1986, selected professionals saw about 300,000 physically abused children, another 140,000 sexually abused children, and 700,000 who were neglected or otherwise maltreated (Sedlak, 1987). According to the study, the surveyed professionals reported only about half of these children to child protective authorities. The surveyed professionals failed to report almost 40 percent of the sexually abused children, nearly 30 percent of fatal or serious physical abuse cases, and almost 50 percent of moderate physical abuse cases. The situation was even worse in neglect cases: About 70 percent of fatal or serious physical neglect cases went unreported, as did about three-quarters of the moderate physical neglect cases. This means that in 1986, at least 50,000 sexually abused children, at least 60,000 children with observable physical injuries severe enough to require hospitalization, and almost 184,000 children with moderate physical injuries were *not* reported to child welfare agencies (Sedlak, 1989, pp. 3–19). And, of course, failure to report can be fatal to children.

❖ THE PROBLEMS OF INAPPROPRIATE REPORTING

In brief, child abuse reporting laws have been effective in bringing more cases of abuse and neglect into the social service system. At the same time, there remain cases that go unreported, and that is most definitely a problem. Yet while many abused children go unreported to authorities, an equally serious problem further undercuts efforts to prevent child maltreatment: The nation's child protective agencies are being inundated by "unfounded" reports. Although rules, procedures, and even terminology vary, an "unfounded" ("unsubstantiated," "not indicated") report is one that is dismissed after an investigation finds insufficient evidence upon which to proceed.

In the past, in a misguided effort to shield child protective programs from criticism, a few advocates quarreled with estimates that I and others had made that the national unfounded rate was between 60 percent and 65 percent (Finkelhor, 1990, pp. 22–29). Emphasizing various inconsistencies in the data, they claimed either that the problem of unfounded reports was not so bad or that it always had been that bad. They did not associate the problem of unfounded reports with increased reporting. Table 18.1, based on the best available data, should settle the matter. It shows a declining substantiation rate from 47 percent in 1976 to 29 percent in 1999.

It is important to stress that an unfounded report does not necessarily mean that the report was inappropriate. There are many reasons why appropriate reports might nonetheless be classified as unfounded. For example, evidence of child maltreatment is hard to obtain and may not be uncovered; a case might be labeled as "unfounded" when no services are available to help the family; cases are closed because the child or family cannot be located. A certain proportion of unfounded reports, therefore, is an inherent—and legitimate—aspect of reporting suspected child maltreatment and is necessary to ensure adequate child protection.

That said, it remains that unfounded rates of the current magnitude go beyond anything reasonably justifiable: In some states, fewer than 1 in 4 reports are substantiated. We must ask about the price paid for so many investigations that yield so little.

The Price of Inappropriate Reporting: Needless Family Intrusions

The determination that a report is unfounded can be made only after an investigation that can be traumatic and that is, inherently, a breach of parental and family privacy. To determine whether a particular child is in danger, caseworkers must inquire into the most intimate personal and family matters. Friends, relatives, neighbors, schoolteachers, day care personnel, doctors, clergy, and others who know the family often are interviewed by CPS workers. Richard Wexler (1985) wrote of what happened to Kathy and Alan Heath (not their real names):

> Three times in as many years, someone—they suspect an "unstable" neighbor—has called in anonymous accusations of child abuse against them. All three times, those reports were determined to be "unfounded," but only after painful investigations by workers. . . . The first time the family was accused, Mrs. Heath says, the worker "spent almost two hours in my house going over the allegations over and over again. She went through everything from a strap to an iron, to everything that could cause bruises, asking me if I did

those things. [After she left] I sat on the floor and cried my eyes out. I couldn't believe that anybody could do that to me." Two more such investigations followed. . . . The Heaths say that even after they were "proven innocent" three times, the county did nothing to help them restore their reputation among friends and neighbors who had been told, as potential "witnesses," that the Heaths were suspected of child abuse. (pp. 19, 22–23)

Laws against child abuse are a recognition that family privacy must give way to the need to protect helpless children. But in seeking to protect children, it is all too easy to ignore the legitimate rights of parents. Each year, about 700,000 families are put through investigations of unfounded reports. This is a massive and unjustified violation of parental rights.

In response, a national group of parents and professionals formed to represent those falsely accused of abusing their children. Calling itself VOCAL (Victims of Child Abuse Laws), the group has thousands of members in chapters across the country. In Minnesota, VOCAL members collected 2,000 signatures on a petition asking the governor to remove Scott County Prosecutor Kathleen Morris from office because of her alleged misconduct in bringing charges, subsequently dismissed, against 24 adults in Jordan, Minnesota.

The Price of Inappropriate Reporting: Endangering Children

While it is possible to argue that infringing on family privacy is a price we should be willing to pay for bringing more cases of child abuse and neglect into the social service system, we pay another price for inappropriate reporting. Inappropriate reporting can *endanger children who experience child abuse or neglect.* By law, workers must perform extensive investigations of every report received. This takes workers' time. Forced to allocate a substantial portion of their limited resources to inappropriate reports, child protective agencies are less able to respond promptly and effectively when children are in serious danger. Some reports are not investigated for a week or more after they are received; dangerous home situations receive inadequate supervision as workers ignore pending cases to investigate the new reports arriving daily. Decision making also suffers: With so many cases of insubstantial or not proven risk to children, caseworkers are desensitized to the obvious warning signals of immediate and serious danger.

These nationwide conditions help explain why 25–50 percent of child abuse deaths involve children previously known to the authorities (Besharov, 1988, chap. 9). Tens of thousands of other children suffer serious injuries short of death while under child protective agency supervision because supervision is inadequate. In one Iowa case, for example, the noncustodial father reported to the local department of social services that his 34-month-old daughter had bruises on her buttocks; he also told the agency that he believed that the bruises were caused by the mother's live-in boyfriend. While the agency investigated and substantiated the abuse, a decision was made against removing the child from the mother's custody, and, instead, to make follow-up visits coupled with day care, counseling, and other appropriate services. *But no follow-up visit was made.* Eight days later, the child was hospitalized in a comatose state, with old and new bruises over most of her body. Three days later, the child died. Yes, workers should have made follow-up visits, yet they did not have the time given legal mandates to investigate all cases reported.

Ironically, by weakening the system's ability to respond, *inappropriate* reports also discourage *appropriate* reports. The sad fact is that many responsible individuals are not reporting endangered children because they feel the system's response will be so weak that reporting will do no good or possibly even make things worse by subjecting fragile families to traumatic investigations. A study of the impediments to reporting concluded:

> Professionals who emphasize their professional judgment have experienced problems in dealing with the child protective agency, and are more likely to doubt the efficacy of protective service intervention and are more likely not to report in some situations, especially when they believe they can do a better job helping the family. (Alfaro, 1984, p. 66)

If workers could spend less time on inappropriate reports, they could do a much better job of responding to the appropriate reports.

❖ TOWARD RESOLVING THE TWIN PROBLEMS OF UNDERREPORTING AND OVERREPORTING

Underreporting therefore remains a problem, as all too many children experiencing abuse or neglect fail to reach the attention of professionals who might well help them. Overreporting likewise is a problem. First and foremost, given legal mandates that workers must investigate all reported cases, overreporting takes away resources from serious cases of neglect and abuse. Overreporting also raises issues about family privacy and the traumas with ensuing problems investigations can inspire. Underreporting and overreporting hence are twin problems, where one problem cannot logically be resolved without attention to the other.

Enhanced Public and Professional Education

Few people fail to report because they don't care about an endangered child. Instead, they may be unaware of the danger the child faces or of the available social services. A study of non-reporting among teachers, for example, blamed their "lack of knowledge for detecting symptoms of child abuse and neglect" (Levin, 1983, p. 14). Likewise, few inappropriate or unfounded reports are deliberately false statements. Studies of sexual abuse reports, for example, suggest that only 4–10 percent are knowingly false (Berliner, 1988; Jones & McGraw, 1987). Most inappropriate reports involve an honest desire to protect children, coupled with confusion about what conditions are reportable.

Given this general confusion, the best way to encourage more complete and more appropriate reporting is through increased public and professional understanding. Recognizing this, almost half of the states have specific statutes mandating professional training and public awareness efforts; most states lacking specific statutes nonetheless offer such training.

However, these educational efforts need much better focus. Confusion about reporting is largely caused by the vagueness of reporting laws, aggravated by the failure of child protective agencies to provide realistic guidance about deciding what should be reported. Educational materials and programs should (1) clarify the legal definitions of child abuse and neglect, (2) give general descriptions of reportable situations (including specific examples), and (3) explain what to expect when a report is made. Brochures and other materials for laypersons, including public service announcements, should give specific information about what to report—and what not to report (Besharov, 1988, p. 346).

Defining "Reasonable Suspicions"

To fulfill this recommendation of more focused education, educational materials must explain, clearly and with practical examples, the legal concept of "reasonable cause to suspect" child maltreatment.

Reporting laws do not require people who report abuse or neglect to have "proof" that a child is being abused or neglected. Rather, in all states, reports are to be made when there is "reasonable" cause to suspect or "reasonable" cause to believe that a child is abused or neglected. Yet what is a "reasonable" suspicion? Too often, "reasonable" is taken to unreasonable lengths. Potential reporters are frequently told to "take no chances" and to report *any* child for whom they have the *slightest* concern. There now also is a tendency to tell people to report children whose behavior suggests they may have been abused—even in the absence of any other evidence of maltreatment. These "behavioral indicators" include a child's being unusually withdrawn or shy as well as a child's being unusually friendly toward strangers. However, only a small minority of children exhibiting such behaviors actually have been maltreated. Thirty years ago, when professionals were construing their reporting obligations narrowly to avoid taking action to protect endangered children, this approach to report any suspicion may have been needed. Now, however, it all but ensures that child abuse telephone hotlines will be flooded with inappropriate reports.

The legal injunction to report suspected maltreatment should not be interpreted as an open-ended invitation to call in the slightest suspicion or "gut feeling." A vague, amorphous, or unarticulable concern over a child's welfare is not a sufficient reason to report. Sufficient objective evidence of possible abuse or neglect should exist to justify a report. Such evidence may be either "direct" (firsthand accounts or observations of seriously harmful parental behavior) or "circumstantial"(concrete facts, such as the child's physical condition, suggesting the child has been abused or neglected). Educational materials for public and professional audiences as well as materials for agency staff should use such specific examples to illustrate when there may be evidence of suspected child abuse or neglect.

In summary, the few attempts to define "reasonable suspicion" have floundered on the fear that an overly strict definition will leave some children unprotected. These attempts therefore encourage overreporting. That an overly broad definition encouraging such overreporting might likewise hurt children is often overlooked.

Upgraded Screening Capacity

No matter how well "reasonable cause to suspect" is defined and taught to the public in general and to professionals in particular, there will remain a tendency for people to report cases that do not legally warrant investigation. In fact, we *want* people to err on the side of caution in deciding whether to call child protective agencies. But what should be phoned in to an agency is not necessarily what should be investigated: Efforts to educate the public and professionals on what must be *reported* must be backed up with clear agency policies about what must be *investigated*.

Many child abuse and neglect reporting hotlines accept reports even when the caller cannot give a reason for suspecting that the child's condition is a result of the parent's behavior. For example, I observed one hotline worker accept a report involving a 17-year-old boy found in a drunken stupor. When asked whether there was reason to suspect the parents were in any way responsible for the child's condition, the caller said "No." Clearly, I don't dispute that the boy, and perhaps his family, might benefit from counseling. But that should not justify the initiation of an involuntary child protective investigation. Hotline workers receive calls from tens of thousands of strangers; they must screen reports. Investigating all reports, regardless of their validity, immobilizes agencies and violates family rights.

For many years, most states did not have formal policies and procedures for determining whether to accept a call for investigation. For example, the American Humane Association (1983) found that in 1982 only a little more than half the states allowed their hotline workers to reject reports, and that even those that did usually limited screening to cases that were "clearly" inappropriate. Now, many states have general intake policies, and it is possible to state them with some precision (Besharov, 1985, p. 60). Reports should be rejected when:

- The allegations clearly fall outside the agency's definitions of *child abuse* and *child neglect,* as established by state law (prime examples include children beyond the specified age, alleged perpetrators falling outside the legal definition, and family problems not amounting to child maltreatment).

- The caller can give no credible reason for suspecting that the child has been abused or neglected.
- The unfounded or malicious nature is established by specific evidence. (Anonymous reports, reports from estranged spouses, and even previous unfounded reports from the same source should be evaluated carefully rather than rejected automatically.)
- Insufficient information is given to identify or locate the child. (The information should be kept for later use, should a subsequent report be made about the same child.)
- In questionable circumstances, the agency should recontact the caller before deciding to reject a report. When appropriate, rejected reports should be referred to other agencies that can provide services needed by the family.

While these are very practical guidelines, the difficulty comes in implementation. First, there are always political pressures to accept reports from influential agencies or individuals concerned about a child's welfare or eager to obtain social services for a family. There also is the very real fear that an appropriate report about a child in real danger will be rejected. Hardest to assess are reports that appear to be falsely—and maliciously—made by an estranged spouse, quarrelsome relatives, feuding neighbors, or even by an angry child. As a general rule, unless there are clear and convincing grounds for concluding that the report is being made in bad faith, any report falling within the agency's legal mandate must be investigated. Reports from questionable sources are not necessarily invalid; many anonymous reports are substantiated following an investigation.

Even a history of past unsubstantiated reports is not a sufficient basis, on its own, for automatically rejecting a report. There may be a legitimate explanation why previous investigations did not substantiate the reporter's claims. Therefore, a subsequent report containing enough facts to bring the case within statutory definitions must be investigated—unless there is clear and convincing evidence of its malicious or untrue nature. The key, in such situations, is to insist that the person reporting provide the specific information that aroused the suspicion. If the agency determines that the report was made maliciously, consideration should be given to referring the case for criminal prosecution or to notifying the parents so that they can take appropriate action.

Many reports that do not amount to child abuse or child neglect nonetheless involve serious individual and family problems. In such cases, CPS intake workers should be equipped to refer callers to other, more appropriate, social service agencies. All hotlines and agencies should possess this capability. Therefore, before making a referral, CPS intake staff should have some assurance that these other agencies will provide the necessary services. Unfortunately, such referrals frequently are made without notifying the other agencies of the practice and without checking to ensure that these agencies have the services to help the people referred to them.

The keys to successful implementation of a rigorous intake policy are the quality of intake staff and the degree of support they receive from agency administrators when exercising their professional judgment in screening cases. Unfortunately, reporting hotlines all too often are staffed by untrained or poorly trained clerical personnel who record basic information about situations and assign cases to caseworkers for subsequent investigation. Yet it is obvious that the kind of sophisticated intake decision making described cannot be performed by such untrained workers. Intake staff should be experienced and highly trained personnel with the ability to understand complex situations quickly; they must be granted the authority to make decisions.

We need to do a much better job at identifying suspected child abuse. Children are dying because they are not being reported to the authorities. At the same time, we need to reduce inappropriate reporting. Child protective agencies do not have the resources to investigate an unlimited number of reports—and they never will.

❖ CONCLUSION

To call for more careful reporting of child abuse is not to be coldly indifferent to the plight of endangered children. Rather, it is to be realistic about the limits of our ability to operate child protective systems and to recognize that inappropriate reporting is also harmful to children. If child protective agencies are to function effectively, we must address both problems. The challenge is to strike the proper balance. The effort will be politically controversial and technically difficult, but we owe it to our children to resolve these twin problems of underreporting and overreporting.

❖ REFERENCES

Alfaro, J. (1984). *Impediments to mandated reporting of suspected child abuse and neglect in New York City.* New York: Mayor's Task Force on Child Abuse and Neglect.

American Association for Protecting Children. (1989). *Highlights of official neglect and abuse reporting: 1987.* Denver: American Humane Association, 5, 10.

American Humane Association. (1983). National substantiation and screening practices. *National Child Protective Services Newsletter, 7,* 3, 10.

Berliner, L. (1988). Deciding whether a child has been sexually abused. In B. Nicholson (Ed.), *Sexual abuse allegations in custody and visitation cases* (pp. 48–69). Washington, DC: American Bar Association.

Besharov, D. J. (1985). *The vulnerable social worker: Liability for serving children and families.* Washington, DC: National Association of Social Workers.

Besharov, D. J. (Ed.). (1988). *Protecting children from abuse and neglect: Policy and practice.* Springfield, IL: Charles C. Thomas.

Finkelhor, D. (1990). Is child abuse overreported? *Public Welfare, 48,* 23–29.

Jones, D., & McGraw, J. M. (1987). Reliable and fictitious accounts of sexual abuse in children. *Journal of Interpersonal Violence, 2,* 27–45.

Levin, P. G. (1983). Teachers' perceptions, attitudes, and reporting of child abuse/neglect. *Child Welfare, 62,* 14–20.

McCurdy, K., & Daro, D. (1994). *Current trends in child abuse reporting fatalities: The results of the 1994 annual fifty state survey.* Chicago: National Committee to Prevent Child Abuse.

Sedlak, A. (1987). *Study of national incidence and prevalence of child abuse and neglect.* Rockville, MD: Westat.

Sedlak, A. (1989). *Supplementary analysis of data on the national incidence of child abuse and neglect.* Rockville, MD: Westat.

U.S. Children's Bureau. (1966). *Juvenile court statistics.* Washington, DC: U.S. Department of Health, Education, and Welfare.

U.S. Department of Health and Human Services. (1980). *Vital statistics of the United States for 1980: Advance report of final mortality statistics.* Washington, DC: Government Printing Office.

U.S. Department of Health and Human Services, Administration on Children, Youth, and Families. (1993). *National child abuse and neglect data system: Working paper 2—1991 summary data component.* Washington, DC: U.S. Government Printing Office.

U.S. Department of Health and Human Services, Administration on Children, Youth, and Families. (1994). *Child maltreatment 1992: Reports from the states to the national child abuse and neglect data system.* Washington, DC: U.S. Government Printing Office.

U.S. Department of Health and Human Services, Administration on Children, Youth, and Families. (1995). *Child maltreatment 1993: Reports from the states to the national child abuse and neglect data system.* Washington, DC: U.S. Government Printing Office.

U.S. Department of Health and Human Services, Administration on Children, Youth, and Families. (1996). *Child maltreatment 1994: Reports from the states to the national child abuse and neglect data system.* Washington, DC: U.S. Government Printing Office.

U.S. Department of Health and Human Services, Administration on Children, Youth, and Families. (1997). *Child maltreatment 1995: Reports from the states to the national child abuse and neglect data system.* Washington, DC: U.S. Government Printing Office.

U.S. Department of Health and Human Services, Administration on Children, Youth, and Families. (1998). *Child maltreatment 1996: Reports from the states to the national child abuse and neglect data system.* Washington, DC: U.S. Government Printing Office.

U.S. Department of Health and Human Services, Administration on Children, Youth, and Families. (1999). *Child maltreatment 1997: Reports from the states to the national child abuse and neglect data system.* Washington, DC: U.S. Government Printing Office.

U.S. Department of Health and Human Services, Administration on Children, Youth, and Families. (2000). *Child maltreatment 1998: Reports from the states to the national child abuse and neglect data system.* Washington, DC: U.S. Government Printing Office.

U.S. Department of Health and Human Services, Administration on Children, Youth, and Families. (2001). *Child maltreatment 1999: Reports from the states to the national child abuse and neglect data system.* Washington, DC: U.S. Government Printing Office.

Wang, C.-T., & Daro, D. (1997). *Current trends in child abuse reporting fatalities: The results of the 1996 annual fifty state survey.* Chicago: National Committee to Prevent Child Abuse.

Wexler, R. (1985, September). Invasion of the child savers. *The Progressive,* pp. 19–26.

❖ ADDITIONAL SOURCES

National Committee for Prevention of Child Abuse. (n.d.). *Child abuse and neglect fatalities: A review of the problem and strategies for reform.* Chicago: Author.

U.S. National Center for Health Statistics. (1999). *National vital statistics reports, 47.* Hyattsville, MD: National Center for Health Statistics, p. 19.

19

The Main Problem Is Underreporting Child Abuse and Neglect

David Finkelhor

No, child abuse is not overreported. The evidence suggests that large numbers of seriously abused and neglected children are still not coming to the attention of child protective authorities. To remedy this, professionals and members of the public need to be sensitized to recognize and report child abuse. If, in concert with these increased reports, child protective authorities improve their triage and investigatory skills and expand their treatment services, we may get closer to identifying and helping all the children at risk.

When the mandatory reporting system was first established in the United States in the 1970s, few people fully envisioned the results. In 1976, an estimated 669,000 cases of abuse were reported nationwide. In 2001, the reporting level was 2.67 million (U.S. Department of Health and Human Services, Administration on Children Youth and Families, 2003). Although some see a contemporary epidemic of abuse, most authorities think that what primarily happened is that many kinds of widespread and serious abuse that went undetected in the past are now being reported because professionals and ordinary citizens have a greater awareness about the problem (Gelles & Straus, 1988; Sedlak, 1991; Finkelhor, Hotaling, Lewis, & Smith, 1990; Peters, Wyatt, & Finkelhor, 1986; Russell, 1986).

In spite of this dramatic increase in reporting, however, most researchers and clinicians believe that a large quantity of abuse is still not being reported. This also is the conclusion of the best national studies of child abuse reporting that we have to date—the National Incidence Study (NIS) (Sedlak, 1991). One of the main functions of the NIS was to look at how much child abuse known to professionals still was not recognized by state child protective services (CPS) agencies. The results show the majority of serious abuse known to professionals was not known by CPS agencies. In spite of increased reporting, the NIS shows an enormous reservoir of serious child abuse that is not reported.

But even these figures, as high as they are, underestimate the amount of unreported child abuse and neglect: The study's statistics are based only on what professionals know. A certain quantity of child abuse does not come to the attention of *any* professional. Although it is virtually impossible to count something so hidden, most experts believe this quantity is also vast, probably two to three times higher than those currently reported (Finkelhor, 1984; Finkelhor et al., 1990). All of this suggests a major problem of *underreporting*.

There is another view, however, that the large and increasing number of reports is not necessarily progress toward revealing the full extent of the problem, but rather is evidence of an overreaction. In this view, the level of current reporting is too high, not warranted, and harmful to children and families (Besharov, 1988b). The answer, in this view, is a new policy that would define child abuse more narrowly, applying more stringent harm requirements before a report is made, and discourage reports by nonprofessionals.

Although this analysis has challenged policymakers to evaluate current practices, it is nonetheless misguided. Child abuse is *not* overreported. Reporting, even of uncertain suspicions, is crucial to our ability to identify serious child abuse. Moreover, the proposed reforms would inevitably result in the weakening of our ability to identify abused children. The myths of the overreporting argument can be broken down into three claims, which I take up in order:

1. A large and increasing proportion of what is reported as child abuse is not serious and not really child maltreatment.

2. The determination that a report is unfounded can be made "only after an unavoidably traumatic investigation which is, inherently, a breach of parental and family privacy" (Besharov, 1993, p. 264).

3. The current level of unfounded cases is patently "unreasonable" and necessitates a radical revision in current practice.

❖ ALLEGATION: REPORTS ARE
    NOT ABOUT "SERIOUS" ABUSE

One tenet of the overreporting argument is that much of what is now being identified, reported, and treated as child abuse consists of "minor situations that simply do not amount to child maltreatment" (Besharov, 1988b, p. 83). According to this argument, child abuse professionals and the public have gone beyond their mandate and now search for minor kinds of bad parenting or cases of simple poverty (Christensen, 1989).

For example, in an article in the *Wall Street Journal,* Besharov (1988a) dismissed 80 percent of all substantiated cases because they involved types of behaviors—such as excessive corporal punishment, educational neglect, emotional maltreatment—that do not lead to serious physical danger. This is a rhetorical minimization of the problem. For example, in the 80 percent rejected category, Besharov dismisses "emotional maltreatment," but this could include such things as children locked for weeks or months in their rooms and children threatened with death. Besharov also excludes from the "serious" category physical neglect where no serious physical injury occurs, yet this might include a mother who abandons her three-month-old child in an alley or a mother who regularly leaves three unsupervised children under six years old for the day—as long as these children are rescued before any actual physical injury occurs. It would rule out nine-tenths of all physical abuse victims, because they do not suffer injuries severe enough to require professional care; for example, a child who had been shot at by his father, as long as the father missed.

There is a major flaw in this argument that seeks to curb the reporting of maltreatment without actual physical injury. One of the most important reasons for a child abuse reporting system is to discover abusive situations *before* serious injury occurs. Thus the presence of injury is not the proper criterion of what should be reported. Under such a criterion, the child protective system does not have a "protective" function at all.

The overall portrait one gets from the available data is *not* of a system casting an increasingly large net by expanding the meaning of "child abuse." Rather, the picture is of a large reservoir of serious child abuse that families and abusers have managed in past years to hide from detection. Many of these serious cases are still, for one reason or another, not getting into the CPS system. The big overload of new cases does indeed make it difficult for CPS to work efficiently. However, to deal with these problems, the system needs to be expanded; reports of abuse do not need to be cut back.

❖ ALLEGATION: CONFUSION ABOUT SUBSTANTIATION

A second argument about overreporting concerns the so-called substantiation rate for child abuse reports. *Substantiated* means that sufficient evidence is found to conclude that maltreatment occurred or that the child is, indeed, at risk for maltreatment. *Unsubstantiated* means either that no such evidence was found or that the case was not investigated. Critics argue that the percentage of unsubstantiated cases is too high and poses an intolerable threat to family privacy, not to mention civil liberties.

There is a great deal of confusion about what is involved when a child welfare agency declares a case "unsubstantiated" or "unfounded." The overreporting argument rests in part on a claim that unsubstantiated cases generally involve unavoidably traumatic investigation(s) that are a breach of parental and family privacy and constitute massive and unjustified violation of parental rights (Besharov, this volume). These, of course, are reasons to rein in the child welfare system and discourage child abuse reporting. Although the true situation obviously is complex, it remains that the available evidence does not support this claim.

A first rebuttal of the "unavoidably traumatic" argument is the fact that for many child abuse reports that are classified as unsubstantiated, the family is never even contacted, let alone "invaded." Cases might not be investigated if the allegation was vague, the event described happened too long ago, the perpetrator was not a caretaker, or the family could not be located or had left the CPS jurisdiction (Wells, 1989).

According to the first National Incidence Study, no investigation at all was conducted in 11 percent of unsubstantiated cases (U.S. Department of Health and Human Services, 1981). Another study examining 12 counties in five states found that 32 percent of all reports of maltreatment were "screened out" without any investigation at all (Wells, 1989). So, one cannot make the claim that an unfounded report means a family is investigated. In reality, unsubstantiated cases frequently are cases in which, for many reasons, no investigation was made at all.

But even when contact with a family is made, this contact is not necessarily "unavoidably traumatic." According to child protection officials, in the typical unsubstantiated investigation, a worker goes out to visit a family; talks with the parent and the child about the incident; looks at physical evidence (injuries); and, on the basis of the explanation, the evidence, and the demeanor of the child, decides that the report has an insufficient basis. There are, of course, horror stories and terrible miscarriages of the investigatory process, but the important point here is that there is no evidence that these are widespread.

The generally benign quality of child protection investigations is supported by a study conducted by researchers at the C. Henry Kempe Center (Fryer, Bross, Krugman, Benson, & Baird, 1990) who did a "consumer satisfaction" survey on a sample of 176 Iowa families who had been the objects of both substantiated and unsubstantiated child welfare investigations. Among many reassuring findings, 74 percent of the respondents rated the quality of the services as excellent or good, and 72 percent said the intervention changed their family life for the *better.* Only 11 percent rated the intervention as poor. Although a low response rate to this mailed survey means the responses are not necessarily representative of all CPS-investigated families, it is nonetheless interesting that satisfaction levels were the *same* for those with both substantiated and unsubstantiated outcomes. Considering that virtually nobody wants to be the object of an investigation, these levels of satisfaction with CPS investigations are remarkable and belie the characterization of them as necessarily and always "unavoidably traumatic."

Complaints about the traumatic nature of investigations also can allege that these investigations are troublesome because they are a "breach of *family* privacy" (Besharov, this volume). Yet in this case, family units are not the proper unit of analysis: Children and parents have different interests at stake in these matters. What may indeed be an intrusion for parents may be rescue for a child. Even in cases where abuse is not substantiated, the investigation may result in improving conditions for a child by alerting parents to the potential for intervention or about the availability of services.

In brief, the strongest argument that can honestly be made at the present is that the intrusiveness of child abuse investigations is currently unknown and that isolated violative incidents have been reported. But empirical data and also information from CPS agencies refute the claim that investigations are necessarily "unavoidably traumatic."

Another problem with the alarmist argument about unsubstantiated cases is that it assumes that the parties involved in all unsubstantiated investigations are innocent, and therefore any intrusion is unjust. But this also is not the case. In many unsubstantiated investigations, workers were simply unable to make a determination. Some of these children were being abused and will later be reported again. According to one study, approximately 25 percent of unsubstantiated cases will be reported again within a four-year period (Wells, cited in Eckenrode, 1988). In other situations, a case is labeled unsubstantiated as part of a negotiated settlement with the child protection authorities in the same way that a criminal conviction may be plea-bargained. That is, in some agencies, if parents admit to the maltreatment and agree to a course of action, workers may declare the case unsubstantiated in return (Eckenrode, Powers, Doris, Munsch, & Bolger, 1988). Given all this, it is unfortunate that some observers continue to equate an "unsubstantiated" case with a "false allegation" (Wexler, 1985).

❖   ALLEGATION: THE LEVEL OF UNFOUNDED
     CASES IS PATENTLY UNREASONABLE

Aside from the controversies about whether unsubstantiated reports are traumatic, however, there is no question that they are numerous. If the substantiation rate is as low as 30 percent, we are discussing perhaps more than 2 million unconfirmed reports annually. Is this evidence of inefficiency, at least, if not overreporting? Not necessarily. If these numbers are considered from a larger perspective, the child abuse detection process seems relatively efficient. Like any other problem detection system—from PAP smears for cancer detection, to urine testing for drug use, to fire alarms—large numbers of screening trials come back negative. The question is whether the costs of these negative screenings are somehow disproportional to the worth of discovering the positive cases.

One of the best and most direct standards against which to compare the child abuse detection system is the criminal justice system. Although there are important differences, there are also many similarities: both are trying to detect antisocial behavior, both receive reports directly from the public, both deal with acts that are not always clearly defined, both have procedures for differentiating "substantiated" ("guilty") from "unsubstantiated" ("not guilty") cases, both have unpleasant sanctions for those whose deviance is substantiated, and involvement in both is stigmatizing.

The criminal justice system is not a very efficient system at any level. Take, for example, the number of crime reports to the police that result in arrests. In 1986, only 19 percent of all crimes reported or known to the police resulted in arrests (Flanagan & Jamieson, 1988). This number had been *declining* steadily over the previous 10 years and was down 33 percent since 1977. The number of crimes known to police resulting in convictions was even lower.

To look at the efficiency of the most stigmatizing portion of the criminal justice system, we should examine the arrest-to-conviction component. Being arrested but not convicted has some parallels to being reported but not substantiated for child abuse. The numbers are revealing. For example, of all persons arrested on rape charges, only 50 percent were convicted (of rape or any lesser charge). For persons arrested on assault charges, the rate of conviction (for that or any charge) was 51 percent (Flanagan & Jamieson, 1988, Table 5.1). Someone just looking at the numbers might say, What appalling inefficiency! How do we tolerate so many arrests of innocent people?

Very few people interpret the operation of the criminal justice system in the same way that the overreporting critics interpret the operation of the child welfare system. If one applied the critics' analysis of child abuse reporting to the criminal justice system and its large number of reported crimes without arrests and arrested criminals without convictions, one might say that overzealous law enforcement officials, without clear definitions of what constitute crimes, encourage too many people to report crimes and arrest too many people on insufficient evidence, and end up wasting time on minor offenses while the serious crimes are not attended to.

But that is not how most people interpret the operation of the justice system. They believe people reported to or arrested by the police probably were doing something wrong. They see the low conviction rate as a reflection of the high standards that are needed to convict.

According to public opinion polls, Americans want more people arrested, not fewer. They want more aggressive control of crime (Flanagan & Jamieson, 1988, p. 142) and are willing to tolerate ineffi- ciency and intrusion if these are the costs.

The point here is not that one view of the criminal justice system is true and the other is false. There is some truth to both. Rather, the point is that a degree of inefficiency and serious intrusion into the privacy and freedom of individuals seems perfectly rational and justifiable *if the goal is important enough.* The issue is balancing individual rights with the need to protect innocent victims.

Two other examples are relevant. Every year the Internal Revenue Service audits more than a million tax returns. In many of these cases, the intrusion into people's private lives is severe, and no wrongdoing is found. In fact, the IRS randomly selects returns for detailed audits in which every line on a tax return is scrutinized, and citizens are required to bring in canceled checks and receipts to justify everything. This is an enormous random invasion of people's financial and per- sonal privacy for no reason other than research on how people fill out their tax returns.

Another example: Millions of people are frisked every day and have their baggage X-rayed, opened, and examined in the airports of this country. Almost nobody is found to be carrying a weapon. This is an invasion of privacy people would have had a hard time imagining a generation ago, yet few people complain. No one wants to be the victim of an airline hijacking or a terrorist attack.

Policymakers are willing to implement, and the public is willing to tolerate, very inefficient systems of deviance detection that sometimes entail serious invasions of privacy when the objective is important enough. People are frightened about crime and terrorism; they don't want their neighbors and fellow citizens cheating on their tax returns, and they are afraid of airline hijackings.

By comparison, the child welfare system is certainly more efficient at rooting out problematic behavior than the criminal justice system and the airline security system, and probably the tax audit system as well. It is also arguably less invasive under most conditions for those unfairly targeted. But the key issue highlighted by this comparison is that the degree of inefficiency and intrusion tolerated is a function of the importance of the objective. Ultimately, the overreporting argu- ment appears to be reflecting the philosophy that *child abuse is not worth it.* Child abuse detection and the cases that are uncovered are not important enough for us to tolerate a million unsubstantiated cases a year.

In this, I think the critics are clearly out of step with the American public. The public has again and again (and increasingly) in national public opinion surveys urged that more be done about the problem of child abuse. In one national survey, respondents specifically endorsed the idea: "Public child welfare agencies should investigate all reports of child abuse regardless of the seriousness of the charge" (67 percent) over a proposal consistent with aims of the overreporting critics: "Parents should be reported as child abusers only when there is clear evidence of serious harm or injury to a child" (30 percent) (Schulman, Ronca, & Bucuvalas, Inc., 1988). This suggests that there is strong public support for the current level of reporting.

❖ CONCLUSION

It is very misleading to say that overreporting and underreporting are "equally serious" problems. The consequences are vastly different. Once a case is reported, we can always choose to take no action. But without a report at all, there is no possibility of any help.

The goals of making the child protection system more efficient, effective, and fair are laudable ones. The system has many problems and many faults. The premise that child abuse is overreported is wrong, but the idea that the system could devote a greater portion of its effort to identifying and treating the most serious cases is a good one. Many people inside and outside the system believe that reports could be much better prioritized, so that the investigators' time is spent on the most serious cases most likely to need intervention. There is hope that certain kinds of risk assessment instruments can direct attention to the most threatened children. But prioritizing is far different from calls to cut back on reports.

Nonetheless, some critics want to increase this efficiency by eliminating or severely limiting reports by nonprofessionals (Besharov, 1988b). In spite of claims, there is *no* evidence that reports by nonprofessionals are made lightly. Meanwhile, it is likely that many serious cases would also never get reported, because they are known to family and friends but not to professionals. It makes much more sense to improve the way that the investigators respond to the reports than to limit the choices available to them. If the research shows that lay reporters are less reliable, then risk assessments can take the sources of reports into account. But this is far different from discouraging laypersons from reporting altogether.

Other suggestions from the overreporting critics do have merit. For example, there is broad support for the idea of defining child abuse more clearly, particularly in vaguely defined areas such as emotional abuse (Garbarino, Guttman, & Wilson, 1986), so that workers can decide which reports warrant intervention. Of course, as emotional maltreatment is better defined, it may spark more, rather than fewer, reports. States also are moving toward procedures giving more rights and options to families subjected to child abuse investigations.

But these reforms are tinkering around the edges compared with the major restructuring of the child protective system that is required. First, the system needs a better-trained, better-paid, and more professional workforce to improve decision making and public and professional confidence and esteem. Child welfare work needs to be honored, welcomed, and rewarded. Second, the public clearly wants to combat child abuse, and people need to be educated that this means accepting increased social and financial costs, including a modest level of outside scrutiny into the affairs of families. Not infrequently, agencies fail to intervene in these cases because they are being overly cautious about the breach of parental rights. Thus attacks on the system for violating "family privacy" arguably are a contributor to child fatalities.

Third, by almost everyone's analysis, the increase in serious child abuse cases coming to CPS attention has not been matched by accompanying increases in staffs and budgets to deal with these cases (Daro & Mitchel, 1989; Salovitz & Keys, 1988). The system cannot respond to increasing reports with decreasing resources. One reason for unsubstantiated reports is that too few workers have too little time to do adequate investigations. Many of the children who die from child abuse and neglect are already known to CPS authorities. Overreporting has little to do with these deaths: Insufficient services have been a chronic problem from the very beginning of the child protection system. The child welfare system also needs to do a far better job, not just of detecting child abuse, but of protecting the children who are discovered to be at risk. This means providing support services for parents, respite care, foster homes, counseling for parents and children, financial aid, and social work assistance to deal with the crises that put families on the brink of abuse and neglect. If we have nothing to offer when abuse is reported, it is silly to argue about whether we are reporting too little or too much. And if we are truly offering help, rather than stigma, blame, and punishment, what would there be to complain about?

❖ REFERENCES

Besharov, D. (1988a, August 4). The child-abuse numbers game. *Wall Street Journal.*

Besharov, D. (1988b). The need to narrow the grounds for state intervention. In D. Besharov (Ed.), *Protecting children from abuse and neglect: Policy and practice* (pp. 47–90). Springfield, IL: Charles C. Thomas.

Besharov, D. (1993). Overreporting and underreporting are twin problems. In R. Gelles & D. Loseke (Eds.), *Current Controversies on Family Violence* (1st ed., pp. 257–272).

Christensen, B. J. (1989, February). The child abuse "crisis": Forgotten facts and hidden agendas. *The Family in America,* 1–8.

Daro, D., & Mitchel, L. (1989). *Child abuse fatalities continue to rise: The results of the 1988 annual fifty state survey.* Chicago: National Committee for Prevention of Child Abuse.

Eckenrode, J., Powers, J., Doris, J., Munsch, J., & Bolger, N. (1988). Substantiation of child abuse and neglect reports. *Journal of Consulting and Clinical Psychology,* 56(1), 9–16.

Finkelhor, D. (1984). *Child sexual abuse: New theory and research.* New York: Free Press.

Finkelhor, D., Hotaling, C. T., Lewis, I. A., & Smith, C. (1990). Sexual abuse in a national survey of adult men and women: Prevalence, characteristics and risk factors. *Child Abuse and Neglect, 14,* 19–28.

Flanagan, T., & Jamieson, K. (Eds.). (1988). *Sourcebook of criminal justice statistics: 1987.* Washington, DC: Government Printing Office.

Fryer, C. E., Bross, D. C., Krugman, R. D., Benson, D. B., & Baird, D. (1990). Good news for CPS workers. *Public Welfare, 69,* 38–41.

Garbarino, J., Guttman, E., & Wilson, J. (1986). *The psychologically battered child.* San Francisco, CA: Jossey-Bass.

Gelles, R. J., & Straus, M. A. (1988). *Intimate violence: The causes and consequences of abuse in the American family.* New York: Simon & Schuster.

Peters, S., Wyatt, C., & Finkelhor, D. (1986). Prevalence. In D. Finkelhor & Associates (Eds.), *A sourcebook on child sexual abuse* (pp. 15–59). Beverly Hills, CA: Sage.

Russell, D. (1986). *The secret trauma: Incest in the lives of girls and women.* New York: Basic Books.

Salovitz, B., & Keys, D. (1988, Fall). Is child protective services still a service? *Protecting Children,* 17–23.

Schulman, Ronca, & Bucuvalas, Inc. (1988). *Public attitudes and actions regarding child abuse and its prevention: 1988.* Chicago: National Committee for Prevention of Child Abuse.

Sedlak, A. (1991). *Study findings: Study of national incidence and prevalence of child abuse and neglect: 1988.* Washington, DC: U.S. Department of Health and Human Services.

U.S. Department of Health and Human Services. (1981). *Study findings: National study of the incidence and severity of child abuse and neglect.* Washington, DC: Author.

U.S. Department of Health and Human Services, Administration on Children Youth and Families. (2003). *Child maltreatment 2001: Reports from the states to the National Child Abuse and Neglect Data System.* Washington, DC: U.S. Government Printing Office.

Wells , S. J. (1989). *Screening and prioritization in child protective services intake.* Grant status report, Grant No. 90-CA-1265. from the National Legal Resource Center for Child Advocacy and Protection.

Wexler, R. (1985, September). Invasion of the child savers. *The Progressive,* 19–22.

20

Family Preservation Is the Safest Way to Protect Most Children

Richard Wexler

- In Orange County, California, an impoverished single mother can't find someone to watch her children while she works at night, tending a ride at a theme park. So she leaves her eight-, six-, and four-year-old children alone in the motel room that is the only housing they can afford. Someone calls Child Protective Services. Instead of helping her with baby-sitting or day care, they take away the children (Saari, 1999).

- In New York City, a former boyfriend assaults the pregnant woman carrying his child. She already has separated from him and has even bought a plane ticket to take her and the baby to the other side of the country. But two days after the baby is born, caseworkers and police officers take the child away because the mother had been beaten "in the presence of the subject child"—who had not been born at the time of the beating. For the first seven weeks of his life, the infant is prevented from living with his mother (Sengupta, 2000b).

- In Los Angeles, the pipes in a grandmother's rented house burst, flooding the basement and making the home a health hazard. Instead of helping the family find another place to live, child protective workers take away the granddaughter and place her in foster care. She dies there, allegedly killed by her foster mother. The child welfare agency that would spend nothing to move the family offers $5,000 for the funeral (Riccardi, 1999).

If the popular press, and even some academics, are to be believed, the past 20 years were the era of family preservation in child welfare. But the number of children in foster care has risen dramatically, from 243,000 in 1982 (Pelton, 1989) to at least 542,000 in 2001 (U.S. Department of Health and Human Services, 2003a). And that is just the number of children in foster care on any given day. Over the course of a typical year, 290,000 children are taken from their parents (U.S. Department of Health and Human Services, 2003a), and more than 800,000 children spend time in foster care (Geen, 2003). If we advocates of family preservation are so all-powerful, how did all those children get into foster care?

The answer, of course, is that there was *no* "era of family preservation." From the 1850s, when Protestant minister Charles Loring Brace first started snatching away the children of poor Catholic immigrants whom he deemed loathsome and genetically inferior (Brace, 1872), to today, the ethos that dominates child welfare can be boiled down to a single sentence: "Take the child and run."

An enormously powerful child welfare establishment, with both a philosophical and a financial interest in the status quo (private agencies are paid for each day a child is in foster care), has blocked any effort at real reform. As a result, thousands of children have been deprived of the opportunity to grow up in safe, loving homes—their own—because some of the safest, most effective child welfare innovations in decades have been marginalized.

❖ WHO IS IN THE SYSTEM?

Understanding why family preservation is safe and effective requires an understanding of who is in the child welfare system. In 2001, the vast majority of more than 3 million reports were false. The child welfare establishment says these false reports are cases in which workers couldn't "prove" maltreatment, but for statistical purposes, no proof is required. In most states, workers declare a case substantiated if they believe there is "some credible evidence" of abuse, even if there is more evidence of innocence. Workers do this with no judicial review and no opportunity for the accused to defend themselves. A federal study found that workers were two to six times more likely to wrongly label innocent parents guilty than they were to wrongly let guilty parents off the hook (U.S. Department of Health and Human Services, 1988).

In 2001, 6.2 percent of reports were "substantiated" victims of physical abuse in any form (U.S. Department of Health and Human Services). Another 3 percent were "substantiated" victims of sexual abuse (U.S. Department of Health and Human Services, 2003b). In the vast majority of the remaining cases, the allegation is "neglect." State neglect laws are so vague that this can mean anything from deliberately starving a child to death to leaving a 12-year-old home alone for a few minutes. For example, New York State guidelines declare that "school aged children (age six to twelve years) may not be ready for the responsibility of being on their own for even short periods of time" (New York State Department of Social Services, 1983).

❖ VERY OFTEN, "NEGLECT" MEANS POVERTY

• A study of "lack of supervision" cases in New York City by the Child Welfare League of America found that the service needed most in 52 percent of the cases studied was day care or babysitting. But the "service" offered most often was foster care (Jones, 1987).

• Courts in New York City (*Cosentino v. Perales*, 1988) and Illinois (Karwath, 1990; Poe & Kendall, 1995) have found that families are repeatedly kept apart solely because they lack decent housing.

• Welfare recipients on New York's Long Island are thrown out of homeless shelters and their children threatened with foster care if the parents make even the slightest slip in complying with myriad, complex work requirements (Bernstein, 1999a, 1999b).

Gelles (this volume) argues that the number of children in foster care should be regarded as low because child protective workers have the power to take away even more, but they don't. But the number of children trapped in foster care for at least part of a year is greater than the entire population of San Francisco. And even such a large aggregate number underestimates the devastation wrought in poor and minority communities. For example, on any given day in Central Harlem in 1998, nearly 1 of out 10 children was in foster care (Child Welfare Watch, 1998). In Minnesota, nearly 1 in 25 black children was taken from his or her parents and thrown into foster care just in one year (U.S. Department of Health and Human Services, 2001a).

Indeed, in America's poor neighborhoods, fear of Child Protective Services is a daily fact of life. It's a constant topic of conversation on the street. There are mothers who never leave their homes without carrying with them yellowed papers exonerating them from some allegation of abuse or neglect, fearful that their children could be taken from them at any time (Sengupta, 2000a).

❖   WHAT IS FAMILY PRESERVATION?

To know whether family preservation is safe and effective, one must first know what it is. That used to be easy enough. The term "family preservation" was invented specifically to denote a particular kind of intervention, an Intensive Family Preservation Services (IFPS) program that follows the model of the first such program, Homebuilders, invented in Washington State in the mid-1970s.

Through the early history of family preservation, this was well understood. But in the early 1990s, when it looked as though IFPS might grow large enough to threaten the child welfare establishment, that establishment gave the term a whole new meaning: all-purpose scapegoat. Whenever something went wrong after any decision to leave any child in any home under any circumstances it was blamed on "family preservation"—whether the family had been anywhere near a family preservation program or not. And Gelles (this volume) now has broadened the definition further, labeling it an act of "family preservation" if a child protection worker goes to a home, finds absolutely nothing wrong, and doesn't take away the children.

Can IFPS programs actually reduce the number of children placed in foster care?

Several studies have documented considerable success:

• Michigan's Families First program sticks rigorously to the Homebuilders model. The Michigan program was measured by comparing children who received family preservation services because of abuse or neglect with a comparison group of similar children who did not. After one year, the comparison group children were nearly twice as likely to be placed in foster care as the Families First children (Berquist, Szwejda, & Pope, 1993).

• An experiment in Utah used an overflow comparison group. After one year, 85 percent of the children in the comparison group were placed in foster care, compared to only 44 percent of the children who received Intensive Family Preservation Services (Fraser, Pecora, Haapala, 1991).

• A California study (cited in Bath & Haapala, 1994) found that 55 percent of the overflow comparison group children were placed, compared to only 26 percent of the children who received Intensive Family Preservation Services.

Gelles (this volume) counters that another study (U.S. Department of Health and Human Services, 2001b) found IFPS ineffective and this study supposedly examined programs "that rigorously followed the Homebuilders model." But they didn't.

A rigorous critique (Kirk, 2001) notes that the programs in this study actually diluted the Homebuilders model, providing service that was less intensive and less timely. At the same time, the "conventional" services given to families in the control groups sometimes were better than average. In at least one case, they may well have been just as intensive as the IFPS program—so it's hardly surprising that the researchers found little difference between the two.

Furthermore, efforts to truly assign families at random to experimental and control groups sometimes were thwarted by workers in the field who resisted assigning what they considered to be "high risk" families to control groups that would not receive help from IFPS programs.

Given all these problems, writes Kirk, "a finding of 'no difference between treatment and experimental groups' . . . is simply a nonfinding from a failed study" (Kirk, 2001). In contrast, according to Kirk, "there is a growing body of evidence that IFPS works, in that it is more effective than traditional services in preventing out-of-home placements of children in high-risk families" (Kirk, 2000).

Even studies purporting to show that IFPS is ineffective do not claim that is it unsafe. Rather, they find that similar numbers of children are kept at home in both experimental and comparison groups. That is, though IFPS should be used only when there is "imminent risk" that a child will be placed in foster care, sometimes it is used when the risk isn't really imminent. This has been called the "targeting" problem, and a study from Michigan used an innovative way to solve it.

For this study, judges gave permission to researchers to "take back" some children they had just ordered into foster care and place them in Families First instead. Thus, it is clear that in this case 100 percent of the children would have been placed in foster care if not for Families First. Instead, one year later, only 7 percent of the children receiving Families First services were placed in foster care (Blythe & Jayaratne, 1999).

❖ OTHER ALTERNATIVES TO SUBSTITUTE CARE

IFPS is the innovative alternative to substitute care that has been around the longest and has the largest body of evaluation literature. But there are other promising innovations in placement prevention. Indeed, several states and counties have successfully rebuilt their entire child welfare systems to emphasize a series of safe, proven approaches to keeping families together.

- In Alabama, the number of children taken from their parents in 2001 was 20 percent lower than in 1997. At the same time, children are safer. Since 1996, re-abuse of children left in their own homes has been cut nearly in half (Groves, 2002). An independent, court-appointed monitor concluded that children in Alabama are safer now than before the system switched to a family preservation model. The monitor wrote that "the data strongly support the conclusion that children and families are safer in counties that have implemented the . . . reforms" (Groves, 1996).
- Since 1997, the foster care population in the county-run system in Allegheny County (Pittsburgh), Pennsylvania, has been cut by 32 percent. When children must be placed, more than half of children placed with families stay with relatives or close friends, and siblings are kept together 80 percent of the time (Allegheny County Office of Children, Youth, and Families, 2002). As in

Alabama, children are safer. Re-abuse of children left in their own homes has declined (Pennsylvania Department of Public Welfare, 1996–2001).

- Recognizing the connection between child maltreatment and poverty, El Paso County, Colorado, effectively turned its Temporary Assistance for Needy Families program into a child abuse prevention program and its child welfare program into an anti-poverty program. The results: a 22 percent decline in out-of-home placements since 1998—and a lower rate of re-abuse of children after cases are closed than either the state or national average (Hutson, 2003).

Illinois also found that it could dramatically reduce its foster care population while increasing child safety. The biggest change in Illinois was simple: The state changed the way private child welfare agencies are paid. Instead of paying them for each day they hold a child in foster care, these agencies now are paid for permanence—they are rewarded both for adoptions and for returning children safely to birth parents. As a result, suddenly the "intractable" became tractable, the "dysfunctional" became functional, and the Illinois foster care population was cut by more than 58 percent, from 50,735 in 1997 (Illinois Department of Children and Families, 2003a) to 20,991 as of May 31, 2003 (Illinois Department of Children and Families, 2003b).

Though Illinois officials like to emphasize the adoption side of the equation, because that is more popular politically, the major reason for the reduction in numbers is that the state is taking away fewer children in the first place. In 1995, 9,037 Illinois children were taken from their parents (Illinois Department of Children and Families, 1998). By 2002, the number had fallen to 4,947, and the re-abuse of children left in their own homes has declined by 37 percent (Illinois Department of Children and Families, 2003a). Says University of Illinois Professor Mark Testa, "Children are safer now than they were when the state had far more foster children" (Franck, 2003).

All of these real-world successes show that family preservation is not merely more humane and less expensive than foster care. For *most* children *most* of the time, it is safer as well. In contrast, opponents of family preservation have yet to offer any proof that family preservation is dangerous—or even that foster care is safe. That's not surprising.

First, of course, there is the emotional abuse inherent in foster care placement. If children are young enough, they may experience the event as akin to a kidnapping. Or they may believe they have done something terribly wrong, and now are being punished. Thus, a three-year-old, dragged literally kicking and screaming by a Sheriff's deputy from her parents, cries out, "I'm sorry! I'm sorry!" (Pollock, 1986).

In a study of children exposed to cocaine in utero (Wobie, Eyler, Behnke, & Garvan, 1998), one group was placed in foster care, another with birth mothers able to care for them. There also was a control group of infants in the care of birth mothers who did not abuse drugs. The Psychomotor scores at six months (measured by the Bayley Scales of Infant Development) for the control group and the cocaine-exposed infants left with their birth mothers were virtually identical—and significantly higher than the scores for the infants placed in foster care. For those infants, removal from their mothers was more toxic than the cocaine. This does *not* mean that children can simply be left with drug addicts. It *does* mean that drug treatment for the parent often is a better option than foster care for the child.

Unfortunately, any invocation of the emotional harm of foster care tends to produce a "Yes, but" response—as in, "Yes, but at least in foster care, the children are physically safe." But often, that is not true.

A study of reported abuse in Baltimore found the rate of substantiated cases of sexual abuse in foster care more than *four times higher* than the rate in the general population (Benedict & Zuravin, 1992). Using the same methodology, an Indiana study found *three times more* physical abuse and *twice* the rate of sexual abuse in foster homes as in the general population. In group homes there was more than *10 times* the rate of physical abuse and more than *28 times* the rate of sexual abuse as in the general population, in part because so many children in the homes abused each other (Spencer & Knudsen, 1992).

In connection with a class-action lawsuit, Children's Rights, Inc., commissioned a study by researchers at the University of Maryland of investigations of alleged abuse in New Jersey foster homes. The researchers found a lack of "anything approaching reasonable professional judgment" and concluded that "no assurances can be given" that *any* New Jersey foster child is safe (Kaufman & Lezin Jones, 2003).

A lawyer representing children in Florida has said in a sworn affidavit that over a period of just 18 months, he was made personally aware of 50 cases of child-on-child sexual abuse involving more than 100 children in the foster homes of Broward County. The official count during this same time period: seven—because the child abuse hotline refused to take reports of foster children abusing each other

(*Ward v. Feaver*, 1998). Furthermore, a study examining case records in Baltimore found abuse in 28 percent of the foster homes studied—more than 1 in 4 (*L.J. v. Massinga*, 1987).

Even what is said to be a model foster care program, where case-loads are kept low and workers and foster parents get special training, is not immune. When alumni of the Casey Family Program were inter-viewed, 24 percent of the girls said they were victims of actual or attempted sexual abuse in foster care. Furthermore, this study asked only about abuse in the one foster home where the children lived longest. A child who had been moved from a foster home precisely because she had been abused there would not even be counted (Fanshel, Finch, & Grundy, 1990).

This does not mean that all, or even most, foster parents are abusive. But the abusive minority is large enough to cause serious concern. And abuse in foster care does not always mean abuse by foster parents. As the Broward County and Indiana data make clear, it can be caused by foster children abusing each other.

❖ FOSTER CARE PANICS

The scenario generally goes like this: A child "known to the system" dies. Either politicians or media or both immediately cite the death as proof that the local child welfare system is fanatically dedicated to family preservation and that this is unsafe—even if the child in ques-tion never was anywhere near a real family preservation program. The message then goes out to caseworkers: Leave a child in her or his own home, and if anything goes wrong, you face dismissal, possible crimi-nal charges, and sometimes a lynch mob mentality in the local press. Remove hundreds of children needlessly, and the children may be traumatized, but the worker is safe. So foster care placements soar, and suddenly systems that are overwhelmed in the best of times are inun-dated with new cases. Children wind up sleeping on office floors or jammed into hideous shelters. Standards for foster homes are lowered and the homes are overcrowded. Abuse in foster care gets even worse.

Gelles (this volume) does not even try to defend the safety record of foster care, arguing instead that returning children to birth parents is, on average, worse. But this argument fails on two counts:

First, he argues that between 20 and 40 percent of children remain-ing with their parents are re-abused. But he also acknowledges that up to 30 percent of foster children may be abused, so abuse in foster care could be more likely. More critically, he talks about "averages," not individual children. Even though advocates of family preservation believe it is, on average, safer than foster care, we do not believe that it is right for every child. When caseworkers are sure that a child has been brutally beaten or sexually assaulted or tortured, the odds of safety—for that particular child—are better in foster care. Conversely, in the many cases in which poverty is confused with "neglect" and many of the "in between" cases, the odds of safety are *better* in a real family preservation program. Rhetoric about averages obscures that reality.

Second, foster care panics—such as those that swept through Illinois in 1993, New York City in 1996, and Florida in 1999—increased deaths of children previously "known to the system." That is not surprising, because even in the best of times child welfare systems are arbitrary, capricious, and cruel. Underprepared, undereducated, undertrained, and underpaid workers are given overwhelming caseloads and sent out to make life and death decisions. They err, often, in both directions. They do indeed leave some children in dangerous homes—even as they remove other children from safe ones. A foster care panic ratchets up the pressure. Now there are even more cases and even less time to make good decisions. So more mistakes are made in both directions. That is why abolishing, or drastically curbing, family preservation makes all children less safe. In contrast, when fewer children are taken away, workers have more time to find children in real danger and safety outcomes improve.

Gelles's claim that one must have more "false positives" in order to avoid "false negatives" does not take into account the dynamics of a foster care panic and its impact on workers' ability to evaluate any case with care. In child welfare, reducing false positives is, in fact, an essential *prerequisite* for reducing false negatives. Or to put it more plainly: What is wrong with child saving? Simple. It doesn't save children.

Other Options

Opponents of family preservation know that defending foster care as an alternative is impossible. So they have sought to co-opt the foster care issue. Indeed, the debate has taken an Orwellian turn.

The blame for children languishing in foster care now is placed on the very initiative designed to prevent it: family preservation. It is argued that children are stuck in foster care while workers supposedly lavish services on their ne'er-do-well parents. Often the blame is placed on a 1980 law, never enforced, that required nothing more than "reasonable efforts" to keep families together.

It will, no doubt, come as news to most workers in child welfare that they have services to lavish. In fact, they usually have few or none. So children languish in foster care not because workers do "everything" for parents, but because they do almost *nothing*. And once the children are placed, they are filed away and forgotten as workers rush on to the next case. Indeed, if a fanatical dedication to enforcing a 1980 law accounts for the large number of children in foster care, why were there at least as many children in foster care, relative to the total child population, in the late 1970s? (Pelton, 1989).

But the revisionist history of child welfare easily carried the day with Congress, prompting passage of the so-called Adoption and Safe Families Act (ASFA) of 1997. The law includes broad, vague, catchall clauses that blow huge holes in what little was left of the "reasonable efforts" requirement. Get those fanatical family preservationists out of the way, Congress was told, and millions of childless Americans would rush forward to adopt the children now trapped in foster care. Indeed, ASFA turns the American child welfare system into the ultimate middle-class entitlement: Step right up and take a poor person's child for your very own. Yet despite desperate efforts to promote adoption and federal cash bounties to states for adoption increases, not that many Americans wanted to step right up.

When ASFA passed, foster child adoptions were not on the decline. They actually had been rising steadily for four years and stood at 31,030 (Maza, 2003). The increase in foster child adoptions attributable to ASFA is fewer than 12,200 per year. That is well under 2.5 percent of the total number of children in foster care on any given day. And by 2001, there was actually a slight *decrease* in foster child adoptions from the previous year (Maza, 2003). Meanwhile, ASFA encourages states to take away many more children in the first place. So the number of children trapped in foster care on any given day actually increased from 520,000, when ASFA was passed, to 542,000 as of September 2001 (U.S. Department of Health and Human Services, 2003a).

America is not going to adopt its way out of the foster care crisis. Indeed, Gelles told the New York City publication *Child Welfare Watch* (2000) that "the adoption component was a way of sanitizing the bill, to make it more appealing to a broader group of people. Adoption is a very popular concept in the country right now" (p. 5). In his book, Gelles (1996) acknowledges that adoption alone is not enough—drastically curbing family preservation will bring so many more children into the system that housing them will require orphanages. He argues that orphanages don't have to be grim, Dickensian warehouses. It's true—they don't have to be. Yet they do keep ending up that way.

Yes, there are a few luxury orphan resorts around, places with endowments that seem to rival the gross domestic product of Third World Nations. But far more common are not just institutions but whole systems of institutions that warehouse children at best, or, at worst, brutalize them. Even more important, there is a strong consensus in the research literature that even "good" institutions are inherently harmful to children. The younger the child, the greater the harm (Frank, Klass, Earls, & Eisenberg, 1996). In fact, the research on the harm of institutionalization is so overwhelming that the federal government now rates state child welfare systems in part on their ability to *reduce* the number of children under age 12 in institutions (U.S. Department of Health and Human Services, 2000).

❖ CONCLUSION

Success stories are rare in child welfare, but they do exist. Alabama is one. Pittsburgh is another. Illinois is a third. That is because it is the family preservation movement that truly takes an unyielding "child-centered" approach to child welfare.

In contrast, what do those who scapegoat family preservation have to offer? Orphanages that effectively become baby warehouses. Children sleeping on office floors. Epidemics of abuse in substitute care. Increases in child abuse deaths. And a law—ASFA—that traps more children in foster care. There is not one single place in the United States where a successful campaign against family preservation has made children happier, healthier, or safer. And there are plenty of places where such a campaign has left child welfare systems far, far worse.

Gelles writes that "child safety, child well-being, and permanence are the most important goals in child abuse and neglect." Those are exactly the right goals. And for most children most of the time, family preservation is the best way to achieve them.

❖ REPLY TO GELLES

As long as we are dealing with human beings and not laboratory mice, as long as we are trying to measure happiness and well-being and not the size of a tumor, and as long as frontline practitioners think it is unethical to deny help to families destined for a "control" group, the perfect study is unlikely to be achieved.

One must, therefore, use the best available evidence. That evidence includes two studies of Michigan's Families First program, studies showing this large-scale *replication* of the Homebuilders model to be safe and effective. The evidence on behalf of family preservation, both in the form of Intensive Family Preservation Services and other, newer initiatives, is far superior to that presented for foster care—or Gelles's preferred option, orphanages.

Gelles puts the burden of proof in the wrong place. In any civilized society, that burden should fall on those who feel children *don't* belong in their families. The proponents of foster care and orphanages have had 150 years to prove the safety and efficacy of *their* interventions of choice. We're still waiting.

So, what is left when you remove the anecdotes from my chapter (and a whole slew of very-good-but-not-quite-perfect studies)?

- *Data* showing that when Illinois abandoned family preservation, child abuse fatalities increased.
- *Data* showing that when New York City abandoned family preservation, child abuse fatalities increased.
- *Data* showing that when Florida abandoned family preservation, child abuse fatalities increased.
- *Data* showing that when Illinois reversed course and rebuilt its system to emphasize family preservation, child safety improved.
- *Data* showing that when Alabama rebuilt its system to emphasize family preservation, child safety improved.
- *Data* showing that when Allegheny County, Pennsylvania, rebuilt its system to emphasize family preservation, child safety improved.

Gelles's article also is critically short on alternatives. Elsewhere he has written that "the child welfare system is effective in 20 to 30 percent of cases, and some reunifications are in the best interests of children. But what of the children in the other 70 to 80 percent of cases?" (Gelles, 1999).

What, indeed? Every year, at least 290,000 children are taken from their parents. If even 70 percent should never go home, that's 203,000 children. Get 50,000 adopted, and 153,000 still are left. And, unless the system is changed to do more to preserve families, there will be at least 153,000 more next year and the year after that and the year after that.

Where does Gelles propose to put all those children?

❖ REFERENCES

Allegheny County Office of Children, Youth, and Families. (2002). *A world where every child has a place to call home.* Retrieved April 3, 2003, from http://www .county. allegheny.pa.us/dhs/brochures/Permanency.pdf

Bath, H., & Haapala, D. (1994, September). Family preservation services: What does the outcome research really tell us? *Social Services Review,* 386–404.

Bernstein, N. (1999a, November 29). Strict shelter rules force many families out. *New York Times,* A1.

Bernstein, N. (1999b, December 20). In Suffolk, shelter rules force two into foster care. *New York Times,* B5.

Benedict, M., & Zuravin, S. (1992). *Factors associated with child maltreatment by family foster care providers.* Baltimore, MD: Johns Hopkins University School of Hygiene and Public Health, 28, 30.

Berquist, C., Szwejda, D., & Pope, G. (1993). *Evaluation of Michigan's Families First program.* Lansing, MI: University Associates.

Blythe, B., & Jayaratne, S. (1999). *Michigan Families First effectiveness study: A summary of findings.* Lansing, MI: State of Michigan Family Independence Agency.

Brace, C. L. (1872). *The dangerous classes of New York and twenty years work among them.* New York: Wynkoop and Hallenbeck.

Child Welfare Watch. (1998). *The race factor in child welfare.* New York: Center for an Urban Future. Retrieved April 3, 2003, from http://www.nycfuture. org/content/reports/report_view.cfm?repkey=9

Child Welfare Watch. (2000). *Too fast for families.* New York: Center for an Urban Future.

Cosentino v. Perales. (1988). New York State Supreme Court, New York County. 43236–85.

Fanshel, D., Finch, S., & Grundy, J. (1990). *Foster children in a life course perspective.* New York: Columbia University Press.

Franck, M. (2003, February 1). The pendulum. *St. Louis Post-Dispatch,* B1.

Frank, D., Klass, P., Earls, F., & Eisenberg, L. (1996). Infants and young children in orphanages: One view from pediatrics and child psychiatry. *Pediatrics, 97*(4), 569–578.

Fraser, M., Pecora, P., & Haapala, D. (1991). *Families in crisis: The impact of intensive family preservation services.* New York: Aldine De Gruyter.

Geen, R. (2003). *Improving child welfare agency performance through fiscal reforms: An assessment of recent proposals.* Paper prepared for the Joint Center on Poverty Research Conference, Child Welfare Services Research and Its Policy Implications, Washington, DC.

Gelles, R. (1996). *The book of David: How preserving families can cost children's lives.* New York: Basic Books.

Gelles, R. (1999, August 30). Early adoptions vs. family reunification. *Christian Science Monitor.* Retrieved December 4, 2003, from http://www.csmonitor .com/cgi-bin/wit_article.pl?script/1999/08/30/p9s1.txt

Groves, I. (1996). *System of care implementation: Performance, outcomes and compliance.* Tallahassee, FL: Human Systems and Outcomes, 3.

Groves, I. (2002). *Status report on implementation of the R.C. Consent Decree from January 2000 to January 2002.* Tallahassee, FL: Human Systems and Outcomes.

Hutson, R. (2003). *A vision for eliminating poverty and family violence: Transforming child welfare and TANF in El Paso County, Colorado.* Washington, DC: Center for Law and Social Policy. Retrieved July 9, 2003, from http://www.clasp .org/DMS/Documents/1043875845.58/ El_Paso_ report.pdf

Illinois Department of Children and Family Services. (1998). *Executive statistical summary.* Springfield, IL: Author.

Illinois Department of Children and Family Services. (2003a). *Signs of progress in child welfare reform.* Retrieved July 10, 2003, from http://www.state.il. us/dcfs/SignsProg.pdf

Illinois Department of Children and Family Services. (2003b). *Executive statistical summary.* Retrieved July 10, 2003, from http://www.state.il.us/dcfs/ com_communications_execstats.shtml

Jones, M. A. (1987). *Parental lack of supervision: Nature and consequences of a major child neglect problem.* Washington, DC: Child Welfare League of America.

Karwath, R. (1990, January 19). DCFS hit on family separation. *Chicago Tribune,* sec. 2, p. 2.

Kaufman, L., & Lezin Jones, R. (2003, May 23). Report finds flaws in inquiries on foster abuse in New Jersey. *New York Times,* p. A1.

Kirk, R. (2000). *Tailoring intensive family preservation services for family reunification cases: Research, evaluation and assessment.* Retrieved April 3, 2003, from http://nfpn.org/resources/articles/tailoring.html

Kirk, R. (2001). *A critique of the evaluation of family preservation and reunification programs: Interim report.* Retrieved April 3, 2003, from http://www.nfpn .org/resources/articles/critique.html

L. J. v. Massinga. (1987). Civil No. Jh-84–4409, United States District Court for the District of Maryland.

Maza, P. (2003). *Adoption data update.* Presentation to Child Welfare and Mental Health Coalition, Washington, DC.

New York State Department of Social Services. (1983). *Child abuse and maltreatment: Allegations and determinations.* Albany, NY: Author.

Pelton, L. (1989). *For reasons of poverty: A critical analysis of the public child welfare system in the United States.* New York: Praeger.

Pennsylvania Department of Public Welfare. (1996–2001). *Annual report on child abuse.* Harrisburg, PA: Author.

Poe, J., & Kendall, P. (1995, December 24). Cases of neglect may be only poverty in disguise. *Chicago Tribune,* p. 1.

Pollock, K. (1986, August 4). The child protectors: Flawed guardian of young. *Sacramento Bee,* p. 1.

Riccardi, N. (1999, June 15). Grandmother blames county in latest death of foster child. *Los Angeles Times,* p. 1.

Saari, L. (1999, January 17). Checking up on the children. *Orange County Register,* p. E1.

Sengupta, S. (2000a, May 31). Parents in poor neighborhoods wary of child welfare agency. *New York Times,* p. A1.

Sengupta, S. (2000b, July 8). Tough justice: Taking a child when one parent is battered. *New York Times,* p. A1.

Spencer, J. W., & Knudsen, D. (1992). Out of home maltreatment: An analysis of risk in various settings for children. *Children and Youth Services Review, 814,* 485–492.

U.S. Department of Health and Human Services. (1988). *Study findings: Study of national incidence and prevalence of child abuse and neglect: 1988* [NIS-2]. Washington, DC: U.S. Department of Health and Human Services, Administration for Children, Youth and Families, Chart, chap. 6, p. 5.

U.S. Department of Health and Human Services. (2000). *Child welfare outcomes 1998: Annual report.* Retrieved April 13, 2003, from http://www.acf.dU.S. Department of Health and Human Services gov/programs/cb/publications/cw098/

U.S. Department of Health and Human Services. (2001a). *Child welfare outcomes 1999: Annual report.* U.S. Department of Health and Human Services. Retrieved April 3, 2003, from gov/programs/cb/publications/cw099/index.html

U.S. Department of Health and Human Services. (2001b). Evaluation of family preservation and reunification programs. U.S. Department of Health and Human Services. Retrieved April 10, 2004, from http://aspe.hhs.gov/hsp/fampres94/chapter1.htm

U.S. Department of Health and Human Services. (2003a). *The AFCARS report: Preliminary FY 2001 estimates as of March 2003.* Retrieved April 14, 2003, from http://www.acf.U.S. Department of Health and Human Services. gov/programs/cb/publications/afcars/report8.htm

U.S. Department of Health and Human Services. (2003b). *Child maltreatment 2001*. Retrieved July 6, 2003, from http://www.acf.dU.S. Department of Health and Human Services.gov/programs/cb/publications/cm01/

Ward v. Feaver. (1998). United States District Court, Southern District of Florida, Ft. Lauderdale Division, Affidavit of David S. Bazerman, December 16, p. 4. #98–7137.

Wobie, K., Eyler, F. D., Behnke, M., & Garvan, C. W. (1998). *To have and to hold: A descriptive study of custody status following prenatal exposure to cocaine.* Paper presented at the joint annual meeting of the American Pediatric Society and the Society for Pediatric Research, New Orleans, LA.

21

Protecting Children Is More Important Than Preserving Families

Richard J. Gelles

It is difficult to disagree with the way this controversy is phrased. Family preservation should be *an* important goal in child abuse and neglect intervention. Parents in the United States have constitutional rights and are afforded constitutional protection in the raising of their own children. U.S. law and tradition grant parents broad discretion in how they rear their children. In *Smith v. Organization of Foster Families for Equality and Reform* (1977), the U.S. Supreme Court held that the 14th Amendment gave parents a "constitutionally recognized liberty interest" in maintaining the custody of their children "that derives from blood relationship, state law sanction, and basic human right" (846). This interest is not absolute, however, because of the state's power and authority to exercise *parens patriae* duties to protect citizens who cannot fend for themselves. The state may attempt to limit or end parent–child contact and make children eligible for temporary or permanent placement or adoption when parents (1) abuse, neglect, or abandon their children; (2) become incapacitated in their ability to be a parent; (3) refuse or are unable to remedy serious, identified problems in caring for their children; or (4) experience an extraordinarily severe breakdown in their relationship with their children (for example, owing to a long prison sentence). Cognizant that severing the parent–child relationship is an extremely drastic measure, the U.S. Supreme Court held in *Santosky v. Kramer* (1982) that a court may only terminate parental rights if the state can demonstrate with clear and convincing evidence that a parent has failed in one of these four ways. Most state statutes also contain provisions for parents to voluntarily relinquish their rights. The state also has the authority to return a child to his or her parents. Ideally, this occurs once a determination is made that it would be safe to return the child home and the child's parents would be able to provide appropriate care.

Although it may sometimes appear that states are in the throes of what Richard Wexler calls "foster care panic," in general, the removal of children from their parents by state child welfare agencies is a relatively rare event. On average, during the past five years, states received some 3 million reports of child abuse and neglect each year. State, county, and local child welfare agencies investigated nearly all of these reports and substantiated about 45 percent of them. In 2002, for example, of the 2.5 million children reported as suspected victims of child abuse and neglect, a little more than 900,000 were found to be victims of abuse or neglect by state child protective service investigators (U.S. Department of Health and Human Services, 2004). Parenthetically, I want to explain that the other 1.6 million reports of children suspected to be victims of maltreatment should not be considered false reports—rather, there was insufficient evidence discovered by child protective service investigators to substantiate that the suspected victim was in fact at risk of harm due to abuse and neglect.

Of the 900,000 or so substantiated victims, about 1 in 5 (200,000) were removed from their parents or caregivers and placed into some form of out-of-home care—with a relative, in a licensed foster home, or in some form of institutional setting.

Statistically speaking at least, it is clear that family preservation is the main consequence of state action when it comes to child abuse and neglect. The vast majority of families are preserved, even when they come to the attention of a child welfare agency for child abuse and neglect. Families are preserved by default when a state agency does not substantiate a report, and families are preserved even after a report is substantiated when a child welfare agency offers or requires a family to receive support services rather than remove a child who is believed to have been abused or neglected.

Even if a child is removed, child welfare agencies are obligated, and often prefer, to minimize the length of the removal and to keep a child close to his or her legal caregivers. The Federal Adoption Assistance and Child Welfare Act of 1980 (Public Law 96–272) requires states to place children in the least restrictive setting. Ideally and by law, state child welfare agencies try to place children with relatives before they place children with foster families or in institutions.

In principle, I believe it is generally appropriate to maintain a "high bar" that restrains and restricts state intervention into the parent–child relationship. This has been the law of the land for more than 200 years, and it has worked reasonably well for the majority of families and children.

The controversy, I believe, involves what the goal should be for the minority of children whose well-being is compromised by the actions and inactions of their caregivers. Here, I think, the singular goal of family preservation is misguided because of two empirically supported facts: (1) Family preservation efforts for children at risk are not widely successful; and (2) family preservation efforts, if they last too long and are unsuccessful, compromise children's safety, well-being, and opportunity to be raised in a safe and permanent home.

❖ FAMILY PRESERVATION EFFORTS

Efforts for Children at Risk Are Not Widely Successful

The goal of preserving families is certainly well intended. The reality is that if a family has abused or neglected a child or children, it is extremely difficult to help the family and be assured that the abused or neglected child is safe from harm. In saying this, I am assuming that those who support family preservation as a goal do so provided that the family can be preserved without causing harm or damage to befall a child. I dismiss out of hand the notion that parents' liberty interests are inviolable and that the state should never remove a child from a home or terminate parents' parental rights. Despite the fact that there is controversy about the goal of child welfare, I know of no professional involved in this controversy who supports unregulated parental rights and the complete subordination of children's rights.

In the past 20 years, an intervention named "Intensive Family Preservation Services" (IFPS) was developed and promoted as the best alternative to the "business as usual" family preservation child welfare casework that had been used by child welfare agencies since the early 1900s. The IFPS movement began in Tacoma, Washington, with "Homebuilders." The goal of IFPS is to work intensively with families *before* a child is removed. There are now many variations of IFPS in use across the country. The core goal of such programs is to maintain children safely in the home or to facilitate a safe and lasting reunification. IFPS programs were designed for families that have a serious crisis that threatens the stability of the family and the safety of the family members.

The initial evaluations of IFPS were uniformly enthusiastic. The programs were claimed to have reduced the placement of children, reduced the cost of out-of-home placement, and, at the same time, assured the safety of children. Foundation program officers and program administrators claimed that families involved in IFPS had low rates of placement and "100 percent safety records" (Barthel, 1991; Forsythe, 1992). Program administrators also claimed success in reducing placement and assuring safety. Susan Kelley, Director of the Division of Family Preservation Services, Office of Children and Youth Services for the state of Michigan, testified before Congress that of 2,505 families who participated in Michigan's Families First program in the first year, one incident of abuse was reported (Barthel, 1991).

There were, however, major methodological and design limitations of the early evaluations of IFPS. The vast majority of the evaluations of IFPS either employed no control group or used a comparison group that was not an appropriate match for the group receiving treatment. Moreover, there were questions raised about whether "placement avoidance" was the appropriate outcome measure for the evaluations. Peter Rossi (1992) cautioned that "placement avoidance" was not a proper outcome variable, because placement avoidance was itself the treatment. Moreover, in his 1992 review, Rossi concluded that the evaluation studies did not convincingly demonstrate that IFPS reduced placement or reduced child welfare costs. The claim that children were safe was not actually evaluated in these early studies.

By 1996, there had been at least 46 evaluations of IFPS of one form or another (Heneghan, Horwitz, & Leventhal, 1996; Lindsey, 1994). Of these 46 evaluations and of nearly 850 published articles on intensive family preservation, only 10 studies actually evaluated IFPS, included outcome data in the report, and used a control group of some kind. In California, New Jersey, and Illinois, the evaluations used randomly assigned control groups, included outcome data, and had large enough samples to allow for rigorous evaluation. In all three studies, there were either small or insignificant differences between the group receiving IFPS and the control group receiving traditional casework services. Even in terms of placement avoidance, there was no difference between the two groups, thus suggesting that earlier claims that IFPS were successful in reducing placement obtained those results because of the low overall rate of placement in child welfare agencies. These results also point to how difficult it is for child welfare caseworkers to accurately classify a family as "high risk" for being placed, since 80–90 percent of the children in the control group were not placed, even though these children were theoretically selected for the study because they were at high risk of being placed.

The empirical case that abusive and neglectful families can be preserved using IFPS has yet to be made. Amid the claims and counterclaims on intensive family preservation and following the funding of the Family Preservation and Support Act of 1993, the Department of Health and Human Services funded a national evaluation of family preservation and support services. This evaluation, conducted by Westat, the Chapin Hall Center for Children, and James Bell Associates examined a full range of family preservation and support programs at a number of sites across the country. The study used a randomized trial design with a variety of outcome measures, including placement, cost, and family functioning. More important, the study evaluated IFPS that rigorously followed the Homebuilders model. The multiyear project concluded that intensive family preservation programs do not reduce placement, do not reduce cost, do not improve family functioning, and, most important, do not improve child safety. It is not that such programs serve no useful purpose; it is that they offer no broadly effective solution to the vexing problems confronting those in the child welfare system (U.S. Department of Health and Human Services, 2001).

There are a number of reasons why intensive family preservation services, specifically, and the broader policy of family reunification are not effective, and I review these in a number of other publications (see, for example, Gelles, 2001). For this chapter, I simply conclude that while IFPS are certainly well-intended, and may even be effective for certain families, by and large they do not succeed in preserving families and protecting children.

Family preservation efforts, if they last too long and are unsuccessful, compromise children's safety, well-being, and opportunity to be raised in a safe and permanent home

Despite the lack of evidence for the effectiveness of IFPS or even more generic family preservation efforts, the American child welfare system still maintains the goal of preserving families. Now, it is certainly true that some 500,000 children are in foster care, and it is also true that the majority of federal child welfare funding can be used only for foster care (this is the result of a policy and legal tradition that would take another chapter to spell out). Nonetheless, children are generally placed in foster care with the goal of being reunified with their parents. Of the 500,000 children in foster care, there will be about 50,000 adoptions a year (this compares to 20,000 four years ago prior to the enactment of the Adoption and Safe Families Act of 1997—see next part of chapter for more on this). Thus, for the vast majority of children taken into care and who are in foster care, the goal is reunification with their families and thus, family preservation. However, given that family preservation services are not generally effective, the end result of the goal of preservation is that (1) many children reunited with their parents will be re-abused or re-neglected and end up back in foster care; or (2) the reunification may never take place, and children will linger in foster care with the goal of reunification but little likelihood that reunification will take place.

And here is how good intentions pave the road to hell. The longer children stay in temporary care, the less likely they are to receive permanent care. The lack of permanent care and the many moves children may make in and out of foster care or from foster home to foster home produces the most detrimental outcome for children.

A single-minded goal of family preservation, without the tools to accomplish a lasting preservation, results in children being abused and neglected again, some even killed, and many other children growing up in a situation that has been called "orphans of the living" (see Toth, 1997).

❖ CURRENT CHILD WELFARE POLICY AND PRACTICE

Current child welfare policy and practice is governed by two main factors: (1) federal and state child welfare legislation, and (2) the culture and ideology of the child welfare system. Both policy and practice are influenced by concerns for families and children—concerns that often create irresolvable contradictions.

As I noted at the beginning of the chapter, parents and caregivers have a constitutionally supported liberty interest to raise their children without unwarranted government interference. When there is evidence that the parents or caregivers are unable or unwilling to meet their children's needs, state and local child welfare agencies may intervene.

For at least 100 years, state intervention has been guided by two goals: (1) assure the safety and well-being of the child and (2) preserve the family. Sometimes the most appropriate action that ensures the safety and well-being of a child is to allow the child to remain in the home; but other times the child's safety cannot be assured if the child is left with his or her caregivers.

Since 1980, federal law has required states, as a condition of eligibility for federal child welfare funding, to make "reasonable efforts" to keep a child in his or her home or reunite the child with his or her caregivers as soon a possible and practical (Public Law 96–272, the Adoption Assistance and Child Welfare Act of 1980). State laws have been consistent with federal law, in large part because without legislative consistency and consistent practice, states would be ineligible for more than $5 billion in annual child welfare funding.

Federal and state law has been generally consistent with the underlying values of child welfare workers and administrators. The major value of the child welfare system is to work with families to protect children. By and large, this means that families and caregivers are seen as the clients of child welfare workers. Family preservation and reunification are not only the legal goal for the child welfare system, but are believed to be the most appropriate goal by those who work within the system. Thus, until 1997, when the Adoption and Safe Families Act (Public Law 105–89) was enacted by Congress, the nearly uniform case goal for children in the child welfare system was family preservation and reunification.

Thus, the child welfare system worked very hard to meet the goal of family preservation, even if this goal was difficult or impossible to achieve. The majority of children removed from their homes were ultimately reunited with their parents. Unfortunately, the reunification was very often fragile, and between 20 and 40 percent of children reunited with their parents were returned to out-of-home placement within 18 months of the reunification. For a small number of children, family preservation was deadly—nearly half of the children killed by parents or caregivers are killed after the children come to the attention of the child welfare system (Gelles, 1996). Some children are killed when left in the homes; others are killed after a reunification.

The goal of family preservation produced another adverse consequence for children. On average, approximately half of the more than 500,000 children residing in foster care have been in out-of-home care for more than 18 months. They remain in foster care while child welfare workers work toward family reunification, or they remain in foster care because a reunification is not possible, but the child has not been adopted.

Each year approximately 20,000 children "age out" of the child welfare system. That is, they reach the age of majority in their state, and their foster parents or other caregivers are no longer eligible for foster care payments. Another important statistic is that, prior to the enactment of the Adoption and Safe Families Act of 1997, the number of adoptions of children from the foster care system was about 20,000, and the number of adoptions was in decline (Bevan, 1996). The main adverse consequence for children was that while they were awaiting reunification—a reunification that might never occur—they were deprived of permanency.

The legal mandate for child welfare was revised in 1997. The Adoption and Safe Families Act of 1997 changed the main goal of the child welfare system from family preservation to the child's health and safety. The mandate for reasonable efforts was tempered with language that stipulated that there were circumstances in which child welfare agencies did not have to make any efforts toward family preservation. These included aggravated circumstances, such as when a parent has committed a murder of another child, when a parent has committed or aided in voluntary manslaughter of another child of the parent, when a parent has committed an assault that resulted in serious injury to a child or another child of the parent, of when a parent has had his or her parental rights involuntarily terminated for a sibling of the child. In addition, timelines were established for reunification efforts in order to remove barriers to adoption and reduce the time children would stay in foster care awaiting an improbable or questionable reunification.

The Adoption and Safe Families Act of 1997 changed family preservation from *the* goal of child welfare systems to *a* goal, albeit the central and main goal of child welfare. The initial impact of the Adoption and Safe Families Act of 1997 has been an increase in yearly adoptions from 20,000 per year to more than 50,000 in 2001. There are little other empirical data that can be used to assess additional impacts of the Adoption and Safe Families Act.

❖ WHAT IS WRONG WITH "CHILD SAVING"?

Critics, including Richard Wexler, of my child-centered position regarding child welfare label me a "child saver." The more negative criticism is that I am "anti-family."

Beyond the name calling, the focus of the criticism is that I take an unyielding "child-centered" approach to child welfare. I place child safety, child well-being, a child reaching his or her developmental potential, and permanency as the central goals of child welfare. If these can be accomplished by more services for the family, fine. But the family should not be preserved at the expense of these goals.

Some of the more common criticisms of my child-centered approach, and my responses to these criticisms, are as follows:

• *The child welfare system is most heavily funded for out-of-home care, thus emphasizing placement over services or prevention.* It is true that Title IV-E, the federal government's primary child welfare budget, is an open-ended entitlement that can be used only to fund out-of-home placement. It is true that Title IV-E funding is more than $5 billion, while federal funding for prevention and support services hovers around $300 million each year. Yet, the funding does not totally determine the structure and goals of the child welfare system, as the case goals for children who are in foster care almost always begin with an attempt at a reunification.

• *There is not enough funding for prevention and intervention services.* The essence of this argument is that if there was more money available for supportive or helping services for families, children would not have to go into out-of-home care and parents would not have their rights terminated. Clearly, federal funding for prevention and support services is minimal. Certainly, more funding to assist families might help. However, for the past 30 years, states have spent more and more on intervention services with little actual payoff in terms of reduced recidivism. Perhaps money alone is not enough to change caregiving behavior. In fact, behavior change is not a direct function of how many or even the quality of services that are available (Gelles, 1996, 2001).

• *Children are harmed in foster care.* Children are abused in foster care, and some children are killed. The rate of abuse in foster care has been reported as being as high as 30 percent—1,000 times greater than the abuse rate in the general population. But the general population is the inappropriate comparison group for this comparison. The proper comparison group is substantiated abused and neglected children left in their homes or returned to their homes from foster care. We do not have adequate data on the former, but we do know that the maltreatment rate for children returned home from foster care is at least 40 percent. Thus, reunification or preservation abuse is actually greater than abuse in foster care. So, too, is the fatality rate for preservation or reunification compared to the fatality rate in foster care.

- *Too many children are taken inappropriately from their parents in the name of child saving.* The issue here is what statisticians call "false positives." That is, instances when maltreatment and risk are substantiated and a removal occurs when it is not necessary. There is no question that children are inappropriately removed from their caregivers in the name of reducing presumed risk that may not exist. On the other hand, it is a basic law of probability theory that one can reduce false positives or false negatives (children who are left with or returned to parents deemed safe, but who turn out to re-abuse or neglect their children). If one wants to limit the number of children removed from their homes, this will be at the expense of false-negatives—the abuse of children left or returned to dangerous parents. Given the choice, I choose to reduce false negatives and accept that resulting problem of false positives.

❖ CONCLUSION

My conclusion is simple: I believe that the child welfare system's over-commitment to the goal of family preservation places too many children in harm's way. Family preservation is an important goal, but it should not be the overriding or only goal of child welfare. For me, child safety, child well-being, and permanence are the most important goals in child abuse and neglect.

❖ A RESPONSE TO WEXLER

Everyone is entitled to his or her own opinion. Everyone is not entitled to his or her own facts. While I can respect and even agree with Richard

Wexler's opinion (this volume) that family preservation should be the goal for child abuse and neglect interventions, the empirical facts just do not support his claim that intensive family preservation services are effective and safe.

First, let me state that no matter how sad and emotional the anecdote or case example, data are not the plural of anecdote. Now, I have been guilty of using anecdotes or case examples to punctuate a point or introduce a paper or presentation. I even used a single case as the framework of my book, *The Book of David: How Preserving Families Can Cost Children's Lives* (1996). But I do not confuse the story with the data, and neither should those who want to assess the effectiveness and usefulness of family preservation as the core child welfare intervention.

The facts are that, to date, there has still not been a study that meets the normal standards of evidence for evaluation research (a random clinical trial) that supports the hypotheses that intensive family preservation services are effective or enhance child safety. Richard Wexler rightfully cites Ray Kirk's critique of the national evaluation of IFPS. As I note in my chapter, these random clinical trials did not support the hypotheses that IFPS are effective and enhance child safety. It is indeed true that there was a fidelity problem in the most recent national evaluations, just as there was in Schuerman, Rzepnicki, & Littell's (1994) random clinical trial evaluations of family preservation programs in Illinois. By fidelity problem, I mean that those who implemented intensive family preservation programs in the experiments did not or were not able to follow the Homebuilders model. But this fidelity problem is data. If in nearly 10 years, those who implement Homebuilders-type programs cannot duplicate the Homebuilders model, this means that the model, however good it is in theory, cannot be implemented as designed. In short, Homebuilders is a wonderful program in theory, but no one has figured out how to implement it so that it is effective.

The facts regarding risks in foster placement or even adoption are compelling. Children in foster care or even those who are adopted are more likely to suffer abuse and neglect than are children in the general population. But, as I point out in my chapter, children in the general population are not the appropriate comparison group. Abused and neglected children who stay with or are returned to their biological caregivers have a higher rate of abuse, neglect, and fatalities than children in placement.

When the anecdotes and the unsubstantiated claims of effectiveness are removed, Wexler's chapter is reduced to his opinion. It is an opinion I would like to share, and in fact do share often, but the facts simply do not support Wexler's deep commitment to the effectiveness of family preservation services.

❖ REFERENCES

Barthel, J. (1991). *For children's sake: The promise of family preservation*. New York: Edna McConnell Clark Foundation.

Bevan, C. (1996). *Foster care: Too much, too little, too early, too late: Child protection: Old problem, new paradigm*. Washington, DC: National Council for Adoption.

Forsythe, P. (1992). Homebuilders and family preservation. *Children and Youth Services Review, 14*, 37–47.

Gelles, R. J. (1996). *The book of David: How preserving families can cost children's lives*. New York: Basic Books.

Gelles, R. J. (2001) Family preservation and reunification: How effective a social policy? In K. White (Ed.), *Handbook of youth and justice* (pp. 367–376). New York: Plenum.

Heneghan, A., Horwitz, S., & Leventhal, J. (1996). Evaluating intensive family preservation programs: A methodological review. *Pediatrics, 97*, 535–542.

Lindsey, D. (1994). *The welfare of children*. New York: Oxford University Press.

Rossi, P. (1992). Assessing family preservation programs. *Children and Youth Services Review, 14*, 167–191.

Santosky v. Kramer, 455 U.S. 745, 766 (1982).

Schuerman, J., Rzepnicki, T. L., & Littell, J. (1994). *Putting children first: An experiment in family preservation*. New York: Aldine de Gruyter.

Smith v. Organization of Foster Families for Equal Rights & Reform, 431 U.S. 816 (1977).

Toth, J. (1997). *Orphans of the living: Stories of America's children in foster care*. New York: Simon & Schuster.

U.S. Department of Health and Human Services, Administration on Children, Youth and Families. 2004. *Child maltreatment 2002 : Reports from the states to the National Center on Child Abuse and Neglect*. Washington, DC: U.S. Government Printing Office.

U.S. Department of Health and Human Services. (2001). Evaluation of Family Preservation and Reunification Programs. Retrieved April 10, 2001, from http://aspe.hhs.gov/hsp/fampres94/chapter1.htm

Conclusion

Social Problems, Social Policy, and Controversies on Family Violence

T he chapters in this volume have only touched upon the many controversies among experts concerned with the problems of family violence. We begin this conclusion by examining how characteristics of this topic lead to controversies that can be deep, long lasting, and resistant to change.

❖ SOURCES OF CONTROVERSY

In the Introduction to this volume we speculated that there are many characteristics of family violence that fuel the controversies swirling around it. Here we offer further speculations about four of those characteristics:

1. Family violence simultaneously is an *academic* puzzle to be *studied* and a *social* problem to be *resolved*.

2. Studying or intervening in family violence requires making *moral* distinctions about what is tolerable and what is intolerable, about which values are more important than others.

3. Studying or intervening in family violence often leads to strong *feelings*, which influence thinking.

4. There are *high practical consequences* associated with "winning" or "losing" controversies.

Is family violence first and foremost an academic puzzle to be *studied* or a social problem to be *resolved?* A commonsense answer is that it is both. Academic study, after all, depends at least in part on social problem consciousness: Why would we study the various forms of family violence unless a significant number of people evaluated them as problems? Family violence, in its many forms, arose as an academic puzzle to be studied only after advocates had made notable progress in their efforts to change public opinion that previously had led to ignoring or even applauding violence in homes. For the most part, what is studied—child abuse, wife abuse, elder abuse—is what has been defined as a social problem. What is much less researched— sibling violence, child and teen violence toward non-elderly parents, the "normal" violence found in American homes—are forms of violence that have not achieved the status of social problems for the general public. Research depends on social advocacy.

Just as certainly, efforts to do something about social problems such as family violence should be based on knowledge from research. A condition cannot be changed unless we know how common it is, who is affected by it, what causes it, and what its consequences are. Just as clearly, only research can show which social interventions are effective and should be continued and which are ineffective and are therefore a waste of resources. Social advocacy depends on research to define the size and shape of the problem, to isolate the problem's cause and, therefore, its potential solution, and to evaluate the effectiveness of all forms of social interventions.

At times, contributors to this volume demonstrate how science and social action can mutually reinforce one another. In these instances, social advocates have done research themselves, and they also cite the research of others to support their calls for practical action. In turn, several authors identify themselves as researchers but nonetheless argue that the results of their studies support particular forms of social change.

While it makes sense to maintain that research and practical action can be mutually reinforcing, it sometimes is difficult to blend science and social activism, because the goals of each are different. At least in their ideal images, the goal of *science* is to *produce knowledge,* while the goal of *social activism* is to *change the world.* What is required to produce knowledge can be very different from what is required to convince a disbelieving public that an intolerable condition exists and must be eliminated. This difference in goals is seen in the recurring controversies in this volume surrounding what constitutes "good evidence" to support arguments. Some authors promote the primary value of science when they talk about the importance of "further scientific studies," when they criticize counter views by arguing that the evidence for those views rests on "biased samples," on "hope" rather than on "research," or on "advocacy research" rather than on "scientific research." Simultaneously, others promote the primary value of social activism and complain that calls for "more research" are merely a convenient rhetoric disguising intentions to discredit efforts at social change, that the scientific measurement of violence misrepresents the complexity of violence in lived reality, that the results of scientific research are used to roll back social change. Herein lies a seed of controversy: When the goals and methods of science and social action are incompatible, which should be privileged? Should the goal of accumulating knowledge be actively pursued even if the uses of this knowledge lead to negative practical consequences? Should social interventions receive continued funding although their effectiveness has not been—and perhaps cannot be—scientifically measured?

The first divide among family violence experts stems from the dual definition of this violence as something to be studied and as something to be changed. The second divide is more subtle: studying or changing family violence require social activists and scientific researchers alike to make *moral* decisions. Because we have an image of science as an "objective" search for knowledge, it might seem odd to claim that researchers identifying their work as scientific must make moral decisions. While moral decision making seems to have no place in the scientific endeavor, scientific researchers must make moral decisions, two types of which are illustrated in these chapters.

First, what should be studied, and how should it be defined and measured? Clearly and most certainly, *none* of the authors of these chapters argues that we need more violence in our world; *none* applauds the use of violence nor maintains that violence is preferable to no violence. At the same time, these authors offer very different answers to questions about what should be studied and how it should be defined and measured. Such decisions are inherently *moral*, because by examining only some types of violence, others are left unexamined. Are we interested in minor violence or only extreme violence? What specific behaviors should be condemned as those of rape? Is spanking discipline or abuse? What specific behaviors are those of elder abuse? When is it moral to excuse a battered woman for killing her abusive partner? Such choices are consequential in the world of practical action, where the public tends to accept—or at least to tolerate—some forms of violence. If the focus is on studying and condemning only extreme cases of violence, are seemingly more minor types of violence unintentionally evaluated as morally tolerable? If the focus is on studying and condemning all violence in all forms, then is the seriousness of extreme cases unintentionally diminished? Deciding what to study is every bit as much a moral decision as is deciding what to change.

A second type of moral decision is reflected throughout many chapters: Which important American values surrounding families should be preserved, and which can be ignored in order to stop violence? The answers to such questions reflect *moral* judgments about the power and the purposes of government authorities, the value of family privacy, and the balance of the rights of victims, offenders, and families. What rights should be expanded? Which should be preserved? Which can be reduced or even suspended? What are the costs and benefits of expanding or reducing rights? Who experiences those costs? Who experiences the benefits?

A third divide in studying family violence that fuels controversies is that what we think about this violence is as much related to our *feelings* as to our cognitive appraisals. While contributors to this volume did not elaborate on their own experiences while doing their research or in accomplishing social advocacy, strong feelings are to be expected when research involves long interviews with people, such as the stressed caregivers of elderly people, battered women, or victims of date rape. Likewise, focusing on horrors such as those of children left with abusive parents or children in the chaotic foster care system will lead researchers to accumulate example after example after example of individual stories. Of course, when researchers or advocates write their findings for a volume such as this, their experiences are sanitized, and they report only the "data" they collected. Yet behind these data are the researchers' experiences, and these often can lead to very strong feelings: of sympathy for victims, hatred of offenders, complete frustration with the organization and characteristics of social services of all types. Controversies can be far more than dispassionate disagreements about "facts." Behind debates about the facts can be the strong feelings of researchers and advocates alike, and these fuel controversies.

A fourth characteristic of the topic of family violence that fuels controversies is that "winning" or "losing" debates leads to very practical consequences. This is not always obvious. For example, arguments in some chapters in this volume might seem to plod along in dense academic prose, with opposing authors offering "dueling statistics," and disputing what might seem to be very minor points of research methodology or offering conceptualizations that are so subtle in their differences that readers might not even notice the differences. In such instances, readers might wonder why authors often seem so intent not just in winning the debate but on completely demolishing the arguments made by their opponents. It is because the stakes are high indeed.

Being convinced that one or another side wins a debate can lead to changing *attitudes*. It is possible, for example, that some readers of chapters in this volume have changed the ways they think about violence in general, or how they think about wife abuse, date rape, spanking, or elder abuse in particular. Depending on which "side" of these arguments was the most convincing, readers might make sense of their experiences and the experiences of others in new ways. Changing the public's attitudes about violence is consequential.

More concretely, convincing arguments can change *behaviors* in daily life. For example, parents might willingly stop spanking their children if they are convinced that spanking does no good and, in fact, does harm; parents might willingly send their children to child sex abuse education programs if they are convinced such programs are worthwhile, or they might refuse to do so if they are convinced these programs are ineffective and possibly even harmful. Members of the public who are on juries might be able to understand the complexity of the self-defense claims of battered women who kill their abusive partners and therefore vote to acquit such a woman, or they might understand self-defense claims as inappropriate and vote to convict her. How people evaluate controversies is consequential, because it can change how people act.

Finally, but critically, sometimes it does not matter how members of the public evaluate the soundness of arguments. Regardless of whether or not the majority of people agree, winning—or losing—the debate about a controversy can convince legislators or courts to change *social policies*. Depending on which side wins controversies in this volume, for example, it could become more difficult—or easier—to initiate investigations for suspected child abuse. More children—or fewer children—could be taken from their homes; more money—or less money—could be spent to change the characteristics of abusive or neglectful parents. The government might declare spanking to be a crime. Each and every controversy in this volume might become a topic of public policy. Although controversies sometimes seem esoteric, they are fueled by the understanding that who wins—and who loses—determines social policies. Clearly, this is consequential.

❖ REFLECTIONS ON CONTROVERSIES

Such are a few of the many seeds of specific controversies surrounding family violence in its many forms. Controversy is a common characteristic of professional groups of *all* types. Indeed, there will be tendencies for a great deal of controversy whenever a professional group is composed of people who seek to study and those who seek to change, whenever a group draws attention from a wide variety of professionals, whenever the topic is political in its consequences. We could, therefore, just as easily make similar comments about groups of experts on homelessness, education, drug abuse, crime, gun control, and so on. While extreme disagreements characterize many professional groups, and while such disagreements are social rather than individual in their nature, too much controversy nonetheless has at least two negative consequences.

First, and as several of our contributors noted, far too little is known about the causes of violence, or about what works to stop it. Extreme controversy hinders the possibility of gaining more knowledge. Debate and learning are not possible when experts approach their work with the a priori attitude that another set of arguments need not be seriously considered; nothing results from dismissing the work of some people as "merely politically correct" or as "politically incorrect." Nothing comes from dismissing research findings simply because the research is "not real science." Too much controversy yields professional fragmentation: Particular conferences organized to expand knowledge are attended only by like-minded others; some people will publish their thoughts in professional journals read only by like-minded others. Indeed, in putting together this volume we found that some experts on family violence refused to have their work included in a volume that also would contain the work of particular others. Little is learned in these small groups of like-minded others, because the only ideas allowed to enter the group are those supporting what group members already believe. Too much controversy hinders the chance of increasing knowledge. This is unacceptable when so little is known about so important a topic.

Second, extreme controversy is destructive when it enters the sound-bite world of the mass media. While the chapters in this volume have demonstrated how disagreements most often are very complex, the world of the mass media does not allow subtlety, complexity, or detail. Furthermore, although there is much upon which the authors of these chapters agree, the mass media tends to ignore agreements and rather to amplify disagreements. This leads to a lack of public trust in what experts say. Why should members of the public trust what experts say if these experts are so adamant about not trusting one another?

Do we believe that family violence experts can become one big happy family characterized by solidarity, assistance, and trust? Unlikely. Do we believe our simple call to "talk about it" will resolve controversies? No. The complexity of the topic and the very different moral evaluations underlying both research and social activism make it improbable that this group of people will cooperatively develop a shared vision of the best theoretical perspectives, definition of the problems and its causes, and routes to social change. Nonetheless, discussion must be encouraged, because the alternatives of divisiveness, animosity, and isolation lead to no political, moral, or social good.

If we lived in a world where people felt sympathy for every human trouble no matter how small, if we lived in a world of unlimited resources to resolve all problems great and modest, it would not be necessary to resolve the controversies contained in this volume. We could, for example, simultaneously conceptualize violence as a problem of psychology, of gender, and of the organization of the social order. We could simultaneously treat individuals, create gender equality, reduce poverty, create community. We could drastically increase the number of social service providers and foster homes while working diligently to make children's own homes safer. In this perfect world, battered women would not kill their abusers, because wife abuse would be stopped long before it reached its horrific conclusions. In this perfect world, there would be no need for programs to educate young children about child sexual abuse, because there would be no child sexual abuse. And so on.

Yet our world is not perfect. Our imperfect world is characterized by a lack of sympathy for all but the most extreme victims of abuse and by increasingly limited social resources for any form of intervention into violence. In this imperfect world, women's violence toward men becomes a justification for withdrawing sympathy and support from battered women. In this imperfect world, money is used to increase the number of child abuse allegations coming into the system, but no new money is given to do anything about these calls. In this imperfect world, children must be educated to protect themselves against child sexual abuse because adults do not protect children. In the present—and in the future—sympathy and resources will be directed only to particular people suffering particular problems. Who gets this sympathy and resources—and who doesn't—will be a consequence of how controversies such as those contained in this volume are resolved. The choice is whether this will happen through debate or through the exercise of sheer political power.

We again thank the contributors to this volume for showing that debate is possible, and we hope our comments and speculations will encourage readers to examine further how particular controversies might be surrogates for underlying, often vaguely articulated, disagreements. The chapters in this volume can be read as mirrors of general controversies within the modern-day United States. It should not be surprising that family violence experts do not agree on what types of violence warrant attention and concern, because Americans in general do not agree. Given that Americans in general do not agree about the compromises we should be willing to make in order to do something about violence—or any other social problem—it is not surprising that these experts likewise disagree. Such professional disputes echo cultural controversies: They are about Americans' failures to agree about what the characteristics of a good society should look like, and how that good society should be achieved.

Donileen R. Loseke

Richard J. Gelles

Mary M. Cavanaugh

Author Index

Subject Index

About the Editors

Donileen R. Loseke received her Ph.D. from the University of California-Santa Barbara and is Professor of Sociology at the University of South Florida. Her books include *The Battered Woman and Shelters*, which won the 1994 Charles Horton Cooley Award from the Society for the Study of Symbolic Interaction, and *Thinking About Social Problems: An Introduction to Constructionist Perspectives*. She has been the coeditor of the *Journal of Contemporary Ethnography*, the President of the Society for the Study of Symbolic Interaction and Theory Division Chair, and member of the Board of Directors of the Society for the Study of Social Problems. Currently she is an advisory editor for *Social Problems* and *The Sociological Quarterly*.

Richard J. Gelles received his Ph.D. in Sociology from the University of New Hampshire. He is Dean of the School of Social Work at the University of Pennsylvania and holds the Joanne and Raymond Welsh Chair of Child Welfare and Family Violence in the School of Social Work at the University of Pennsylvania. He is Director of the Center for the Study of Youth Policy and Co-Director of the Center for Children's Policy, Practice, and Research. His book *The Violent Home* was the first systematic empirical investigation of family violence and continues to be highly influential. He is the author or coauthor of 23 books and more than 100 articles and chapters on family violence. His latest books are *The Book of David: How Preserving Families Can Cost Children's Lives* (1996) and *Intimate Violence in Families, 3rd Edition* (1997).

Mary M. Cavanaugh, M.F.T., M.S., is currently a doctoral candidate in both Social Welfare and Criminology at the University of Pennsylvania. She has been involved with numerous research projects on intimate violence that have been submitted to the National Institute of Justice and the National Institute of Mental Health. She is a practitioner in the field of domestic violence facilitating batterer intervention service programs in cooperation with adult probation and parole departments and victim service agencies. She has served as a consultant and trainer on offender risk assessment and treatment services to state and local victim service agencies and youth and family service departments. She has recently completed a project for the U.S. Army on "The Evaluation of Domestic Violence Prevention and Intervention Strategies." She also serves as a consultant to the Violence Against Women and Family Violence Research and Evaluation Program for the National Institute of Justice.

About the Contributors

Jill Antonishak is a doctoral student in the Department of Psychology at the University of Virginia. She received her undergraduate degree from Goucher College and her master's degree from UVA. Her research focuses on adolescent risk taking and problem behavior, with an emphasis on peer relations. Other research interests include the application of developmental psychology to law and public policy, especially juvenile justice issues and the prevention of child abuse and neglect.

Douglas J. Besharov, a lawyer, is Professor at the University of Maryland School of Public Affairs. He also holds the Joseph J. and Violet Jacobs Chair in Social Welfare Studies at the American Enterprise Institute for Public Policy Research. He was the first director of the U.S. National Center on Child Abuse and Neglect. His books include *Recognizing Child Abuse: A Guide for the Concerned; Family Well-Being after Welfare Reform; America's Disconnected Youth: Toward a Preventive Strategy; Enhancing Early Childhood Programs: Burdens and Opportunities; When Drug Addicts Have Children: Reorienting Child Welfare's Response; Legal Services for the Poor: Time for Reform; The Vulnerable Social Worker: Liability for Serving Children and Families;* and *Juvenile Justice Advocacy.*

Mark Bodnarchuk is the staff psychologist for an intensive group psychotherapy program for high-risk spousal assaulters with the Correctional Service of Canada, a position he has held since 2002. He has also provided group treatment for community resident spousal assaulters, and has conducted research on the personality and behavioral typologies, treatment evaluation, and the assessment of risk with this population. He received his Ph.D. in Counseling Psychology from the University of British Columbia in 2002.

Sarah L. Cook is Associate Professor of Community Psychology and Director of Undergraduate Studies in the Department of Psychology at

Georgia State University in Atlanta, Georgia. Her research interests focus on how social scientists measure women's experiences, and the role of conflict and coercion in women's responses to abuse, incarcerated women's abuse experiences, and the perceptions and effects of street harassment on higher education students. Before beginning her academic position at GSU, she confronted the problem of violence against women as a peer educator, rape crisis advocate, child protection social worker, and consultant to local and state advocacy organizations. She received her Ph.D. from the University of Virginia.

Donald A. Downs is Professor of Political Science, Law, and Journalism at the University of Wisconsin, Madison. He also has taught at the University of Michigan and at Notre Dame. He specializes in public and constitutional law, political and legal theory, and American politics. He is the author of numerous articles and five books dealing with such topics as free speech, criminal law, and academic freedom and politics. He has lectured nationally and internationally, and has been interviewed by national and international media. His book, *More Than Victims: Battered Women, the Syndrome Society, and the Law,* was published in 1996.

Donald G. Dutton is Professor of Psychology at the University of British Columbia. He co-founded the Assaultive Husbands Project in 1979, a court-mandated treatment program for men convicted of wife assault. He has published more than 100 papers and three books, including the *Domestic Assault of Women* (1995), *The Batterer: A Psychological Profile (1995),* and *The Abusive Personality (1998).* He frequently has served as an expert witness in civil trials involving domestic abuse and in criminal trials involving family violence, including his work for the prosecution in the O. J. Simpson trial (1995). He received his Ph.D. in Psychology from the University of Toronto.

David Finkelhor is Director of the Crimes against Children Research Center, Co-Director of the Family Research Laboratory, and Professor of Sociology at the University of New Hampshire. He is well known for his conceptual and empirical work on the problem of child sexual abuse, reflected in publications such as *Sourcebook on Child Sexual Abuse* (1986) and *Nursery Crimes* (1988). He has also written about child homicide, missing and abducted children, Internet victimization, children exposed to domestic and peer violence, and other forms of family violence. He is editor and author of 10 books and more than 75 journal articles and book chapters on the victimization of children.

James Fisher is Assistant Professor of Political Science and Criminal Justice at Edinboro University of Pennsylvania. He received a law degree from William and Mary School of Law and is a doctoral candidate in political science at the University of Wisconsin-Madison.

Jerry P. Flanzer is known for his work on drug abuse, alcoholism, and family conflict as an author, clinician, program consultant, and researcher. He currently is a senior social scientist with the Services Research Branch, Division of Epidemiology, Services and Prevention Research at the National Institute on Drug Abuse. Before coming to NIDA, he served as Professor of Social Work at the University of Wisconsin, University of Arkansas, and as CEO and Director of Recovery and Family Treatment, Inc. He is a licensed clinical social worker and a certified substance abuse and relapse prevention counselor who has authored two books and numerous articles. He received his Ph.D. from the University of Southern California.

Neil Gilbert is Chernin Professor of Social Welfare at the University of California-Berkeley and Co-Director of the U.C. Berkeley Center on Child and Youth Policy. He has served twice as a Fulbright Fellow studying European social policy and was awarded the University of Pittsburgh Bicentennial Medallion of Distinction. His publications include 25 books and more than 100 articles. His works have been translated into Chinese, Japanese, Korean, and Italian, and reviewed in the *New York Times, Wall Street Journal, New York Review of Books, New Republic, Society, Partisan Review,* and leading academic journals. Gilbert is the Oxford University Press U.S. Delegate for Sociology and Social Work. He is chair of the Board of Directors of Seneca Center. He received his Ph.D. from the University of Pittsburgh.

Jeffrey J. Haugaard is Associate Professor in the Department of Human Development and Family Studies at Cornell University. He is Chair of the Working Group on Implications for Education and Training of Child Abuse and Neglect Issues of the American Psychological Association, author of several professional articles and papers on child maltreatment, and, with N. Dickon Reppucci, is coauthor of *The Sexual Abuse of Children: A Comprehensive Guide to Current Knowledge and Intervention Strategies.* He received his Ph.D. from the University of Virginia in Clinical Psychology.

Mary P. Koss is Principal Investigator of the RESTORE Project and is Professor of Public Health on the faculty of the Mel and Enid Zuckerman

Arizona College of Public Health at the University of Arizona. She works to prevent violence and improve policy responses through service to boards such as the Governor's Commission on Prevention of Violence against Women, and on the management Committee of the Sexual Violence Research Initiative based at the World Health Organization. She has worked in sexual assault for more than 25 years, in recognition of which she received the American Psychological Association Committee on Women in Psychology 2003 Leadership Award.

Demie Kurz is Co-Director of Women's Studies at the University of Pennsylvania with an appointment in the Sociology Department. Her primary research and teaching interests are contemporary issues of gender and the family. She has written extensively on issues of domestic violence in the United States. Her book on divorce, *For Richer, For Poorer: Mothers Confront Divorce* (1995), analyzes the social and economic impact of divorce on a diverse group of divorced mothers, and also includes an analysis of the role of domestic violence in the causes and consequences of divorce. She received her Ph.D. in Sociology from Northwestern University.

Holly Maguigan is Professor of Clinical Law at New York University School of Law. She has litigated and consulted on battered women's criminal trials since 1979 and has published many articles on the subject. She is a member of the Family Violence Prevention Fund's National Advisory Committee on Cultural Considerations in Domestic Violence Cases. She serves on the National Advisory Council of the National Clearinghouse for the Defense of Battered Women, and is on the Board of Directors of the Society of American Law Teachers and the William Moses Kunstler Fund for Racial Justice. She received her J.D. degree from the University of Pennsylvania.

Sue Osthoff is Director of the National Clearinghouse for the Defense of Battered Women, a Philadelphia-based organization designed to enhance the quality of legal representation and personal support to battered women facing trial and to incarcerated battered women. She began work with the National Clearinghouse full-time in 1987 when she co-founded the organization. She has been working in the battered women's movement since 1979 when she was a counselor/advocate in Massachusetts.

Karl Pillemer is Professor of Human Development at Cornell University and Director of the Cornell Gerontology Research Institute.

His major research interests lie in the family relationships of the elderly, including projects relating to family caregiving, relationships of family members to nursing homes, and elder abuse and neglect.

Carol A. Plummer is the author of *Preventing Sexual Abuse*, a prevention curriculum first published in 1984 and still widely used in schools and communities. She has conducted several studies of child sexual abuse prevention programs and on program effectiveness. Most recently, her research and writing has focused on the nonabusive mothers of sexually abused children. She is a founding member and current board President of the Association for Sexual Abuse Prevention. She received her Ph.D in Social Work and Personality Psychology from the University of Michigan.

N. Dickon Reppucci is Professor of Psychology at the University of Virginia, a position he has held since 1976. He received his Ph.D. from Harvard University and was Assistant and Associate Professor at Yale University from 1968 to 1976. He is an author, coauthor, or editor of more than 135 books, chapters, and articles. His major research interests include children, families, and the law, especially juvenile justice and adolescent development, and the prevention of child abuse and neglect.

John Rosemond is a family psychologist who directs the Center for Affirmative Parenting in Gastonia, North Carolina. His nationally syndicated parenting column appears weekly in more than 200 newspapers. He has written nine books, including *A Family of Value*, on various parenting and family issues. His Web site is located at www.rosemond.com.

Suzanne K. Steinmetz is Professor of Sociology at Indiana University, Indianapolis. She received her doctorate in Sociology from Case Western Reserve University. Steinmetz is the author of *Cycle of Violence: Assertive, Aggressive and Abusive Family Interaction* (1977) and *Duty Bound: Elder Abuse and Family Care* (1988). She is the coauthor of *Marriage and Family Realities* (1990), and co-editor of several books including *Violence in the Family* (1974), *Family and Support Systems throughout the Life Span* (1988), *Sourcebook of Family Theories and Methods: A Contextual Approach* (1993), *Pioneering Paths in the Study of Families: The Lives and Careers of Family Scholars* (2003).

Murray A. Straus. is Professor of Sociology and Co-Director of the Family Research Laboratory at the University of New Hampshire. He has served as President of the National Council on Family Relations (1972–73), the Society for the Study of Social Problems (1988–89), and the Eastern Sociological Society (1990–91). He was awarded the Ernest W. Burgess Award of the National Council on Family Relations for outstanding research on the family in 1977. He is the author or coauthor of more than 150 articles and 15 books, including the *Handbook of Family Measurement Techniques, Four Theories of Rape in the American Society,* and *Physical Violence in American Families* (with Richard J. Gelles).

Richard Wexler is Executive Director of the National Coalition for Child Protection Reform (www.nccpr.org), a nonprofit child advocacy organization. He is the author of *Wounded Innocents: The Real Victims of the War against Child Abuse* (1990, 1995). His interest in child welfare grew out of 19 years of work as a journalist. During that time, he won more than two dozen awards, many of them for stories about child abuse and foster care. He is a graduate of the Columbia University Graduate School of Journalism, where he was awarded the school's highest honor, a Pulitzer Traveling Fellowship.

Kersti A. Yllö is the Henrietta Jennings Chair of Sociology at Wheaton College in Norton, Massachusetts. She received her Ph.D. in Sociology from the University of New Hampshire. She has published *License to Rape: Sexual Abuse of Wives* (with D. Finkelhor) and *Feminist Perspectives on Wife Abuse* (with M. Bograd) as well as numerous articles on domestic violence, sexual assault in marriage, and feminist theory and methodology. She has conducted evaluation research on violence programs at Boston Children's Hospital and the U.S. Marine Corps. She is currently working on the problem of marital rape as a human rights issue and an important aspect of the HIV/AIDS pandemic.